The Visitor's Guide to the Birds of the Rocky Mountain National Parks

UNITED STATES AND CANADA

Roland H. Wauer

ILLUSTRATIONS BY MIMI HOPPE WOLF

John Muir Publications
Santa Fe, New Mexico

John Muir Publications, P.O. Box 613, Santa Fe, New Mexico 87504

© 1993 by Roland H. Wauer
Cover © 1993 by John Muir Publications
All rights reserved. Published 1993.

Printed in the United States of America
Printed on recycled paper

First edition. First printing September 1993.

Library of Congress Cataloging-in-Publication Data
Wauer, Roland H.
     The visitor's guide to the birds of the Rocky Mountain national
     parks : United States and Canada / by Roland H. Wauer
               p.   cm.
     Includes bibliographical references and index.
     ISBN 1-56261-101-1 : $15.95
     1. Bird watching—Rocky Mountains Region—Guidebooks.
     2. National parks and reserves—Rocky Mountains Region—
     Guidebooks. 3. Birds—Rocky Mountains Region. I. Title
QL683.R63W38 1993
598'.0723478—dc20   93-1773
                                                 CIP

Design: KenWilson
Illustrations: Mimi Hoppe Wolf
Typeface: Minion
Typography: Ken Wilson
Printer: Malloy Lithographing

Distributed to the book trade by
W. W. Norton & Company, Inc.
New York, New York

Cover photo: Photo Researchers, Inc., © E. R. Degginger
Interior photographs by Roland H. Wauer

Contents

Foreword

It is with much pleasure that I write this foreword to *The Visitor's Guide to the Birds of the Rocky Mountain National Parks: United States and Canada*. The Humane Society of the United States (HSUS) is proud to provide, through this important book, an expanded opportunity for wildlife appreciation to those who visit our national parks.

The HSUS has been known widely for its proactive and advocacy-oriented programs to protect animals. We have championed the cause of companion animals, urging those who acquire pets to treat them with consideration and care. We have worked to eliminate the suffering of animals used in laboratories and have aggressively advanced the use of alternatives. We have challenged the all too prevalent inhumane rearing of farm animals and successfully helped promote reforms within the industry while at the same time urging a reduction and replacement of meat and other farm products in one's diet.

Our wildlife programs have been equally forceful and proactive. Among them are the elimination of commercial killing of fur seals on Alaska's Pribilof Islands and the slaughter of the world's great whales; halting the sale of elephant ivory; protecting from destruction animals that would have been destined for fur fashions; and saving millions of animals from brutal elimination caused by predator control programs.

The HSUS, an organization of more than a million and a half constituents, is equally committed to promoting an appreciation and enjoyment of wild animals and wild places. This book opens the doors to that appreciation in a unique and authoritative way. Ro

Wauer, drawing amply on his lifelong interest in and love for animals, walks each visitor through the national park units of the Rocky Mountains with the skill and accomplished grace of a dedicated birder and naturalist. Firsthand, the reader is drawn into the habitat and environment of each park and its bird life. Through these pages, the reader feels the interrelations and interaction of the animals and plants and the enjoyment of a lifetime spent in studying the intricacies of nature.

For my family, this book, with its invitation to sight a particular bird and then move quickly on to discover another, is far more important than a field guide. This book encourages the reader to know a park and understand its animal life in a way that all concerned citizens must if essential qualities of our parks are to be preserved for future generations.

Finally, the HSUS is pleased and gratified to have a book of this quality which actively encourages wildlife enjoyment and environmental appreciation. To protect wildlife, people need to understand wild creatures more thoroughly and to appreciate the subtleties of their interaction with the environment that sustains them. This book provides the knowledge and information that can make these values truly available to each reader.

Ro Wauer has done a magnificent job of integrating his own special interest in wildlife and his personal commitment to environmental quality into a readable text that will make park exploration a delightful and unique experience. I wish you many delightful visits.

April 17, 1993   John A. Hoyt
Washington, D.C.   Chief Executive,
                          The Humane Society of the United States
                          President, Humane Society International

Preface

The national parks of the United States and Canada possess the best examples of the continent's natural heritage, complete with the grandest scenery and most stable plant and animal communities still in existence. In a large sense, North America's national parks represent a microcosm of our last remaining wildlands.

The Visitor's Guide to the Birds of the Rocky Mountain National Parks: United States and Canada describes the bird life within each of the Rocky Mountain national parks. This book is intended to introduce the park visitor to the most common and obvious birds and also to provide an introduction to the fascinating world of bird identification and behavior. This book can be used as a reference to the park and its bird life during a park visit, as well as a valuable tool in preparing for that visit.

Birds of the Rocky Mountains National Parks is not intended to be used as a field guide or a book on bird identification per se. Several excellent field guides are already available; they should be used as companion volumes to this book. Nor is this book intended to help the birder find the rarities or the out-of-the-way specialties. Its purpose is to help the park visitor better appreciate the park and its bird life. If in making new acquaintances, the park visitor should become interested in birds and more concerned about their well-being, all the better.

Forty national parks are included in this book, from Jasper in the northern Rocky Mountains south to Chiricahua in Arizona and Big Bend in West Texas. The forty national parks are divided into three geographic or biotic regions: those that occur in the Northern and Central Rocky Mountains, the Southwestern Rocky Mountains, and the Southeastern Rocky Mountains. The three categories provide continuity in discussion of both the national parks and the biotic communities they contain, as well as a perspective for anyone planning a trip.

Each chapter begins with a personalized experience that might happen to anyone visiting the park. At Yellowstone National Park, for example, the reader is introduced to that park through an early morning visit to the Old Faithful Geyser Basin. Each chapter then continues with a description of the national park itself, including the plant and animal communities that exist there, visitor facilities available within the park, interpretive activities, and where one can write or telephone for additional park information. The chapter then returns to the bird life, describing common birds within several of the area's most popular and accessible places to visit. Each chapter ends with a summary of the park's bird life and a list of a few key species.

A visit to any of the national parks should begin with a stop at the park's visitor center or information station to obtain a park brochure and activity sheet. These will contain basic information about the roads and trails, locations of accommodations, campgrounds, picnic sites, hiking routes, details of interpretive activities, descriptions of the park's key resources, and so on. The numerous sites mentioned in the book can best be located by using the area map found in the park brochure.

Common bird names that are used throughout the book, including a comprehensive checklist on pages 393 to 399, are taken from the most recent checklist of birds published by the American Ornithologists' Union (AOU) and used in all the up-to-date field guides. In the case of plants, because common names vary so much from one part of the country to another, a list of all common plant names used, along with their scientific names, is included after the bird checklist.

A bibliography begins on page 403. It includes all the references used by the author in the writing of this book, in hopes that the reader will utilize these sources for continued study of Rocky Mountain bird life.

Enjoy!

—Roland H. Wauer

Acknowledgments

This book would not have been possible without the kind assistance of dozens of employees of the U.S. and Canadian national park systems: superintendents, rangers, naturalists, resource specialists, scientists, and a few other individuals. I especially want to thank the following individuals: Christine Beekman at Arches; Craig Allen at Bandelier; Heather Dempsey, Doug Leighton, and Mark Tierney at Banff; Rick LoBello, Jeff Selleck, and Keith Yarborough at Big Bend; Superintendent Bill Binnewies and Terry Peters at Bighorn Canyon; Craig Murphy and Hugh Wight at Black Canyon of the Gunnison; Susan Colclazer at Bryce Canyon; Jane Belnap, Damian Fagan, and Larry Thomas at Canyonlands; Sandy Borthwick, Rick Nolan, John Spence, and Larry Vensel at Capitol Reef; Geoffrey Smith at Capulin Volcano; Bobby Crisman and Steve West at Carlsbad Caverns; Allan Myres at Cedar Breaks; Walt Saenger at Chiricahua; Bill Row and Henry Schoch at Colorado; Superintendent John Chapman, Mitzi Frank, and Phil Zichterman at Curecanti; Chris Fuco at Glacier (Canada); Steve Gniadek, Gary Gregory, Cliff Martinka, and Lucy Walter at Glacier (U.S.); Greer Price and John Ray at Grand Canyon; Steve Cain, Katy Duffy, Marshall Gingery, and Sheila Willis at Grand Teton; Bill Haviland, Katrina Walker, and Roberta Williams at Great Sand Dunes; Brent Wauer at Guadalupe Mountains; Larry Halverson at Kootenay; Anne Landry, Roy Richards, and Cleone Todgham at Jasper; Steve Budd-Jack, Marilyn Colyer, and Pat Oppelt at Mesa Verde; Babs Monroe at Montezuma Castle; Bob Brade at Mount Revelstoke; Stephanie Helline and Jeff Maugans at Rocky Mountain; Liz Bellantoni, Linda Booth, Tom Denton, Acting Superintendent Art

Eck, Jeff Kartheisser, Meg Weesner, and Loretta Wyatt at Saguaro; Bruce Anderson and Superintendent Sam Henderson at Sunset Crater, Wupatki, and Walnut Canyon; Eddie Colyott, Dessamae Lorrain, and Faye Morrison at Tonto; Janice Smith at Waterton Lakes; Stu Coleman and Terry McEneaney at Yellowstone; Paul Kutzer and Ken Walker at Yoho; Sheri Fedorchak and Vic Vieira at Zion.

I also want to thank Jan Hartke and President John Hoyt of the Humane Society of the United States (HSUS). The monetary assistance provided by HSUS was necessary for the travel and research required in the production of this book. Their contributions were most appreciated.

This project was the idea of my friend Bob Cahn, who provided encouragement throughout. Pat Cahn also lent her editorial expertise in the initial development of ideas and review of early chapters. Other manuscript reviews and suggestions were provided by Mark Elwonger, Victoria, Texas, and Brent Wauer, Guadalupe Mountains National Park. And information on the most recent changes in common bird names was kindly supplied by Greg Lasley and Van Remsen, Austin, Texas, and Louisiana State University, respectively.

Last and certainly not least, I thank my wife, Betty, who supported this project with editorial advice and assistance as my "trailer slave" throughout the approximately 19,400 miles we traveled gathering first-hand and up-to-date information for this book.

1

Birds—What They Are and How to Find Them

The bond between birds and man is older than recorded history. Birds have always been an integral part of human culture, a symbol of the affinity between mankind and the rest of the natural world, in religion, in folklore, in magic, in art—from early cave paintings to the albatross that haunted Coleridge's Ancient Mariner. Scientists today recognize them as sure indicators of the health of the environment. And as modern field guides make identification easier, millions of laymen watch them just for the joy of it.
—Paul Brooks

How often I have wished I could fly. To soar high over the mountains and valleys. To explore secluded places that are impossible to reach any other way. To escape this earthbound existence with the ease of a bird. These were among my secret desires as a youngster. How I envied the hawks and the swallows and even the tiny hummingbirds. They were the masters of my universe.

Only birds and bats, of all the warm-blooded creatures, can fly for more than a few yards. Only birds possess the combination of feathers, powerful wings, hollow bones, a remarkable respiratory system, and a large, strong heart. They are truly magnificent flying machines. The power of a wing beat, due to the marvelous flight feathers, allows a bird to cruise at speeds of 20 to 40 miles (32-64 km) per hour while flying nonstop across the Gulf of Mexico or the Arctic tundra. The tiny hummingbird has been clocked at 50 miles (80 km) per hour. And the powerful peregrine falcon is thought to stoop at speeds in excess of 200 miles (322 km) per hour.

A blue-winged teal banded in Quebec, Canada, was killed by a hunter less than four weeks later in Guayana, South America, more than 2,500 miles (4,023 km) distant. A Manx shearwater, taken from its burrow on Skokholm Island, Wales, and carried by airplane to Boston, Massachusetts, returned to its burrow on the thirteenth day, having flown 3,000 miles (4,828 km) across the Atlantic Ocean. And a lesser yellowlegs banded in Massachusetts was captured six days later 1,900 miles (3,058 km) away on Martinique, in the Lesser Antilles. That bird had averaged 317 miles (510 km) per day.

Migrating birds usually fly below 3,000 feet (914 m) elevation, but observers at 14,000 feet (4,267 m) in the Himalayas reported storks and cranes flying so high overhead, at an estimated 20,000 feet (6,096 m) elevation, they could barely be seen through binoculars.

Other marvelous features of birds are their bill shapes and sizes. Anyone who has watched birds for any time at all cannot help but notice the diversity of feeding methods. Hummingbirds, for example, have long thin bills that they utilize to probe into flowers to feed on nectar, sometimes deep inside tubular flowers. Their bills are especially adapted to this type of feeding. Many shorebirds, such as dowitchers and common snipes, also have long bills, but they are much heavier for probing for food in mud. The long-billed curlew's bill can reach into deep burrows to extract its prey.

The many insect feeders have dainty bills for capturing tiny insects. Vireos and warblers are gleaners that forage on trees and shrubs, picking insects off leaves and bark. A careful examination of feeding warblers will further suggest the size of their preferred food on the basis of their bill size. Flycatcher and swallow bills are wider to enhance their ability to capture flies in midair. Woodpecker bills are specialized so they are able to drill into insect-infested trees and shrubs to retrieve the larvae there.

Finch bills are short and stout, most useful for cracking seeds or crushing armored insects. Crossbills are able to extract seeds from conifer cones. And grosbeaks are able to feed on much larger fruit, actually stripping away the husk from fleshy seeds. Fruit becomes particularly abundant in late summer and fall and provides food for a host of birds, many of which feed on insects at one time of year and fruit at other times of the year.

And then there are the predators, with their variety of bill shapes and sizes. Raptors possess short and stout bills with a specialized hook used for tearing apart their prey. The wading birds possess large, heavy bills for capturing their prey. And diving birds possess bills that are hooked for catching fish and serrated on the edges for a better grip.

Feet are another fascinating feature of a bird's anatomy, also helpful to understanding a bird's requirements. Webbed feet suggest its adaptation to water for swimming, and flattened toes help birds walk on soft mud. Tiny, flexible toes suggest an ability to perch on small twigs and branches. And large, powerful feet with sharp talons are required to capture and grip prey.

There are approximately 9,600 kinds of birds in the world; about 900 of those are found in North America. And every one has slightly different characteristics that permit it to utilize a slightly different niche (the combination of its needs) from any other species. Whenever two or more species have the same needs, in all likelihood only one will survive.

A bird is a very specialized creature, indeed, but its bill and feet are usually less obvious than its plumage, the sum total of its feathers. A bird's plumage is unquestionably its most obvious and usually its most attractive characteristic. This is especially true for the more colorful and contrasting birds, such as warblers, hummingbirds, some waterfowl, and some finches. Birds are the most colorful of all vertebrates.

Feathers reveal every color in the rainbow. The colors we see are the product of pigments and the reflection and refraction of light due to feather structure. The concentration of pigments produces the intensities of color, as in the vivid red of a male vermilion flycatcher and the diluted red of a female northern cardinal. The total lack of pigment production results in white plumage. Many of the colors we see are due to the light that may be reflected or absorbed by the feathers. The bright blues of Steller's jays or bluebirds are due to a particular arrangement of cells in the feather. Iridescence is also due to feather structure, not pigments. A dull velvet color is the reversal of iridescence.

Of all the aesthetically pleasing characteristics of birds, bird song may be the most enduring. Louis Halle wrote, "As music is the purest form of expression, so it seems to me that the singing of birds is the purest form for the expression of natural beauty and goodness in the larger sense, the least susceptible of explanation on ulterior practical grounds."

Who has not paused to watch an American robin or cedar waxwing feeding on berries, or the wild dives of an osprey, brown pelican, or tern? And who has not stopped to admire a humming-bird feeding from a particularly colorful flower?

But birds possess additional values that are sometimes ignored, perhaps because they are often taken for granted. For instance, certain birds are extremely adept at catching and consuming large quantities of insects, many of which are considered pests. These include obnoxious insects as well as those that are a serious threat to various crops on which we humans depend for our sustenance.

Human beings have utilized birds from earliest history. Birds were worshipped by many early civilizations. Cormorants were ringed for catching fish. Pigeons carried our messages. Songbirds were taken into mines and brightened our homes with their wonderful songs. In literature, Coleridge has immortalized the albatross, Shelley the lark, and Poe the raven. The concept and development of manned flight was derived from our observations of birds. Every state and province has an official bird, many of which highlight flags and seals. The majority of Canadian coins and paper money display common bird species. And the most powerful country in the world utilizes a bird as its symbol: America's bald eagle is one of the most visible symbols in the United States.

Birds truly are an intricate part of the human ecosystem, an important link to nature. Birds, more than any other creatures, are obvious and omnipresent members of our natural community.

Birding for Fun

There comes a time when those of us with a natural curiosity and appreciation for the outdoors want to know the names of the various creatures we see around us. The initial spark to identify birds may be kindled by some exceptional happening or a special sighting. Watching a family of gray jays at a campground as they actively investigate you and your food supply or suddenly being mobbed by a flock of cliff swallows at a nest site is likely to foster interest in those species and what they are about.

But identifying those birds can be somewhat difficult unless you know where to begin. Although the average park visitor usually can identify more birds than he might first assume, further bird identification requires some basics, just like any other endeavor. With bird identification, the basics include two essential pieces of equipment: a field guide and a pair of binoculars.

There are several very good field guides available which utilize the bird identification technique developed by Roger Tory Peterson. Peterson's field guides and those published by the National Geographic Society and Golden Press utilize bird paintings. These guides are preferred over those with photographs, because the paintings highlight key features that only occasionally are obvious in photographs.

Binoculars are absolutely essential for identifying, watching, and enjoying most birds. Binoculars vary in power, illumination, and field of vision, as well as price. The most popular birding binocular is an 8x35 glass. "8x" is the power or magnification; "8x" magnifies a bird eight times, and "7x" magnifies a bird seven times, etc. "35" is the diameter of the objective lens in millimeters and is used to illustrate illumination. Illumination (brightness) can be determined by dividing the magnification into the size of the optical lens; a 7x50 binocular produces a brighter image than an 8x35 binocular by 7.1 to 4.4. However, although the larger 50mm binocular provides a brighter image than the 35mm binocular, and is best in dim light, it usually is too heavy for a full day in the field. Also, binoculars 9x and above are often too powerful for beginners who are not yet comfortable with holding binoculars perfectly still. Pocket-sized, lightweight binoculars (those with a small objective lens) are good for occasional use but continuous use can cause eyestrain. Select binoculars that are best suited for you.

Field of vision, determined by the binocular design, usually is also marked in degrees (angle visible out of 360 degrees) or feet (width visible out of 1,000 ft). The 7.3 degree field of vision (out of

360 degrees), for my wife's 9x35 Discoverer binoculars, and the 395 feet of vision (out of 1,000 ft), for my old 9x35 Burton binoculars, will remain the same no matter the distance of the bird being observed.

In addition, central-focus binoculars are a must. And the minimum focusing distance is important, as well, for focusing on a bird that may be as close as 12 to 15 feet (4-6 m). Binoculars come in all prices, but the moderately priced ones usually work just as well as the most expensive, which may be more water resistant, less inclined to fog, and armored for rough use.

Using binoculars usually requires some experimentation, but the skill is easy to learn. First, make sure that the right ocular is set at "0" for 20-20 vision. Then, while looking directly at an object, bring the binoculars up into position without changing your position or looking elsewhere, and use the center wheel to focus on the object. A few tries will produce immediate success.

The next step is to get acquainted with your field guide. Start with leafing through the entire guide and locating the first page of tyrant flycatchers (just beyond the woodpeckers). The flycatchers and all the birds illustrated beyond are perching birds (songbirds). All the nonperching birds (seabirds, waders, waterfowl, raptors, shorebirds, gulls and terns, grouse, hummingbirds, woodpeckers, etc.) are located within the first portion of the book.

Next, read the introductory section of your field guide, especially the discussion about field marks. Your field guide will also include a drawing of a typical bird showing basic field marks. Look these over so that you possess a good idea of where the bird's crown, eye line, eye ring, chin, upper and lower mandibles, flank, upper tail and under tail coverts, wrist, wing bar, and so on, occur. Be ready to refer back to this illustration for help when necessary.

Now that you have discovered the value of a field guide, it is time to start identifying real-life birds. You should now have an idea of what features to look for in live birds. The following suggestions provide an identification strategy of sorts:

1. Size. It is a good idea to relate bird size to those species you already know. For instance, consider five categories: sparrow-size, robin-size, pigeon-size, duck-size, and heron-size. With a few

exceptions, such as the common raven, any bird the size of a duck or larger is a nonperching bird and will be found in the first half of the field guide. By thinking size, you immediately know where to start your search. Also, one can often pick out odd-sized birds in a flock for further attention or recognize different species that might be foraging together. For example, a tiny bird within a party of warblers will more than likely be a chickadee, kinglet, or brown creeper.

2. Shape and behavior. Does your bird possess any outstanding features? Is it a wader with long legs and an upright posture? Possibly a heron. Is it walking along the shoreline? Possibly a shorebird. Is it swimming on a lake or river? Probably a waterfowl or gull. Is it soaring high in the sky? Possibly a turkey vulture or hawk. Is it perched on a wire or tree limb? Certainly a perching bird. Is it a perching bird eating seeds at a feeder? Probably a sparrow or finch. If it is smaller than a sparrow, is creeping up a tree trunk, and is all-brown, it is sure to be a brown creeper.

3. Color and pattern. Many birds possess an obvious plumage that is an immediate giveaway. Cardinals, crows, robins, yellow warblers, and red-winged and yellow-headed blackbirds are the first to come to mind. These are easily identified species requiring only a minimum of observation time. Their bold and obvious color and/or pattern stands out like a sore thumb. But many of their neighbors will require a little more study. Do the all-white underparts extend onto the back, or does your bird possess only white wing bars? Does its white neck extend only to the lower mandible or onto the face? Does its reddish color extend onto the back, or is it limited to the tail and wings? Do the yellow underparts include the throat and belly or only the chest? The answers to these questions will eventually become second nature to you.

Field Techniques

Bird-finding techniques are often personal ones, and you will need to discover your own preferred methods. For example, I like to move very slowly through a particular habitat, trying to discover all of the birds present within that immediate area. I personally find that part of birding to be the most enjoyable and a very special challenge. Other birders often prefer to move along at a faster clip, stopping only to watch those birds that become obvious. This method is based on the concept that they will find more birds by covering more ground. That is definitely the reason for visiting as many habitats as possible, but I believe that the largest number of species can be found by slowly moving through each habitat, making yourself part of the scene, both physically and mentally.

There are definite clues to bird finding that you can use to your advantage. First and foremost are bird sounds. During the breeding season, bird song is the very best indicator of a bird's presence and location. Songbirds often sing throughout the day. They almost always sing at dawn and dusk, but a few species sing only at dawn. The more serious birders will find themselves out at dawn to experience the dawn chorus while other birders are still asleep. The majority of the birds, however, can usually be found throughout the day.

A rustling of dry leaves in the underbrush can be another valuable clue. Leaf rustling can be caused by numerous creatures, but when the leaves seem to be thrown back as if being cleared away for finding food underneath, the originator is likely to be a thrasher, fox sparrow, or rufous-sided towhee.

Songbirds tend to ignore intruders who are quiet and move slowly, unless they get too close to a nest or fledgling. You can get surprisingly close to songbirds by moving slowly and not making any sudden motions. Also, wearing dull clothing, instead of bright and contrasting clothing, helps you to blend into the bird's environment, usually permitting closer viewing.

Some of the nonperching birds will permit a slow, cautious approach, but the wading birds, ducks, and raptors are not as trusting. You will need to observe these birds from a distance, and you may want to use a spotting scope for these observations. Or you may be able to use a blind, sometimes installed at bird-viewing sites.

During the nonbreeding portion of the year, birds often occur in flocks or in parties. Flocks of waterfowl or blackbirds can number in the hundreds or thousands and be readily visible from a considerable distance. But a party of songbirds moving through the forest will require quiet study for identifying all the members. It is possible to wander through the woods for some time before discovering a party of birds that may include a dozen or more species.

Migrant songbirds usually travel in parties that can include hundreds of individuals of two or three dozen species. When finding such a party, it is best to be still and let the party continue its feeding activities without disturbing it. In the few cases when a bird party is just beyond good viewing distance, you can sometimes attract a few of the closer individuals by spishing—making low, scratchy sounds with your teeth together and mouth slightly open—a few times; attracting the closer individuals often entices the whole flock to move in your direction. However, I find that spishing within a bird party tends to frighten some species off or to move the party along faster that it might otherwise go.

At times, a bird party is concentrated at a choice feeding site, such as flowering or fruiting trees and shrubs. So long as they are not frightened or unduly agitated by noises or movement, they may remain and continue feeding for some time, once they overcome their initial concern over your presence. Also, their activities will tend to attract other birds, allowing you to see a broad spectrum of birds at one spot.

Generally, birding along a forest edge, often along the edge of a parking lot, can produce excellent results in the early morning. Bird parties prefer sunny areas at that time of day, to take advantage of greater insect activity. Within two or three hours, however, feeding birds tend to move into the cooler vegetation, especially on hot, sunny days.

Birds may then need to be enticed into the open; many species respond well to some sounds. Spishing often works very well. Squeaking sounds made with your lips against the back of your hand or finger may work at other times. Birds are naturally curious and will often come to the sounds to investigate. At other times, spishing or squeaking seems to frighten birds away. And some species will be attracted once but will be difficult to fool twice. So always be prepared to focus your binoculars on the bird immediately when it pops up from a shrub or out of a thicket.

As mentioned above, the best way to find a large number of birds is to visit a variety of bird habitats. All birds occur in preferred habitats, especially during their nesting season. But they tend to frequent a broader range of sites in migration and in winter. Learning where species can most likely be expected is very helpful. For instance, boreal chickadees occur only in the northern coniferous forests; this species cannot be found at Big Bend National Park. And one cannot expect to find a roadrunner in the boreal forest. A new birder should learn to take advantage of the range map and habitat description for each species that are included within the field guides. It can save time and considerable embarrassment.

Birding by song is often left to the experienced birder, but many novices are as well equipped to utilize bird songs as many of the experts. Some birders have poor hearing or a "tin ear." So for anyone with an ear for melody, there is a wide range of records, tapes, and CDs available to help you learn the bird songs. And during the spring and summer, there is no better method of bird identification. When tiny passerines are singing from the upper canopy of the forest, finding and observing those individuals can be most difficult. But their songs are an instant method of recognition that does not involve eye and neck strain from staring into the high canopy for hours on end. And observing rails can also be trying, if not outright dangerous. Fortunately, rails and other marsh birds also sing their own unique songs that can usually be easily identified.

Much of the knowledge required to make quick bird identifications comes from field experience. An excellent shortcut is spending time with an experienced birder who is willing to share his or her knowledge. That person can pass on tidbits of information that otherwise might take years to acquire. Most national parks have staff naturalists who give bird talks and walks during the visitor season. This kind of assistance can be extremely worthwhile for bird finding and bird identification.

Birding Ethics

As with any other activity, there are certain rules of the game. Birding should be fun and fulfilling. It can be a challenge equal to any other outdoor endeavor. But it should never become so all-consuming as to threaten the bird's health or habitat. Any time we are in the field, we must realize that we are only visitors to that habitat on which a number of birds depend for their existence. We must not interfere with their way of life. Disturbing nests and nestlings, for whatever reason, cannot be tolerated. Tree whacking to entice woodpeckers and owls to peek outside is not acceptable.

Most national parks are adequately posted, but sometimes just plain thoughtlessness can lead to severe impacts on the environment. These acts range from shortcutting to actually driving over a tundra or meadow. Respect closures within the park; they are there for a very good reason. The survival of nesting swans or peregrines may depend upon them.

The hobby of birding can be a most enjoyable pastime. And it is one that costs very little and can be done with little or no special training. It can be pursued alone or in a group and at any time of the day or night. And there is nowhere on earth where birds are not the most obvious part of the natural environment.

Early naturalist Frank Chapman, in his *Handbook of Birds of Eastern North America*, summarized the enjoyment of birds better than anyone else. Chapman wrote that birds "not only make life upon the globe possible, but they may add immeasurably to our enjoyment of it. Where in all animate nature shall we find so marvelous a combination of beauty of form and color, of grace and power of motion, of musical ability and intelligence, to delight our eyes, charm our ears and appeal to our imagination?"

2

Parks as Islands

*The wild things on this earth are not to do with as we
please. They have been given to us in trust, and we must
account for them to the generations which will come after
us and audit our accounts.*

—William T. Hornaday

The last viable peregrine falcon populations anywhere in North
America south of Alaska were those in national parks in the
Rocky Mountains, Colorado Plateau, and West Texas. The discovery
that populations of this and several other high-level predators were
being decimated by DDT and other chlorinated hydrocarbons, and
the eventual banning of DDT use in the United States and Canada
in 1972, came too late to save any of the eastern peregrines. The last
active aerie in the Appalachian Mountains was at Great Smoky
Mountains National Park. The entire population of that subspecies
became extinct in three decades. By 1975, fewer than 30 pairs were
known to exist in the United States. Peregrines in Big Bend, Black
Canyon, Dinosaur, Grand Canyon, Mesa Verde, and Zion, however,
were well enough isolated and had sufficient numbers to ensure the
survival of an adequate breeding population.

These examples demonstrate the value of national parks as natural refuges. The western parks provided the last strongholds for
peregrine populations to withstand human-induced pollutants. In
most cases, those peregrines fed primarily on resident bird life that
had not been subjected to DDT elsewhere. In the case of the Great
Smoky Mountains population, those birds relied on prey that had
picked up DDT from adjacent farmlands or during migration. The
eastern peregrines disappeared forever.

During the 1980s, when peregrine restoration programs were being implemented, park sites in the Great Smoky Mountains and at Bighorn Canyon, Capitol Reef, Colorado, and Dinosaur were among the first selected. Nearly 2,500 peregrines were released in the West, according to James Enderson, leader of the Western Peregrine Recovery Team. By 1990, peregrines once again began to frequent their old haunts, including the actual nesting of pairs at several areas. The finding of 58 active aeries at Grand Canyon in 1989 suggests that peregrine populations have recovered sufficiently to consider delisting the species. The current populations highlight the importance of national parks to species' recovery.

In spite of an apparent peregrine "fix," many other bird populations continue to decline. The most serious losses are occurring in Neotropical species, long-distant migrants that nest in the U.S. and Canada and winter to the south in the Greater Antilles, Mexico, Central America, and, to a lesser extent, in northern South America. According to U.S. Fish and Wildlife Service Breeding Bird Survey data, 44 of 72 Neotropical species declined from 1978 to 1987. These include almost all the warblers, five vireos, five flycatchers, and various thrushes, buntings, orioles, tanagers, cuckoos, grosbeaks, and the blue-gray gnatcatcher.

The reasons for the declines are varied. Neotropical migrants are less adaptable than most resident species. They have a shorter nesting season, with only enough time to produce one brood before they must depart on their southward journeys. Long-distant migrants tend to arrive on their breeding grounds later and to depart earlier. They also produce smaller clutches than the full-time residents. And most of the Neotropical species place their nests in the open, either on the ground or in shrubs or trees. Their nests, therefore, are more susceptible to predators and to brood parasitism by cowbirds than those of the full-time residents, many of which are cavity-nesters (woodpeckers, chickadees, titmice, wrens, and bluebirds). If a racoon, skunk, or fox were to destroy the nest of a full-time resident, the bird could start over again, but one episode of predation or parasitism can destroy an entire breeding season for a Neotropical bird.

Breeding bird studies within the fragmented environment of Rock Creek Park, Washington, D.C., from 1947 through 1978 revealed that six Neotropical species (yellow-billed cuckoo, yellow-throated vireo, and parula, black-and-white, hooded, and Kentucky warblers) could no longer be found to nest. And several other species, including Acadian flycatcher, wood thrush, red-eyed vireo, ovenbird, and scarlet tanager, had declined by 50 percent.

Conversely, at Great Smoky Mountains National Park, with its 494,000 acres (200,000 ha) of mature forest, breeding bird censuses conducted in the late 1940s and repeated in 1982 and 1983 "revealed no evidence of a widespread decline in Neotropical migrants within the large, relatively unfragmented forest" of the park, according to the National Fish and Wildlife Foundation. These divergent examples, peregrines in Big Bend and Neotropical breeders in the Great Smoky Mountains, demonstrate the value of large natural parks as preserves for the perpetuation of wildlife resources.

Threats to the Parks

North America's national parks are not immune, however, to the abundant threats. Every park has experienced impacts that threaten its ecological integrity. Although its exterior shell may appear unchanged, and the average visitor may find the scenery looks pretty much the same from year to year, the park's fragile ecological web possesses a number of damaged strands.

During the early years, most of the natural parks had sufficient buffers around them to insulate the heart of the parks from the development and pollution occurring outside their borders. But with continued population growth and increased adjacent land uses, the park's buffer zones dwindled. Many of today's parks are bordered by farmlands that are maintained by chemicals, forests that are clear-cut, and increasing numbers of industrial centers, malls, and housing developments. Widespread air pollution reaches great distances and affects even the most remote parkscapes.

Long-term monitoring of air quality values in remote areas such as Big Bend and Grand Canyon reveals that prevailing winds, especially in the summer, carry pollutants from urban and industrial areas in northern Mexico and the U.S. Gulf Coast to Big Bend, and from urban and industrial areas in southern California, Arizona, and northern Mexico to Grand Canyon.

Inside the parks can be found roadways, trails, campgrounds, and other facilities, all designed to permit greater human use of the resources. But they often are poorly sited and designed, and so increase fragmentation and stress resources already threatened by external disturbances.

Habitat degradation within the parks by improper management can have serious consequences to the park's bird life. Any fragmentation reduces the integrity of the ecosystem, lowering its value for wild species. New sites increase access to the forest interior for predators that feed on birds and their eggs; parasitic cowbirds that lay their eggs in other species' nests; exotic house sparrows, European starlings, and other invaders that compete for nesting space and food; and exotic plants that can drastically change the habitat.

A number of recent studies suggest that cowbird parasitism can affect songbirds even in large forest tracts and may be the major cause of the decline of many Neotropical migrants. Researchers have concluded that cowbirds "will commute up to seven kilometers [4.35 mi] from feeding areas to search for nests to parasitize." John Terborgh reports in the May 1992 issue of *Scientific American* that "[a] seven-kilometer [4.35 mi] radius describes a circle of 150 square kilometers [58 sq mi], equal to 15,000 hectares [37,065 acres]. It is disturbing to think a forest that might offer at its center a haven from cowbird parasitism would have to be at least that size."

Cuts into the forest interior also increase populations of other open area birds, such as American crows, jays, magpies, and grackles, which prey on other birds and their eggs and hatchlings.

Once a park's natural ecosystem has been damaged by fragmentation and pollution, all the resources become more susceptible to impacts from natural disasters, such as hurricanes, floods, fires, and diseases. These catastrophies can seriously affect small bird populations that already have been reduced by pollution, predators, parasites, and competitors.

Wildland Fires and Their Effect on Bird Life
Nature is never static. Environmental changes are part of every natural system. But a healthy bird population is better able to withstand those changes. Wildland fires, which occur within most of

our forest, shrub, and grassland communities, are one example. Indeed, many plants and animals are fire-dependent. Some pinecones must burn to open, drop their seeds, and regenerate. Woodpeckers frequent freshly burned sites to feed on various wood-boring beetles that are attracted to trees weakened by natural fires. Many raptors are attracted to prairie fires to feed off the displaced rodents and insects.

Wildland fires have received considerable scrutiny by the public and government officials since the highly visible Yellowstone National Park fire of 1988. Almost one million acres (404,694 ha) of Yellowstone's parklands were affected by that burn. Although park officials readily point out the negative affects of fire, largely in areas where the fuel loads have built up in excess over too many years without burning, they also are eager to discuss the benefits of fire to the Yellowstone ecosystem. Fire is a natural part of the ecosystem. Old age forests do not have the diversity of wildlife that occur in mixed-aged forests created by fires. Fire opens the forest so that new vegetation, such as grasses, aspens, and a variety of shrubs, that had been overcome by the old-age forest, can contribute to the mix of habitats. Terry Rich's article, "Forests, fire and the future," in *Birder's World*, includes a good summary of the Yellowstone fire and its affects on the park's bird life.

From my own research at Bandelier National Monument, the 1977 La Mesa fire initiated a series of changes that continue 15 years later. All three of my study sites, initiated prior to the fire, revealed increased numbers of bird species and populations following the fire. Significant population increases occurred almost immediately in woodpeckers, with minor increases in all the other insect feeders, such as violet-green swallows, nuthatches, and warblers. Seed feeders, such as sparrows, juncos, and finches, initially declined in varying degrees, but soon increased with the newly available grass seed. Once woodpeckers became established, other cavity-nesters, such as ash-throated flycatchers, violet-green swallows, mountain chickadees, nuthatches, and bluebirds increased to take advantage of vacated nest-holes. Predators also increased with the additional prey base and more open character of the landscape. A few lowland species, such as mourning doves, ash-throated flycatchers, Say's phoebes, scrub jays, and rufous-sided towhees, moved in to take advantage of the open and warmer terrain. Snag-fall provided increased habitats for house wrens. Although the initial influx of downy, hairy, and three-toed woodpeckers and northern flickers tapered off by the fifth year, Lewis' woodpeckers appeared to utilize some of the vacated nest-holes. And vireos, Virginia's warblers, black-headed grosbeaks, towhees, and dark-eyed juncos were soon able to take advantage of the young aspens and oak thickets.

The Future

Although extinction is part of the natural process, the rate of extinction has never been so swift as it is at present. The International Union for the Conservation of Nature and Natural Resources (IUCN) predicts that by the year 2000 the world will have lost 20 percent of all extant species.

The greatest losses are occurring within the tropical forests, where many of our songbirds spend their winters. *The Global 2000 Report to the President* stated, "Between half a million and 2 million species—15 to 20 percent of all species on earth—could be extinguished by 2000, mainly because of loss of habitat but also in part because of pollution. Extinction of species on this scale is without precedent in human history. . . . One-half to two-thirds of the extinctions projected to occur by 2000 will result from the clearing or degradation of tropical forests."

In North America, at least 480 kinds of plants and animals have become extinct since the arrival of the first Europeans. Seven species have disappeared since 1973, when the United States Congress enacted the Endangered Species Act. Canada established a Committee on the Status of Endangered Wildlife in Canada in 1977. More than 600 species have since been listed as "threatened" or "endangered." Endangered species are those in danger of becoming extinct; threatened species are those on the verge of becoming endangered. Howard Youth of the Worldwatch Institute reports that worldwide "about 1,000 bird species—more than 11 percent—are at risk of extinction, while about 70 percent, or 6,300 species, are in decline."

Today, the concept of threatened and endangered species is an accepted part of our world. Significant decisions are based on whether a species is "listed" or not. And many of our "T and E" species have become household terms. Who has not heard of the plight of the peregrine falcon, humpback whale, and snail darter?

The shortcoming of the Endangered Species Act is that it addressed individual species instead of communities of plants and animals. Attempts to restore species do not always give adequate attention to the natural processes on which they depend. And at a time of inadequate funding and moral support, only the more charismatic species receive attention.

An Endangered Ecosystem Act would have much greater success in protecting species, if large tracts of intact landscape (at least 58 sq mi or 150 sq km) that contain several threatened and endangered species were given adequate protection. These larger areas are the essence of the national parks.

The bottom line is that our North American birds are losing their breeding grounds, winter habitats, and many of the stopover places in between.

What Is Being Done within the Parks

Much has been written about the threats to park resources. The National Park Service itself has been in the forefront of expressing concern about those threats. A major "State of the Parks" initiative was undertaken in 1980 and 1981 to identify the threats and to establish a program for preventing additional threats and mitigating current impacts. Parts of that strategy continue to the present, but other portions were eliminated, reduced, or ignored due to in-house bureaucracy or insufficient funding.

In Canada, the National Parks Act was amended in 1988 to require the Minister of the Environment to report to the Parliament on the "State of the Parks" every two years. In response, Canada's "Green Plan" was developed and includes the goal of setting aside 12 percent of Canada's total lands and waters as protected space. The Green Plan includes targets and specific actions, including five new national parks by 1996 and completion of the Canadian Parks System by the year 2000.

In addition, many of the Rocky Mountain national parks, from Jasper in the northern Rockies, to Big Bend and Chiricahua along the Mexican border, are involved in one way or another with bird-oriented research, monitoring, and restoration activities.

Park research activities include the long-term effects of fire on birds at Bandelier and Yellowstone; long-term effects of cattle grazing on Capitol Reef grassland communities; changes in riparian communities along Grand Canyon's Colorado River; riparian corridor avifauna at Zion; effects of human impacts on cavity-nesters at Saguaro; American white pelican feeding ecology on Yellowstone Lake; harlequin duck and bald eagle ecology at Glacier; cave swallow ecology and migration at Carlsbad Caverns; and spotted owl studies at Bandelier, Canyonlands, Capitol Reef, Chiricahua, Mesa Verde, and Zion. Radio transmitters have been placed on spotted owls at Capitol Reef to learn more about this bird's ecological requirements.

Monitoring projects include an abundance of Christmas Bird Counts, numerous breeding bird surveys, and several involving threatened or endangered species. These include peregrine falcons at Big Bend, Bighorn Canyon, Black Canyon of the Gunnison, Bryce Canyon, Capitol Reef, Curecanti, Dinosaur, Grand Teton, Guadalupe Mountains, Yellowstone, and Zion. Bald eagle populations are being monitored at Bighorn Canyon, Canyonlands, Glacier, Grand Teton, and Yellowstone. Further monitoring programs include trumpeter swans at Yellowstone and Grand Teton, whooping cranes at Grand Teton and Yellowstone, ospreys at Grand Teton, and great gray owls at Glacier and Grand Teton.

The majority of the large national parks were involved with peregrine restoration programs until about 1988. Those projects successfully restored birds to the ecosystem; it is now up to the birds to fill the vacant niches as they mature. Nesting has now been recorded in a few of the parks and is expected in all suitable sites during the next few years. Current avian reintroduction activities involve Montezuma quail at Guadalupe Mountains and the use of floating nest platforms for trumpeter swans at Yellowstone and Grand Teton.

In addition, the U.S. National Park Service and Canadian Parks Service are participating in the Neotropical Migratory Bird

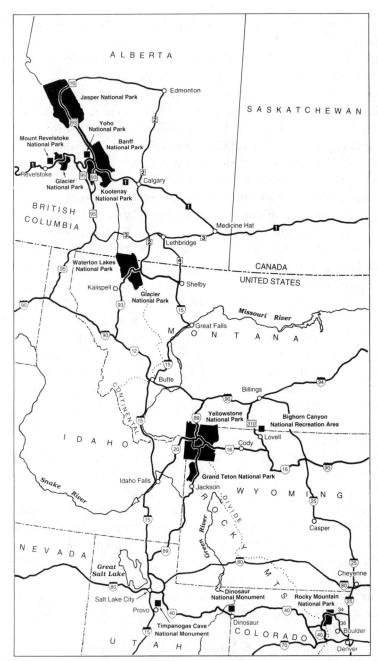

Northern and Central Rocky Mountain National Parks

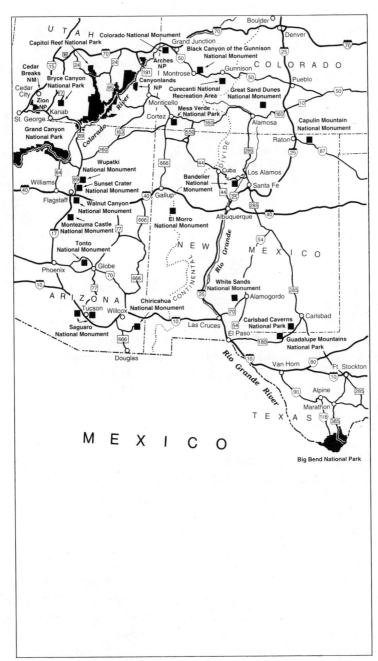

Southwestern and Southeastern Rocky Mountain National Parks

Conservation Program, as coordinated by the National Fish and Wildlife Foundation. The primary focus of this program will be to "integrate research, monitoring, and management (including ecological restoration activities) on behalf of migratory nongame birds" for "the conservation of Neotropical migratory birds."

Many Rocky Mountain parks also are participating in "Partners in Flight," a consortium of government agencies and private organizations. This is an international program to identify and conserve species of birds and their habitats that are in peril.

Early emphasis has been placed on the development of a network of parks and protected areas in the Western Hemisphere that are linked by Neotropical migratory birds. Migratory bird watch programs have begun in more than thirty parks as another way to develop linkages between pertinent park units.

Yet in spite of the parks' mandates for unaltered ecosystems, the dual charge of "protection and enjoyment" has too often been interpreted to mean that the parks are meant primarily for people instead of the resources they contain. And so even the largest of the parks have undergone changes to benefit the human visitor while they create more chinks in the park's ecological integrity. These incremental bites may seem insignificant separately, but together they have eaten into the essential fabric that keeps parks viable. Many of our national parks are little more than skeletons of their former selves.

Today's national parks more and more are becoming islands within a great sea of disturbance. They can be equated with sea islands, with few connections to continental sources for species renewal. The longer an island is isolated, the less its flora and fauna have in common with other communities, and the greater likelihood of species loss.

The Value of National Parks

How important are national parks for the perpetuation of our North American bird life? Except for a very few of the largest and most remote of the public forests and refuges, and an insignificant scattering of private preserves, only the national parks are dedicated to the preservation of complete ecosystems. The vast majority of other managed areas are primarily dedicated either to the perpetuation of only one or a few species or to the area's multiple use values. The perpetuation of unaltered ecosystems too often is given secondary importance.

In spite of changes, the national parks still represent some of the finest of our natural environments in existence. Many of the units contain some of the least disturbed habitats in North America. And each national park increases in value with every passing day.

The national parks contain far more than tracts of natural landscape, scenic beauty, and places of inspiration. The parks literally serve as biological baselines for the continent. There can be found gene pools of diversity that have disappeared almost everywhere else. The national parks contain our last remaining outdoor laboratories in which we can learn about the past in order to prepare for the future. There can be found the last reasonably intact examples of what North America was like before our resources were exploited for the benefit of a few.

A survey of the national parks, however, quickly reveals that the park systems of the U.S. and Canada are far from complete. Many of North America's major biotic communities have been left unprotected. Both the United States and Canada have recognized this shortcoming, have taken steps to identify the needs, and are trying to complete the systems.

In addition, only a few of the parks and reserves are large enough to represent complete ecosystems. Few parks contain a complete spectrum of natural processes that shape the ecosystem, so that the nutrient, hydrologic, fire, and other natural cycles are allowed to function unfettered by human constraints.

The key to long-term perpetuation of native species is the complete protection of intact ecosystems. They must be fully protected from all degrading activities, including grazing, timber cutting, mining, all forms of pollution, fragmentation by overdevelopment or overprotection (such as fire roads), and various forms of recreation that are not compatible with the purpose of the park.

C. F. Brockman understood the greatest value of the parks when he wrote:

> The national parks are charged with the obligation of preserving superlative natural regions, including wilderness areas, for the benefit of posterity. Attentiveness to the pleasure and comfort of the people is essential but it cannot mean catering to absolutely unlimited numbers unless the second function is to destroy the first. In a theatre, when the seats in the house have been sold out and the available standing room also has been preempted, the management does not jeopardize the main event by allowing still more onlookers to crowd upon the stage and impede the unfolding of the drama. ᔭ

NORTHERN AND CENTRAL ROCKY MOUNTAINS

Conservationists owe a tremendous debt of gratitude to the United States of America, for the creation of Yellowstone National Park started a movement that has, with steadily growing momentum, embraced the whole world, jumping all barriers of nationality, creed, ideology and race. It has paid off handsomely in preserving intact many of the most magnificent scenic displays and in saving numerous species of animals and plants from certain extinction.

—C. A. W. Guggisberg

3

Banff and Jasper National Parks, Alberta, and Kootenay and Yoho National Parks, British Columbia

The Clark's nutcracker is the self-proclaimed good-will ambassador at Lake Louise, Banff National Park. No other native attempts to compete with this busy and vociferous creature. Nutcrackers occur everywhere along the lakeshore and hotel grounds, and park visitors from around the world receive equal welcome from these avian diplomats.

Clark's nutcrackers are, without a doubt, one of the bird world's most fascinating members. Not only do they frequent areas of high human use, such as Lake Louise and Jasper's Mount Edith Cavell parking area, where they thrill park visitors with their aerial acrobatics, boldness, and apparent curiosity, but they also possess an exceptionally keen memory. Nutcrackers are able to remember the location of about 1,000 seed caches from one season to another.

In fall, when conifer seeds ripen, nutcrackers pry the seeds from the cones in crowbar-fashion with their sharp, heavy bills, then hide the seeds on south-facing slopes for winter use. They possess a special pouch under their tongue in which they are able to carry up to 95 seeds per trip. A study by ornithologist Stephen Vander Well, of Utah State University, proved that nutcrackers were able to recall where they had cached their seeds. John Ehrlich and colleagues described that study thusly: "The birds remember where the seeds are in relation to central landmarks, such as rocks. If the landmarks are moved, the areas the birds search are displaced an equivalent amount."

This ability to cache food is not unique to Clark's nutcrackers. Several other bird species store food, including woodpeckers, titmice, chickadees, shrikes, jays, and owls. But only nutcrackers are able to store food in such large quantities. Some jays, members of the same family (Corvidae) as nutcrackers, are able to store lesser amounts of seeds in the ground, but only nutcrackers possess a sublingual pouch; pinyon and Steller's jays carry smaller amounts in their expandable esophagus. What's more, only nutcrackers bury their caches at a perfect depth so that the seeds that go undiscovered (approximately 30 percent) can germinate and produce more trees. Ehrlich wrote that "pines appear to have evolved cone and seed structures and fruiting times that increase the chance for their seeds to be buried (planted) by the birds."

Clark's nutcracker

The amazing Clark's nutcrackers are medium-sized birds (about 12 in. or 30 cm in length) with all-gray bodies and black wings with white patches, and black feet, eyes, and bills. In flight, the white trailing edges of their wings and broad, white outer tail feathers are conspicuous. Often, their almost continuous calls, a guttural and drawn-out "kra-a-a," are heard even before the bird appears. In the backcountry, the nutcracker's "kra-a-a" or "chaar" calls are commonplace, even if a bird is not seen.

The scientific name for this bird is *Nucifraga columbiana*: the genus is Latin for "nut-breaker," and the species name was derived from the Columbia River, the place where William Clark, of the Lewis and Clark Expedition, was the first to collect one in about 1804.

Except during the most severe winters, when the depth of the snowpack prevents the birds from digging out their food caches and they move to lower elevations, nutcrackers stay true to their territories. Nest-building may begin as early as February and young are on their own by June.

As might be expected for a Corvid, nutcrackers are one of the most curious and opportunistic of birds. They learn very soon where they can expect handouts, and their presence about campgrounds, picnic areas, and overlooks, as well as the Lake Louise Hotel grounds, can be attributed to those expectations.

The Park Environments

The four national parks share boundaries as well as flora and fauna; they were declared a comprehensive World Heritage Site by UNESCO (United Nations Educational, Scientific, and Cultural Organization) in 1985 because "they include all four geological zones of the Rocky Mountains in an outstanding setting of exceptional beauty." World Heritage Site designation is truly an honor; it includes only about 325 sites worldwide. Each is considered of universal value; their protection is considered the responsibility of all humankind. As of January 1, 1990, 111 countries had signed the World Heritage Convention, an agreement to cooperate in providing aid for protecting all the World Heritage Sites.

Although the four parks were given world recognition as a comprehensive unit, each has its own identity. Banff was established in 1885, as Canada's first national park, and is the best known; beautiful Lake Louise has long been a favorite of travelers. The Canadian Parks Service brochure for the four parks describes the 1,640,960-acre (664,087 ha) Banff National Park as an area "of mountains, valleys, glaciers, forests, alpine meadows, lakes and wild rivers along the Alberta flank of the Continental Divide." The highest elevation is 11,500 feet (3,505 m), and much of the area is above treeline.

Jasper National Park also lies along the eastern slope. It is one of Canada's largest parks, at 2,688,000 acres (1,087,819 ha), and is 98 percent wilderness. It contains "broad valleys and rugged mountains" and a parkway that is "unparalleled for beauty as it runs alongside a chain of massive icefields straddling the Continental Divide." The park's maximum elevation is 12,294 feet (3,747 m) at the summit of Mount Columbia, which is also the highest point in Alberta. Jasper's lowest river valleys are approximately 3,000 feet (914 m) in elevation, producing the greatest relief in any of Canada's Rocky Mountain parks.

Kootenay National Park (347,520 acres or 140,839 ha) is described in the brochure as "a land of startling contrasts of towering summits and hanging glaciers, narrow chasms and color-splashed mineral pools." The 324,480-acre (131,315-ha) Yoho National Park is "a park with snow-topped mountain peaks" (more than 25 are over 10,000 ft or 3,048 m elevation), "roaring rivers and deep silent forests," and nearly 8,400 feet (2,560 m) of relief. "Yoho" means "awe" in the Cree Indian language. These latter two areas are located along the western slope of the Rocky Mountains in British Columbia.

The combined area of the four parks includes over 6½ million acres (approximately 2,700,000 ha) of magnificent scenery. Although a highway crosses through the center of each park, only a fraction of the total land area is visible along the major roadways. These parks also offer 2,315 miles (3,725 km) of hiking trails: 950 miles (1,529 km) at Banff, 930 miles (1,514 km) at Jasper, 185 miles (297 km) at Kootenay, and 250 miles (402 km) at Yoho.

Plant life within the four parks can be divided into three broad vegetative zones: alpine, subalpine, and montane. The harsh alpine area lies above treeline where low-growing plants, such as purple saxifrage, heartleaf arnica, and dryad, and lichens and mosses are dominant. All the alpine plants possess short growing seasons; they must flower and seed in only a few weeks.

Below treeline, approximately 7,500 feet (2,286 m) elevation, subalpine vegetation prevails, but it takes a variety of forms, depending upon the stage of succession and various environmental conditions. Engelmann spruce and subalpine fir occur nearest treeline. Much of this vegetation shows the effects of continuous wind, which causes plants to grow in a windblown, flattened posture called "krummholz," a German word for "twisted wood." Scattered areas of alpine larch and whitebark pine may exist just below treeline. Shrubby meadows occur in some valley bottoms that retain cold air, producing dwarf willows, birch, and spruce. Thick stands of willows and alders dominate avalanche slopes.

The subalpine forest is usually dominated by Engelmann and subalpine fir. This habitat often produces extensive dark-green forests, often so thick that sunlight only partially penetrates the thick canopy. Feather-mosses often form deep green carpets, and dominant shrubs include heathers, bunchberry, and wintergreens.

White spruce usually dominates the valley bottoms, and dense stands of lodgepole pine occur in areas following fires, such as the old railroad bed along the Bow River. Stands of aspens exist on well-drained and drier soils, and black cottonwoods often dominate the riverbanks. Typical undergrowth in the lower areas include grasses, horsetails, Labrador tea, and Canada buffaloberry.

Douglas fir is a good indicator of the montane zone and often forms savannah-like stands, interspersed with grasslands. Common understory montane species include grasses, common and creeping junipers, shrubby cinquefoil, and bearberry. Montane wetlands occur at scattered locations, such as near the townsites of Banff and Jasper and downriver. Often, these habitats are the most productive within any of the four parks.

The Canadian Parks Service maintains a number of information centers: at Banff townsite and Lake Louise in Banff, at the

Columbia Icefield and Jasper townsite in Jasper, at West Gate and Marble Canyon in Kootenay, and at Field in Yoho. Each of these centers contains an information desk and orientation exhibits. Bird checklists are available for Banff and Kootenay National Parks; Jasper has its own bird book, *Birding Jasper National Park*, by Kevin Van Tighem.

Interpretive activities vary within the four parks, but each area has orientation programs at its information center and naturalist-guided walks in season; Lake Louise and Jasper's Icefield information centers also contain exhibits. Evening talks at pertinent locations are also provided. Schedules vary within the four parks and are included within the parks' mini-newspapers, available for the asking.

In addition, the Jasper Institute and Friends of Yoho offer a variety of natural history courses, including several on birding. Further information can be obtained from the Jasper Institute, Box 2337, Jasper, Alberta T0E 1E0; and Friends of Yoho, Box 100, Field, BC V0A 1G0.

Additional park information is available from the following superintendents: Banff National Park, Box 900, Banff, Alberta T0L 0C0; (403) 762-1550; Jasper National Park, P.O. Box 10, Jasper, Alberta T0E 1E0; (403) 852-6161; Kootenay National Park, P.O. Box 220, Radium Hot Springs, B.C. V0A 1M0; (604) 347-9615; Yoho National Park, Box 99, Field, B.C. V0A 1G0; (604) 343-6324.

Bird Life

The Clark's nutcracker is but one of seven Corvids that reside within the parks; they are some of the most obvious and personable birds in the entire Rocky Mountains. The other Corvids include the common raven (largest), American crow, black-billed magpie, and three jays: gray, Steller's, and blue. There are 18 species of Corvids in North America and 103 species worldwide. John Terres, in his wonderful book *The Audubon Society Encyclopedia of North American Birds*, calls them the most bold, active, noisy, and aggressive of all birds. They also are considered among the most intelligent of birds. Some individuals can count, mimic sounds as if to talk, and learn to perform tricks and solve puzzles.

The **black-billed magpie** resides throughout the montane portion of Banff, Jasper, and Yoho; it is especially common in Banff and Jasper townsites and Lake Louise Campground, and somewhat less numerous along the Banff Highway and Yellowhead Highway east of Jasper townsite. Magpies are long-tailed, black-and-white birds with loud "chaeck" or "cack cack cack" calls. They are rarely alone but usually in family groups. And magpies are one of the few songbirds that form long-term bonds with their mates. During courtship, a male's display before the female is a thing to behold. He will strut, flash his wings, and chase the female from place to place, all the time calling in cackles and musical whistles. Diet-wise, magpies are opportunists and will eat almost any kind of meat, dead or alive, found along the highways and in the forest. For additional information on their diet and personality, see chapter 25 on Great Sand Dunes.

Common ravens and American crows are also common in the parks. Ravens enjoy the widest distribution and can be expected almost anywhere from the lowlands to the tundra, but crows are restricted to grassy areas below the alpine zone and are especially common at campgrounds and along the entrance roads. Both are all-black birds that sometimes can be difficult to tell apart. However, there are some easy keys to identification. Besides the raven's larger size and heavy-set appearance, its bill is huge in comparison with the crow's; ravens possess loose feathers about their heads that give them a shaggy appearance, while crows have a slicker look; and ravens' tails are wedge-shaped in flight, while crows' tails are squared.

A pair of **common ravens** put on a wonderful show of aerial maneuvers over The Whistlers at Jasper National Park, diving, twisting, and riding the thermals. The two dozen or so hikers, who had just ascended from the Athabasca Valley to treeline by tram, could not help but admire these vociferous Corvids. Except for the numerous, much smaller horned larks, which sang their tinkling songs along the Summit Trail, ravens are usually the only birds in evidence at this high alpine area. White-tailed ptarmigans, Clark's nutcrackers, Townsend's solitaires, and gray-crowned rosy finches can also be found with persistence.

And then there are the three jays. Blue jays, the crested, blue-and-white jays common to eastern North America, are rare vagrants at Banff and Jasper. The Steller's jay, the royal blue bird with a blackish crest, is the jay of the montane forests; it is most numerous along the western slopes, and rare on the east side. At Kootenay's Sinclair Pass Overlook, Steller's jays replace nutcrackers as that park's welcoming agent. And gray jays, locally known as "whiskey jacks," are present in substantial numbers in the subalpine zones of all four parks.

Gray jays greeted me at the start of the Johnston Canyon Trail in Banff, floating through the spruce and firs like silent ghosts. They came so close I was almost able to reach out and touch one or two. It was immediately evident that this was a family group of light-colored adults and much darker youngsters. Their calls, low-pitched whistles and "cla cla cla" sounds, seemed muffled in comparison with other loud-mouthed Corvids. I couldn't help but admire the adult's dull beauty: gray underparts with darker back and wings, and coal black bills and eyes against an almost silvery white cheek and forehead. Their bold manner reminded me of a camping trip during which these brazen "camp robbers" actually stole food I was eating.

Like nutcrackers, gray jays store food for the winter. But rather than hiding food underground like their longer-billed cousins, they cache seeds, fruit, bugs, carrion, and unattended nestlings on conifers. They store partially digested food coated with sticky fluids from their mouth glands that helps it to stick in place. This storage system permits them to remain in their territories throughout the cold winter months when little fresh food remains. It also allows gray jays to nest in late winter, when the snow is still deep, prior to the arrival and/or growth of a new food supply.

The alpine portions of the four parks share many of the same bird species. Typical Rocky Mountain tundra birds include white-tailed ptarmigan, water pipit, horned lark, and rosy finch. See chapter 5 on Glacier and Waterton for a description of these birds. An additional alpine species, **willow ptarmigan**, occurs in Jasper, where it is at the southern edge of its range. This grouse-like bird nests from above treeline and down to the willow and alder thickets of the subalpine zone. Maligne Range, Signal Mountain, and Tonquin Valley are the most likely sites to observe this northern species, according to Van Tighen.

Willow ptarmigan

Willow ptarmigans are larger than their white-tailed cousins and possess an all-black tail; even in mid-winter, when their plumage turns all-white to help hide them from their enemies, their tails, eyes, and bills remain black. Summer plumaged birds are brown with a reddish tint, and have white wings. During courtship, the male's bright red comb, the bare skin above the eyes, swells to four times the normal size. Willow ptarmigan courtship can be a wild affair. Terres described it and the male's attentiveness during nesting as follows:

> Each male selects a bare spot of ground and with swollen red combs begins to strut and call; frequently flies into air; uttering barking notes as he flutters to ground; many fierce battles between males, with feathers plucked, blood flowing; females

loiter in cover nearby; after mating with a male, later make nest; unlike other species of ptarmigans, male remains with female throughout incubation period; he hides in thickets close to female while she is on nest; he defends her, flying viciously at gulls, sometimes knocking them over to prevent them from getting at mate's eggs; has even attacked grizzly bear that stumbled over mate's nest, and male will attack persons who catch one of the chicks.

The Bow Lake area lies along the Icefields Parkway in northern Banff National Park, 25 miles (40 km) north of Lake Louise; it provides the visitor with a smorgasbord of subalpine habitats. One morning in June, I walked the Bow Glacier Trail that passes through thickets of pussy willows, skirts the forested lakeshore to the glacier runoff, and then follows the flood plain to where it climbs over a series of moraines to the falls. The willow-dominated wetland was alive with birdsong. **White-crowned sparrows**, typical wetland species in all four parks, were most numerous, singing their songs of clear whistles and buzzing trills, sometimes described as a plaintive whistle followed by "more more cheezies please." Their bold black-and-white head patterns, gray collars and underparts, and mottled backs were easily visible in the bright sunshine. I found three individuals hopping about in the center of the trail, occasionally scratching the ground with both feet as if they were searching for seeds.

A similar willow thicket at Sunwapta Pass was also dominated by white-crowned sparrows, which shared the area with Brewer's sparrows and American robins. The robins had adapted to this dwarf vegetation very well; I discovered a pair of birds feeding youngsters in a nest built only about 2 feet (60 cm) above the ground in an alpine fir that reached only about 4 feet (122 cm) tall. And Brewer's sparrows were actively singing from several of the adjacent fir and willows. These little sparrows with whitish underparts, grayish eyebrows, and finely streaked crowns, were singing wonderfully varied and bubbly songs, actually in chorus with one another. The best description of this elaborate song comes from David DeSante, in *The Audubon Society Master Guide to Birding*: "Canary-like series of long, sweet, musical or buzzy trills that seem endlessly varied in speed, pitch, and quality. A typical song may last 10 seconds or more."

A musical song of a Lincoln's sparrow exploded from a taller willow next to the little stream that wove through the thicket toward Bow Lake. I listened intently as it sang its gurgling melody, "churr-churr-churr-wee-wee-wee-wah." This perky little sparrow possessed a buff wash on its finely streaked breast and flanks, bold gray eyebrows, and obvious whitish eye rings.

Then suddenly I heard the winnowing of a common snipe flying high above the wetland. It took me several minutes to locate this medium-sized, long-billed shorebird, little more than a dot in the blue sky. I watched it circle the area; every 15 to 20 seconds it would dive slightly and spread its tail feathers, producing a strange winnowing sound as the wind blew through its feathers. Several days later, at Cottonwood Slough near Jasper townsite, I found two individuals perched at the top of black spruce trees, calling nasal "scaip" calls over and over. I couldn't decide if their defensive behavior was targeted toward me or each other. See chapter 23 on the Black Canyon of the Gunnison and Curecanti for an explanation of this bird's behavior.

Other birds found about the wetland and adjacent Num-Ti-Jah Lodge included a noisy killdeer, numerous barn swallows (they were nesting on the lodge building), American robins, black-capped Wilson's warblers, and brightly marked pine siskins. Scoping the lake, I found two pairs of common mergansers, a pair of lesser scaups, and a lone red-necked grebe. A male green-winged teal was located along the near shoreline. Then, an adult bald eagle appeared over the north shore; it crossed over the lodge, followed the east shoreline over the highway, and disappeared to the south. What a beautiful bird it was; its snow white head and tail contrasted with its dark brown body.

A spruce-fir forest covers much of the south slope beyond the wetland and could well represent most of the spruce-fir forests in the four parks. I paused below the forest and listened to the bird sounds coming from the dark green slope. The persistent songs of ruby-crowned kinglets rang from the high conifers; their "tee tee tee, tew tew tew, teedadee teedadee teedadee" notes were extremely loud for such tiny songsters. The toy horn calls of red-breasted nuthatches were evident as well. The nasal "tseek-a-day-day" song of a boreal chickadee descended from the forest. Yellow-rumped warblers joined the morning chorus. The rising "zzzhrreeee" notes of pine siskins were common. And high on the ridge Clark's nut-crackers called.

I suddenly realized that both varied and hermit thrushes were singing as well. The **varied thrush** song was a strange bell-like buzz that varied in pitch from one song to another, a little like a series of quavering whistles that changed pitch every now and then. The hermit thrush song was very different, constructed of flutelike phrases on different pitches.

On another day I walked around Yoho's beautiful Emerald Lake, slightly lower in elevation and surrounded by a dense spruce-fir forest with scattered mountain hemlocks and western redcedars, evidence of the Pacific slope influence. Most of the bird species were the same as those near Bow Lake, but the composition was very different. For example, varied thrushes were abundant, and their lovely, bell-like songs were evident throughout the 3.2-mile (5.2 km) circuit. The few glances I got revealed it to be a lovely bird. Varied thrushes are robin-sized and possess orange underparts with a black chest-band, orange cheeks divided by bold black eye lines, and bluish back and wings with orange wing bars. See chapter 5 on Glacier and Waterton Lake for additional information on this wonderful species.

Townsend's warblers were common along the Emerald Lake Trail as well. Like the varied thrush, this is another western species that is generally more numerous on the west slope of the four parks than it is to the east; it is also common in Bow Valley. Its very unique song, a series of hoarse "see" notes, was especially evident near the lodge buildings. Its song does not match this very dynamic and bright, black-and-yellow warbler. Males possess coal black throats, upper breasts, and cheeks, bright yellow eyebrows and bold slashes below the cheeks that form a collar, yellow breasts, streaked flanks, white belly, and black wings with two white wing bars. It is a gorgeous bird, indeed!

Winter wrens sang a continuous and rapid melodious trill from the heaviest undergrowth. Ruby-crowned and golden-crowned kinglets sang from the treetops. The very high-pitched song of brown creepers was evident on several occasions. American robins, yellow-rumped warblers, dark-eyed juncos, and pine siskins were common throughout. Lesser numbers of rufous hummingbirds, olive-sided flycatchers, gray jays, Swainson's thrushes, Wilson's warblers, and pine grosbeaks were also found.

On the far side of the lake, several streams form wetlands where they enter the lake and produce a very different habitat. The area reminded me of the moss-draped rainforest of the Olympic Peninsula. And this is where I found four territorial **northern waterthrushes**, spaced out every few hundred feet. Each was singing from near the top of a spruce or fir, telling its neighbor to stay out of its territory. The northern waterthrush is not a very colorful species, with dark olive-brown upperparts, bold whitish eye lines, and light-buff underparts that are heavily streaked with black. But its song is loud and clear, an emphatic melody that can be written as "sweet sweet sweet swee-wee-wee chew chew chew."

I couldn't help but wonder where this bird had spent its winter months, somewhere in the West Indies, Mexico, or Central America. It is one of our Neotropical songbirds that divides its time in half between its nesting grounds in North America and its winter home in the tropics. The loss of either habitat may result in the decline and eventual extirpation of this wonderful songbird.

Emerald Lake also contained a number of water birds: pairs of common loons, common mergansers, and white-winged scoters. The scoters, like the loons, are seabirds that spend the majority of their lives at sea but come inland to nest on the grassy shores of northern lakes during their breeding seasons. Alberta and British Columbia encompass their southernmost nesting grounds.

Emerald River flows into the Kicking Horse River 4.8 miles (7.7 km) below Emerald Lake, at a point near where the Amiskwi River also joins the Kicking Horse, and eventually flows into the Columbia River and on to the Pacific Ocean. Many of the upper watercourses are glacier melt that are aqua-blue in color, a product of light reflecting on the fine silt particles from the glaciers. But in

spite of the water's milky color, these streams support high populations of **American dippers**. These plump, dark gray birds spend
much of their time in the swift currents, feeding on the insect larvae they find on the river bottoms. They have adapted to these
habitats to such an extent that they actually can swim through the
swift currents and walk underwater. They are amazing birds to
watch. Betty and I watched a dipper one afternoon at Kootenay's
Marble Canyon. We were intrigued by its constant dipping behavior. It was busy searching for food in the swift stream near the start
of the trail, but as soon as it had a mouthful of food it flew up the
gorge, under the little bridge, and disappeared in the deep chasm of
Marble Canyon. We assumed it was feeding young in a nest tucked
in a crevice or under an overhang.

The American dipper is our only truly aquatic songbird, and it
can swim to 20 feet (6 m) below the surface while feeding. John
Ehrlich and colleagues described their feeding habits thusly:

American dipper

Although dippers occasionally glean their prey from streamside rocks or even flycatch, they extract most of their prey from the water. Often they wade along the stream with their heads beneath the surface snapping up prey. They also stride along the bottom completely submerged and "fly" underwater using powerful beats of their wings as they search for food.

Dippers may also feed on floating insects, on frozen insects found on snowbanks, and occasionally they take clams, snails, and trout fry. They possess special adaptations for their unique behavior: much larger oil glands than other songbirds and scales that close their nostrils when underwater.

Banff's Bow River flows southeast through the park, increasing in size with each tributary, and finally forms a series of shallow lakes near Banff townsite. These lakes, especially the three Vermilion Lakes, and the surrounding mixed forest, provide superb montane habitats for birds. Common waterfowl on these lakes in summer include common loons, red-necked grebes, Canada geese, mallards, and blue-winged teal.

Dozens of **Canada geese** were present along the near shore and feeding on the shallow lakes one June morning. Small flocks of birds were also moving from place to place, probably en route to preferred feeding sites. Their large size, black necks and obvious white chins, and loud honking calls made identification easy.

Canada geese populations at Vermilion Lakes vary considerably through the year. Although they usually are absent in winter, once the lake freezes over until the spring thaw in late February or early March, highest numbers occur in spring and early summer. The Vermilion Lakes' birds generally spend their winters in the inter-mountain region of Washington and Oregon and south to Nevada and central California. And according to Frank Bellrose, in *Ducks, Geese & Swans of North America*, during mild winters, when open water prevails, many also overwinter in western Montana, Wyoming, and Colorado.

I spotted several other birds during my morning visit to the Vermilion Lakes and adjacent Cave and Basin Marsh. Common species included the western wood-pewee; violet-green swallow; American crow; black-billed magpie; American robin; ruby-crowned kinglet; warbling vireo; orange-crowned, yellow, and yellow-rumped warblers; common yellowthroat; red-winged blackbird; chipping, song, white-crowned, and Lincoln sparrows; dark-eyed junco; and pine siskin. Lesser numbers of bald eagles, killdeers, common snipes, northern flickers, belted kingfishers, willow and alder flycatchers, Clark's nutcrackers, winter wrens, solitary vireos; Tennessee, Townsend's, and MacGillivray's warblers; American redstarts; western tanagers, and brown-headed cowbirds were present.

Yoho National Park has a smaller wetland habitat, called Leanchoil Marsh, near its western entrance, along Kicking Horse River at the Wapta Falls Road junction. I found many of the same birds there but with some interesting additions. Six species of swallows were feeding over the wetland: tree, violet-green, cliff, northern rough-winged, bank, and barn. A pair of eastern kingbirds participated in the flycatching frenzy. And at least five willow flycatchers sang their loud and distinct "fitz-bew" songs from widely spaced trees over the marsh.

The waterfowl assemblage at Leanchoil was also very different from the Vermilion Lakes. Ring-necked ducks were most numerous, a few mallards, and a lone American coot were detected. Other wetland species found there included a lone great blue heron, perched on a tall Douglas fir; common snipes and solitary sandpipers were courting; soras called their loud whinny notes; and a belted kingfisher sat on a stump sticking out of an ancient beaver lodge.

Another very birdy wetland, Cottonwood Slough, exists on the bench just above Jasper townsite. This area consists of two lakes, several ponded areas, and connecting waterways. One morning in mid-June, I found many of the same birds that had been present at Banff's Vermilion Lakes and Yoho's Leanchoil Marsh, but differences were most interesting. Jasper's montane wetlands contain a stronger eastern affinity than is found in the other three parks: Tennessee and blackpoll warblers, and swamp sparrows, and three species of eastern affinity were actively involved with territorial responsibilities.

Other common songbirds found in and about Cottonwood Slough included five *Empidonax* flycatchers (alder, willow, least,

Hammond's, and dusky); northern rough-winged and barn swallows; black-capped chickadees; ruby-crowned kinglets; Swainson's thrushes; American robins; cedar waxwings; warbling vireos; orange-crowned, yellow, and yellow-rumped warblers; northern waterthrushes; chipping, clay-colored, song, and Lincoln's sparrows; dark-eyed juncos; red-winged blackbirds; brown-headed cowbirds; and pine siskins. Less numerous songbirds that morning included red-breasted nuthatches, varied thrushes, solitary vireos, MacGillivray's warblers, American redstarts, western tanagers, and Cassin's finches.

Several black swifts were present high over the wetland in early morning but disappeared soon afterwards. The dull drumming of a ruffed grouse echoed from the aspen grove. Two male calliope hummingbirds chased one another along the shore of the larger pond. A lone common loon flew over, calling its crazy, laughing songs while in flight. Spotted sandpipers called from the shore. A belted kingfisher perched on various snags about the wetland. And an osprey flew by, circled the ponds, and then continued on to another fishing site.

Jasper's **yellow-rumped warblers** came in two forms: the yellow-throated "Audubon's," typical of the Rocky Mountains and western North America, and the white-throated "myrtle" warbler, typical of eastern North America. I had finally discovered a place where the two forms overlap, where they interbreed, and where ornithologists gained sufficient insight to lump these two different-appearing birds into a single species.

I spent two full weeks in the four parks, visiting the most heavily visited sites as well as a few places slightly off the main routes. My favorite memories included: hiking to above Larch Valley in Banff, where two dozen gray-crowned rosy finches walked around me, calling to one another as if I was not there; finding a bright red male and two female pine grosbeaks feeding on new, green foliage above Emerald Lake in Yoho; seeing four pairs of gorgeous harlequin ducks at the outlet of Maligne Lake; and watching a dozen black swifts wheeling overhead at Cottonwood Slough in Jasper.

Wintertime presents a very different situation for birds. Local birders undertake Christmas Bird Counts each year to tally the various species that are present. Although count success depends primarily on local weather conditions, most of the censuses tally 1,100 to 2,250 individuals of 13 to 52 species. In 1991, the Yoho and Jasper counts produced 20 and 39 species, respectively. The dozen most numerous species, in descending order of abundance, were common raven, house sparrow, evening grosbeak, black-capped chickadee, pine grosbeak, gray-crowned rosy finch, gray jay, white-winged crossbill, boreal chickadee, mountain chickadee, European starling, and American dipper.

In summary, a comprehensive list of birds for the four parks include 284 species, of which 143 have been found to nest. Twenty-five of the 143 species are water birds (loon, grebes, heron, waterfowl, rails, and shorebirds), 17 are hawks and owls, and 12 are warblers. Only three species—pygmy nuthatch, rufous-sided towhee, and hoary redpoll—have been recorded only during winter.

Birds of Special Interest

Canada goose. This large water bird, with its black neck and white throat, is common in montane wetlands such as Banff's Vermilion Lakes.

Willow ptarmigan. It is most likely to be found in the Maligne Range, Signal Mountain, and Tonquin Valley. Its summertime plumage is reddish brown with white wings and a black tail.

Gray jay. Watch for this grayish jay anywhere within the subalpine zones of the four parks. Young birds are much darker in color. It is locally known as "whiskey jack."

Clark's nutcracker. There is no better place to find this black, gray, and white bird than at Banff's Lake Louise, but it is common in all the parks.

Black-billed magpie. This is the black-and-white bird with a long tail that is most numerous about Banff and Jasper townsites and Lake Louise Campground.

Common raven. Its large size, all-black plumage, heavy bill, and wedge-shaped tail help to separate this bird from the smaller, sleeker American crow.

Varied thrush. Its bell-like songs, sung at different pitches that fade at the end, are common in the parks' moist conifer forests in spring and summer.

American dipper. It is fairly common along all of the parks' fast-rushing streams. It is a plump, gray-brown bird that dips up and down.

Northern waterthrush. This medium-sized, rather nondescript warbler sings a loud and spirited song within the low- to mid-elevation wetlands.

Yellow-rumped warbler. Both the yellow-throated "Audubon" and white-throated "myrtle" warblers occur together at Jasper and Banff. They otherwise look alike: yellow caps, sides, and rumps.

White-crowned sparrow. Its black-and-white striped head help to identify this active, vociferous bird of willow shrubbery along the streams and subalpine wetlands.

4

Mount Revelstoke and Glacier National Parks, British Columbia

A myriad of bird songs greeted me on my early morning visit to the Skunk Cabbage Nature Trail. The descending, flutelike song of a veery, the rich caroling of American robins, the melodious warblings of yellow and MacGillivray's warblers, and the "fee-bee" call of a black-capped chickadee provided a welcoming chorus at the parking area.

I crossed the little wooden bridge and entered the moist canopy of black cottonwoods and western redcedars. Mountain alders, willows, elderberries, honeysuckles, and red-osier dogwoods dominated the undergrowth. Suddenly, the spirited song of an American redstart erupted from the willows to my left. A few seconds later a black and orange male appeared; it flew to an open limb and serenaded me with a rapid series of thin notes: "zee-zee-zee-zawaah." It was active and animated, and I watched that butterfly-like warbler for several minutes as it gleaned the foliage for insects. Every now and then it put its head back and sang its sibilant song. I couldn't help but think how often I had seen this lovely bird in eastern landscapes, but here it was in the Columbia forest of the far West. The theory that this little songbird may be the most numerous warbler in all of North America now made a little more sense.

The boardwalk of the Skunk Cabbage Trail began just ahead and wound through a wetland that contained a multitude of skunk cabbage plants. This large-leafed arum bore bright yellow flower-coverings that stood a foot high; inside was a thick rootstock that contained hundreds of minute flowers. Swamp horsetail stalks, many with swollen cones, were also abundant in the shallow water.

Immediately on entering the marsh, a **song sparrow** announced its presence. It was abundantly obvious that this was the dominant bird of Skunk Cabbage Marsh; song sparrows were everywhere. They sang from the boardwalk and the elevated overlooks, from the low shrubbery, the higher shrubs, and from the very tops of the adjacent trees. Their vocal renditions varied as much as their singing posts. Their most common song was three or four short, clear notes, like "sweet sweet sweet," followed by a buzzy "tow-weee," then a trill. Their unique "chimp" call was also commonplace.

Song sparrows are not the most colorful of birds, but they more than make up for their drab appearance by their constant activity and wonderful repertoire of songs. In fact, this bird's scientific name is *melodia*, Greek for melody or melodious song. The species was the subject of a 1943 study of bird songs by Margaret Nice, who discovered that an Ohio song sparrow sang a total of 2,305 songs during a single day in May. Its reputation for being a remarkable songster is well-deserved.

Song sparrows possess brown plumage with darker streaks; the heavy streaks on their whitish breasts form a black stickpin that is not always visible. When flying from one singing post to another, they will pump their rather long tails up and down, as if to get cranked up for their next series of songs.

Unlike most sparrows, song sparrows may nest several times during a single breeding season, occasionally using the same nest or building another one nearby at a slightly higher elevation. Males and females actually divide up their nestlings for feeding, each caring for their own set. But as soon as the young are able to fly, they become the male's responsibility; the female begins the next clutch.

The Park Environment

Mount Revelstoke and Glacier national parks are not actual parts of the Rocky Mountains. They occur in the Selkirk Range to the west, part of the Columbia Mountains of British Columbia, a region of North America often referred to as the "interior wet belt." Average annual precipitation at Revelstoke, BC, is about 28 inches (70 cm), compared with only 12 inches (30 cm) at Calgary, Alberta, on the eastern flanks of the Rocky Mountains. However, because of their proximity to the four Rocky Mountain parks, Banff, Jasper, Kootenay, and Yoho, visitors to one area often stop at the other.

Although Mount Revelstoke and Glacier are physically separated by 10 miles (16 km), they are connected by the Trans-Canada Highway and railway that runs from Vancouver to Calgary and eastward. Their close association is due to joint administration and operations, as well as to a number of joint descriptive superlatives: the two parks possess 422 glaciers that cover a tenth of the landscape; permanent snow and ice cover 12 percent of the two parks; 13 peaks rise over 8,200 feet (2,500 m) in elevation; more than 1,500 avalanches affect the highway passing through the parks each winter; and John Woods, in *Glacier Country*, wrote that the dual parks possess "the steepest and wildest mountain terrain on the continent."

The 64,000-acre (25,900 ha) Mount Revelstoke is best known for its topographic relief that runs from 1,500 feet (457 m) at the town of Revelstoke, on the Columbia River, to 8,681 feet (2,646 m) elevation at the summit of Mount Coursier, the park's highest point, providing a total relief of 7,180 feet (2,189 m). The summit of Mount Revelstoke is 6,358 feet (1,938 m) elevation. The park includes more than 50 miles (80 km) of trails, including the spectacular but short Mountain Meadows Interpretive Trail at the summit. That trail passes through a subalpine meadow, where wildflowers provide an array of colors in summer, reaching their peak during late July and early August. The Mount Revelstoke summit is accessible by a 16-mile (26-km) roadway from the town of Revelstoke.

The much larger Glacier National Park encompasses an area of 333,333 acres (134,898 ha) east of Mount Revelstoke and 50 miles (80 km) west of Yoho. Ann and Myron Sutton, in *Wilderness Areas of North America*, regard Glacier as "a place almost classic in its arrangements of lofty mountain." Half of Glacier National Park lies above 5,900 feet (1,800 m), and more than a tenth of the area is permanently bound in ice and snow.

Three rather distinct vegetation zones exist within the two parks: alpine tundra, subalpine forest, and montane forest. Tundra occurs above treeline, approximately 6,600 feet (2,000 m) in elevation, where high winds, cold temperatures, and thin soils prevail. The Canadian Parks Service's little booklet, *Alive in the Wet Belt*, points out that this area is "a land of specialists. Low-growing alpine plants often escape high winds behind ridges or boulders. Lichen-encrusted rock and glacial ice cover much of the alpine."

The subalpine zone is generally dominated by a dense forest of Engelmann spruce, subalpine fir, and mountain hemlock. In moist, cool sites at mid-elevation can be found Pacific slope communities, the "interior rainforest," that are dominated by western redcedar and mountain hemlock, with lesser numbers of Pacific yew and false box. Understory plants include lady fern, devil's club, thimbleberry, and early blueberry. Typical understory plants of the upper areas include feather mosses, Rocky Mountain rhododendron, and heathers. At lower elevations, grasses, horsetails, labrador tea, and false azalea are more common.

Avalanches play an extremely important role in determining plant communities within the subalpine zone of the Columbia Mountains because of the extensive snowpack that they receive during normal winters; fire is less common there than it is in the drier Rocky Mountains. Windthrows, fungal rots, and insect infestations affect forests to varying degrees, but avalanches are the most widespread influence on the ecological diversity of these forests. Without avalanches the landscape would consist of more even-stand forests with less diversity. Avalanches create clearings within the forest so that new growth can begin. The resultant grasses and shrubs, mainly alders and willows, form early communities that contain a surprisingly rich flora and fauna.

The montane zone is limited to the lower, warmer valleys and slopes of Mount Revelstoke National Park. Douglas fir is the best indicator tree of this zone, although stands of aspens, birch, and alders occur in scattered localities. The lower portion of the Mount Revelstoke Summit Road passes through this vegetative zone.

The Trans-Canada Highway cuts directly through Glacier but only skirts the southeastern edge of Mount Revelstoke. The Canadian Parks Service operates information centers at Rogers Pass in Glacier and in the town of Revelstoke. A sales outlet at Rogers Pass is operated by the Friends of Mount Revelstoke & Glacier; bird field guides and a comprehensive *Wildlife Checklist* (which includes a bird list) are available.

Interpretive activities include daily nature walks from Glacier's Illecillewaet (pronounced Illa-silla-wet; a Shuswap Indian name for "rushing waters") Campground, special flower walks at the summit of Mount Revelstoke in August, and evening movies at Rogers Pass Center. In addition, five self-guided trails are available: Abandoned Rails and Loop Brook trails at Glacier, and Giant Cedars, Skunk Cabbage, and Meadows-in-the-Sky trails at Mount Revelstoke. All of the park's interpretive activities are described in *Selkirk Summit*, which is available for the asking.

Two campgrounds are maintained in Glacier, at Illecillewaet and Loop Brook, but none at Mount Revelstoke. Overnight accommodations are available at Glacier's Rogers Pass.

Additional information on the two parks can be obtained from the Superintendent, Mount Revelstoke and Glacier National Parks, Box 350, Revelstoke, B.C. V0E 2S0; (604) 837-7500.

Bird Life

The **common yellowthroat** is almost as numerous as are song sparrows along the Skunk Cabbage Trail. Males are bright yellow birds with coal black masks below a grayish forehead; females are rather plain olive-brown birds with yellowish throats. I watched four males participating in a wild chase that must have lasted for two or three minutes. I never was sure which bird was defending which territory. But from their vigorous behavior and constant singing, nesting was undoubtedly underway. Their "witchity witchity witchity" songs emanated from every part of the marsh.

I was so busy tracking song sparrows and yellowthroats that the harsh "fitz-bew" songs of the **willow flycatchers** were not at first apparent. I suddenly realized that at least four birds were within hearing distance, each one singing its own version of the fitz-bew song. It took me several minutes before I found one of these little, nondescript songsters at the very top of a mountain alder. "Fitz-bew."

In spite of having an excellent look at this little flycatcher, I knew that the best way to identify this bird in the field is by its distinct song. And in the course of three hours that I spent in and around Skunk Cabbage Marsh, I also identified an alder flycatcher, singing from among mountain alders in the marsh, and a dusky flycatcher singing from an adjacent cottonwood. The alder's song was the typical, descending "fee-beo." The dusky flycatcher's song was less distinct; it sang both a clear "sillit" and a "chrip bic" song. Kenn Kaufman's *Advanced Birding* book contains the best descriptions of these troublesome *Empidonax* flycatchers.

Other birds were found in and adjacent to the marsh that morning: warbling vireos were singing their rambling whistle notes; a lone red-eyed vireo scolded me from the foliage of a cottonwood tree; yellow warblers were represented by bright yellow males with chestnut streaks on their breasts; a lone northern waterthrush sang one vigorous song and then remained silent; and a hairy woodpecker was busy extracting breakfast from an old alder snag.

I detected a few additional birds in the nearby forest: the distinct call of a pileated woodpecker; a pair of American crows with two offspring that were begging for a handout; the obnoxious "kweesch" calls of Steller's jays; loud, nasal honking calls of red-breasted nuthatches; distant, ascending flutelike songs of Swainson's thrushes; rapid tinkling songs of winter wrens; eight cedar waxwings flying from one tall tree to another; rapid trills of orange-crowned warblers; and dozens of pine siskins.

A more extensive wetland occurs along Bear Creek in the Beaver River Valley, near the east entrance to Glacier. Bear Creek Marsh contains all of the same birds found at Skunk Cabbage Marsh, as well as a number of other wetland species that are likely to be found there in spring and summer: green-winged teal, Barrow's goldeneye, common merganser, solitary sandpiper, and common snipe.

The Giant Cedars Interpretive Trail is located a short distance above the Skunk Cabbage Marsh and provides the visitor easy access to the interior rainforest. This very wet, moss-draped environment does not support a large assortment of birds, and those species that do occur there often stay high in the canopy of the giant trees. These birds include chestnut-backed chickadees, Steller's jays, brown creepers, golden-crowned kinglets, and hermit and varied thrushes. Winter wrens and dark-eyed juncos prefer the shadowy undergrowth.

Winter wrens are more often heard than seen. Their almost constant chippering calls from the dense undergrowth, and their reluctance to venture out into the open, can often persuade one to give up the chase. But patience eventually will prevail, and the wait is well worth the time and effort, for the winter wren is one of the park's loveliest creatures. Its tiny, plump frame, short tail, and reddish plumage give it a personality all of its own. Its song is a "loud series of tinkling trills and tumbling warbles, often ending on a high note or trill," writes Wayne Peterson.

Steller's jay

Nevertheless, the **Steller's jay** is the area's most charismatic bird. It is so popular in British Columbia that it was named the official province bird by a vote of the people. *Alive in the Wet Belt* dubs it "the bird of flimflam," and describes it as "alert, intelligent, inquisitive, handsome and carefree. They are also a pest—mischievous, noisy and even unscrupulous." But whatever they may be, Steller's jays produce a wide variety of sounds that can fool even the avid birder. Arthur C. Bent, ornithologist and author of the extensive Life History series, reported that they "utter low-pitched raucous squawks different from other kinds of jays; calls harsh 'waah, waah, shaack, schaak, schaak,' and mellow 'klook, klook, klook,' and shrill hawklike cries: 'kweesch, kweesch, kweesch,' has sweet soft song somewhat like 'whisper song' of robin; female has a rolling click call; is superb at imitating scream of red-tailed hawk."

Steller's jays sport royal-blue plumages, with tall, blackish crests, and tiny white eyebrows. And they can occur almost everywhere below treeline; they are especially common in the rainforest. During courtship, males feed the females and perform courtship flights that include bobbing up and down before their ladies. A mated pair builds large, bulky nests, cemented together with mud, usually in the crotch of an evergreen tree, 8 to 15 feet (2-4.5 m) high. Bent reported one nest in a giant fir at 100 feet (30 m) above the ground.

Like other members of the crow (Corvidae) family, Steller's jays are opportunists, and consume a wide variety of foods. They can be extremely aggressive toward smaller birds, taking eggs and fledglings when available. John Terres reports that this jay forages "in treetops and on ground, eats many acorns, pine seeds, some wild and cultivated fruit, beetles, wasps, bees, grasshoppers, caterpillars and moths, spiders, sow bugs, frogs, eggs and young of small birds; sometimes attacks and kills snakes." They also cache food and are able to transport small quantities of food in their esophagus.

Steller's jays rarely migrate to warmer climates in winter although they do move to lower elevations during periods of heavy snowfall. John Woods reports that these jays "line the highways" during November and April, probably representing some form of altitudinal movement.

Pine siskins also gather along the roads in winter to feed on road salt. Woods described a larger than normal siskin congregation in November 1984: "hundreds of thousands of siskins moved into the parks. It was not unusual to see a single flock of a thousand or more, and hundreds were killed daily on the highway." Park naturalist Bob Brade told me that so many siskins are struck down on the highways that the locals refer to them as "grill birds," because they get caught in the grills of their vehicles. Brade once observed a truck strike and kill 208 siskins at once, and another time he watched a common raven capture and eat nine wounded siskins.

Pine siskin

Woods continued: "The following April the big flocks dispersed, and siskins set up breeding colonies in the dense coniferous forests. Until mid-June, you could see or hear siskins almost anywhere. Then, with the first days of summer, they vanished. Nor did they return that autumn. Forests which had teemed with life one winter were completely silent the next. In the decade from 1975 to 1985 siskin invasions followed by a total exodus have been observed twice in Mount Revelstoke and Glacier parks."

What happens to these tiny mites? No one knows for sure, but Woods noted that "a siskin killed on the highway in the spring of 1984 at Mount Revelstoke had been banded two winters earlier at Whiting, New Jersey, 3,500 km (2,175 mi) away near the Atlantic coast."

Pine siskins are one of the smallest of birds, barely larger than a hummingbird. They have prominent streaking on their backs and breasts, and possess bright yellow wing bars that show up best in flight. But because of their tiny size, they usually are most often detected by their rising "schreeee" calls.

The subalpine forest dominates the slopes of both parks, forming extensive dark green forests above the lush valleys, between avalanche paths, and below the high gray cliffs. Glacier's Illecillewaet Campground is situated at the base of the subalpine zone and provides an excellent introduction to its bird life. The campground entrance road passes through an avalanche thicket where common species include rufous hummingbirds; willow flycatchers; yellow, MacGillivray's, and Wilson's warblers; and song and fox sparrows.

The **fox sparrow** is the largest of North America's 38 sparrows and is blessed with one of the most beautiful but complicated of songs. Terres calls it "clear, exultant, melodious, flutelike," and Dennis Martin, in *The Audubon Society Master Guide to Birding*, described its song thusly: "usually begins with introductory whistle followed by series of sliding notes, whistles, and slurs." They possess three or more song types, and if uninterrupted will sing all types one after the other until their entire repertoire is completed; it will then start over. One June morning I described a series of fox sparrow songs thusly: "tee-de-dee-dee-dee, sweet sweet-tree," with emphasis on the "tree"; then, "swee-dee-deet, che-che-che"; "sweede, dee-de-de-de, chip chip"; and finally, "tur-de-wee-dee, tzee, chip chip, de."

Fox sparrows are best identified by their large size, uniform dusky-brown plumage, and lighter, heavily streaked underparts. Song sparrows, which occur in the wetter portion of the thicket, are smaller and possess striped heads.

The campground proper and the trails beyond offer good examples of subalpine bird life. Steller's jays are commonly found visiting campers to check on available food supplies. Dark-eyed juncos patrol the adjacent thickets. The liquid gurgling songs of winter wrens resound from the denser undergrowth. Yellow-rumped warblers, with their black chests and five yellow spots (throat, cap, sides, and rump) flycatch from the tall spruce and hemlocks. Hammond's flycatchers call their low-pitched "chi-pit" songs from dense stands of conifers. The high, thin "tsee" notes of golden-crowned kinglets can be heard almost everywhere. The quavering whistles of warbling vireos are common along the edges. And **Townsend's warblers** sing their slurred hoarse "wee wee wee weez eah" (the last note drops) songs high overhead. Their songs have been described as being drowsy or wheezy, deliberate, and persistent—a lazy, five- to seven-note song.

Townsend's warblers are one of the area's most colorful songbirds; males are bright yellow with olive green backs, two white wing bars, and coal black throats and cheeks that are surrounded with bold yellow markings that form a collar. This is one of the parks' true western birds, a species considered analogous to the black-throated green warbler of the eastern forests.

Three thrushes can be heard from the campground and along the trails: Swainson's, hermit, and varied. Their flutelike renderings are some of the most exquisite in the bird world, and to have three (actually four if the American robin is included) singing their songs at the same time is a true delight. Swainson's thrush songs possess an upward-rolling series of phrases, written as "wip-poor-wil-wil-eez-zee-zee." These birds are dusky olive-brown with dark streaks on their lighter breasts, and buff spectacles.

The hermit thrush song, as described by Terres, "opens with clear flutelike note, followed by ethereal, bell-like tones, ascending and descending in no fixed order, rising until reach dizzying vocal heights and notes fade away in silvery tinkle." These birds possess all-brown upperparts except for reddish tails, spotted breasts, and whitish eye rings. Betty and I walked a mid-elevation portion of the Mount Revelstoke Summit Road one day in June, before the road was completely open, and during our three-hour walk we were never out of range of one or two hermit thrushes. We found one individual at the very tip of a tall, stately Engelmann spruce; it sang continuously for at least ten minutes.

The **varied thrush** may have the most unusual of all thrush songs. It has been described as a "protracted, nasal, whistled note" of varying pitches, or "a melancholy, long quavering whistle, a pause, then another succession of vibratory notes, sometimes high, then low, fading away at end" (Terres). Ehrlich and colleagues describe its song as "an eerie, bell-like, prolonged whistle that slowly fades away from the listener." Its appearance is just as unusual: orange underparts with a broad, black breastband, blackish back and head, except for a bold, orange eyebrow stripe, and orange wing bars. Females are duller than the brightly marked males. See chapter 5 on Glacier and Waterton Lakes for further details about this lovely thrush.

I found an **American dipper** along the river just above the campground. I was able to watch it search for food in the swiftly flowing waterway. It used a combination of feeding techniques: either walking over the protruding boulders and picking up insects above the waterline, sticking its head and shoulders below the water's surface to search for food, or diving completely underwater and finding insects on the stream bottom. Each time it surfaced it held an insect or larvae tightly in its bill. It bobbed or dipped its entire body time and again (hence its name), and each time I could see its eyelid slide over its black eye. Its all-gray-brown plumage and plump body was easy to lose among the rounded stream boulders as it progressed upstream. See chapter 3 on Banff, Jasper, Kootenay, and Yoho for additional information about this bird's behavior and adaptations.

American crows and their look-alike cousins, the common raven, also frequent the campground and roadways. Crows prefer the grassy roadsides and meadows, and rarely venture into the higher portions of the forest. The larger common raven, however, is equally as at home in the alpine meadows as it is patrolling the highways in search of breakfast. The raven is one of the parks' most fascinating creatures. In spring, courting birds can put on spectacular displays of aerial acrobatics, diving, twisting, and soaring in a fashion that would compete with almost any of the better known, high-flying hawks and swifts. Later in the summer, when thermals rise out of the deep valleys, ravens can soar to unbelievable heights:

their all-black plumage, pointed wings, and wedge-shaped tails may be barely visible against the deep blue sky.

Most years the Mount Revelstoke Summit Road is clear of snow by mid-July, and then the alpine meadows appear in all their glory. The Mount Revelstoke alpine zone is one of the few that can be so easily reached by vehicle. Alpine bird life is usually limited to a handful of species: golden eagle, white-tailed ptarmigan, American pipit, and rosy finch. The adjacent subalpine firs and spruce provide habitat for a few additional high-country species: gray jay, Clark's nutcracker, boreal chickadee, Townsend's solitaire, and fox and white-crowned sparrows. See chapter 3 on Banff, Jasper, Kootenay, and Yoho for a discussion of these alpine species.

Wintertime is a low ecological ebb in the highlands, although a variety of birds remain in the warmer lowlands. Christmas Bird Counts taken at Revelstoke provide a perspective on that time of year. The 1990 Revelstoke count tallied 3,138 individuals of 47 species. The most numerous species, in descending order of abundance, included Bohemian waxwing, pine siskin, Canada goose, evening grosbeak, common raven, American goldfinch, varied thrush, American crow, black-capped chickadee, red crossbill, and the Steller's jay and dark-eyed junco were tied.

In summary, the two-park checklist of birds includes 183 species, of which 112 are either full-time or summer residents, and assumed to nest. Ten of the 112 species are water birds (waterfowl, rail, and shorebirds), 13 are hawks and owls, and 13 are warblers. Three species are listed as winter residents only: Bohemian waxwing, and common and hoary redpolls.

Birds of Special Interest

Steller's jay. This is the royal-blue jay with a blackish crest; it is the official province bird of British Columbia and is most common in the montane and lower subalpine zones.

Winter wren. This is the little reddish bird of the forest undergrowth that sings a rapid bubbling, tinkling song.

American dipper. Watch for these chubby gray-brown birds at watercourses, where they actually feed underwater.

Varied thrush. Robin-sized, it has orange underparts with a black chestband and sings eerie, bell-like songs that vary in pitch from one phrase to another.

Townsend's warbler. One of the most colorful songbirds, it can be identified by its black throat and cheeks, bright yellow underparts, olive green back, and two white wing bars.

Common yellowthroat. This is the yellow bird with a black mask that is so numerous at Skunk Cabbage Marsh. It sings a loud "witchity witchity witchity" song.

Song sparrow. It is abundant at Skunk Cabbage Marsh and less numerous at other wetlands; it has all-brown plumage with darker streaks, and its breast streaks form a dark stickpin.

Pine siskin. Only slightly larger than a hummingbird, it can be abundant throughout the parks. It is an all-grayish bird with dark streaks and yellow wing bars.

5

Glacier National Park, Montana, and Waterton Lakes National Park, Alberta

I followed the boardwalk across the open expanse of Rocky Mountain tundra. Millions of alpine flowers dotted the landscape. Their bright reds, purples, and yellows were in sharp contrast to the velvety-green sedges, lichens, mosses, and algae growing at ground level. The 2-mile (3.2 km) Hidden Lake Trail, which starts just behind the Logan Pass Visitor Center, provided easy access to the alpine tundra and the high-country bird life. Almost immediately I detected bird songs resounding across the open terrain.

The songs of white-crowned sparrows were most obvious. I located one individual perched atop a subalpine fir. Its boldly striped black-and-white head gleamed in the morning light as it sang a variable song of thin whistle-notes followed by a twittering trill. Further away, a pair of fox sparrows chased one another about an isolated stand of fir. Then nearer, an American pipit suddenly flew up from the tundra and shot up almost vertically to about 150 feet (146 m). Through binoculars, I watched it reach the apex of its flight, and then, spreading its wings and tail, it seemed to float downward. Throughout its descent it sang a weak but melodic song, a "che-whee, che-whee, che-whee." When it landed on the ground it ran a few feet, and then pumped its tail down and then up before it disappeared among the tufts of tundra where I assumed it was nesting.

Not until then did I realize that only a few feet away from the boardwalk was a **white-tailed ptarmigan**, much larger than the sparrows and pipits, but it blended so well into the ground cover that I had not noticed it before. Its mottled plumage of blacks, browns, golds, and whites provided it with amazing camouflage. Through my binoculars I could also see the scarlet eye combs (bare skin patches) above each eye. Its snow white belly and wings were partially hidden from view by its crouching position.

White-tailed ptarmigan

What a marvelous bird is the white-tailed ptarmigan, a hardy creature that exemplifies the alpine character of the dual parks better than any other species. In some areas it is known as "Rocky Mountain snow partridge" or "snow quail." It lives on the alpine tundra during all but the most severe winters, and molts into a snow white wintertime dress (except for the scarlet comb and black bill) to match its surroundings. It also grows "snowshoes," dense mats of stiffened feathers on its toes that help in walking over fresh snow. Traveling ptarmigans have been seen descending rocky slopes by sliding with legs forward and tail spread behind and used as a rudder. In addition, its nostrils are closed by dense feathers that keep out winter snow. John Terres reports that ptarmigans "fly directly into soft snowbanks to sleep; dozens may roost close together, but none walks to the roosting places because their tracks could be followed by weasels, foxes, lynxes, or other predators which might catch ptarmigans in their sleep." It feeds on twig tips and buds that protrude above the snow in winter, and adds flowers, leaves, and insects to its summertime diet.

In spring, as soon as open ground appears, males begin their courtship displays, strutting before females with alternating speeds, their red combs swollen four times their normal size. Nests are little more than shallow depressions, lined with grasses, lichens, leaves, and feathers, under low shrubs or directly on the open tundra. When approached, incubating females will usually remain on their nest until the very last moment; they sometimes can be touched before flying. John Ehrlich and colleagues reported that sitting hens will actually eat white feathers and retrieve pieces of egg shell to reduce the conspicuousness of their nests.

The bird's cryptic coloration and general lack of predators are usually adequate for their nesting success. It is not unusual, from mid-June to late July, to find females with broods of three to 12 chicks near the boardwalk. But except for those birds seen there or accidentally found by alpine hikers, white-tailed ptarmigans usually go undetected.

The Park Environments

Glacier and Waterton Lakes national parks are inseparable, from a biogeographic perspective. In spite of the parks' separate international affiliations, resource management activities usually are comprehensive in nature. The two park units form a single core area within the greater Glacier and Waterton Lakes Biosphere Reserves, sponsored by a UNESCO program known as "MAB," or Man and the Biosphere. The core area, the two national parks, of the Biosphere Reserve is surrounded by a zone of cooperation, which includes adjacent federal and private lands that are most affected by the national parks. An advisory committee, made up of government and private citizens, including local ranchers and business people, participates in park planning and decision-making at Waterton Lakes. The purpose is greater understanding of all parties' objectives and needs.

Waterton Lakes National Park was established in 1895, and Glacier 15 years later. The combined area consists of more than 1,400,000 acres (566,572 ha) and ranges in elevation from approximately 3,200 feet (975 m) at Lake McDonald to nearly 10,500 feet (3,200 m) at the summit of Mt. Cleveland. The area contains more than 650 lakes and 50 glaciers. Glacier's 19 principal valleys drain into three distinct waterways: north into Hudson Bay, west into the Pacific Ocean, and south into the Gulf of Mexico. The Glacier/Waterton Lakes area has been called the "crown of the continent" and "land of shining mountains."

The dual parks also are the crossroads of a variety of floristic regions that result in a higher diversity of plant and animal species than occurs anywhere else in the northern Rocky Mountains. Pacific Coast influences are most obvious along the lower, western slopes, where various prairie grasses, golden aster, moss phlox, early cinquefoil, and prairie rose are common. Boreal and arctic alpine species migrated into the area after glaciation, and are best represented by fireweed, wintergreens, bunchberry, twinflower, and yellow avens of boreal affinity; and by mountain sorrel, alpine cinquefoil, dryad, and moss campion of arctic alpine affinity. Cordilleran species, original flora that evolved here before glaciation, include Indian paintbrushes, arnicas, spring beauty, snow buttercup, beargrass, and fairybells.

Five or six broad and sometimes overlapping habitat types are evident in the two parks. Each contains rather distinct flora and fauna: alpine or mountain tundra and rock, subalpine forest, montane or mixed coniferous forest, aspen parkland, prairie grassland, and water or aquatic. Mountain tundra and rock habitats dominate the highlands and include everything above treeline. The windblown fir and spruce at this elevation are sometimes called "krummholz," a German word for "twisted wood." Lichen and alpine mosses, sedges, heath, laurel, and creeping willow are the most common plants of this windswept and exposed environment. Indicator birds include white-tailed ptarmigan, American pipit, and rosy finch.

Forest occurs below approximately 7,500 feet (2,286 m) elevation, starting with a subalpine habitat that is dominated by subalpine fir and Engelmann spruce. Other common woody plants include whitebark pine, alpine larch, and willows. Indicator birds include blue grouse, Clark's nutcracker, Townsend's solitaire, and white-crowned sparrow. Below the spruce-fir zone is a montane

forest where lodgepole pine, white spruce, and Douglas fir are usually dominant; whitebark pine can also be common, and limber
pine is often present in patches on the eastern slopes. In the
McDonald Creek watershed on the west side, where the Pacific
influence is greatest, western redcedar and western hemlock are
abundant. Shrubs are plentiful in these zones, being represented by
Canada buffaloberry, black and red twinberry, elderberry, rusty-leaf
menziesia, and others. The common birds of the mixed coniferous
forests include the violet-green swallow, Steller's jay, Swainson's
thrush, golden-crowned kinglet, yellow-rumped and MacGillivray's
warblers, and pine siskin. Two indicator birds of the redcedar-
hemlock forests are the varied thrush and Townsend's warbler.

Prairie grasslands occur on the lower eastern slopes and are
most extensive in Waterton Lakes National Park; lesser amounts of
prairie are also present near St. Mary in Glacier. Grasses and a
number of shrubs are common. Kathleen Wilkinson, in *Trees and
Shrubs of Alberta*, reports that sagebrush, rabbitbrush, and greasewood are common in drier prairie areas, and buckbrush, wolf-
willow, serviceberry, hawthorn, and chokecherry are common in
shaded ravines. Indicator birds of the prairie habitat include prairie
falcon, black-billed magpie, western meadowlark, and savannah,
vesper, and clay-colored sparrows.

The aquatic areas can be divided into mountain lakes, mountain streams, and a wetland category that Lloyd Parrot, in his 1970
out-of-print book, *Birds of Glacier National Park*, divided into
marshes, willow thickets, wet meadows, ponds, and bogs. Willows,
alders, white spruce, waterbirch, aspen, and black cottonwood are
most abundant. The entrance road to Waterton Lakes passes excellent examples of mountain stream and wetland habitats. Barrows'
goldeneye and spotted sandpiper best represent mountain lakes; the
harlequin duck and American dipper represent mountain streams;
and the common snipe, eastern kingbird, yellow warbler, red-
winged blackbird, northern waterthrush, common yellowthroat,
and song sparrow are good representatives of the park's wetlands.

Access to many of these habitats is limited, as these parks primarily are hiking areas. There are 732 miles (1,175 km) of trails in
Glacier and 158 miles (255 km) of trails in Waterton Lakes. The

only cross-mountain road is Glacier's Going-to-the-Sun Road that runs for 50 miles (80 km) between West Glacier and the St. Mary entrance on the east side. It provides the traveler with some of the most spectacular scenery in all of North America. The overpowering vistas and alpine surroundings are second to none. Two other roads penetrate Glacier's eastern slope: the 9-mile (14 km) road into Two Medicine, and the 12-mile (19 km) road into Many Glacier. At Waterton Lakes, Highway 5 to Townsite continues for 10 miles (16 km) to Cameron Lake, and the 9-mile (14.5 km) side road to Red Rock Canyon contains sweeping vistas that blend the prairie with montane habitats.

Glacier's visitor centers are located at Apgar on the west end of Lake McDonald, at Logan Pass, and at St. Mary. Waterton's information center is located at the Townsite. All these centers have an information desk and sales outlet for books, videos, and maps; bird field guides and checklists are also available. Several campgrounds and overnight accommodations are available within the two parks.

Interpretive activities include evening talks and nature walks, occasionally highlighting the park's bird life, during the summer season, and a number of self-guided nature trails at pertinent locations. Summer schedules are available for the asking. In addition, the Glacier Institute, a private, non-profit organization, provides a number of educational field seminars, including those on birds in general and birds of prey. Additional information is available from the Glacier Institute, P.O. Box 1457B, Kalispell, MT 59903. Waterton's Heritage Education Program also offers a variety of activities, including one program on birds. Further information on this program is available from the Waterton Natural History Association, P.O. Box 145, Waterton Park, Alberta T0K 2M0.

Additional information on the parks is available from the Superintendents, Glacier National Park, West Glacier, MT 59936; (406) 888-5441; or Waterton Lakes National Park, Waterton Park, Alberta T0K 2M0; (403) 859-2224.

Bird Life

Gray-crowned rosy finches also occur on the mountain tundra and are usually found along the edge of snow fields and rocky ledges.

They can be incredibly tame; a hiker can sometimes walk right up to a feeding bird. Although they are about the same size as a white-crowned sparrow, their appearance and behavior are very different. Rosy finches possess cinnamon-brown plumage tipped with a rose color on their rumps, shoulders, and underparts, and a gray crown with a black forehead. In sunlight, at the edge of a glistening snow patch, they possess a subtle but marvelous beauty.

Gray-crowned rosy finch

The gray-crowned rosy finch is a true tundra species in summer. It feeds on seeds of tundra plants, walking in a rather jerky fashion over the terrain. It possesses a pair of gular sacs in the upper throat capable of carrying food; although adults feed almost exclusively on seeds, young are fed insects. Breeding males display before females but, unlike most birds, courtship centers on the female. Terres points out that "wherever she moves, her mate goes to drive away other males (males outnumber females 6 to 1); male does not have true song; he and mate communicate with call notes: a harsh chew or tsew similar to chirping of house sparrow, a low sharp pert, and a high piercing peent."

After nesting, rosy finches usually congregate in large and rather compact flocks. When a flock is disturbed they will fly up together, with quick wing strokes, and then glide in an undulating flight back to the tundra. They remain in the high country until winter when heavy snow covers the available food sources; they then move into the lowlands. There they often roost together in tight-knit groups, and winter roosts of up to 1,000 individuals have been reported in abandoned cliff swallow nests, cave entrances, mine shafts, and other artificial structures. Rosy finches sometimes overwinter in and about the villages of Townsite and East Glacier.

Mixed forest habitats provide some of the best bird-finding sites. The Swiftcurrent Nature Trail at Many Glacier, the Akamina Parkway at Waterton, and Avalanche Lake Trail in the McDonald Creek watershed provide some of the best access to this habitat. One day in late May, Glacier Park resource specialist Gary Gregory and I walked the 2.4 mile (3.9 km) loop-trail around Swiftcurrent Lake. Red-breasted nuthatches, American robins, ruby-crowned kinglets, warbling vireos, and yellow-rumped warblers were most numerous. Fewer numbers of calliope hummingbirds, gray jays, boreal chickadees, mountain bluebirds, golden-crowned kinglets, and MacGillivray's warblers were found. A lone common loon, pairs of Barrow's goldeneyes and common mergansers, and three pairs of Canada geese were found on the lake; one pair of geese was escorting four or five goslings. Spotted sandpipers were present along the shoreline. We frightened an American dipper, feeding near the shoreline, that flew off with an agitated rattle-call. And in the wetlands near the parking area we recorded a whinny call of a sora and found several singing yellow warblers, a pair of MacGillivray's warblers, a lone common yellowthroat, and a pair of red-winged blackbirds.

One of the most common of the forest birds was the little **yellow-rumped warbler**, a black, yellow, and white bird with five distinct yellow patches: on its cap, throat, sides, and rump. Many of the yellow-rumps we detected were in full song, apparently on their nesting territory among the mixed forest. Their songs, a musical trill that can be written as "chwee-chwee-chwee-ah-chwee" or "tsil-tsil-tsil-tsi-tsi-tsi," often changes to a higher or lower pitch near the end.

The songs of the ruby-crowned kinglets also were evident along the trail, emanating from the taller firs and spruce. Their songs, surprisingly loud for such tiny mites, often start with "heby-jeby" notes, and are followed by a more extensive series of notes, like "tee tee tee, tew tew tew, teedadee teedadee teedadee."

On another day I hiked to Avalanche Lake, 2.4 miles (3.8 km) above the Avalanche Campground. It had rained the night before and the trail was wet; the streamside vegetation was still dripping with rainwater. But the sky was crystal clear and bright blue. Patches of snow still clung to crevices and ridges on the cliffs that rose several thousand feet above the narrow valley in which the trail lies.

Varied thrush

From almost anywhere along the trail the eerie, bell-like songs of **varied thrushes** were heard. Most of the songs rang from the foliage of western redcedars, and most of the birds were hidden from view. But on two occasions a brightly colored male sang from an open perch near the treetops. These glamorous, robin-sized birds looked all the world like bright ornaments atop a green Christmas tree. The varied thrush sports a bright orange breast with a coal black chest band, orange eyebrows over bold black cheeks, and gray-blue back and wings that possess two orange wing bars. It is usually shy and frequents the shadowy areas of the forest. If it were not for its wonderful song, it might be ignored. Terres describes its song as a "rich, melancholy long quavering whistle, a pause, then another succession of vibratory notes, sometimes high, then low, fading away at end." The varied thrush is Glacier's best Pacific Coast representative; the park is the eastern edge of the bird's summer range. Park biologist Steve Gniadek told me that it is a "harbinger of spring," one of the park's "first migrants we hear in the early spring."

Not far up the trail, winter wrens became commonplace, their rapidly delivered songs emanating from many of the woody thickets. The songs of red-breasted nuthatches, American robins, Swainson's thrushes, golden-crowned kinglets, warbling vireos, yellow-rumped and Townsend's warblers, and dark-eyed juncos joined the chorus.

I spent considerable time among the willow and alder thickets along the streamside, trying to coax a MacGillivray's warbler into view. It stayed in the dense foliage at first, but I eventually was able to spish it close enough to see its gray and yellow plumage and white partial eye ring. A moment later it hopped onto a higher willow branch so that the sunlight highlighted its rich colors. Its gray head suddenly became a dazzling blue-gray color that contrasted with its blackish throat and bright yellow underparts. Then it put its head back and sang a liquid melody that Bent described as a series of "double notes likened to swee-eet, swee-eet, swee-eet, peachy, peachy, peachy."

About halfway to the lake I began hearing high-pitched tinkling sounds high overhead. At first I looked in the higher canopy for a flock of migrants but soon realized that I was hearing the chatter of Vaux's swifts flying over the forest. They undoubtedly were nesting in cracks and crevices of the mature conifers. Their cigar-shaped bodies with swept-back wings and pale underparts were more easily seen near the lake where they were flycatching in large numbers. Once, I detected a larger, all-black black swift flying over the lake. Gniadek later told me that the airshed over Avalanche Creek is the best locality in the park to see this large swift. Both are western species; the Vaux's swift reaches the eastern-most edge of its range at Glacier National Park.

The bright green vegetation surrounding Avalanche Lake was filled with bird song. I added the rufous hummingbird, Hammond's flycatcher, violet-green swallow, brown creeper, Wilson's warbler, fox sparrow, and pine siskin to my day's list of birds.

I sat at the edge of the lake admiring the beauty of the crystal-clear waters and the amphitheater-like surroundings, a matrix of white snow, black and gray cliffs, green vegetation, and blue sky. Then suddenly, less than 50 feet (15 m) away was an **American dipper** floating on the lake's surface, consuming a rather large insect larva of some sort. Then, just as suddenly, it dived beneath the surface. When it bobbed up a few seconds later, it had captured another larva. When it dived again, I stood up so that I was able to watch it swim below the surface of the crystal-clear lake. It actually propelled itself through the water with its wings; its feet hung unused. I watched it grab another larva and swim to the surface. It immediately consumed its catch. But this time it paddled to a nearby log protruding above the surface, walked a few inches up the log, and proceeded to preen. It was a remarkable bird, very plump and short-tailed, with all-gray-brown plumage. See chapter 4 on Mount Revelstoke and Glacier, BC, for more details about this bird's ability to feed underwater.

Four pairs of **Barrow's goldeneyes** were also present on the lake, spaced several hundred yards apart as if they had already divided up their breeding territories. The birds near the outlet, where I was watching, kept their distance, but nevertheless were close enough for me to admire their lovely plumage. The male was the brightest of the two with snow white underparts and neck, black back with several white bars on its wings, and a large white crescent in front of its golden eyes that are set on its oval-shaped, glossy purple head.

Goldeneyes usually are tree-nesters, utilizing cavities in mature conifers, which they line with their own feather-down. They also can nest on the ground, on cliffs, and, when necessary, in a variety of other sites. Frank Bellrose, in his informative book *Ducks, Geese & Swans of North America*, reported it nesting in nest-boxes and once in a crow's nest in British Columbia. Normal clutch sizes rarely exceed 15 eggs, but egg "dumping," other females laying a few eggs in a central nest, is commonplace. As many as 24 eggs have been found in one goldeneye nest. After hatching, females lead their broods to a rearing area, but by six weeks of age the young are on their own. Males go off in small flocks, usually by June, and spend their summers molting their plumage on quiet, out-of-the-way lakes.

In spite of the Barrow's goldeneye being one of nature's most exquisite ducks, the **harlequin duck** is even more glamorous. It occurs on high-country lakes and along the swiftly flowing streams of the parks. Its name is derived from the comic Italian character in multicolored tights, but it hardly does justice to this brightly colored, almost gaudy duck. Their slate-blue head, numerous white slashes at various places and angles, chestnut flanks, and gray-blue bodies are one of a kind. To discover this lovely creature perched along one of the park's rushing streams, where they are able to swim and walk underwater like a dipper, is one of life's great wonders. Gniadek told me that six to 16 pairs of these birds nest each year along one section of Upper McDonald Creek. They, too, are tree-nesters and follow a life cycle similar to Barrow's goldeneyes.

The most productive streamside and wetland bird habitats of the two parks exist along the entrance route to Waterton Lakes, especially in and around Maskinonge and Lower Waterton lakes. One June morning I found more than 50 bird species on the lakes, along the shore, and in the adjacent aspen groves. A pair of ospreys were nesting on an old utility pole north of the highway; Waterton Lakes interpreter Janice Smith told me this nesting site has been used for at least 15 years, and that "the ospreys return annually at about Easter; they are our sign of spring." One bird was sitting on the nest and its mate was fishing the adjacent riverway. A red-tailed hawk seemed to have claimed the grove of aspens across the lake. Several hundred cliff swallows were busy nest-building under the highway bridge at the junction. They were swarming like bees over the muddy pools along the highway, where they were gathering nesting materials.

Several pairs of waterfowl were scattered at preferred places. Most numerous were the **mallards**, the drab hens and brightly marked drakes with their bright green heads and necks, white necklaces, and chestnut breasts. One hen was already escorting a half-dozen ducklings, little balls of yellow fuzzy feathers. Other common waterfowl included ring-necked ducks, with their upright stance and white rings on their bills; American wigeons with the male's white foreheads, green eye lines, and buff bellies; blue-winged teals with the males' bold, white crescent face patch; and seven hooded mergansers, the males' black-and-white crested heads gleaming in the early morning light. Both Barrow's and common goldeneyes were also present in numbers, and Canada geese were plentiful as well. These large birds were found along the lakeshore, on the banks, and in the shallow areas of the lake. One group of five adults near the park's entrance station were accompanied by eight goslings.

Other wetland species present included pied-billed grebes, a lone great blue heron, soras, killdeers, common snipes, spotted sandpipers, black terns, common yellowthroats, and yellow-headed and red-winged blackbirds. The **black terns** stayed along the southeastern edge of Maskinonge Lake, but from their numbers (10 or 12 individuals) and behavior I assumed they were nesting. I watched a few individuals make acrobatic flights, up and down, and then hover in midair. Once, I detected a bird carrying a fish in its bill, probably to offer to its mate, an indication of courtship. Their graceful flight was very swallow-like for such a large bird. Their all-black bills and plumage, except for their whitish upperwing coverts and wing linings, give them a stately appearance. During the summer months, black terns feed mostly on insects captured in flight, but in the winter, which they spend at sea, they feed only on small fishes.

The aspen grove at Maskinonge Picnic Area was alive with song-birds that morning. Most numerous were house wrens, American robins, cedar waxwings, European starlings, warbling vireos, and yellow warblers. Less numerous were ruffed grouse, red-naped sapsuckers, downy woodpeckers, western wood-pewees, willow flycatchers, black-capped chickadees, veeries, northern waterthrushes, black-headed grosbeaks, and American goldfinches.

McDonald Creek and Apgar Campground, below Glacier's Lake McDonald, provide yet another and somewhat different habitat for bird-finding. The deciduous vegetation along the flood plain provides suitable habitat for downy woodpeckers, willow flycatchers, violet-green swallows, black-capped chickadees, red-eyed and warbling vireos, yellow and MacGillivray's warblers, American redstarts, northern waterthrushes, and song sparrows. Cliff swallows build their nests under the Apgar Bridge, and the bare dirt bank downriver on the left is utilized by nesting belted kingfishers and northern rough-winged swallows.

The mixed forest of deciduous and coniferous trees, such as that at Apgar Campground, is utilized by a few additional nesting species: pileated and hairy woodpeckers, Hammond's and dusky flycatchers, gray jays, yellow-rumped and Townsend's warblers, western tanagers, chipping sparrows, and dark-eyed juncos.

I also spent a morning on Waterton's prairie grasslands, where I walked a wide loop-route over the undulating terrain just above the Red Rock Canyon Road junction. At least a hundred Columbian ground-squirrels "inked" at me. They got especially excited when a golden eagle cruised by only 20 to 30 feet (6-9 m) above the ground. Western meadowlarks were most obvious due to their loud, ringing songs. And four kinds of sparrows were detected: vesper, savannah, clay-colored, and Brewer's. The vesper sparrows were most numerous, singing their rapid trills, sometimes described as "here-here, where-where all together down the hill," from low shrubs. Vesper sparrows are rather plain, striped birds with rusty shoulders, narrow white eye rings, and white edges on their tails that are most noticeable in flight.

Savannah sparrows were fairly common as well, identified by their striped bodies, yellow eyebrows, and short tails. Clay-colors were next in abundance; they sang their low-pitched, buzzing songs from small patches of shrubbery. And a lone Brewer's sparrow, with its canarylike song, was detected but once.

I kept watching for **sharp-tailed grouse** that frequent these prairies, but to no avail. Sharp-tails breed there, according to Smith, and perform their courtship displays during April and May. My June visit was too late to experience their wild dances. Ehrlich and colleagues described sharp-tails courtship thusly: "Males occupy lek, usually on small knoll; male inflates sac on sides of neck, with tail erect and wings dropped, then rapidly drops head and deflates sacs with a weak 'coo.' Jumping displays follow, males run at each other with tail and neck tufts erect, sacs inflated." "Dancing" usually involves a few to 20 males, and includes ritualistic or actual fighting, according to ornithologist Paul Johnsgard; the best performer breeds with the females.

Sharp-tails are a northern prairie-chicken that lack the elongated pinnate feathers on each side of the throat, and possess an all-dark, pointed tail with white outer feathers. In flight, they appear to have pale, frosted wings.

Colder weather, starting in late September to early October, brings migrant waterfowl to the Waterton Lakes wetlands, where they can occur by the thousands. Fifty-five species of water birds are listed on Waterton's bird checklist for the fall months. The abundant bird feeders at Townsite attract numerous land bird migrants as well.

Bald eagles, a beautiful raptor with an all-white head and tail, can be numerous at choice feeding areas during the fall, although a few also nest each year along the parks' larger lakes. Southbound migrants congregate along Waterton and McDonald creeks. At McDonald Creek, the bald eagle's fall appearance has coincided with the kokanee (landlocked sockeye salmon) spawning runs for over 50 years; a peak count of 618 adults and subadults was recorded in November 1978. But more recent numbers have hovered between 22 and 40 birds. This decline resulted from the collapse of the nonnative kokanee population that, according to biologists Craig Spencer, Riley McClelland, and Jack Stanford, was brought about by the 1968 and 1975 introductions of nonnative opossum shrimp into the Flathead River ecosystem. These researchers found that opossum shrimp feed on the same organisms as the kokanee and were able to out-compete them. The result was a collapse of the kokanee population, its annual McDonald Creek spawning runs, and therefore the massive congregation of migrating bald eagles.

Bird-finding in the Glacier/Waterton Lakes parks in winter is only a fraction of what it is in summer. Christmas Bird Counts are taken annually to assess those populations. At Glacier, 315 individuals of 52 species were found on the 1990 Christmas Count. The dozen most abundant species, in descending order of abundance, included evening grosbeak, mallard, black-capped chickadee, bufflehead, mountain chickadee, dark-eyed junco, red-breasted nuthatch, common goldeneye, pine siskin, common raven, bald eagle, Steller's jay, and (equal counts) American wigeon and hairy woodpecker. At Waterton, counters tally 18 to 37 species each year; of the 37 species found in 1987, the dozen most abundant species were, in descending order of abundance, Canada goose, snow bunting, black-capped chickadee, common redpoll, black-billed magpie, mountain chickadee, common goldeneye, pine grosbeak, common raven, evening grosbeak, red-breasted nuthatch, and pine siskin.

In summary, the combined bird checklists for Glacier and Waterton Lakes national parks include 287 species. One hundred and fifty-nine species are known to nest: 17 are water birds, 18 are hawks and owls, and 9 are warblers. Only one, the northern hawk-owl, considered accidental, is known only for winter.

Birds of Special Interest

Barrow's goldeneye. Males possess snow white underparts and necks, black backs with white bars, and a large white crescent in front of their golden eyes.

Harlequin duck. This brightly colored duck of the swiftly flowing streams is most numerous along upper McDonald Creek in spring and summer; occasionally birds occur at high lakes.

Black tern. Look for this medium-sized tern at Waterton's

Maskinonge Lake in summer; it possesses an all-black body, pale gray underwings, and darker upperwings.

Bald eagle. A few nest along the larger lakes, but they are most numerous in the fall when they congregate along McDonald Creek.

White-tailed ptarmigan. Watch for this grouse along the Logan Pass boardwalk; it is a true alpine bird that turns snow white in winter, but sports black, brown, gold, and white colors in summer.

Sharp-tailed grouse. This "prairie-chicken" occurs on Waterton's prairie grasslands; it can be recognized by its dark, pointed tail, edged with white, and its white-spotted wings.

Varied thrush. It is most common within the McDonald Creek watershed. It is robin-sized with an orange breast that is banded with a bold black line. Its eerie song sounds like high-pitched bells.

American dipper. This plump, gray-brown bird lives along the streams and highland lakes; it actually swims and walks underwater in search of insect larvae.

Yellow-rumped warbler. This is the common mixed forest warbler, identified by the five yellow patches: rump, throat, crown, and sides.

Gray-crowned rosy finch. Watch for this alpine species, with its rosy-brown plumage and jerky gate, along the edge of snowbanks in summer. After nesting it may occur in large flocks.

6

Bighorn Canyon National Recreation Area, Montana and Wyoming

The views from Devil Canyon Overlook are truly spectacular, whether one is looking up or down Bighorn Canyon. The more than 1,000 foot (305 m) canyon walls tower over the sparkling blue waters of the Bighorn River and Lake, a narrow ribbon far below. Occasionally, bighorn sheep, for which the mountains, river, lake, and park were named, can be seen from the overlook, grazing at patches of grasslands on the open benches above the cliffs. But the most prominent wildlife visible from the overlook are the birds.

White-throated swifts are most numerous; they zoom by at more than 100 miles (160 km) per hour, sometimes so close one can feel the wind from these black-and-white speedsters. Their cigar-shaped bodies and swept-back wings are perfect adaptations for their aerial maneuvers. As many as two dozen of these 6½-inch (16.5 cm) birds are usually present at any one time of day throughout the spring and summer. The slightly smaller violet-green swallows, identified by their violet-green colored backs and snow white underparts and rumps, can also be common.

The master of the high cliffs and canyons at Devil Canyon Overlook, however, is a much larger, faster, and more powerful bird than the swifts and swallows. This is the peregrine falcon, considered one of the speediest birds in the world; they have been clocked at more than 200 miles (322 km) per hour in a dive. Peregrines are approximately the size of red-tailed hawks but possess pointed rather than rounded wings, light underparts with faint streaks, and dark backs; males can be slate gray but females are lighter colored. They also possess dark hoods and moustachial stripes, heavy black sideburn markings on their cheeks.

Peregrines are native to the Rocky Mountains and have long been an integral part of the Bighorn Canyon ecosystem. But by the mid-1970s, peregrine populations in all of western North America had been reduced by 80 to 90 percent due to DDT poisoning. By 1972, peregrines were placed on the endangered species list, and DDT was banned from use in the United States and Canada. A special captive breeding program was initiated by Dr. Tom J. Cade at Cornell University in 1970, and captive-bred peregrines hatched successfully three years later. Bighorn Canyon released its first captive-reared birds in 1989; during the next three years a total of 16 peregrines were introduced into the park. Some of those birds are expected to serve as a nucleus for a new breeding population of these incredible birds at Bighorn Canyon.

Peregrines hunt by diving on their prey from above and can easily kill pigeons and ducks with a single blow. They actually strike their prey on or near the back of the skull with a partly open fist, either severing the spine or crushing the skull. They even take the smaller, but swifter, white-throated swifts. Their ability to time their dive so perfectly that they are able to hit a swift flying at 100 miles (160 km) per hour is difficult to conceive. And then, instead of letting their prey fall to the ground, they actually turn and retrieve their kill in midair. They then carry their prey to a high perch or to their nest to either consume it or feed it to their nestlings. The weight of a swift is nothing compared with a mallard or common merganser, more typical prey of peregrines at Bighorn Canyon. The ability to carry that added weight upward 1,000 feet (305 m) to its perch is mind-boggling. See chapter 16 on Grand Canyon for additional information about this incredible falcon.

Devil Canyon Overlook is undoubtedly the most likely site to watch for this speedy raptor. Although peregrine observations are rare, they are expected to increase as the species begins to utilize the high cliffs for nest sites once again.

The Park Environment

The Bighorn/Pryor Mountains of north-central Wyoming and south-central Montana are the first high mountains that a traveler coming east is likely to encounter. They are the easternmost range of the Rocky Mountains and rise directly out of the vast prairie grasslands. The Bighorn/Pryor Mountains are sliced in two by the Bighorn River, the Pryors on the west and the Bighorns on the east.

Bighorn Canyon National Recreation Area (120,000 acres or 48,563 ha) extends for 65 miles (104 km) from near Lovell, Wyoming, to near Hardin, Montana. The meandering, 71-mile-long (113 km) Bighorn Lake, dammed by Yellowtail Dam near Fort Smith, Montana, is the centerpiece of the park. The National Park Service administers the national recreation area, but much of the park lands in Montana are controlled by Crow Indians and are closed to the public. Another portion of the area is jointly managed by the National Park Service and Bureau of Land Management as part of the Pryor Mountain Wild Horse Range.

Access to the area is limited. The southern district can be reached off Wyoming Highway 14A, from a 20-mile-long (32 km) paved road that provides access to Horseshoe Bend, Devil Canyon Overlook, and Barry's Landing. The northern district of the park can be reached from Montana Highway 313 to Fort Smith, and then from a 10-mile-long (16 km) paved road as far as Ok-A-Beh Marina on Bighorn Lake, with side roads to the Afterbay and Yellowtail Dam.

Three visitor centers exist within or adjacent to the park: Bighorn Canyon Visitor Center, with exhibits, at Lovell; Fort Smith Visitor Center near Fort Smith; and Yellowtail Dam Visitor Center, operated by the Bureau of Reclamation, at Yellowtail Dam. Each of these centers has an information desk and sales outlet where one can obtain bird guides and other interpretive materials. A checklist of park birds is available for the asking. This list is largely based upon a thorough inventory of the park's birds and mammals that was undertaken in 1984 by Craig T. Patterson. Also available is *Canyon Echoes*, an interpretive newspaper that includes an interpretive schedule for both districts of the park and other pertinent information.

Campgrounds are available at both ends of the park, but hiking trails are limited to three in the north and four in the south; two are nature trails: Beaver Dam Nature Trail at the Yellowtail Visitor Center, and Crooked Creek Nature Trail off loop C at Horseshoe Bend Campground.

Vegetation within the park varies with elevation and rainfall; the southern portion is much drier than it is in the north because it falls in the rain shadow of the higher and more massive Absarokee–Beartooth Mountains to the west. The dry, southern slopes of the Bighorns are dominated by Utah juniper and big sagebrush. Curl-leaf mountain mahogany is common at slightly higher elevation. Limber and ponderosa pines and Douglas fir are present on cooler, north slopes of the higher canyons. Larger stands of ponderosa pines occur in the north. The common shrubs of this community include littleleaf sumac, holly-grape, common juniper, poison ivy, and yucca.

Above the ponderosa pine stands on the rounded mountain tops is a vast grassland community, much of which is on Crow Indian land and grazed by cattle and bison. Arrowleaf balsamroot is abundant in places, and low-growing wild rose, yucca, and prickly pear cacti occur throughout.

Riparian habitats occur along the open lake shore and streams, and within side drainages that form fingers of dense vegetation that often extend high up the slopes. These communities usually are dominated by eastern cottonwood and box elder. Common undergrowth species include chokecherry, golden current, silver buffaloberry, and dogwood.

The southern end of Bighorn Lake contains a very different riparian environment that is dominated by eastern cottonwoods, willows, Russian olives, and tamarisks. A tract of 11,600 acres (4,694 ha) of this area is managed as the Yellowtail Wildlife Habitat Unit of the park, administered by the National Park Service and managed by the Wyoming Game and Fish Department.

Additional information can be obtained from the Superintendent, Bighorn National Recreation Area, P.O. Box 458, Fort Smith, MT 59035; (406) 666-2412.

Bird Life

The high cliffs along the lake provide nesting sites for a number of birds: white-throated swifts, violet-green swallows, American kestrels, and prairie falcons. **American kestrels**, once called sparrow hawks, are one of the park's most colorful and charismatic raptors.

They are fascinating birds to watch when they are hunting. They will hover in midair, wings flapping to hold their stationary position, while they search for prey below. Suddenly, they will dive with wings folded back to gain speed and, just before they reach their target, they will pull out their sharp talons and grasp their prey. Rodents are preferred, but they also will take small birds and snakes, as well as a variety of insects. The American kestrel is almost as dynamic as its larger cousin, the peregrine, but because of its smaller size and abundance it is too often taken for granted. This little falcon also nests in cavities on cottonwoods in riparian zones and in conifers in the upland forest communities, but they are most numerous along the canyon. Their reddish backs, the slate gray wings of the males, and black-and-white face patterns are commonplace throughout the park.

Prairie falcons also occur along the canyons. This falcon is almost as large as a peregrine but inhabits drier, more open country, preying upon birds, rodents, lizards, and insects. It is easily recognized by its pale, instead of slate gray, plumage, its narrower moustachial stripes, and its black underwing markings, like black wingpits.

Then there are the **golden eagles**, the largest of the park's raptors, with a wingspan of up to 88 inches (224 cm). These are all-dark-brown birds, except for their golden head-feathers that seem to have a bronze cast when viewed from the right angle on a sunny day. Immature birds possess whitish tails with black terminal bands, and they are sometimes confused with bald eagles. Most of the time golden eagles build their nests in out-of-the-way places on the walls of the inner canyon. But in 1992, a pair nested on the high cliff directly across the river from the Yellowtail Dam Visitor Center. On June 20, I found four youngsters, almost large enough to leave home, exploring the open ledge; I wondered how often nonflying birds fall to their doom. Through my spotting scope, I could see that one individual had not yet finished breakfast; 10 to 12 inches (25-30 cm) of a snake protruded from its beak. It took several deep gulps before it finally managed to swallow the whole thing.

Golden eagles are extremely adaptable birds, occurring from the Arctic to central Mexico. Pairs develop long-term bonds that

Golden eagle

may result in lifetime affairs; they often hunt in pairs. Jackrabbits are their favorite prey in the West, although they will take almost any kind of mammal, including skunks, large birds, and snakes. Only when food is scarce will they eat carrion.

I watched a lone golden eagle from Devil Canyon Overlook. It was flying over the grassy ridge directly across the canyon, apparently hunting. It appeared to be making a number of passes over one particular area. I assumed it was attempting to dislodge a prey species that it knew was present but hunkered down out of sight.

Eagles will spend long periods of time soaring low over their hunting grounds in an attempt to frighten some prey into making a run for it. This technique apparently works very well.

A common raven suddenly appeared overhead, a large, all-black bird with pointed wings, a wedge-shaped tail, and a large, heavy bill. Its bill was grasping a rock dove squab, undoubtedly taken from a nest on the adjacent cliff face. I had heard considerable "cooing" of rock doves below me and had seen several birds, alone or in small flocks, flying far below the overlook. I had recognized the value of these large pigeons as peregrine food, but I had not thought of other birds utilizing this abundant food base. When I mentioned my raven/rock dove sighting to Terry Peters, the park's resource management specialist, Terry told me that ravens often take squabs, and on one occasion a visiting biologist observed a raven with an adult rock dove.

When I walked out onto Yellowtail Dam to better view the eagle nest, I was swarmed by **cliff swallows**. Their buff rumps and darker throats were obvious on these square-tailed swallows. Their low "chrrr" and nasal "nyew" calls were everywhere. I discovered dozens of birds clinging to an adjacent wet cliff that apparently contained sufficient mud for nest-building. They were extremely busy, flying back and forth, from their mud source to various nesting sites along the cliffs.

The largest cliff swallow colony I found in the park was on the point of rock that juts out into Bighorn Lake directly across from the Ok-A-Beh Marina. When a boat passed near the cliff, the air was suddenly blackened with moving dots. Through my spotting scope I could see that there were at least 800 cliff swallows in that one congregation. They swarmed up over the water, flew in a wide circle, and then many returned to their nests, which were plastered on the cliff 30 to 40 feet (9 to 12 m) above the water.

Waterfowl are never common inside the canyon, although substantial numbers occur on the southern and northern ends of the lake, in the Yellowtail Wildlife area and below Yellowtail Dam, respectively. The only waterfowl common inside the canyon is the **common merganser**, a large, mostly white duck with an orange bill and legs. Males possess a deep green head, while females have chestnut-colored, crested heads and white throats. This is one of the few ducks able to live in the confines of the canyon; most ducks require ponds or rivers with streamside vegetation. The common merganser does very well inside the canyons, however, for two good reasons: it is a fish-eating duck that does not require pond weeds and grasses, and it is able to nest on cliffs. See chapter 23 on Black Canyon of the Gunnison and Curecanti for further details about this extraordinary fisherman.

The open water and grassy shores of the Wildlife Management Unit can be superb bird-viewing areas during most of the year. The best ponds are accessible via a 2-mile (3 km) dirt road that runs south from the west side of the Highway 14A bridge. Trails follow levees between the ponds that provide easy access to cattail-dominated wetlands and open water. Almost any kind of dabbling duck can be expected during the summer months, and during migration one can expect almost any of the water birds.

During my mid-June visit to the area, I found more than 400 American white pelicans on the far shore. Peters explained that their nesting attempts at Pathfinder Reservoir, near Casper, Wyoming, had probably failed, and they had moved to Bighorn Lake to fish its rich waters. Eight sandhill cranes were present, too; two or three individuals were courting, performing their wonderful crane dance, suggesting that these birds were nesting nearby. Ring-billed gulls and Caspian terns were also present over the lake or perched along the shore near the pelicans.

Other birds found about the ponds and lake included a lone common loon; nesting pied-billed grebes; several great blue herons feeding along the shore; three wood ducks; four redheads; numerous American coots and killdeers; a flock of 12 American avocets; marsh wrens singing their musical trills and rattles from the cattails; common yellowthroats singing their "witchity witchity witchity" throughout the area; a few yellow-headed blackbirds and many red-winged blackbirds; and song sparrows calling "chimp" from adjacent thickets.

The riparian habitats that persist along the open lakeshores and streams, as well as in the narrow draws, contain a very different assortment of birds. But one species is all-prevailing; the **yellow warbler** can be found in numbers in every location. I discovered that it readily responded to spishes or squeaks. These bright yellow birds reacted with surprising boldness and aggression, sometimes approaching to within a few feet of me. The male's chestnut streaks on its golden breast, all-yellow body, and coal black eyes made identification easy.

They also filled the air with song, a lively, cheerful melody that has been written as "tseet-tseet-tseet sitta-sitta-see" or "wee wee wee witita weet." It undoubtedly was the most common bird song along the streams and lake in the park. Nesting was well underway in mid-June, and the boldness of these 5-inch (13 cm) golden songsters in defense of their territories was beautiful to behold.

Other common songbirds of the riparian thickets included western wood-pewees, house wrens, cedar waxwings, yellow-breasted chats, lazuli buntings, song sparrows, and American goldfinches. Fewer numbers of eastern and western kingbirds, least flycatchers, black-capped chickadees, gray catbirds, American robins, warbling vireos, American redstarts, northern orioles, brown-headed cowbirds, black-headed grosbeaks, and rufous-sided towhees were encountered.

I know of no other place where one can find eastern and western kingbirds living so close together, actually singing from the very same tree, than at Bighorn Canyon. Although I found several nests of both species, I did not find both nests in the same tree, although I tried. The eastern kingbird is a most attractive black-and-white bird that often sits at the top of trees and shrubs and calls loud "dzeet" notes; it sings stuttering "kip-kip-kipper-kipper" songs. Its clear white underparts and black cap, back, and tail, except for a rather distinct white tip, give it a rather dramatic appearance.

Western kingbirds seem to have many of the same personality traits; they will sit at the top of trees or on wires and call loud, sharp "whit" notes, or sing harsh "ker-er-ip-ker-er-ip" songs. Western kingbirds possess gray throats and breasts, yellow bellies and crissums (undertail coverts), and black tails with white outer edges.

The most numerous bird of the draws is the **rufous-sided towhee**, easily identified by its black head with blood-red eyes, dark back, white belly, and rufous sides. It is one of the best known of America's bird life, and so its presence may go unnoticed. But it is difficult to ignore this bird when it is courting and in full song. Males are adamant in their courtship, chasing females from shrub to shrub, or sometimes high in adjacent trees. They will fan their tails to display the large white spots on the outer edges, rapidly spread and fold their tails and wings to flash their white spots, raise their wings, fluff their feathers, and persistently sing loud warbling songs that end in a series of musical thrills. Watching towhees in their spring mating rituals is an experience not soon forgotten.

The juniper woodland that occurs along the warmer slopes in the park's south district is one of the area's most unusual habitats. The presence of territorial black-throated sparrows gave this community a desert flavor; the number of singing Brewer's sparrows suggested sageflats; and territorial blue-gray gnatcatchers suggested pinyon-juniper woodlands of the Southwest. Several other birds were found within this community: mourning doves called from various perches on the low-growing junipers and adjacent rocky outcroppings; mountain chickadees called their hoarse "chick a-dee a-dee a-dee" songs; family groups of bright-blue mountain bluebirds were present (they may have nested at higher elevations and afterwards moved into the area); rock wrens were abundant at rocky areas; and chipping sparrows added their trills to the bird chorus. But the colorful, boldly marked lark sparrows were the most numerous.

Lark sparrows are reasonably large sparrows with very distinct plumage: they possess all-white underparts except for a prominent black spot in the center of their breasts; black, white, and chestnut streaks on their heads; and black tails with obvious white corners. They are curious sparrows that are easily attracted by spishing and will walk about the ground with little regard for one's presence. They also produce a lovely, musical song that includes a high-pitched opening, with two clear notes and a trill, given in various sequences.

The upper grasslands in the north also hold a special appeal to the naturalist, not only because of the abundant bird life but also because of its aesthetics. Early morning views across the grassy slopes with backdrops of reddish cliffs and dark green patches of forest can be spectacular. Bird song can also be appealing, although species are usually limited to the abundant western meadowlarks and Brewer's blackbirds, and to lesser numbers of American kestrels, common ravens, and vesper, savannah, and lark sparrows.

Western meadowlarks often perch on fence posts or shrubs so that their bright yellow underparts and contrasting black V-shaped breast bands actually glow in the morning light. But their plumage cannot compare with their wonderful songs, typical of the western grasslands and fields: a series of rich, gurgling, flutelike, double-notes that Arthur C. Bent stated had "the flutelike quality of the wood thrush with the rich melody of the Baltimore oriole." When I was a kid growing up in Idaho, my mother often told me that the western meadowlark was singing, "Salt Lake City is a pretty little city."

Meadowlark nests are rather special. They are constructed of grass and other plant materials on the ground but are woven into the surrounding grasses with an opening on one side; they are lined with fine grasses and hair. Meadowlarks feed principally on insects, including several kinds considered pests by farmers, such as weevils and Mormon crickets. They also have been found to feed on some seeds, bird eggs, and road kills.

Winter birds are limited to the hardier species that remain full-time or move into the area from more northern localities. Peters has initiated annual Christmas Bird Counts in the southern portion of the area, and these counts provide the best perspective of what species can be expected at that time of year. In 1991, Peters and colleagues found 4,479 individuals of 47 species on count day. The dozen most abundant species tallied during the 1990 and 1991 counts, in descending order of abundance, included European starlings, rock doves, house sparrows, Canada geese, mallards, cedar waxwings, American tree sparrows, red-winged blackbirds, Townsend's solitaires, Bohemian waxwings, American goldfinches, and black-billed magpies.

In summary, Craig Patterson's inventory of birds and mammals documented 212 bird species within the national recreation area, of which 90 were found to nest and an additional 58 species were listed as "probably breeders." Of these 148 species, 27 were water birds (grebe, cormorant, waders, waterfowl, rails, and shorebirds), 19 were hawks and owls, and 8 were warblers. Only three species—rosy finch, common redpoll, and snow bunting—were found only during winter.

Birds of Special Interest

Common merganser. One of the few ducks of the inner canyons, its white body and wing bars, the male's green head, and the female's chestnut head, help identify this large diver.

Golden eagle. This is the area's largest raptor; adults are all-dark with golden heads and fly with wings held straight out.

Peregrine falcon. Although currently rare, watch for it along the canyon rim from the Devil Canyon Overlook. Its medium size, pointed wings, and black-and-white head pattern help identify this fastest of all birds.

American kestrel. This little falcon can be found throughout the area; it possesses a reddish back, pointed wings, and black-and-white face pattern.

White-throated swift. It is abundant about the cliffs, always in flight; its black-and-white body and swept-back wings help to identify this aerial acrobat.

Cliff swallow. These square-tailed swallows usually are found in large numbers along the cliffs; they possess buff-colored rumps and throats.

Yellow warbler. Probably the area's most common bird; males are all-yellow with chestnut chest-streaks.

Western meadowlark. It occurs in grasslands and is best identified by its song or by its bright yellow breast, crossed by a bold, black V-shaped band.

Rufous-sided towhee. This robin-sized bird prefers thickets along the river or lakeshore. It has an all-black head, black-and-white back, white belly, and rufous sides.

Lark sparrow. It occurs in dry grassy areas throughout and is best identified by its black, white, and chestnut head, and bold white corners on its otherwise black tail.

7

Yellowstone National Park, Montana, Wyoming, and Idaho

The steam and fog rising from the numerous geysers, pots, and vents gave the scene a ghostly appearance, like a gigantic abstract painting. Boiling, gurgling, and hissing sounds dominated my hearing, while the more subtle sounds of the Firehole River, flowing through the little valley, and a few distant bird songs were barely audible as I began my circle walk of the Old Faithful Geyser Basin that early summer morning.

The appearance of a coal black common raven, which suddenly burst out of the fog and soared overhead, was almost expected. Its huge size, pointed wings, wedge-shaped tail, and heavy bill, seemed very much in place within Old Faithful's surrealistic setting. It suddenly wheeled and dropped to the ground amid a caldron of steam. A few seconds later it flew up with some morsel of food held tightly in its massive bill. I wasn't sure what it had found, probably one of the numerous young birds recently fledged, too naive of the dangers that existed out of the nest. The common raven gave a loud, deep-throated "craaw" call as it flew off into the adjacent forest.

Then, directly in front of me, perched on the boardwalk, was a brightly colored, almost turquoise-blue mountain bluebird. It, too, held something tightly in its bill. A second later, with the aid of binoculars, I could see the insect that it had captured. I also was able to admire its gorgeous plumage, darker on its back than its underparts, and black bill and eyes. Beyond it on the boardwalk was its mate; she possessed more subtle colors of blues and grays but was also a beautiful creature, a species typical of the high Yellowstone plateau. A moment later they both took flight, each calling flutelike "veer" notes as they crossed over gurgling caldrons and landed on a naked snag of a thermally killed lodgepole pine.

As I neared the green forest beyond, additional birdsongs greeted me. Loudest was the rich caroling of American robins. I located one individual perched at the very top of a pine; its orange-red breast shined brightly as it caught the early morning light. The warbling melody of a yellow-rumped warbler was evident nearby, and further away I detected the trembling whistle of a western tanager. The "chick a-dee a-dee a-dee" songs of mountain chickadees resounded from the adjacent foliage. One individual was singing a slightly different version that sounded more like a drawled "you are here, right here." This little bird of the conifers, identified by its black throat, cap, and eye patch, with a narrow, white eye line, continued its singing as Betty and I progressed around the circle.

Patches of grassy areas, scattered along the edge of the steaming waters, had attracted other songbirds that morning. The long-tailed blackbirds with white eyes were male Brewer's blackbirds; the browner females possessed black eyes. The smaller birds with black hoods, brown backs, white bellies, and black tails with distinct white edges, were dark-eyed juncos. I found an entire family of juncos searching for seeds surprisingly close to the superheated water of a nearby thermal spring. Juncos also sang their musical trills from the forest, sometimes changing pitch half-way through their songs. A pair of even smaller chipping sparrows, their reddish caps obvious through binoculars, were also searching for seeds. Others were singing from the forest; their drawn-out trills had little change in pitch.

We followed a side trail up the slope toward Solitary Geyser, passing through forest that had not yet been disturbed by the thermal activities below. Ruby-crowned kinglets sang from the upper foliage, a rollicking "jibby jibby jibby" and "tsee tsee tsee." A hermit thrush sang its incredibly beautiful series of flutelike phrases, one after the other, from the top of a nearby conifer. Few songs possess the deep-forest quality of the hermit thrush's song.

We walked as far as Morning Glory Pool; its deep blue color matched that of the mountain bluebird. Then we circled back toward Castle Geyser and on toward the Old Faithful Inn and Visitor Center. Across from Hamilton Store, inside the walkway, was a reasonably large marshy area, open water surrounded by an acre or two of lush cattails and rushes.

The most obvious bird of the Geyser Basin Marsh was the red-winged blackbird; the male's all-black body with bright red epaulets helped to identify this common species. Less obvious of the marsh birds were the common snipe, Wilson's phalarope, and sora. We first detected the snipe by its winnowing flight, high above the marsh. See chapter 23 on Black Canyon of the Gunnison and Curecanti for details about this bird's amazing courtship display. The phalarope female was standing alone at the edge of the marsh grasses; I assumed its mate was sitting on a well-hidden nest among the dense vegetation. I was reminded that phalaropes reverse roles in that the males possess the dullest plumage and spend more time tending the nest; females are brightest and apparently do more guard duty. The sora, the park's smallest rail, was detected only by its occasional calls from the marsh grasses: loud "eeek" notes, and a high-pitched whinny-song, like distant horse whinnies.

The Park Environment

No other national park has received the adoration, respect, and attention that Yellowstone has. Set aside by the United States Congress as the world's first "national" park in 1872, it is also recognized as both a Biosphere Reserve and a World Heritage Site. These prestigious titles were awarded the park by UNESCO, largely because of its more than 10,000 thermal springs and geysers and its concentration of large mammals. Yellowstone is one of the half-dozen most popular destinations for travelers throughout the world. But in spite of tremendous summer visitation, much of the park is still pristine wilderness.

Reader's Digest's *Our National Parks* pointed out that "[t]here are many Yellowstones. Each in its own way is something of a miracle. That each should all exist together—here in this one place, at this moment in time—is among the major miracles of this truly fabulous country of ours." Larger than the states of Delaware and Rhode Island combined, Yellowstone National Park (2,219,823 acres or 898,350 ha) contains an incredible assemblage of plant and animal communities, most of which are little disturbed by human development and use. The exceptions to this are scattered along the 350 miles (563 km) of paved roads and at eight visitor-use hubs, all arranged along a great figure-8 route: Mammoth, Canyon, Norris, Madison, Fishing Bridge, Lake, Old Faithful, and Grant. The park also maintains over 1,000 miles (1,600 km) of trails.

The majority of Yellowstone National Park lies on a high central plateau between the Absaroka Range on the east and Gallatin Range on the northwest. Most of the park falls between 7,000 and 9,000 feet (2,100 and 2,700 m) elevation, although elevation extremes in the park range from a low of 5,265 feet (1,604 m) along the Yellowstone River at the park's northern border, to 11,358-foot (3,462 m) Eagle Peak in the southeastern corner.

Biologists and geologists divide the park into five broad geovegetation provinces: the dominant central plateaus (34% of the park), southwest plateaus (18%), the Absaroka Range (32%) that extends along the entire eastern and southeastern borders, and two smaller provinces: Yellowstone-Lamar Valleys (9%) in the north-central area, and Gallatin Range (7%) in the northwest.

The park's vegetative zones fall within four broad types: alpine, subalpine, montane, and foothills. In 1990, Yellowstone's research biologist, Dr. Don Despain, further divided the park's vegetation into various plant communities, habitat types, and cover types.

The alpine zone lies above treeline, beginning at about 10,000 feet (3,050 m) elevation, on Mount Washburn and on the higher peaks in the Absaroka and Gallatin ranges. Vegetative cover is dominated by a thick turf of grasses mixed with dwarf willows.

The subalpine zone makes up far-and-away the largest portion of the park and includes everything between approximately 7,600 feet (2,316 m) elevation and the lower edge of the alpine zone. The forested slopes are dominated by Engelmann spruce and subalpine fir near treeline; whitebark and lodgepole pines and Engelmann spruce dominate much of the mid-elevation areas, with scattered aspen groves at lower elevations. Common understory plants within the various habitats include heartleaf arnica, grouse whortleberry, globe huckleberry, twinflower, Cascade mountain ash, western meadowrue, and elk sedge.

The montane zone, generally between 6,000 and 7,600 feet (1,830 and 2,316 m) elevation, contains forested habitats that are dominated by Douglas fir as well as large areas of aspen. Lodgepole pine also occurs in scattered stands. Chokecherry, serviceberry, and mallow ninebark are common understory species.

Each of the park's eight visitor hubs offers a visitor center, campground, and, in most cases, a variety of visitor services. Each visitor center has an information desk, exhibits, and a sales outlet where one can purchase videos, maps, and publications such as bird guides, checklists, and a Yellowstone bird book, *Birds of Yellowstone*, by park biologist Terry McEneaney.

National Park Service interpretive activities range from evening talks, nightly in season at 9:30 p.m., to daily nature walks, including bird talks and walks to choice bird habitats, and other scheduled events. The *Yellowstone Today* newspaper contains pertinent information and activities; it is available from any of the visitor centers for the asking.

In addition, the Yellowstone Institute provides a number of field courses from May through October, including those on bird identification and ecology. Further information about this program can be obtained from the Yellowstone Association, P.O. Box 117, Yellowstone National Park, WY 82190.

Additional information about the park can be obtained from the Superintendent, P.O. Box 168, Yellowstone National Park, WY 82190; (307) 344-7381.

Bird Life

Cliff and violet-green swallows were also present in substantial numbers flying over the Old Faithful Geyser Basin. The buff rumps and maroon throats of the square-tailed cliff swallows helped to separate it from the slightly forked-tailed violet-green swallows, with their violet-green backs, white rumps, and snow white underparts.

I found a few other bird species there as well: a lone belted kingfisher made several over-flights, rattling its displeasure at any human disturbance; spotted sandpipers were fairly numerous along the river, and their numerous "sur-weet" and "weeet" calls were heard several times; a pair of hairy woodpeckers called from a little island of conifers amid the steaming basin; a brilliantly colored, male rufous hummingbird was found feeding at columbines at the edge of the forest; a family of gray jays lurked among the outer conifers, making strange, weird sounds all the while; and several Clark's nutcrackers called their nasal "cra-a-a" calls from the forested slope.

The flock of **Clark's nutcrackers** at Old Faithful consisted of both adults and youngsters, birds that nested earlier in the spring and may have been wanderers in search of an adequate seedcrop. Nutcrackers are big, white, gray, and black birds that show flashes of white on their wings and tails in flight. They are more numerous at higher elevation in summer, but they may descend into the lower valleys during periods of deep snow in winter. They normally remain true to their breeding grounds where they cache large amounts of food underground in summer and fall to sustain themselves through the winter months. See chapter 3 on Banff, Jasper, Kootenay, and Yoho for further information about this bird's hoarding behavior.

Nutcrackers are usually abundant on Mount Washburn, where one can hike to the summit via either the 3.2-mile (5 km) Dunraven Pass Trail or by following the supply roadway from the Mount Washburn Overlook. Snow still lay on the high ridges and in protected crevices during my mid-June hike from Dunraven Pass. It was a bright, beautiful day. I imagined I could see a hundred miles or more; there was no pale of smog along the horizon as there are so many other places in the western mountains.

Songbirds serenaded me from the adjacent forest as I moved upward along the wide, easy trail. Hermit thrushes, American robins, ruby-crowned kinglets, mountain chickadees, dark-eyed juncos, and chipping sparrows formed a welcoming chorus. From the open slopes below the trail were singing white-crowned sparrows.

Then, from the rocky outcropping on the slope ahead came the "too too too too too" and buzz song of a rock wren. This all-gray songster bobbed up and down, then flew to a slightly higher rocky perch, bobbed up and down again, and called "tick-ear tick-ear." I preferred its earlier, more melodious song.

Suddenly, less than 50 feet (15 m) ahead, along the edge of the trail, a **blue grouse** appeared. Its sooty black tail formed an open fan; its breast feathers were spread to display its bulging, bare, orange-yellow skin, like a bull's-eye with white feathers tipped with black; and its orange combs, one above each eye, were swollen and extended in full courtship. I froze in place, so as not to frighten it. Through binoculars I watched it strut ever so slowly along the side of the trail; then it walked over the edge into the shrubbery. Each step it took was so smooth it seemed to float. Once it entered the adjacent vegetation, it was next to impossible to see, its protective coloration blended so perfectly into its surroundings.

It remained still, feathers and tail back to normal. So in a few minutes I moved on up the trail. But I wasn't more than 200 feet (61 m) away before it moved back onto the trail and continued its courtship display. It again spread its tail and feathers and strutted like a rooster, with its wings dragging the ground and its head pulled in and back. Then it suddenly jumped up about two feet and made a loud fluttering sound with its wings, ending with several strange grunts. It was an altogether engrossing display. Later that morning, when we stopped at one of the pull-outs overlooking Antelope Creek, primarily to scope the open meadows for grizzly bears, we found four more blue grouse. Each had chosen open, rocky ground below the roadway to strut its stuff.

I continued up the Mount Washburn Trail, stopping several places to photograph the wonderful vistas to the east. The Grand Canyon of the Yellowstone formed a long cut beyond the green meadows and darker green forest; several snow-capped peaks of the Absaroka Mountains highlighted the far background.

"Pretty, pretty, pretty" echoed from the slope behind me. I turned just as a **Townsend's solitaire** flew from a nearby perch to one further up the rocky slope. I could clearly see its grayish body, buff wing bars, and the white, outer edges of its tail in flight; when it landed I could also see its bold white eye ring. It is a typical songbird of the high, forested, subalpine zone. But then it sang a song that was more lovely than any of the others I had heard that morning, a song filled with melody and reminiscent of other members of the thrush family. Its song was a prolonged, melodious series of rapid, warbling notes that were sweet, clear, and rich in their delivery. And then it flew off its perch, almost straight up for 100 feet (30 m) or so, fluttered at the top of its ascent, and then slowly descended, singing another lovely flutelike rendition while in flight.

See chapter 9 on Timpanogos Cave for more information about this wonderful songster.

The open alpine tundra habitat that lies along the upper slopes of Mount Washburn, especially south and east of the summit, supports only a few bird species. Horned larks, American pipits, and black rosy finches nest among the grasses, arctic sandwort, and lanceleaf stonecrop vegetation. Golden eagles (occasional), common ravens, and Clark's nutcrackers patrol the sky.

The **black rosy finch** is a dark, sparrow-sized, gray-black bird with a pinkish wash on its wings and rump and a gray patch on the back of its head. It frequents the edge of snowbanks, feeding on seeds and insects that it finds among the run-off and even on the snow and ice itself. Rosy finch nests, bulky structures constructed of mosses, grasses, feathers, hair, and the like, may be some distance away among talus slopes or rocky ledges. In order to carry sufficient food to their nestlings, during the nesting season both sexes develop a pair of gular sacs in their upper throats. They therefore are able to carry large amounts of food between their feeding and nesting sites.

This beautiful finch was earlier lumped with two other rosy finches, the gray-crowned rosy finch that occurs to the northwest, and the brown-capped rosy finch that occurs to the southeast. The three species spend their summers within their respective high mountain breeding grounds and often congregate at lower areas in winter.

Yellowstone Lake and River also support important wildlife habitats. And Fishing Bridge, located at the northern end of Yellowstone Lake, where the Yellowstone River begins, is one of the park's best bird-viewing sites. I spent one mid-summer morning at Fishing Bridge and adjacent Pelican Creek, and found more than two dozen birds from the walkways and roadside overviews.

The most outstanding bird of the morning was the **American white pelican**. Five to 14 individuals were visible from the old bridge at any one time. Their huge size, white bodies with black-tipped wings, and yellow-orange bills and feet, make them one of the most obvious birds in all the bird world. Most of the time they remained alone, drifting downriver with the current like huge white corks. They would then come flying or paddling back upriver to where they had started, probably because of the greater abundance

American white pelican

of native cutthroat trout at Fishing Bridge, near the lake outlet, only to drift slowly downriver again, starting their round-trip cycle all over again. To get airborne, a pelican has to use both wings and feet, flapping and running over the water in unison. I wondered how much of their lives are spent moving back and forth.

Occasionally, groups of three or four, and sometimes even up to a dozen individuals, gathered together in very close quarters to participate in a cooperative fishing activity. Unlike the sea-going brown pelicans, white pelicans do not dive underwater for their food but fish from the surface by lowering their long bills and heads below the surface and literally scooping up their prey. I watched five pelicans swimming abreast a couple hundred feet below Fishing Bridge. They suddenly formed a semicircle facing the shore, and with great amounts of splashing and wing move-ment, they herded fish ahead of them to shallower water, where they were then able to capture them by scooping them up into their great gular sacs. I never did see any of the fish, but when one of the pelican tipped its head back, I knew it had already forced the water (as much as three gallons) out of its distendable pouch, and was swallowing its catch. I was reminded of a famous limerick that begins, "A wonderful bird is the pelican / His bill will hold more than his belican."

Yellowstone's white pelicans nest in colonies on small islands on Yellowstone Lake. Four to six hundred pairs utilize the lake sites annually. According to Yellowstone biologist McEneaney, a white pelican's "nest is nothing more than a simple circular scrape in gravel, sometimes intermixed with loose plant material. Nest building and egg laying are nearly simultaneous and occur in early to mid-May." Young are fledged by August, and by the first of October they leave the park for their winter homes "on the coastal lowlands of Mexico." The park's June 1992 aerial survey of white pelicans produced an all-time high of 2,185 individuals.

Double-crested cormorants, California gulls, and Caspian terns also utilize Yellowstone Lake nesting sites. Of these colonial nesters, only the California gull occurs elsewhere in the park with regularity. Its white body, gray mantle, black wing tips, and yellow bill with a red and blackish blotch on the lower mandible can be expected at almost any water area in small numbers. The cormorants and terns are best seen near Pelican Creek. One evening, Betty and I found a variety of birds at the mouth of Pelican Creek, perched on the sandy spit across from the end of the Pelican Creek Nature Trail. There were more than two dozen pelicans, several Caspian terns, two common terns, three California gulls, and, surprisingly, at least 85 Franklin's gulls; this black-headed gull is a prairie pothole nester.

One of the most obvious birds along lower Pelican Creek that evening was the common snipe. Its presence was abundantly obvious throughout our stay, either by its loud "wheet-wheet" calls or by the winnowing sounds it produces in flight. At one time, we detected four separate winnowing displays high over the marsh. Further details of this unique sound can be found in chapter 23 on Black Canyon of the Gunnison and Curecanti.

I was amazed at the large variety of waterfowl that I found from Fishing Bridge. **Canada geese** were scattered all along the river-banks, and a couple dozen individuals, including several goslings, were grazing on the green island a few hundred feet downriver. These large, brownish birds, with black necks and white throat- and cheek-patches, were common all along the grassy banks and islands of the Yellowstone River. I found flocks of 60 or more at various places in the Hayden Valley. For such a large bird, it was surprisingly abundant.

The majority of Yellowstone's honkers, a common name given this goose because of its deep, musical "honk-a-lonk" calls, migrate south in early winter. But many others remain at open water areas in the park, where thermal springs provide sufficient heat to melt the snow and ice. In early April their populations increase once again. Courtship begins immediately and involves wild displays by the males. John Ehrlich and colleagues described these displays thusly: "Courting male hold head 1″ off ground, bill open, tongue raised, hissing loudly, quills shaking, approaches female, and passes neck around hers." Nests are constructed of grasses, moss, sticks, and various plant materials, usually very near the water. By early summer, when park visitors begin to crowd the roads and accommodations, goslings are almost the size of their parents.

Barrow's goldeneye

Barrow's goldeneyes were also common below Fishing Bridge. I discovered numerous flocks of a few to 17 individuals passing overhead, flying from the lake downriver. Most of the flocks were so low that the loud, continuous winnowing sound produced by their wings was easily audible. While the majority of the birds disappeared downriver, a few splashed down within viewing distance from the bridge, and I was able to admire their bright, perky attire. The male Barrow's goldeneye is marked with a snow white chest and neck, black back and tail, and a purplish-black head offset by a white crescent stripe in front of each golden eye. Females possess a similar pattern but are brownish.

The majority of the goldeneyes seen flying by were males. Females remain with their broods after hatching, while the drakes go off to join bachelor parties. Nesting occurs in natural cavities in trees and stumps, or in abandoned and enlarged woodpecker nesting holes, sometimes as high as 50 feet (15 m). They never venture far from water because these ducks feed on aquatic insects, crustaceans, and some plant materials. They, too, spend their winters in the park, at open water along the lake and rivers.

Other waterfowl were found at Fishing Bridge that summer morning: several pairs of lesser scaup were scattered along the waterway, and I was not sure whether their ducklings were hidden on the adjacent grassy shore or they were non-breeders. American wigeon were fairly common as well, and a few were located on the narrow ponds above the bridge. A pair of cinnamon teal occupied one of these little ponds. A few mallards were present along the riverway, and one female was accompanied by five half-grown chicks. Flybys during my visit included a pair of green-winged teals, one male redhead, and two female buffleheads.

Songbirds to be expected about Fishing Bridge in summer include violet-green and cliff swallows (nesting on the bridge), Clark's nutcrackers, common ravens, mountain chickadees, red-breasted nuthatches, house wrens, ruby-crowned kinglets, mountain bluebirds, hermit and Swainson's thrushes, American robins, yellow-rumped warblers, chipping sparrows, and dark-eyed juncos.

A lone osprey also flew by, carrying a fish it apparently had captured in the lake and was taking home to waiting youngsters. The osprey's black-and-white head and body, with its long, narrow wings with black wrist patches, were obvious as it passed overhead. I searched the top of the tall trees along the edge of the river for a nest, but to no avail. Earlier I had seen an osprey nest perched on the top of a tall rock pinnacle on the steep slope of the Grand Canyon of the Yellowstone, downriver from the Lower Falls. The nest was a huge pile of sticks that appeared to have been used for many years.

The deep canyons of the Yellowstone also support **peregrine falcons**, most often seen hunting along the river in Hayden Valley. They can stoop at more than 200 miles (322 km) per hour and are known to prey on waterfowl, shorebirds, and smaller birds. McEneaney told me that as many as eight pairs nested in the park during 1992 and that their recovery in the park is largely a result of a six-year (1983-1988) restoration program. Pesticides, especially DDT, had totally wiped out peregrines from the Greater Yellowstone Park area by 1960; 1984 marked the first time in 24 years that this bird reappeared and nested.

The peregrine's large size (about red-tailed hawk size), long, pointed wings, and brown to slate gray backs with black moustachial stripes on their white cheeks are their most obvious features. They frequent the park from March through early October, and then go south to their wintering grounds in the southern United States, western Mexico, and Central America.

Bald eagles also occur along the lake and rivers, and 16 pairs nested in the park in 1992. They are easiest to find in winter, however, when 20 to 50 individuals gather along the Yellowstone, Madison, and Firehole river, in places that are ice-free so they can catch fish on the open water or feed on winter-killed ungulate carrion.

Watch, too, along the grassy valleys for sandhill cranes. I found several pairs in Hayden Valley, Antelope Creek, and Pelican Creek. They usually give themselves away by their loud and very distinct calls, a rattling "gar-oo-oo" that seems ventriloquistic in quality. They appear all-brown from a distance, but with binoculars or a spotting scope, one can spot the adults' whitish neck and face, and even their reddish cap. This long-legged crane is one of the park's largest birds, with a wingspan of six feet (1.8 m). It flies with its neck stretched forward, unlike the great blue heron, a bird of similar size that normally flies with its neck doubled up. Sandhills reside in the park from mid-April to mid-September, and then go to warmer sites in the south.

Another of Yellowstone's larger birds is the **trumpeter swan**, identified by its all-white plumage, long, graceful neck, and coal black bill and feet. This wonderful bird has declined throughout its range and is having a difficult time within the park, probably due to the fluctuating water conditions and the birds' susceptibility to predators. Nesting birds "need shallow, quiet, fresh-water environments with a relatively stable level and marshy edges," according to Dick Follett in *Birds of Yellowstone and Grand Teton National Parks* (1986). Habitats outside the park provide better nesting conditions for this very specialized bird. However, the more important role of the park in the long-term survival of this graceful creature may be as "a temporary autumn sanctuary," according to Fish and Wildlife Service biologist Ruth Shea (Wilkinson 1991). The most likely swan viewing sites in summer are Beach Springs, east of Fishing Bridge, and Seven Mile Bridge, near the West Entrance. Care should be taken in each area to keep your distance so as not to harass these birds, nor should they be fed. See chapter 8 on Grand Tetons for additional information on this threatened species.

The park's most extensive lowland area, representing the montane zone, is located in the Mammoth Hot Springs area. The valley and adjacent slopes of Douglas fir and aspen support an additional group of birds, different from those found in the higher subalpine zone. McEneaney regards Mammoth as "the best birding area in Yellowstone, whether in summer or winter." The forested slopes, such as those found along the Beaver Ponds Trail, contain populations of western wood-pewees, warbling vireos, black-headed grosbeaks, lazuli buntings, and green-tailed and rufous-sided towhees. The Boiling River streamsides, below Mammoth Campground, is a good place to find red-naped sapsuckers, willow flycatchers, and MacGillivray's warblers. The Mammoth Valley in general contains populations of black-billed magpies and mountain bluebirds. Golden eagles, Swainson's hawks, and prairie falcons can be found overhead.

Yellowstone's Chief of Natural Resources Stu Coleman and I hiked the Lava Creek–Boiling River Trail in late June. The 5-mile (8 km) route contains a microcosm of the lower elevations of the park and includes a surprisingly high diversity of birds, from Townsend's solitaires to MacGillivray's warblers. We also found several American dippers, feeding amid the rushing waters and bobbing up and down on protruding boulders.

The Mammoth Hot Springs area is included in the park's Christmas Bird Count circle that is censused every year around Christmas time. In 1989, 12 counters located 1,172 individuals of 39 species. The dozen most numerous species, in descending order of abundance, included rosy finch, common redpoll, common raven, mallard, Clark's nutcracker, American dipper, black-billed magpie, rock dove, Townsend's solitaire, Canada goose, American tree sparrow, and mountain chickadee.

In summary, McEneaney's bird checklist includes 279 species, of which 144 are listed as "confirmed breeders." Of those, 38 are water birds (loon, grebes, pelican, cormorant, waders, waterfowl, rails, shorebirds, gulls, and terns), 19 are hawks and owls, and 6 are warblers. Only two species, American tree sparrow and hoary redpoll, are listed as being present only in winter.

Birds of Special Interest

American white pelican. This all-white bird with black wing tips and a huge yellow-orange bill and pouch is fairly common on Yellowstone Lake and Yellowstone River.

Trumpeter swan. It is all-white except for a coal black bill and feet; summertime birds usually are found only at Beach Springs and Seven Mile Bridge.

Barrow's goldeneye. This duck can be expected at any of the park's lakes, ponds, and rivers; the male's bold, white crescent patch in front of each eye is its most distinguishing feature.

Osprey. This fish-hawk can be expected anywhere near water areas; it is a large bird with a black-and-white head and black patches on its wrists.

Peregrine falcon. Most sightings are of birds hunting in Hayden Valley. It is a large, powerful raptor with a dark back and cap with a black moustachial stripe.

Blue grouse. It is best found in May and June when males are displaying their finery to attract a mate.

Clark's nutcracker. This black-and-white crow can be found in forest habitats throughout the park in summer. It is usually first detected by its loud "kra-a-a" calls.

Common raven. This is the large, all-black bird with pointed wings, wedge-shaped tail, and heavy bill. The look-alike American crows are rare inside the park.

Townsend's solitaire. It occurs along rocky, forested slopes in summer but moves into the valleys during the colder months.

Black rosy finch. In summer it frequents the alpine slopes, feeding at the edge of snow patches; in winter it is found at lower elevations, where it can be abundant.

8

Grand Teton National Park, Wyoming

An osprey suddenly dropped from its hovering flight, diving almost straight down for about 100 feet (30 m), its great talons extended forward, its tail spread, and wings slightly folded. It hit the water with a huge splash and, for a second or two, totally disappeared underwater. Then it emerged with a great thrashing of wings, and was soon airborne once again. It tightly held a 10- to 12-inch (25-30 cm) trout by both talons. A moment later in midair, it shook vigorously to remove the remaining water from its black-and-white plumage. Then it rearranged its catch so the head pointed forward so as to create less wind resistance. With only a slightly labored flight, the osprey headed for its nest somewhere along the shore.

Osprey

I had been watching that bird for more than an hour as it flew back and forth over the lake. Numerous times it had hovered in flight, searching, no doubt, for fish that were vulnerable to the osprey's lethal dive. The bird's large size, its whitish underparts that reflected the bluish color of the water, its dark brown back, bold white eye lines and cap, and long, slightly bent wings with dark wrists, were all readily apparent. I already had seen ospreys elsewhere in the park, several along the Snake River and the Hermitage Point Trail near Colter Bay. But none had been as cooperative as the one at Leigh Lake.

Just off the Hermitage Point Trail, an osprey nest was located at the very top of a tall Engelmann's spruce. It consisted of hundreds of sticks and various bits of debris, and may have been five feet (1.5 m) across and weighed 100 pounds (45 kg) or more. Older nests, always built at the very top of trees and posts, may be twice that size and weigh up to half a ton (454 kg). Nesting materials range from dead sticks and limbs with bits of foliage, actually broken from adjacent trees or found on the ground, to pieces of sod, animal scat, and anything else that might strike the fancy of the nest-builders. Some nests are used annually for decades, getting larger each year until the tree breaks under the weight or some other catastrophe occurs.

In spite of being found throughout the world, ospreys are truly unique creatures. They are the only member of the hawk subfamily Pandionidae and the only hawk with reversible outer toes. Like owls, they possess two toes in front and two toes in back, which enable them to better grasp their slippery prey. Further, their toe pads are covered with spicules, tiny spines which give them a sandpaper-like texture and help them to hold their catch. The osprey's generic name is *Pandion*, from the legendary King of Athens whose daughters were transformed into birds. Its species name, *haliaeetus*, is Greek for "sea eagle." An earlier common name was "fish-hawk," because they feed almost exclusively on fish.

Approximately 20 pairs of ospreys nest each year in Grand Teton National Park. They remain until early fall and then migrate south to warmer climates, from southern Mexico south to Chile and northern Argentina, for the winter months. By mid-April they reappear at their old haunts, and nest-building or repair begins almost immediately. Territorial calls are melodious, drawn-out whistles or soft whistling and chirping sounds. Courtship flights are undertaken by males that, according to William Clark and Bryan Wheeler in *A Field Guide to Hawks of North America*, include "a series of undulating dives and climbs, usually performed while the bird is carrying a fish and calling constantly." Their nests are defended with much vigor and considerable vocalization. When they are disturbed, their "cheap-cheap-cheap" calls can continue for hours, and adults may even strike an intruder.

The Park Environment

Although Grand Teton National Park is often passed by for the much larger and better-known Yellowstone National Park on its northern border, the Tetons have their share of loyal admirers. Few parks possess such raw beauty that is so readily visible from a major highway. And few mountains change so dramatically from every angle every hour of the day as do the Tetons.

Grand Teton park is of modest size (310,443 acres or 125,635 ha) and consists of two very different parts, the marvelous Teton Range and the eastern lowlands, which consist of extensive sage-brush flats, flood plain, and sparkling lakes. The Tetons, considered by geologists to be one of the most impressive fault-block ranges in the world, rise directly out of the flatlands like a great barrier wall. The range contains 11 principal peaks, the highest of which is the Grand Teton itself at 13,770 feet (4,197 m) elevation; all the others rise over 10,000 feet (3,050 m).

The string of interconnected lakes at the foot of the Tetons vary in size, from the huge, northernmost, dammed Jackson Lake (25,540 acres or 10,336 ha at full pool) to smaller lakes to the south: tiny Bearpaw, larger Leigh, elongated String, and glorious Jenny. More than 100 other lakes and ponds are scattered elsewhere in the park at various elevations. The Snake River begins its long journey to the Columbia and to the Pacific Ocean above Jackson Lake, and flows south, collecting waters from dozens of smaller tributaries.

Much of the Teton Range consists of bare rock; treeline is about 10,000 feet (3,050 m) elevation. Three broad vegetative zones occur within the park: alpine, subalpine, and montane, each containing a variety of plant and animal communities. Alpine grasses, herbs, and sedges form low-growing tundra-like vegetation on soils at treeline. Dwarfed subalpine fir and Engelmann spruce occur in scattered patches above the taller and more extensive spruce-fir forests that range down to about 6,500 feet (1,980 m) elevation. Douglas fir are scattered on lower ridgetops, and lodgepole pines dominate the glacial moraines at the base of the mountains.

The montane zone consists of big sagebrush and bitterbrush communities on much of the flatlands. The Snake River flood plain forms a linear narrowleaf cottonwood-blue spruce forest, interspersed with swampy areas, and smaller tributaries with dense riparian growth. And scattered stands of aspens and limber pine also occur throughout.

The National Park Service operates two visitor centers in the park, at Colter Bay and Moose. Each has an information desk and sales outlet, where bird guides and a park-specific bird book by Bert Raynes. A park checklist and a bird-finding guide are free for the asking. These centers also serve as the hub for the park's interpretive program, which includes a wide variety of activities. Evening talks are presented at Gros Ventre, Signal Mountain, and Colter Bay, and daily nature walks are provided at a number of locations throughout the summer season. In 1992, bird walks were provided twice a week at Willow Flats. Specific locations, dates, and times are available at the visitor centers and posted at the various campgrounds, which are located, south to north, at Gros Ventre, Jenny Lake, Signal Mountain, Colter Bay, and Lizard Creek.

The park also maintains approximately 220 miles (354 km) of trails that reach into every one of the major Teton canyons and form a network of routes across the lower slopes. Five self-guided trails are also available; they vary from the half-mile (.8 km) Menor's Ferry Trail to the much longer Cascade Canyon Trail (15.4 miles or 25 km from the west shore boat dock). Snake River float trips, in the company of concession guides, are offered several times daily in summer.

In addition, the Teton Science School provides a wide range of student and adult programs throughout the year, including several

on birding and ornithology. Further information on these programs can be obtained from the Teton Science School, P.O. Box 68,
Kelly, WY 83011.

Additional park information can be obtained from the
Superintendent, Grand Teton National Park, P.O. Drawer 170,
Moose, WY 83012; (307) 733-2880.

Bird Life

Ospreys can occur almost anywhere in the park, although they are
most numerous in the lowlands, especially along the Snake River.
They often build their bulky nests within the flood plain forest.
Osprey nests, as well as those of the larger **bald eagles** that also frequent the riverway, are similar in appearance. The two birds are
sometimes mistaken for one another. Bald eagles, however, are one-
third larger than ospreys, and the adults possess snow white heads
and tails, all-dark-brown bodies and wings, and yellow feet, eyes,
and bills. And while ospreys leave the park for the winter, bald
eagles remain as long as open water provides places where they can
feed on fish, waterfowl, and carrion. In summer, the best place to
find this royal bird is along the river near Moose. Steve Cain, the
park's wildlife biologist, told me that he knew of eight nesting pairs
of bald eagles in the park in the summer of 1992.

There are few birds with the charisma of bald eagles. Not only
is it America's national bird, but its very appearance creates excitement. It has a fierce and stately demeanor. Finding a pair sitting
quietly along the river, as one floats by, is an experience not soon
forgotten. And a bald eagle's nest is most impressive. Usually built
in the fork of a high tree, they may be 7 to 8 feet across and 12 feet
deep (2-3.7 m). Sticks make up the foundation, and the depression
on top is usually lined with mosses, grasses, pine needles, feathers,
and such. Courtship displays in winter consist of wild aerial flights
that include the locking of their talons and free-falling in a series of
spectacular somersaults. By summertime, chicks are being fed a diet
of fish and carrion, and by early August, the young are flying free.

Other raptors also nest within the flood plain forest: red-tailed
hawks are most numerous; the smaller Cooper's hawks possess dark
backs and reddish, barred underparts; the powerful northern

goshawks have dark backs, whitish underparts with dark gray streaks and white eyebrows; and the dainty American kestrels are the small falcons with reddish backs.

Few birds are as obvious along the river as **belted kingfishers;** they fly ahead of boaters and produce loud, harsh rattle-calls each time they are disturbed. When they finally become still, one can appreciate their large size, all-bluish backs and heads, and white collars and underparts with blue breastbands. Females can be identified by an additional rusty bellyband. These birds also feed on fish, which they capture by diving bill-first into the water. After capturing their prey they will fly to a nearby perch, where they usually kill their prey by beating it on a limb before swallowing it head-first. Fishbones and other indigestible food parts are disgorged as pellets.

Kingfishers nest in dirt banks along the riverway and dig slightly upturned entrance tunnels, usually 3 to 7 feet (1-2 m) long with a 6- to 10-inch-deep (15-25 cm) chamber at the far end. Nest construction may take up to three weeks and is accomplished by both sexes digging with their heavy bills and small feet.

Many of the birds that occur within the flood plain forest in summer also frequent the riparian habitats along the streams. Of the numerous songbirds found in these habitats, none are as abundant as the **yellow warbler**, sometimes incorrectly called "canary" or "golden warbler." Males are bright yellow with chestnut streaks on their chests and black eyes. Their abundant songs are cheerful and lively, a "tseet-tseet-tseet sitta-sitta-sitta," sung over and over again. In addition, these golden songsters will aggressively defend their territories; try spishing at patches of willows, and several individuals will likely respond, perch on the adjacent vegetation and scold you vehemently.

Other songbirds to be expected within the cottonwood groves include black-capped chickadees that sing "chick-a-dee-dee-dee"; white-breasted nuthatches that walk up and down tree trunks in search of insects; house wrens with rapid, bubbling songs; American robins with their reddish breasts; warbling vireos that sing rambling warbles all through the day; black-headed grosbeaks with their heavy bills and brown, black, and orange plumage;

brown-headed cowbirds, the social parasites of the bird world; and pine siskins, tiny streaked birds with yellow wing-markings.

A few additional songbirds can be expected at willow thickets and streamside habitats: willow flycatchers are pert little birds that sing loud "FITZ-bew" songs; MacGillivray's warblers possess yellow bodies, gray hoods, and white spots above and below each eye; lazuli bunting males have turquoise-colored hoods, dark backs, and chestnut and white underparts; Lincoln's sparrows have a perky manner and buff chest with darker stripes; and white-crowned sparrows possess contrasting black-and-white striped heads.

Another bird of these habitats is the **red-naped sapsucker**, a robin-sized woodpecker that can be fairly common. One morning in late June I watched a pair cavorting over Blacktail Ponds, flying here and there with great undulations. They actually were capturing insects over the pond, which I assumed were fed to nestlings in a nearby cavity. Several times one or the other would disappear among the cottonwoods on the far side of the pond, only to return almost immediately, after just enough time to shove a bill-full of insects into the gaping beak of a youngster. The male was a particularly bright and colorful creature. Its black, white, and red head, red patch on the back of the head, black wings with single bold white wing bars, and white rump glistened in the morning light.

Sapsucker adults feed almost exclusively on sap or pitch, with occasional supplements of berries and cambium, but they feed their nestlings insects. Sap is acquired by drilling shallow holes, usually in rows, in cottonwoods and willows, and lapping up the gooey substance that flows from the hole with their specially adapted, long brush-tipped tongues. This behavior gives them a "keystone" role within the bird community; the sap, which they often defend, also attracts other birds and insects. Hummingbirds, kinglets, and warblers drink the oozing sap, and other woodpeckers and warblers feed on the insects that are attracted to the sap.

The various lakes and ponds, and the slow-flowing oxbows of the Snake River, possess a rather distinct assemblage of bird species in summer, several of which are rarely found elsewhere in the park. These habitats are some of the park's richest bird-finding sites. The best of these areas include Christian Pond, across the highway from

Jackson Lodge; Willow Flats, the open flats to the west of the Lodge; and Oxbow Bend, a meandering portion of the Snake River east of the Jackson Lake Junction.

Christian Pond was alive with birds during my early morning visit; several water birds were busy foraging for breakfast or tending to their numerous youngsters. Most abundant were the **American coots**, all-black, except for white tail patches and bills. I had never before seen so many coot chicks as were scattered about the open water and among the cattails and rushes. There was continuous vocalization from these plump rails, an assortment of grunts, groans, cackles, whistles, and croaks. Every now and then two of three adults would suddenly charge one another, sometimes grabbing at the other, and then turning their backs to display their two bright, white rump patches.

Coots, sometimes called "mudhens," are fascinating birds because, in spite of belonging to the rail family, their behavior is duck-like. They usually swim about the open water like ducks instead of sneaking through the marsh grasses like most rails. They feed like ducks, too, tipping up to find aquatic vegetation on the bottom of the pond, or diving down 10 to 25 feet (3-7 m) in deeper water.

Scoping the pond, I detected numerous pied-billed grebes, several with reddish-tinged chicks, and seven species of ducks: most numerous were American wigeons with the male's whitish caps, bold green eye-stripes, and pinkish breasts; ring-necked ducks with the male's all-dark fronts and backs, whitish sides, and white ring on the bills; and the smaller ruddy ducks with the male's cinnamon bodies, black caps, white cheeks, and bright blue bills. Less numerous were green-winged and cinnamon teal, mallards, and redheads.

The bright yellow-headed birds sitting atop the grasses were yellow-headed blackbirds. In flight their white wing patches provided good contrast to their yellow heads and black bodies; I later discovered a few yellow-heads begging for handouts at the Willow Flats Overlook. The "witchity, witchity, witchity" songs of common yellowthroats were commonplace, and the songs of marsh wrens and song sparrows echoed from the willow-dominated edges.

Trumpeter swan

Then, all of a sudden, a pair of **trumpeter swans** appeared out of the tall grasses on the far shore, and with them, a single cygnet, only about one-tenth the size of its parents. What large and majestic birds they were! Their long necks curved gracefully, two feet or more above their snow white backs. Through binoculars I could see their "grin line," a reddish border at the base of their coal black bills. I also could see the red-brown stain on their otherwise snow white necks, colored by the ferrous waters of the pond. The cygnet was almost all gray, except for its black bill. I later learned from Ranger Naturalist Katy Duffy that this pair had hatched two chicks but one had disappeared.

I couldn't help but admire these beautiful creatures, and I wondered if I was watching some of the last members of a dying species. Trumpeters were almost totally eliminated by commercial harvesting in the United States and Canada during the 1800s, and thought to be extinct by 1900. Then, a 1932 survey of the tri-state region of Wyoming, Montana, and Idaho tallied 70 birds, the majority of those were located in the national parks and Red Rock Lakes National Wildlife Refuge.

The tri-state swan population increased to 640 birds by the 1950s but declined afterwards, so that the 1986 count tallied only 392 birds, the fewest since 1950. A three-year study by ornithologists Ruth Gale, Rebecca Griffen, and colleagues revealed that their decline was due to inadequate grains available to them "six to eight weeks prior to nesting when the birds must store the energy necessary for egg production and incubation," according to Rebecca Griffen. The majority of the tri-state birds remain on their breeding grounds full-time instead of migrating to warmer habitats.

Since then, the Red Rock Refuge birds have been given supplementary feed in early spring, and, aided by favorable weather as well, trumpeters have made a significant comeback. In 1987, the tri-state population was 1,710 birds. Griffen reports that swan biologists are now attempting to move swans father south to better winter quarters. Such a shift will allow them to develop their own migratory pattern, provide them with greater diversity of habitats through the year, and reduce the possibility of a catastrophe that could wipe out one entire population.

The survival of the few breeding trumpeters remaining in Grand Teton National Park depends upon the privacy they allowed them. Areas are usually closed to human use during the nesting season. Human disturbance almost always results in swan nest failure.

Antelope Flats provides the best example of the park's sagebrush community. Although its bird life is rather sparse, it includes several species that either do not occur or are rare elsewhere in the park: northern harrier; Swainson's hawk; sage grouse; short-eared owl; mountain bluebird; sage thrasher; Brewer's, vesper, and savannah sparrows; and western meadowlark. And in moist depressions with dense shrubbery, green-tailed towhees and white-crowned sparrows are common.

I searched the sage flats in late June for **sage grouse**, but to no avail. The males had already completed their spring courtship displays and moved away from their leks to nesting grounds at slightly higher elevations. April and May are the best months to see their spectacular dancing. Paul Ehrlich and colleagues described their courtship rites as follows: "Groups of males strut and inflate neck sacs until nearly reaching ground; with tail erect and fanned, rapidly throw head back with wings held rigid and almost touching ground, and deflate sacs with loud popping." Ornithologist Paul Johnsgard also points out, in *Birds of the Rocky Mountains*, that Wyoming supports the nation's largest sage grouse population, and Grand Teton National Park is the only Rocky Mountain park where the species is still reasonably common. Much of their range elsewhere has been converted to irrigated fields.

Most obvious of the birds seen during my late-June visit to Antelope Flats were **northern harriers**. I watched black-and-white males and buff-colored, striped females, each with a bold white rump, slowly flying low over the flats, wings held in shallow V-patterns, and quartering back and forth, as if searching one area at a time. Hunting harriers are one of the few hawks that utilize audio clues in their search for prey. They are able to zero in on sounds, such as rodent squeaks, and then immediately double back and pounce on their prey. Their audio-location ability is performed by an amazing system of triangulation, similar to that used by owls. A close look at a northern harrier will reveal sound-reflecting disks, special facial characteristics that are missing from other hawks.

In addition, studies of nesting harriers have revealed that 25 percent of nesting females, usually subadults, are involved with polygamy, several females mating with one male. However, once incubation begins the male harrier rarely visits the nest, leaving those chores to the hens. He does provide his fair share of food for the nestlings, by transferring prey in flight to the female, who then sneaks back to the nest after several false landings to confuse any watching predators.

Duffy told me that northern harriers also nest on Willow Flats, one of the areas where park interpreters give nature walks twice each week in summer. Park Naturalist Sheila Willis leads some of those walks and normally finds 30 bird species each morning. Besides the abundant yellow warblers, great blue herons, American wigeons, American coots, cliff and tree swallows, common yellowthroats, and red-winged and yellow-headed blackbirds, she also points out some of the less easily found birds: soras, broad-tailed and rufous hummingbirds, willow flycatchers, and marsh wrens. Sandhill cranes are often seen as well. These long-legged birds with grayish plumage, whitish throats and faces, and red caps, usually are brownish stained like the trumpeter swans.

Aspen-dominated communities occur throughout the foothills of the park and may contain their own assortment of birds, although a few species can also be found in the willow-sedge swamps or cottonwood groves. The best representative of the aspen grove communities is the little **warbling vireo**, a nondescript songbird with a gray-green back, lighter underparts, bold whitish eyebrows, and a stubby bill. But what it lacks in color it more than makes up for in personality and song. It will sing throughout the day, even late in the summer when most of the other songbirds are silent. Its song is surprisingly loud and bold for such a little bird. John Terres described its song best: a "long, flowing warble, rhythm like slowly pronounced phrase, brigadier, brig-adier, brigate." And it is one of the first birds to respond to spishing or squeaking sounds. It usually will immediately charge up to the intruder and scold with wheezy "tshay, tshay" notes.

Other reasonably common aspen grove birds include the red-naped sapsucker, western wood-pewee, tree swallow, dusky flycatcher, yellow warbler, and black-headed grosbeak. The undergrowth usually supports calliope hummingbirds, house wrens, MacGillivray's warblers, and Lincoln's and song sparrows.

The park's spruce-fir forests are most accessible around Jenny Lake, String Lake, and on Hermitage Point, beyond Swan Lake. About two dozen birds nest within this community in reasonable abundance. Songbirds include olive-sided and Hammond's flycatchers, tree and violet-green swallows, gray jays, mountain chickadees, red-breasted nuthatches, house wrens, ruby-crowned kinglets, Swainson's and hermit thrushes, American robins, yellow-rumped warblers, western tanagers, chipping sparrows, dark-eyed juncos, pine grosbeaks, Cassin's finches, and pine siskins.

One of the most numerous and most colorful of these is the **yellow-rumped warbler**, a bird that, until it was lumped with the eastern "myrtle" warbler, was called "Audubon's" warbler. It is one of the easiest of all the little songbirds to identify: males possess black faces, backs, and chests, and five bright yellow spots: on their cap, throat, sides, and rump. Females are dull gray with the same lighter yellow pattern. Also, it is one of the most vocal of the forest birds, singing "che che che che che che che," with a slight inflection on the fourth to sixth "che" notes. It usually sings high overhead but will occasionally sing at ground-level, too.

In *Birds of Grand Teton National Park and the Surrounding Area,* Bert Raynes reported that yellow-rumps are "[a] summer resident, a spring and fall migrant. Found nesting mainly in the piedmont and morainal forests and the mountainside forests in the conifers. In migration, yellow-rumped warblers will be found all over the valley floor, except in the sagebrush itself."

But the loveliest sounds of the forests are two thrushes: Swainson's and hermit. These birds occur throughout the spruce-fir communities, even in patches adjacent to the park's principal campgrounds. Their flutelike songs are commonplace, even though the listener may not know where those wonderful renditions originate.

Swainson's thrushes sing an ascending spiral of mellow whistles, while hermit thrushes sing a series of warbling notes that are repeated at different pitches. Both can sing for long periods of time, especially during the morning and evening hours. They are both slightly smaller than their cousin, the American robin, and possess brownish backs with whitish underparts with darker spots or streaks. Hermit thrushes possess reddish tails and whitish eye rings; Swainson's thrushes are slightly larger and have all-brown backs, buff eye rings and lores (between the eyes and bill); they otherwise are difficult to tell apart, especially in the shadowy forests in which they both reside.

Of all the park's wonderful trails, none is as exciting to me as the Cascade Canyon Trail, starting behind Jenny Lake and ending at Lake Solitude (9,035 ft or 2,727 m elev.). Growing up in nearby Idaho, I spent many memorable days in Cascade Canyon. The beauty and wildness of upper Cascade Canyon will always have a very special place in my life. It was also the site of many of my earliest birding adventures.

Cascade Canyon was the first place I ever found and watched American dippers feeding in a rushing stream. I discovered my first Wilson's warblers among the willows there. I once watched a Williamson's sapsucker feeding within a dense thicket. And I clearly remember eating lunch on the edge of Lake Solitude and watching American pipits walking along the shoreline and a number of black rosy finches along an adjacent patch of snow.

Wintertime is very different in the Tetons. The vast majority of songbirds have gone south to warmer climes. Many of the full-time residents congregate at warmer sites that stay relatively snow-free. And a few new arrivals from more northern latitudes put in their appearance. Over the years, the best summaries of winter bird populations have been the Christmas Bird Counts taken in Jackson and the lower edge of the park. The 1990 Christmas count tallied 2,962 individuals of 64 species. The dozen most numerous birds on that count, in descending order of abundance, included mallard, Canada goose, common raven, mountain chickadee, black-capped chickadee, black-billed magpie, Barrow's goldeneye, trumpeter swan, Clark's nutcracker, bald eagle, green-winged teal, and gadwall.

In summary, the Teton/Jackson Hole bird checklist includes 293 species, of which 152 are believed to nest. Of those, 34 are water birds (loon, grebes, cormorant, waders, waterfowl, rails, and shorebirds), 21 are hawks and owls, and 6 are warblers. None are listed for winter only.

Birds of Special Interest
Trumpeter swan. This all-white, graceful bird can best be found at quiet places along the Snake River or at Flat Creek on the Elk Refuge, north of Jackson. Care must be taken so the few remaining park birds are not disturbed.

Osprey. Its long wings with dark wrist patches, all-dark back, and black-and-white underparts distinguish this fisherman from the larger, all-white-headed bald eagle.

Bald eagle. A year-round resident, it is most numerous along the Snake River. Adults possess all-white heads and tails.

Northern harrier. This is a bird of the park's wetlands and sagebrush flats; males are black-and-white and females are buff with dark streaks.

American coot. It is all-black with white tail-patches and bill, best found at Willow Flats and beaver-dammed streams in the lowlands.

Sage grouse. This large bird of the sagebrush flats possesses a black belly and long pointed tail; the males have black throats and bibs.

Belted kingfisher. Watch for this large-billed, greenish-backed bird along the riverway. It produces a harsh, loud rattle-call.

Red-naped sapsucker. A medium-sized woodpecker of the willows and aspens, it possesses a red, black, and white head and yellowish underparts.

Warbling vireo. It is best detected by its loud and melodious songs, and identified by its bold whitish eyebrows, olive-green back, and yellowish belly.

Yellow warbler. Males are all-yellow, including the underside of their tails, and they have chestnut breast-streaks.

Yellow-rumped warbler. This is the common warbler with five distinct yellow patches: on the cap, throat, sides, and rump.

9

Timpanogos Cave National Monument, Utah

There are very few places where one can get personally acquainted with a Townsend's solitaire on its nesting grounds. This western thrush usually spends its breeding season on high, rocky, inaccessible cliffs, often just below treeline. It builds its nest on the ground or in crevices on steep slopes. Most summertime sightings of these birds are at a considerable distance and from awkward angles. But at Timpanogos Cave National Monument, Townsend's solitaires sit on rocky pinnacles, open snags, and treetops along the upper parts of the Cave Trail, and seem oblivious to one's presence. I spent more than 20 minutes at the overlook near the cave exit admiring a solitaire, up close and personal.

Townsend's solitaires are not the most colorful of birds, but what they lack in appearance they more than make up for in personality and song. They are slim, robin-sized birds that possess all-gray plumages, except for their buff wing patches, white eye rings, and white outer tail feathers, which usually are obvious only in flight. Their rather drab appearance helps to camouflage these birds, especially when they fly against the light sky. Solitaires usually fly in a slow and gentle manner, in flycatcher-fashion; they seem to flit from place to place.

A solitaire will often sit motionless for long periods of time, and every now and then give a high-pitched, metallic "tink" call. Then, suddenly, it will sing a rambling, but melodic and rather complex, flutelike song. Arthur C. Bent quotes Aretas A. Saunders' description of its song thusly: "It is a rather prolonged, warblelike series of rapid notes, each note on a different pitch than the last.

Townsend's solitaire

The notes are clear, sweet, and loud, and follow each other almost as rapidly as those of the winter wren."

During my prolonged sighting near the cave exit, I discovered that, unlike most songbirds, it barely opened its bill while singing. And as soon as it had uttered its song, it spent several seconds preening itself, ruffling its feathers, and then sat perfectly still once again. A few seconds later it sang again, a melodious warble, very different from the song of other members of the thrush family. Once it dashed off its perch, flying upward at a rather steep angle after a passing insect, which it missed. Unruffled, it returned to the same perch and sat perfectly still once again.

Its generic name, *Myadestes*, was derived from its flycatching habits. *Myadestes* is Greek for "fly-eater," according to Edward Gruson in *Words for Birds*. Its common name comes from its apparent solitary status during its breeding season. But whatever its preference, there is no better representative of the western highlands.

The Park Environment

Timpanogos Cave National Monument encompasses only 250 acres (101 ha) along a half-mile (.8 km) stretch of the American Fork River and extends 1,200 feet (366 m) up the north-facing slope and 300 feet (91 m) up the south-facing slope of American Fork Canyon. The park brochure states that the park was established in 1922 because of the cave's "unusual scientific interest and importance," and the cave has continued to be the park's principal attraction. Two thousand visitors tour the cave on an average summer weekend, and a record 90,000 people visited during the 1988 summer season (May through October).

The cave entrance is located high up the north-facing slope, at the end of a 1.5-mile-long (2.4 km) trail that climbs a vertical distance of 1,065 feet (325 m). Vegetation along the cool, shaded route consists of northern forest species dominated by Douglas fir, white fir, Rocky Mountain and common junipers, and elderberry, with fingers of Gambel's oak and western mountain and canyon maples in the long, steep drainages. The south-facing slope across the canyon contains a warmer, drier environment, with Rocky Mountain juniper, Gambel's oak, mountain mahogany, littleleaf sumac, big sagebrush, and cliffrose being most abundant. The riparian habitat on the canyon floor contains a very different environment that is dominated by tall narrowleaf cottonwoods, box elders, white firs, and a number of shrubs.

The park's visitor center is located in the canyon (5,665 ft or 1,727 m elev.) at the start of the Cave Trail. There one can find an information desk, where tickets can be purchased for the cave tours, and a sales counter where bird guides are sold; a bird checklist is available for the asking.

Interpretive activities include the popular cave tours and ranger-guided walks on the Cave Trail and along the streamside. The Cave Trail may also be self-guided; guidebooks are available to help one understand the impressive geology, plant life, and scenery along the way.

Additional information can be obtained from the Superintendent, Timpanogos Cave National Park, Rural Route #3, Box 200, American Fork, UT 84003-9803; (801) 756-5239.

Bird Life

The Townsend's solitaire is, without a doubt, the most unusual member of the thrush family. First of all, solitaires are the only thrushes that nest on the ground, building their well-concealed nests among moss, under roots, or in rocky places on steep slopes, up to 12,000 feet (3,658 m) in elevation. Unlike other thrushes that migrate to the tropics for the winter, solitaires only move to lower elevations when freezing temperatures reduce their food supply of insects. Then, they may occur either alone or in scattered flocks, depending upon the availability of fruit. Some winters they are able to survive primarily on juniper and mistletoe berries, with a lesser supplement of insects. The insects are often captured in flight, flycatcher-style, instead of on the ground, as other members of the family catch them.

The steep, rocky slope near the cave entrance and exit is the summer home not only for Townsend's solitaires, but for several other high mountain birds. **Violet-green swallows** are most obvious; they not only are abundant but they flycatch all along the upper trail. These are beautiful swallows with snow white underparts, violet-green backs, and white rumps. If one of the passing birds is in good sunlight, so that its back is highlighted, it can display an almost velvety, purple-green color. All the while, it may be uttering high-pitched calls, either a "chip-chip" or a "tweet."

Violet-greens are common swallows of all the high western mountains. They nest in woodpecker holes and crevices in aspens, cottonwoods, and various conifers, as well as on cliffs. They overwinter to the south, from California to South America, but they return to their nesting grounds just as soon as the earliest insects begin to fly in spring.

White-throated swifts are also present along the higher cliffs in spring and summer, and can be confused with violet-green swallows because of their similar size. Swifts, however, are very different birds, all-black-and-white with narrow, curved wings and a "twinkling" method of flight. They often are described as "flying cigars." Their flight is swifter and bolder than swallows' and includes considerable twisting and turning. They also utter drawn-out, twittering calls in flight. See chapter 22 on Colorado National Monument for a more extensive description of this fascinating bird.

Once the day gets underway and thermals begin to rise from the warmer lowlands, some of the larger soaring birds put in their appearance. Turkey vultures and red-tailed hawks are most numerous, but also watch for an occasional and much larger golden eagle to soar overhead. Peregrine falcons are also rarely seen.

Two kinds of hummingbirds occur along the Cave Trail. From early spring until fall, **broad-tailed hummingbirds** make themselves known by their high-pitched squeaks and aerial acrobatics. Males perform high, U-shaped display flights in spring to attract mates and often hover over a female at the bottom of their dive like a bumblebee buzzing a particularly choice flower. They feed on the sweet nectar of various flowering plants, such as the bright red Eaton penstemons or flowering chokecherries and raspberries. They also feed on insects, sometimes stealing these tiny morsels from spiderwebs.

By July, the slightly larger and more aggressive rufous hummingbirds arrive from their breeding grounds further north. Male rufous hummingbirds can be easily identified by their overall rufous colors, except for white chests and bellies, and loud wing-whistle in flight. Broad-tails possess all-green backs; males have red gorgets and all-white underparts.

Another bird one is likely to see along the Cave Trail in summer is the **western tanager**, a large sparrow-sized bird that sings a song that is robinlike in character, "a series of 1- and 3-syllable languid notes with alternating inflection," according to Larry Ballard in *The Audubon Society Master Guide to Birding*. Western tanagers also have a slurred call, a "pit-er-ick" that can usually be heard along the trail all day long. Males are gorgeous creatures with bright red faces, canary yellow collars and underparts, black backs, and wings that possess two wing bars: a bold yellow upper wing bar and a narrower white one.

The western tanager of the western mountains and the scarlet tanager of the eastern forests are the two northern representatives of a large family of tanagers that includes 236 species, all within the Western Hemisphere. Both of the northern birds join other family members during the winter months in more tropical climes from southern California to Central America. The western tanager, therefore, is a true Neotropical migrant that depends as much upon viable habitats in the tropics as it does on a healthy forest ecosystem in the Rocky Mountains.

I found a few other birds in the coniferous forest habitats along the Cave Trail one day in early June: hairy woodpeckers called out their sharp "peek" calls on a couple occasions; mountain chickadees sang their "chick a-dee a-dee a-dee" songs from the treetops; hermit thrush songs, a series of flutelike phrases on different pitches, echoed from the forested slopes; black-throated gray warblers foraged among the firs and occasionally sang a "wheezy-wheezy-wheezy-weet" song; golden-crowned kinglets were busy among the high foliage; dark-eyed juncos were twittering among the undergrowth; and pine siskins flew here and there, uttering rising "zzzhrreee" calls in flight.

Dark-eyed juncos are relatively scarce in early June while nesting, but once the youngsters are fledged, they become more numerous along the trail. Their gray heads, tails, and underparts, and rufous backs help identify this active little bird. They often call out a sharp "dit" note, and their songs, usually delivered from the treetops, are a musical trill that may change pitch halfway through. This bird was once known as "gray-headed junco," before the three common North American forms—slate-colored, Oregon, and gray-headed—were discovered to interbreed. The American Ornithologists' Union lumped the three together, and they are now collectively called dark-eyed juncos. Another southern junco with pale eyes, which ranges from Guatemala to southeastern Arizona, is known as "yellow-eyed junco."

The fingerlike zones of oaks and maples provide habitats for two warblers that sing their songs surprisingly close to one another, almost in competition, the orange-crowned and Virginia's warblers. Orange-crowned songs are most numerous, identified by their jumbled, rapidly descending melody. Virginia's warblers sing a more musical song that usually ascends at the end. Orange-crowns utilize any of the deciduous vegetation for nesting, but Virginia's are apparently restricted to the Gambel's oaks. On the south-facing slopes of American Fork Canyon, where Gambel's oaks are more abundant, Virginia's warblers are by far the most numerous of the two.

Along the lower streamsides, orange-crowned and Virginia's warblers are replaced by the MacGillivray's warbler, a lovely bird with an all-gray hood, except for white crescents above and below the eyes, olive-brown backs, and lemon-yellow underparts. The thickets of deciduous vegetation above the riparian zones provide nesting habitats for the black-headed grosbeak, green-tailed towhee, and lazuli bunting.

The riparian area contains a more varied environment with a greater number of bird species. Summer residents include many of the same birds already mentioned, but the following species are also common: tiny black-chinned hummingbirds; ash-throated flycatchers that sing "ha-wheer" songs; Steller's jays with royal-blue bodies and a blackish crest; the well-known American robins; warbling vireos, little, nondescript birds with rambling, whistle songs that continue throughout the day; and tiny yellow warblers that sing rapid, cheerful "tseet-tseet-tseet sitta-sitta-see" songs.

Most evident of these is the **American robin**. The Timpanogos robins are some of the most brightly marked birds anywhere. Males possess deep orange-red bellies and black heads; females are slightly duller in appearance. Perhaps because of the noisy competition with the rushing stream, they seemed to sing more loudly and clearly here than they do elsewhere. They sing from the very tops of the trees, producing a familiar caroling song, "cheerily-cheery-cheerily-cheery," which they sing over and over again.

Robins feed on the ground, running over the lawns and beneath the streamside vegetation, searching for insects and earthworms. Although the question of whether robins find earthworms by sight or by sound has never been definitively answered, most ornithologists believe that robins locate earthworms by sight. So, when a robin cocks its head as if listening, it is probably just getting a better look.

One of the most interesting, but less obvious, of the park's birds occurs only in the fast-flowing American Fork Creek. This is the **American dipper**, a medium-sized, short-tailed, plump gray to slate gray bird with a brown tinge on its head. Dippers spend more time foraging underwater than along the streambank and generally are better known to fishermen than they are to those of us who watch for birds among the shrubs and trees.

Their name derives from their habit of dipping up and down with their whole body. Their nests are bulky, oven-shaped structures, usually a foot in diameter and constructed under waterfalls, on ledges, or among exposed tree roots. Females are polygymous, mating with several males and defending their mates against other females. Young of the year are very precocious and can climb, dive, and swim on departing the nest.

Watch for this facinating bird along the stream throughout the half-mile (.8 km) portion of the park. It maintains the same home range whenever possible, moving to lower elevations only during the very coldest winters. See chapter 3 on Banff, Jasper, Kootenay, and Yoho for additional information about this bird's behavior.

In summary, the Timpanogos Cave checklist of birds includes 123 species, of which 32 are full-time residents, 92 are summer residents and assumed to nest, and 15 species are listed for the winter months only.

Birds of Special Interest

Broad-tailed hummingbird. This is the green-backed hummingbird with a bright red gorget, common in spring and summer; the rufous-backed rufous hummingbird is present in July, August, and September.

Violet-green swallow. Its violet-green back and snow white underparts help to identify this common swallow. It is abundant along the upper Cave Trail, often perching on rocky pinnacles and tree-tops, as well as on the wires near the cave exit.

Townsend's solitaire. This is the thin, robin-sized, gray bird with white eye rings and outer tail feathers, and buff-colored wing bars, common along the upper portions of the Cave Trail.

American dipper. Watch for this bulky, dark gray bird in the swiftly flowing stream in the canyon. It feeds underwater and is a fascinating bird to watch.

Western tanager. The male's bright yellow body, red head, and black wings help identify this sparrow-sized songster; it is common in spring and summer.

Dark-eyed junco. This is the little gray bird with a rufous back and white outer tail feathers. It spends most of its time on the ground but sings a loud, melodious trill from the treetops.

10

Dinosaur National Monument, Colorado and Utah

A bright yellow-breasted bird suddenly arose from the riverside thicket, flew straight up 20 to 25 feet (6-8 m) above the vegetation, and then, with wings flopping, tail pumping, and legs dangling, floated back to the same place from where it had first appeared. It sang a remarkable song during its descent, a jumble of whistles, clucks, mews, squawks, and gurgles. A moment later, it let loose with a series of "kuk kuk kuk" notes, very different from any it had produced in flight. I watched it through my binoculars as it preened itself, ruffled its feathers, and then began a completely new series of clucks, mews, yanks, and gurgles. Suddenly, it shot back into the air, and I watched a repeat of its earlier territorial display.

The yellow-breasted chat is an amazing bird. It is one of our most vocal warblers, singing vigorously during mornings and evenings and sometimes late into the night. Its singing behavior is often compared with mockingbirds. One of the best descriptions of the chat was made by Percy Taverner in a 1906 *Bird-Lore* article: "With his stealthy elusiveness, with outpourings of song and fund of vituperation, the Chat is a droll imp. He is full of life and boiling over with animation. It bubbles out of his throat in all manner of indescribable sounds. He laughs dryly, gurgles derisively, whistles triumphantly, chatters provokingly, and chuckles complacently, all in one breath."

The yellow-breasted chat is a bird of the dense thickets that occurs along Dinosaur's rivers and tributaries. It can be loud and obnoxious in spring but quiet and secretive by summer and fall. Riverside campers often find that this large, bright yellow warbler serves as an excellent alarm clock.

Yellow-breasted chat

Its status in the family of wood warblers was recently verified by DNA studies, in spite of its possessing a number of "unwarblerlike" characteristics: a larger overall proportion, a heavy and more curved bill, shorter and more rounded wings, and the ability to hold food with one foot.

But whatever its taxonomy, its bright yellow throat and breast, set off against its olive-green upperparts and white chin and spectacles, give it a distinct appearance. Add its unique territorial display and vociferous characteristics, and no one will question its very special status.

The Park Environment

Dinosaur National Monument is a multidimensional park; one's perspective is shaped by one's approach and use of its resources. River users see the park from the bottom up and learn first to appreciate the flowing rivers, exciting rapids, and patches of lush riparian growth with dramatic backdrops of multicolored walls. Visitors to Dinosaur Quarry and Split Mountain learn of the geological and paleontological significance of the monument. And those folks who visit Harper's Corner Scenic Drive receive their introduction from the top of the park, which is dominated by broad, gray-green sagebrush flats and scenic vistas. Elevations within the park range from 4,735 feet (1,443 m) near the quarry to 9,006 feet (2,745 m) at the summit of Zenobia Peak.

The centerpiece of the park is the confluence of two impressive rivers, the Yampa and Green. The Yampa River flows into the Green River very close to the geographic center of the park. The Green River is impounded above the park by Flaming Gorge Dam, but the Yampa River is free-flowing. It represents the only remaining large tributary in the entire Colorado River system that remains undammed.

Riparian growth along the rivers and side canyons varies greatly but generally is dominated by cottonwoods, especially Fremont cottonwood that may occur in large open groves if space allows, and willows, boxelder, and the nonnative tamarisk. Adjacent flats usually possess sagebrush communities where big sagebrush, rabbitbrush, and two kinds of grasses are dominant: the native ricegrass and the nonnative cheat grass.

Pinyon-juniper woodlands, dominated by pinyon pine and Utah juniper, occur on rocky slopes from just above the riparian zone to 8,500 feet (2,590 m) elevation. Big sagebrush, rabbitbrush, and mountain mahogany are common within these short-tree woodlands. Sagebrush communities dominate the open flatlands between 5,000 and 8,000 feet (1,524-2,438 m). Sherel Goodrich and Elizabeth Neese, in *Uinta Basin Flora*, described five rather distinct sagebrush communities resulting from slope and elevation differences.

Ponderosa pine, Douglas fir, and aspen communities occur above the pinyon-juniper woodlands in scattered localities. The Harper's Corner Trail, which follows a high ridge to an outstanding view into Whirlpool Canyon of the Green River, provides one example where pinyon-juniper occurs on the warmer south-facing slope and Douglar-fir and associated flora dominate the cooler, steep, north-facing slope.

The park's visitor center and administrative offices are located along Highway 40 near Dinosaur, Colorado, at the entrance to the Harper's Corner Scenic Drive. A second visitor center is located at Dinosaur Quarry, just north of Jensen, Utah. Each center has an information desk and sales counter; bird guides and a park checklist are available. Interpretive programs, including evening talks and ranger-guided walks, are provided during the summer season. Schedules are available at all the information stations for the asking. An informative newspaper, *Echoes*, is also available at no charge.

Additional information can be obtained from the Superintendent, Dinosaur National Monument, P.O. Box 210, Dinosaur, CO 81610; (303) 374-2216.

Bird Life

Although the yellow-breasted chat is the flood plain's most exciting summer resident, it has several neighbors that also are loud and colorful. A visit to Green River or Split Mountain campgrounds, or Echo Park and Jones Hole, will likely result in finding most of these riparian specialties. In a little over two hours at Green River and Split Mountain campgrounds one morning in mid-May, I recorded 28 species.

Lazuli bunting males appeared like small, bright jewels among the riverside thickets. Their bright turquoise heads and throats gleamed in the morning light. With their bluish backs, white bellies, and cinnamon sides, they were most distinguished. Their name is very fitting; it is derived from lapis lazuli, an opaque, azure-blue to deep-blue gemstone of lazurite, according to *Webster's*. Females are brownish birds with darker wings, lighter underparts, and bluish rumps. But both sexes were active and easily observed. I watched one especially bright male chase another male away from a patch of saltbushes where I assumed it was nesting. I made a few sharp chip sounds, and almost immediately a female appeared out of the saltbush thicket and chipped back at me, as if agitated by my presence.

A moment later the male lazuli bunting burst forth with song, as if to help solidify its territory against this human intruder. I marveled at its bright and rapid song, a series of varied phrases that John

Lazuli bunting

Terres described as "see-see, sweert, sweert, sweert, zee, see, swert, zeer, see-see." During the 15 to 20 minutes that I watched these lovely and rather aggressive birds, the male sang from several levels: on the low saltbushes, from the lower branches of an adjacent cottonwood, from the top of an adjacent utility pole, and from the apex of a taller cottonwood tree. The female stayed among the dense shrubbery but proclaimed her territory with loud and hard chips.

The numerous cottonwoods within the campground were literally alive with birds. Most numerous were western kingbirds, house wrens, American robins, blue-gray gnatcatchers, and northern (Bullock's) orioles. I counted more than 20 **western kingbirds** at the Green River Campground, either chasing one another among the high foliage, singing from the higher branches, or performing wild courtship flights. Paul Ehrlich and colleagues report that males perform frantic courtship flights: "darting into air, fluttering, vibrating feathers, and trilling." A separate flight song was described by Scott Terrill in *The Audubon Society Master Guide to Birding* as "a pkit-pkit-pkeetle-dot or pkit-pkit-deedle-ot, which is highest pitched." Numerous individuals produced loud, sharp, "kit, whit," or "pkit" calls. The western kingbird is a lovely bird with a yellow belly, grayish throat and breast, gray-brown back, and black tail with distinct white edges. The white edges on the tail are its most distinguishing features; its look-alike cousin, the Cassin's kingbird that normally occurs farther south, lacks the white tail-edges, but possesses white at the tip of its tail as well as a darker breast and back.

A duo of tiny, all-brown house wrens sang their rapid, bubbling songs from the tip-top of two cottonwoods. Two pairs of blue-gray gnatcatchers were busy among the lower branches of the trees; they sang high-pitched, buzzy songs, very insectlike. American robins were also in full song; they produced loud, rich caroling that has been described as "cheerily-cheery-cheerily-cheery." Located 5 feet (1.5 m) up in a big sagebrush near the campground entrance, I found a robin nest with five bright blue eggs. The female flew off the nest as I approached, scolding me with sharp "tut, tut, tut" notes.

I discovered a partially constructed **northern oriole** nest in the outer foliage of one cottonwood tree, approximately 25 feet (8 m) up. Most of the orioles seemed too busy chasing one another about the trees to spend any time nest-building. These large black, orange, and white birds could hardly be ignored for their aggressiveness. The male northern oriole is a lovely bird. In the sunlight its orange underparts and face, black back and throat, and broad white wing bars give it a tropical bird appearance. Females are much duller, with yellowish heads and whitish underparts. The plumage of immature males is a combination of both adults. They possess the black chins and yellow-orange underparts, but their backs are only beginning to darken. All three patterns of this gregarious species were present; all were chasing one another about the Green River Campground. The partially completed nest was a finely woven, oval-shaped cup about 6 inches (15 cm) deep. I watched the adult female carry grasses to the nest, which she wove into the thin matrix. Later, she will line the cup with plant down, mosses, and animal hair.

Another bird in surprising abundance in the Green River Campground was the European starling. This large and aggressive nonnative species is a cavity-nester and seemed to be utilizing most of the choice nesting sites. I wondered how many native cavity-nesters it had replaced since moving into the area. Although starlings are too large to usurp smaller nest-holes, such as those required by house wrens and violet-green swallows, they undoubtedly replace American kestrels, ash-throated flycatchers, and white-breasted nuthatches. Those birds are now relegated to the more arid, adjacent pinyon-juniper woodlands.

Also present in large numbers that morning were brown-headed cowbirds, social parasites that lay their eggs in the nests of other, smaller birds. See the introductory chapter, "Parks as Islands," and chapter 31 on Big Bend National Park, for more information on the effects cowbirds have on native songbirds. I couldn't help but wonder which birds were being affected at Dinosaur.

All the while I wandered through the campground, violet-green and cliff swallows and white-throated swifts flew overhead. The violet-greens were nesting on the cottonwoods, utilizing deserted woodpecker holes and various cracks and crevices not already in service by starlings. The cliff swallows were constructing their own nests on the adjacent cliffs. I located several groupings of old mud nests, some broken and unused, and others that had been repaired and appeared to be in use. And I found dozens of the square-tailed cliff swallows fluttering over the muddy shore, just above Split Mountain Campground, gathering mud pellets for nest-building. The swifts nest in crevices high on the steep cliffs.

Black-billed magpies were also present during the morning, but only flying over, as if their interests were focused elsewhere. I imagined that they would have been more interested if I had been eating lunch. They then would compete with the numerous golden-mantled ground squirrels for snacks and leftovers. Instead, the magpies were mostly involved with nesting on the little island below Split Mountain Campground; several large stick nests were evident in the cottonwoods there.

Several other birds were found that morning in and around the campgrounds: small flocks of Canada geese flew over, honking all the while; six northern pintails flew upriver, circling to gain altitude, and flew off toward the north; a couple pairs of barn swallows were flying around the ranger residence; an *Empidonax* flycatcher, probably a migrant dusky flycatcher, chipped at me from the shrubbery; a solitary vireo sang its rich two- to six-note whistles; two yellow warblers were singing from the high cottonwood foliage at Green River Campground; and a pair of white-crowned sparrows that had not yet moved to their high-country nesting grounds were searching for seeds at the far end of the campground circle.

Within the canyons themselves, one of the most conspicuous birds, judging from sound rather than sight, is the canyon wren. Its descending and decelerating songs are commonplace, and river runners learn to associate them with the river. Canada geese and common mergansers are the most frequently observed waterfowl in the canyons.

The adjacent pinyon-juniper woodlands contained a few additional birds that were evident from the campgrounds: scrub and pinyon jays, plain titmice, rock wrens, black-throated gray warblers, and house finches. I walked the Red Rock Nature Trail, which starts near the entrance to the Split Mountain Campground, follows a cottonwood-filled arroyo, and then circles a juniper-dominated ridge; the trail provided good looks at all those species. I also found several black-throated sparrows singing from big sagebrush. This little sparrow was earlier called "desert sparrow" because of its affinity for the arid lowlands. Its presence within the sagebrush flats on the Red Rock Nature Trail confirmed the desert-like character of the area.

Another day was spent along the Harper's Corner Scenic Drive, walking the Harper's Corner Trail, and visiting Echo Park.

Common ravens were present along the roadway, apparently searching for road kills from the previous night. We found a dead common poorwill that had not yet been claimed by one of the many scavengers. **Brewer's blackbirds** were most abundant along the roadway and flying over the adjacent sagebrush flats. Most were already paired and courtship was in full swing. Males were attempting to impress their ladies by pointing their heads skyward, fluttering their drooping wings, spreading their tails, and uttering a series of whistles, squeaks, and trills. The male's coal black body and white eyes apparently appeal to the more somber-colored females. This blackbird often nests in colonies of up to 20 pairs; they build nests on the ground as well as on sagebrush.

Mountain bluebirds, American robins, sage thrashers, western meadowlarks, green-tailed towhees, and vesper and Brewer's sparrows were all in full song along the roadsides. We found two golden eagles perched on rocky ridges; one flew off as we approached, but the other stayed and allowed us to look it over from our blind inside the vehicle. It was a marvelous bird with a golden sheen to its bulky head.

The bird of the morning was a **sage grouse**, walking along the road shoulder, pecking now and then at green buds or insects that we couldn't detect. This grouse is a large bird, more than 2 feet (.6 m) in length, with long, pointed tail feathers, mottled brown plumage, and a black belly. The park birds overwinter on the lower sagebrush flats and move to higher elevations, along the edge of the aspens and conifers, to nest, according to the park's resource specialist, Steve Petersburg. Once on their nesting grounds, groups of males (usually 20 to 70 individuals) occupy display sites called leks, where they show off their finery in an attempt to impress the females. Ehrlich and colleagues described the courtship displays thusly: they "strut and inflate neck sacs until nearly reaching the ground; with tail erect and fanned, rapidly throw head back and wings held rigid and almost touching the ground, and deflate sacs with loud popping." The same leks are used annually and are said to have been used by a hundred or more generations of sage grouse.

At Echo Park Overlook, we frightened a blue grouse that apparently was feeding along the road shoulder. It took flight and soared off into the adjacent forest. Its bluish color and smaller size were obvious in flight. This grouse is not a lekking species; instead, solitary males display on scattered territories to entice their mates. See chapter 7 on Yellowstone for a description of this bird's courtship behavior.

I walked the 2-mile (3.2 km) Harper's Corner Nature Trail through high-elevation pinyon-juniper woodlands, past outstanding views of Steamboat Rock and Echo Park, to a high perch (7,510 ft or 2,289 m) overlooking the Green River. I found a fascinating mixture of woodland and forest birds along the trail. Pinyon-juniper birds included black-chinned hummingbirds, gray flycatchers, scrub jays, mountain bluebirds, black-throated gray warblers, and chipping sparrows. The black-throated gray warblers were singing a song that seemed quite different from those that I heard in the lower woodlands. It took me several minutes to find this attractive black-and-white warbler with a tiny yellow spot in front of each eye to confirm its identity. Its varied songs have been described as a buzzy "weezy weezy weezy weezt-weet." See chapter 14 on Zion for additional information on this little songster.

Several boreal bird species were found: Clark's nutcrackers were flying over the northern slope; mountain chickadees called their hoarse "chick a-dee a-dee a-dee" songs from the Douglas firs; two red-breasted nuthatches called out from the lower slope, toy trumpet-like "nyak nyak nyak" sounds; a pair of Townsend's solitaires flew by, and a moment later I detected their mellow call notes; ruby-crowned kinglets were vigorously singing from the conifers; two or three yellow-rumped warblers were detected by their distinct chips; a red crossbill flew across the sky, calling "chink-chink-chink"; and a lone Cassin's finch serenaded me from the top of a tall conifer.

Echo Park lies at the end of a 13-mile (21 km) secondary road that starts near the Island Park Overlook on the Harper's Corner Scenic Drive. I found almost all of the same bird species there as I did at Split Mountain and Green River campgrounds, with a couple of exceptions. Most obvious of these was the greater number of **yellow warblers**; they seemed to be singing from every cottonwood and riverside thicket. Their cheerful but rapid songs have been described as "tseet-tseet-tseet sitta-sitta-see" or a musical "wee wee wee witita weet." This little all-yellow bird, with chestnut streaks on the male's breast, goes by a number of other names: "wild canary," "golden warbler," and "summer yellowbird."

I couldn't help but wonder why this warbler was so abundant at Echo Park, after I had found only two individuals in the larger but comparable areas of Split Mountain and Green River campgrounds. The one difference that I could detect was the much greater number of brown-headed cowbirds at the campgrounds. Since cowbirds totally eliminated nesting populations of yellow warblers along the Rio Grande at Big Bend National Park, I wondered if a similar change was occurring at Dinosaur.

But this has not been the case for the endangered **peregrine falcon**; there has been a exciting about-face for this species in recent years. Peregrine nesting sites have increased from a low of only one active aerie in 1976 to ten in 1992. Petersburg told me that the number could be as high as 14, and that biologists are finding sites as close as 4 to 6 miles (6.4-9.6 km) apart. Peregrine recovery is largely due to a 10-year program to restore birds at pertinent locations in the Rocky Mountains. Many of the birds now being found within the canyons of Dinosaur are non-banded birds, undoubtedly the product of those early efforts. The canyon overlooks are the best places to see this swiftest of all birds, which resides within the park from March through September.

Winter birds of the park include a very different assortment from those that occur at other times. The best indications of the wintering bird life are the annual Christmas Bird Counts. The 1990 Christmas count recorded 1,949 individuals of 34 species. The dozen most numerous of those, in descending order of abundance, included red-winged blackbird, house sparrow, horned lark, European starling, black-billed magpie, Brewer's blackbird, dark-eyed junco, ring-necked pheasant, rosy finches, white-crowned sparrow, American goldfinch, and Canada goose.

In summary, the Dinosaur National Monument checklist of birds includes 209 species, of which 54 are considered full-time residents, 85 occur in summer only, and 11 have been reported only during the winter months. Of the approximately 140 species present during the nesting season, 16 are water birds (waders, waterfowl, coot, and shorebirds), 18 are hawks and owls, and 9 are warblers.

Birds of Special Interest

Peregrine falcon. Watch for this large falcon with the slate gray back anywhere along the rivers where cliffs provide high, inaccessible nesting sites.

Sage grouse. It is reasonably common along the Harper's Corner Scenic Drive in late winter and spring. Its large size, long tail-feathers, and black belly are its most distinguishing features.

Yellow warbler. This is a little all-yellow warbler at riparian areas along the rivers; males possess chestnut streaks on their bright yellow breasts.

Yellow-breasted chat. The loud shrieks, mews, rattles, and squawks of this large warbler are commonplace along the river. Watch for its colorful display flights over the vegetation.

Northern oriole. Males possess orange, black, and white plumage. Northern orioles are commonplace along the river and are often seen chasing one another about the trees and shrubs.

Lazuli bunting. Its turquoise-colored head, white belly, and chestnut sides help identify the colorful male. It is most numerous in brushy areas in the lowlands.

Brewer's blackbird. Hundreds of these all-black birds reside among the sagebrush in spring and summer. Males possess white eyes, and females are a gray-brown color.

11

Rocky Mountain National Park, Colorado

The American pipit is one of only five birds that nest on the high, open alpine tundra of Rocky Mountain National Park. It is by far the most abundant of the five and difficult to miss at any of the overlooks and parking areas on Trail Ridge Road between Forest Canyon Overlook and Medicine Bow Curve. Most often, one is first attracted to this sparrow-sized bird by its very distinct song and territorial display. Its repetitive but musical song is a long series of "treet" or "pip-it" notes, from which its name was derived, sometimes sung from a rocky perch but most often sung in flight. Pipits fly upward almost vertically to as much as 200 feet (60 m) and then float downward with their wings out, legs hanging, and tail upward, singing all the while.

American pipit

Their aerial display evolved to conform to the treeless terrain of the tundra, where they do not possess the luxury of singing posts as do forest and woodland birds. Also, because of the open character of their habitat, pipits must blend into the terrain to survive. Until they move, they are next to impossible to locate because of their cryptic coloration. Pipits are relatively slender birds with gray-brown backs with darker streaks, whitish throats, buff underparts with dark-brown streaks, and white outer tail feathers. On the ground, they walk rather than hop, and have a habit of bobbing their tail up and down, or sometimes swinging it from side to side.

These hardy birds arrive on their nesting grounds before the snow has melted, and nesting is well underway by mid-June; snow storms can be expected on the tundra at any time. Nests usually are placed directly on the ground in slight depressions or under the partial protection of a rock or tufts of vegetation, and lined with grasses. The four or five eggs hatch within two weeks, and birds are fledged two weeks later. Almost immediately they form flocks and move to lower elevations, usually frequenting water courses or cultivated fields where they may remain until colder weather forces them further south. Flocks of several hundred pipits are not unusual in fall and winter.

Other tundra nesters include horned larks, brown-capped rosy finches, white-crowned sparrows, and white-tailed ptarmigans. Horned larks look a little like pipits at first glance, because of their similar size and gray-brown backs. But their black-and-yellow streaked faces, throats, and chests, and their tiny black "horns" (actually feathers that extend upright above each eye but are rarely evident on the windy tundra), give them a very different appearance.

Brown-capped rosy finches are heavy-set, sparrow-sized birds with grayish-brown backs, brown heads and gray crowns, and reddish color on their rumps, bellies, and wings. This bird was earlier lumped together with the more northern black rosy finch of the Yellowstone area and gray-crowned rosy finch of the Canadian Rockies. They all feed along the edge of snowfields and sing a descending series of short "chew" notes.

White-crowned sparrows are readily identified by their bold black-and-white head stripes and their song, which John Terres describes as a sad "more wet wetter chee zee." This bird nests in willow and meadow habitats throughout the park, but its "more wet wetter chee zee" songs can be expected in all but the dense forest habitats.

And then there is the **white-tailed ptarmigan**, the size of a small chicken, and one of the park's truly outstanding birds. It is the only one of the five species that remains on its tundra homeland in winter. In the fall it molts its mottled black-and-gold plumage to all-snow white, except for its coal black bill and eyes and red eye combs. It also develops heavily feathered legs and feet that serve as snowshoes. John Ehrlich and colleagues reported that the "feathers increase the bearing surface of the foot by about 400 percent and reduce the distance the foot sinks in snow by roughly 50 percent." Ptarmigans are able to remain warm during winter snowstorms by nestling together in tight circles under the snow, so that there is a minimum loss of body heat.

In summer, their plumage matches the terrain so perfectly, they are next to impossible to find. When one is located, it usually is easy to observe because it seldom will fly, remaining perfectly still, relying upon its natural camouflage to keep it safe. See chapter 5 on Glacier and Waterton Lakes for additional information on this alpine species.

The Park Environment

No other national park provides vehicular access to miles of tundra habitat. Spectacular Trail Ridge Road, which passes over "the roof of the Rockies," remains above treeline for 11 miles (18 km) and reaches an elevation of 12,183 feet (3,713 m). The views are spectacular! To the south is the rugged Front Range while to the north, across Fall River Valley, the view is dominated by the majestic Mummy Range. Far to the west is the Never Summer Range. The park's highest peak, to the south, is Long's Peak (14,255 ft or 4,345 m elevation), but almost 100 peaks within the park's 265,668 acres (107,514 ha) exceed 11,000 feet (3,353 m).

Most of the park is wilderness and can be experienced only by hiking its 355 miles (571 km) of trails. Roads are limited to Trail Ridge Road, Old Fall River Road, a one-way gravel road that parallels a portion of the eastern part of Trail Ridge Road, the 10-mile (16 km) Bear Lake Road, and the Fall River Entrance Road to Deer Ridge Junction.

Ecologists place all of the park's plant and animal communities into three broad vegetative zones: alpine, subalpine, and montane. Treeline occurs at about 11,000 feet (3,353 m) elevation; all of the bare rock and broad expanses of tundra habitat above that falls within the alpine zone. This is the environment that Ann Zwinger and Beatrice Willard wrote so intimately about in their excellent book, *Land Above the Trees*.

An interpretive sign along the Tundra Nature Trail features one of Zwinger's descriptive quotes: "The alpine tundra is a land of contrast and incredible intensity, where the sky is the size of forever and the flowers the size of a millisecond."

Vegetation just below treeline often consists of contorted and dwarfed subalpine fir and Engelmann spruce, often in windblown krumholtz conditions. Below these areas are the more expansive stands of fir and spruce that dominate the subalpine zone. This zone receives the greatest amount of snowfall and it lasts longest in summer, insuring plentiful moisture during the short summers. Many lakes, marshes, and meadows are associated with this zone, as are nearly pure stands of lodgepole pine on old burns, and limber pine on the more exposed slopes. Common understory plants of the subalpine zone include blueberries, grouse whortleberry, and mountain ash; thinleaf alder and twinberry occur along streams.

Everything below approximately 8,000 feet (2,438 m) elevation is within the park's montane zone, but habitats vary with elevation and slope. Ruth Nelson provided a good general description of this zone in her early book, *Plants of Rocky Mountain National Park*. The eastern slope is characterized by open ponderosa pine forest, interspersed with Douglas fir: "It includes moist and dry aspen groves, lodgepole, and Douglas fir forest on the north-facing slopes, open meadows, and barren, rocky ridges." Ponderosa pine may be mixed with Rocky Mountain juniper at lower areas, and "[a]long the streams are found groves of the magnificent Colorado blue spruce associated with willows, alder, and water birch." The western slope receives the greatest precipitation resulting in more continuous and luxuriant growth, although big sagebrush can be dominant on the drier south-facing slopes.

The park's east and west sides, separated by the Continental Divide, differ in a number of respects. The park's newspaper, *High Country Headlines*, highlights those differences. The East Side possesses "2 million visitors/year, glaciers, greenback trout, no moose, no major rivers, ponderosa pine, 13 inches (33 cm) moisture, windy, Abert's squirrel, no otter, wood lily, pricklypear cactus, and mild winters." The West Side possesses "[o]ne-third million visitors/year, no glaciers, Colorado River trout, moose, Colorado River & headwaters, no ponderosa pine, 24-25 inches (61-63 cm) moisture, little wind, no Abert's squirrel, otter, no wood lily, no pricklypear cactus, cold winters."

The National Park Service operates four visitor centers: at Estes Park at the east entrance; at Alpine at Fall River Pass; at Kawuneeche at Grand Lake; and at Lily Lake in the southeast corner. There is also a center at the Moraine Park Museum. All five of these centers have an information desk and sales outlet for publications, including bird guides and a checklist of birds. They also provide orientation programs and serve as a hub for the park's varied interpretive activities. A schedule of all the "Ranger Programs," talks, walks, and hikes, are listed in *High Country Headlines*, which is handed out at the park's entrance stations and available at the visitor centers for the asking. Bird walks and talks are presented on both sides of the park.

In addition, the Rocky Mountain Nature Association sponsors a number of seminars on a variety of topics, including one-day sessions on raptors and birdwatching, and a week-long bird ecology seminar. For further information about this program, write the Seminar Coordinator, Rocky Mountain Nature Association, Rocky Mountain National Park, Estes Park, CO 80517.

For additional information about the park, write the Superintendent, Rocky Mountain National Park, Estes Park, CO 80517; (303) 586-2371.

Bird Life

One of the best places to observe the Rocky Mountain tundra is at the Alpine Visitor Center. One day in early July, following a sprinkling of powdery snow the day before, I watched the comings and goings on the steep slope behind the center. Far below in the lush, green meadows, 35 to 40 cow elk grazed or nursed their calves. Small flocks of pine siskins, tiny, stripped birds with yellowish wing bars, passed by, undoubtedly heading toward the spruce-fir forests below. A common raven, identifiable by its all-black plumage, pointed wings, wedge-shaped tail, and large bill, soared along the high ridge to my right. I had passed a pair of these birds doing roadside cleanup at Many Parks Curve on my way up the mountain earlier that morning.

A pair of tree swallows soared along the rocky cliff far below; through my binoculars I could just barely identify these birds with their all-dark backs and snow white underparts. Then an American pipit soared up from the steep slope below, rising almost to eye level before floating back to its territory on the green tundra.

Suddenly, about 300 feet (90 m) below my perch, a **prairie falcon** appeared, soaring very low over the steep slope, as if searching for an inattentive bird or pika. I watched it hover in midair, wings beating slowly as it maintained zero speed against the sharp breeze. It then settled down on a rocky perch directly below me, so I was able to get a much better view of this medium-sized falcon. It was much lighter in color than prairie falcons that I had seen outside the park at lower elevations. Its back was mottled gray and it had white streaks on its darker hood. But its facial pattern was typical of prairie falcons, buff with dark moustachial lines from below its eyes down to its chest. I had earlier seen its dark wing linings, like dark armpits. Not as large and powerful as its cousin, the peregrine falcon, but a formidable predator nonetheless.

I couldn't help but admire this hardy falcon for making a living at 12,000 feet (3,660 m) elevation. Allegra Collister, in *Birds of Rocky Mountain National Park* (now out of print), reported it to nest above 12,000 feet. Prairie falcons hunt either by diving on their prey and knocking them out of the air with a fatal blow or by plucking them out of the air in flight. It appeared that this bird had already eaten and was satisfied with standing guard over its vast domain.

The subalpine forest forms a lush green cape below the rock

and tundra. Two of the best examples of this environment can be found along the Colorado River Trail, actually the North Fork of the mighty Colorado, on the park's western slope, and at Bear Lake on the park's eastern slope. Both areas support similar bird species.

Willows dominate the Colorado River flood plain, and the songs of three willow residents are obvious throughout: Lincoln's and white-crowned sparrows and Wilson's warblers. **Lincoln's sparrows** are the most numerous of the three but are the shyest and seldom spend much time in the open. But they are curious birds and usually can be attracted by low spishing sounds. Then they may come to within a few feet of the perpetrator to investigate. Their pert manner, buff wash across their streaked breast, and bold gray eyebrows are their most distinguishing features. They will sometimes raise their crests when alarmed, a characteristic few other sparrows possess. And their loud songs are wonderfully rich and varied, reminiscent to my ear of the bubbling renditions produced by house wrens. Wayne Peterson, in *The Audubon Society Master Guide to Birding*, described their songs as having "the gurgling quality and harmonics of Purple Finch's song: kee kee kee, see see, seedle see-dle see-dle, see-see-see-see; starts low, rises, then drops."

Another bird of the willows and river birch thickets, which I found unusually abundant along the Colorado River Trail, was the **red-naped sapsucker**. Its bright red, white, and black head, red patch on the back of the head, and yellowish underparts provided lovely contrasts on this medium-sized woodpecker. I was first attracted to a brightly marked male by its hoarse "churr" call, with emphasis on the "urr." It took me several minutes to locate it as it, uncharacteristically, was collecting insects from the foliage of a dense willow thicket. I watched it glean the underside of leaves, much like warblers do; a half-dozen or more insects stuck out of its bill. It undoubtedly was collecting food for its nestlings. A few minutes later it took flight, and I was able to follow it to an adjacent aspen where it was greeted by its mate; it then entered a nest and delivered the insects to its begging chicks. Even from a distance I could detect the loud, begging cries of the nestlings. Then, almost immediately, it was out the hole and off for another haul. It was a very busy time of year for sapsucker parents.

Other birds were found that July morning: a small troop of gray jays patrolled the parking lot; American robins were common throughout, caroling from the treetops and searching for food on the grassy flats; mountain chickadees sang their "chick a-dee a-dee a-dee" songs from the high conifers; numerous yellow-rumped warblers were evident by their five yellow markings, on their caps, throats, sides, and rumps; dark-eyed juncos flitted about in the undergrowth; and lesser numbers of northern flickers, broad-tailed hummingbirds, cordilleran flycatchers, ruby-crowned kinglets, house wrens, warbling vireos, red crossbills, and pine siskins were also detected.

One evening I circled Bear Lake, following the half-mile-long (.8 km) paved, self-guided nature trail along the rocky shore. And true to the park's brochure, the three common birds were Steller's and gray jays and Clark's nutcrackers. All three greeted me at the trailhead. The jays landed almost at my feet, expecting their usual handout of junk food that, in the long term, makes them more dependent upon human foods and less likely to survive harsh winters. **Steller's jays** were particularly colorful birds, with their dark blue bodies, blackish-blue heads, and tall crests. They were so close I could see the four white streaks on their foreheads.

Steller's jays are one of the forest's most impressive birds, often congregating in large flocks at choice feeding sites, such as at Bear Lake. At their nesting sites, however, it is another matter; a pair will vigorously defend the immediate area against all intruders. Nests, usually placed on horizontal branches or crotches high on conifers, are constructed of twigs and dry leaves, cemented with mud, and lined with rootlets, pine needles, and grass. See chapter 4 on Glacier and Mount Revelstoke for additional details about this fascinating bird.

The Clark's nutcrackers were a little more discreet, remaining beyond reach, perched on the various low-growing conifers at the trailhead. Others called their very distinct, nasal, grating "kra-a-a" calls from the adjacent treetops. Nutcrackers were particularly abundant at Fairview Curve, on the western side of Trail Ridge Road earlier in the day; I counted 26 individuals there, all begging for handouts. I photographed nutcrackers from a distance of 3 feet (1 m), posing, no doubt, for their next handout. A park ranger stopped to chastise the numerous good-willers who were feeding the nutcrackers, golden-mantled ground squirrels, and chipmunks; she stayed until the horde of feeders departed. Later in the day when I passed by, even more visitors and nutcrackers were present; the ranger was elsewhere, attempting, no doubt, to protect the park's valuable resources from another clamoring horde of ignorant critter-feeders.

The numerous jays and nutcrackers at Bear Lake provide a rare opportunity to examine these members of the crow family at the same time. All possess somewhat similar calls, and all are hoarders, storing food for future use. Cones and seeds are cached in the ground as well as in cracks and crevices high in the trees. Nutcrackers are especially adept at hiding their caches underground and can relocate up to 1,000 caches by memory. See chapter 3 on Banff, Jasper, Kootenay, and Yoho for further details about this bird's remarkable behavior.

All along the Bear Lake Trail that evening, two or three **hermit thrushes** serenaded me from the adjacent forest. Their songs are some of the most beautiful in all the bird world, and they provided a wilderness character to the Bear Lake area that somehow was inconsistent with the number of human visitors I encountered along the trail. I wondered if any of the people I passed were aware of the quality of song nature was providing them. I stopped to listen, and the song continued: it opened with clear flutelike notes, "followed by ethereal, bell-like tones, ascending and descending in no fixed order, rising until it reaches dizzying vocal heights and notes fade away in silvery tinkle" (Terres).

Only once did I spot one of these lovely songsters, at some distance at the very top of a tall Engelmann spruce. With binoculars I could see its upright stance, but its spotted breast and whitish throat and eye ring were barely evident in the dimming light. At ground level it would also reveal an all-brown back with a reddish tail. Its glorious, flutelike renditions continued.

Other forest birds encountered along the lake included broad-tailed hummingbirds, northern flickers, cordilleran flycatchers, red-breasted nuthatches, mountain chickadees, ruby-crowned kinglets, warbling vireos, and dark-eyed juncos. Several red crossbills flew overhead, their repetitious "jip jip" notes echoing across the rocky basin. And at the far end of Bear Lake, among the willows, I found a number of Wilson's warblers and Lincoln's sparrows.

Two **Wilson's warbler** males responded to my low spishing sounds immediately, approaching to within a few feet of me, nervously trying to see what kind of intruder they had to deal with. Their bright yellow bodies and coal black caps and eyes provided easy identification. Females are somewhat duller yellow without the obvious black cap. Both were silent at that time of evening, and I was sure that each male was guarding a well-hidden nest among the willows or on the ground among the lush mosses and debris. During most of the daylight hours they will sing rapid, chattering songs that drop in pitch at the end, like "chi chi chi chi chet chet."

Endovalley, beyond the Fall River Entrance Station and Horseshoe Park, contains a wide variety of montane habitats; it represents a microcosm of the park's lower elevations. Harold Holt and Jim Lane, in *A Birder's Guide to Colorado*, write that this area is the park's best birding locality, and they recommend walking the roadside beyond the bridge. That area contains a mixed grove of ponderosa pines, Douglas fir, and aspens; it also includes a narrow lake and meandering stream, at the base of a huge alluvial fan, the result of the 1982 Lawn Lake Dam rupture and flood.

Spotted sandpiper

Except for a pair of ring-necked ducks, a few mallards at the far end, a lone great blue heron and California gull, and several spotted sandpipers calling along the stream and lakeshore, the aquatic habitats were vacant. **Spotted sandpipers** called their loud "weep" sounds from several locations, and I wondered how much territorial confrontation had occurred earlier in the season. Although this shorebird usually is a solitary nester, in some instances they form loose colonies. But what is most interesting about this species is that the females arrive on the breeding grounds first (about April 25) and establish territories prior to the arrival of the males. Once the males arrive, the polyandrous females will actually form their own harem, occasionally competing with other females in fierce combat.

Multiple mates permit the combative female to lay up to five clutches of four eggs, which are then cared for by her male consorts. Ehrlich states that "[m]ultiple mates enable a female to increase her reproduction output by freeing her from the responsibility for incubation and care of the young." Spotted sandpipers, the most widespread of North American shorebirds, are thought of as "pioneering species," quick to take advantage of new sites and opportunities. Apparently, their pioneering method of reproduction has served this robin-sized, spot-breasted sandpiper very well.

The air was filled with violet-green swallows during my morning walk. Many were nesting in used woodpecker nest-holes in the aspens. Their violet-green backs, white rumps, and snow white underparts gleamed in the early morning light. Their constant twittering calls were commonplace. Fewer numbers of tree swallow were present; they possessed all-purple-black backs without the white rump patches of the violet-greens. A few forked-tailed barn swallows, with dark backs and reddish throats, cruised the wetlands. Near the entrance to the valley, nesting on the concrete bridge, was a colony of cliff swallows, distinguished by square tails, dark backs, buff rumps, and chestnut throats.

The willow habitats along the valley floor were filled with birdsong: red-winged blackbirds sang the loudest, their "konk-la-ree" songs echoed across the flats; Lincoln's sparrows were most numerous; Wilson's warblers were also plentiful; black-capped chickadees called their "chick a-dee-dee-dee" song with regularity; several song sparrows were heard as well; and smaller numbers of common snipes, willow flycatchers, black-headed grosbeaks, Brewer's black-birds, and fox sparrows were also detected.

The drier, forested slope to the north of the roadway also contained an assortment of birds. House wrens were most numerous, at least their abundant and continuous cascade of bubbling notes made it seem so. Most of these tiny, short-tailed songsters flew from shrub to shrub, making good sightings next to impossible. I finally located one individual singing from the very top of a ponderosa pine; a long series of "rapid, bubbling chatter that rises in pitch, then falls off toward the end; given many times in succession" (Wayne Peterson).

Several other birds were detected that morning: numerous broad-tailed hummingbirds and a lone male rufous hummingbird; both downy and hairy woodpeckers, and red-naped sapsuckers; loud calls of northern flickers far up the slope; the lazy "peeer" calls of western wood-pewees; the up-slurred "suweet" songs of cordilleran flycatchers near rocky outcroppings; a family of black-billed magpies guarding the old Fall River Road entrance; mountain chickadees and ruby-crowned kinglets singing among the high conifers; the sweet whistle-notes of a solitary vireo; the rambling, whistle-notes of warbling vireos; white-crowned sparrows singing from shrubs along the upper slope; and the social parasite of the bird world, the brown-headed cowbird, also present in substantial numbers.

On one especially bright, sunny morning, I walked the Deer Mountain Trail to sample the bird life of the park's ponderosa pine community. I found this relatively arid environment filled with birds. "Solitaire time" had begun at dawn and continued for another hour; at least a dozen **Townsend's solitaires** were in full song at any one time. Their flutelike renditions went on and on, as if they were part of a great orchestra and were tuning up for a world premiere. Aretas Saunders, in Arthur C. Bent's *Life Histories of North American Thrushes, Kinglets, and Their Allies*, provided the best description of a solitaire song. She wrote that it is "one of the most glorious and beautiful of bird songs . . . a rather prolonged, warblelike series of rapid notes, each note on a different pitch than the last. The notes are clear, sweet, and loud." To me, their rich notes seemed to almost fall over each other in their delivery.

Along the trail, I located several of these thin birds, plain gray except for buff wing bars and white eye rings. Most flew up to an open pine branch as I passed by. Since they are ground-nesters, I wondered if any had chosen the open, nearby slope to build their nest. They may only have been feeding along the trail; more often they will nest on steeper, moister hillsides with more shrubbery. See chapter 9 on Timpanogos Cave for further details about this bird.

As soon as I began my walk, I became aware of a family of **pygmy nuthatches** foraging on the outer branches and foliage of a tall ponderosa pine. These tiny, short-tailed birds, with gray backs, darker caps, buff underparts, and white cheeks and throats, were in continuous communication with one another, twittering as they moved back and forth in their energetic search for insects.

There is no better representative of the ponderosa pine forest than this little nuthatch. It is a full-time resident that spends most of the year in small flocks, actually roosting together in cavities, such as unused woodpecker nests, in winter. In summer, they may share "communal tree trunks with Tree Swallows and Mountain Bluebirds," according to Collister. They are also rather special because they develop long-term pair bonds and live in "breeding units" that consist of the pair and several unmated helpers (usually offspring) that assist with nest-building and maintenance, feeding the female while she is incubating, and also feeding the nestlings and fledglings.

The larger white-breasted nuthatches were also common along the trail, foraging on the ponderosa pine trunks, and a lone, slightly smaller red-breasted nuthatch was detected on the mid-elevation branches. It was obvious that these three nuthatches had selected foraging sites relative to their size, from the large tree trunks to the outer foliage.

Several other songbirds were detected: western wood-pewees sang their slurred songs; Steller's jays called from the northern slope; house wrens sang from a number of shrubs; American robins were common, searching for insects on the ground or caroling overhead; a pair of mountain bluebirds were flycatching below the trail; mountain chickadees were seen on several occasions; western tanagers called slurred "pit-er-ick" notes from the upper foliage; the meow calls of green-tailed towhees resounded from dense shrubbery on the lower slopes; dark-eyed juncos were feeding youngsters in the shade of a bitterbrush; a lovely song of a Cassin's finch echoed down on me from a treetop along the trail; five red crossbills, a bright red male and four yellowish females, were found searching for seeds on the ground; and pine siskins were also present in small flocks.

The majority of the park's songbirds go south for the winter months, leaving only those individuals more adapted to colder conditions. Christmas Bird Counts are undertaken annually in the Estes Park area, and 1990 counters tallied 1,974 individuals of 46 species. The dozen most numerous birds, in descending order of abundance, included pygmy nuthatch, mountain chickadee, mallard, Steller's jay, dark-eyed junco, common raven, black-billed magpie, American crow, rock dove, house finch, Clark's nutcracker, and Bohemian waxwing.

In summary, the park checklist, which also includes adjacent Arapaho National Recreation Area, includes 260 bird species, of which 149 are listed as "all year" or "summer" residents, and are assumed to nest. Of those 149 species, 17 are water birds (grebe, heron, waterfowl, rails, and shorebirds), 19 are hawks and owls, and 9 are warblers. Only three species, American tree and Harris' sparrows and common redpoll, have been found only in winter.

Birds of Special Interest

Prairie falcon. Watch for this medium-sized falcon on the high tundra; in flight it shows black underwing coverts.

Spotted sandpiper. This shorebird lives along the streams and lakeshores in summer; it exhibits a boldly spotted breast and tips back and forth while foraging.

Red-naped sapsucker. A medium-sized woodpecker with a bright red, black, and white face pattern, it prefers willow and aspen habitats.

Steller's jay. This is the royal-blue jay with a blackish crest; it often occurs at trailheads and overlooks.

Pygmy nuthatch. It rarely is found far from ponderosa pines; it is a tiny, short-tailed bird with a gray back, darker cap, buff underparts, and white cheeks and throat.

Townsend's solitaire. This is a thin, grayish bird with buff wing bars and white eye rings and outer tail feathers.

Hermit thrush. Most often detected by its flutelike songs, it has a spotted breast and reddish rump and tail.

American pipit. Watch on the tundra in summer for this little, nondescript bird with white outer tail feathers. It walks on the ground and has a high-flying display.

Wilson's warbler. Its all-yellow body and solid black cap help to distinguish this little bird of the willows and alders.

Lincoln's sparrow. This little sparrow is most often detected by its loud and constant songs from the streamside thickets; it sports a buff chestband, streaked breast, and bold gray eyebrows.

SOUTHWESTERN ROCKY MOUNTAINS

This we know. The earth does not belong to man; man belongs to the earth. This we know. All things are connected like the blood which unites one family. All things are connected. Whatever befalls the earth befalls the sons of the earth. Man did not weave the web of life, he is merely a strand in it. Whatever he does to the web, he does to himself.

—Chief Seattle

12

Capitol Reef National Park, Utah

Chukars stood like sentinels over Fruita Campground. Their loud, coughing "chuck" or "chuck-or" calls resounded off the steep, barren slopes and echoed across the campground. It took me several minutes to find these territorial birds; they blended perfectly into the ancient landscape. One exception had chosen an outcropping where it was silhouetted against the early morning light. It may have been a dominant male because it seemed that each time it called, it set off a series of other "chuck" calls along the lower slope.

I walked through the campground to the entrance road to where I could get a better view of the one chukar that had not yet relinquished its dominant post. From that closer perspective I could see its stocky build, like a very large quail, black-striped head, and barred sides. With binoculars, I could see its pinkish-red bill, eye ring, and legs contrasted with its buff throat and belly. It was an extremely handsome bird. Its upright stance, like a palace guard, gave it additional stature.

Then, realizing perhaps that it was under scrutiny, it began a series of rapid "chuck chuck chuck" notes, and seconds later it took flight. But rather than flying away from me, it crossed the slope in my direction and glided toward the roadway, landing only about 70 feet (21 m) away from me on a low bench partially covered with shadescales and saltbushes. Not until then did I see the covey of 13 additional chukars. They undoubtedly had been there all along but had gone undetected because my attention was focused on the one calling adult. Now I could see that this was a family group with more juveniles than adults. Several produced low chucking sounds, in greeting perhaps to the returning sentinel, but others were only pecking at the seemingly barren ground.

Chukar

    Chukars are not native to North America but have been introduced into several of the western states from Turkey and India as a gamebird by state game departments. They have done very well in areas where the terrain and food are compatible with their requirements. The arid badlands of the southern Rocky Mountains and desert uplands apparently fulfill their needs. And in some places, such as at Capitol Reef, their populations have expanded to the point where they are the dominant quail. The park's biologist, Sandy Borthwick, told me that she believes the chukars have "displaced the native Gambel's quail."

Capitol Reef's chukars have few enemies, so their numbers have greatly expanded in the Fruita area, to the point where the campground, orchards, and immediate area support a dozen or more coveys of ten to 15 birds each. Their numbers are reduced only by natural aging, an occasional highway accident, or by a few of the resident predators, such as coyotes, bobcats, gray foxes, golden eagles, and Cooper's hawks.

The Park Environment

Capitol Reef is a misnomer. The great uplifted monolith of deep canyons, arches, and slickrock is not an ancient reef at all but a weird combination of sandstone and basalt that forms the 100-mile-long (161 km), north-south Waterpocket Fold, a "monoclinal flexure" in the earth's surface. Early settlers reported that the whitish Navajo Sandstone capstone made it appear "like the U.S. Capitol building." But Navajos called the area "land of the sleeping rainbow," after its impressive multicolored formations.

A portion of the area was established as a national monument in 1937 and expanded to 241,904 acres (97,897 ha) as Capitol Reef National Park in 1971. Park elevations range from about 9,200 feet (2,804 m) in the northwest corner, to 3,877 feet (1,182 m) at the southern end of Grand Gulch.

The historic community of Fruita forms the hub of the park. It is situated on Highway 24, which crosses the middle of the park at 5,400' (1,646 m) elevation. Settled in 1881 by Mormons, Fruita (named for the many orchards of apple, peach, and cherry trees) still retains much of its early-day flavor; the many fields and orchards are managed as a historic district. The N.P.S. visitor center and campground are also located there. The visitor center has an information desk, auditorium for orientation programs, exhibits, and sales outlet; bird field guides and a park checklist are available. Interpretive activities include nature walks and evening programs in season. Overnight accommodations and supplies are available in adjacent Torrey, Utah.

Much of the park is wilderness, visited only by those hardy souls who wish to partake of its unique backcountry character. Road access includes the popular, paved 10-mile (16 km) Scenic Drive south of Fruita, and the dirt Notom-Bullfrog Road that runs along the eastern edge of the Waterpocket Fold, crossing into the park only between Cedar Mesa and The Post. The Notom-Bullfrog Road also provides access to the Burr Trail Road that runs west to Boulder, Utah. Fifteen trails traverse the park, ranging from the easy $\frac{1}{10}$-mile (.16 km) Goosenecks Trail to the more strenuous 4.5-mile (7 km) Navajo Knobs Trail.

The vast majority of the park is slickrock, bare but colorful sandstone, with little vegetation. Pinyon-juniper woodlands cover many of the gentler slopes; desert shrubland communities occur on the lower south slopes; and riparian vegetation exists along the streams and in a few protected side canyons. Dominant woodland plants include two-needle pinyon, Utah juniper, and silver buffaloberry; fewer numbers of squawbush, singleleaf ash, and Mormon tea are also present. Desert shrubland plants include shadescale, four-winged saltbush, rabbitbrush, sand sagebrush, and a few grasses. Broom snakeweed, Russian thistle, kochia, and cheatgrass cover disturbed sites. The riparian zones are dominated by Fremont cottonwood, willows, and nonnative tamarisk, with a scattering of Russian olive and squawbush. The Fruita area is transected by the Fremont River with its riparian vegetation, and numerous orchards and fields.

Additional information can be obtained from the Superintendent, Capitol Reef National Park, Torrey, UT 84775; (801) 425-3791.

Bird Life

Spring mornings at Fruita can be alive with birds. Many of the species found there at that time of year are migrants en route north to their nesting grounds. But they often linger in the lush oasis environment, where food and water are plentiful, until they are ready for the next step on their journeys. Almost one-quarter of the park's bird life are migrants only.

One of the park's most obvious residents is the little **house finch** that sings constant and wonderful melodies from all the surrounding high points in spring and summer. They also have a sweet "cheet" flight call. Males sport a bright red breast, throat, and eyeline, brownish backs, and striped bellies; females are duller versions of the males. These heavy-billed finches often occur in large flocks prior to nesting, and they flock again soon after their fledglings appear. House finches are adaptable birds that nest in cavities in trees and man-made structures, as well as in open nests on shrubs, cacti, and even in tin cans and unused bird nests. They have even been found using cliff swallow nests and portions of hawk nests. Their feeding habits also are variable. John Terres, in *The Audubon Society Encyclopedia of North American Birds*, reports that their food consists of about 86 percent weed seeds, "especially thistle, dandelion, noxious weeds, from old fields."

One of the most active spring birds about Fruita's campground and picnic areas is the **northern oriole**, known as "Bullock's oriole" until it was lumped with the eastern Baltimore oriole. Males arrive from the wintering grounds first, sometimes so early that the cottonwoods are not fully leafed out. They immediately begin a diligent defense of a breeding territory in anticipation of their mate's later arrival. The territorial males are noisy and active, chasing one another about with fierce determination. Their fiery orange plumage, with a black crown and orange cheeks, is a thing to behold. By the time the duller-colored females arrive, territories have already been decided, and it is then a matter of courtship, enticing a particular female to take advantage of the male's hospitality. That activity can be equally time-consuming and vigorous. It's a wonder that by the time nesting finally gets underway, the males are able to perform at all.

Yellow warblers also nest among the cottonwoods and willows, but they are far less obvious than the larger orioles. These are the all-yellow birds, including the underside of their tails, that are sometimes called "canaries" or "yellow-birds." Males can be distinguished from females by their chestnut-streaked breasts. And the song of the yellow warbler is very different from that of their oriole neighbors. Areta Saunders described the yellow warbler's song as

Northern oriole

"[a] series of musical notes, about 8 in number, a sort of "see-see-see-see-tititi-see." Peter Vickery, in *The Audubon Society Master Guide to Birding*, described its song as a "lively, cheerful song: usually 3-4 well-spaced "tseet-tseet-tseet sitta-sitta-see." Northern orioles, on the other hand, sing a series of rich whistle-notes, that Terres described as a "loud, clear, flutelike, varied whistle, easy to imitate but difficult to describe."

Other songbirds that nest within Fruita's oasislike environment include black-chinned hummingbirds, northern (red-shafted) flickers, western kingbirds, western wood-pewees, American robins, blue-gray gnatcatchers, and yellow-breasted chats. The thickets of willows and squawbush along the washes also provide nesting habitats for blue grosbeaks, lazuli buntings, rufous-sided towhees, and song sparrows.

The most attractive of these is the **blue grosbeak**, a rather plump bird with a noticeably heavy bill. Males are gorgeous creatures in good light, brilliant blue with a black face and chestnut wing bars. Females are a dull brown with tinges of blue on their rumps and wings. They are often detected first by their loud, almost explosive "chink" calls. Their songs are rich and full, almost robin-like, a series of sweet warbling phrases that rise and fall.

Blue grosbeaks, especially females, can at first glance be confused with the neighboring lazuli bunting females. But grosbeaks are larger and possess a more massive bill while the male lazuli bunting has a lazuli-blue-colored head and back, orange-brown breast and flanks, and whitish belly. Male blue grosbeaks possess all-blue underparts.

Most summers, band-tailed pigeons also frequent the Fruita area, taking advantage of the available fruit. These are large, grayish birds with purplish heads and breasts, yellow legs and bills with a black tip, and gray-banded tails. They may be detected first by their low "coo-cooo" calls. In addition, by early July, rufous hummingbirds can be numerous. The little rufous males are usually bold and aggressive, and often set up feeding territories, keeping other hummers away from choice feeding sites.

The Fremont River provides a niche for one additional songbird seldom found elsewhere in the park, the **American dipper**.

This is a plump, 7- to 8-inch (18-20 cm), all-grayish bird that can actually walk underwater while searching for aquatic insects and larvae. It has evolved special adaptations for this unique behavior: a movable flap over its nostrils, nictating eye membranes, and a large preen gland. Dippers construct oven-shaped nests, with a side entrance, of mosses and grasses at the waterline amid tree roots or under rocks and debris. Their name was derived from their habit of dipping their entire body up and down when they come out of the water or alight on a rock or snag. See chapter 5 on Glacier and Waterton Lakes and chapter 9 on Timpanogos Cave for further details about this amazing bird's behavior.

The park's pinyon-juniper woodlands support a very different bird life than is found within Fruita's riparian vegetation. This is where one can find nesting mourning doves, common poorwills, ash-throated flycatchers, violet-green swallows, scrub jays, plain titmice, bushtits, Bewick's wrens, western bluebirds, blue-gray gnatcatchers, solitary vireos, black-throated gray warblers, Scott's orioles, western tanagers, and chipping sparrows.

The most accessible examples of Capitol Reef's pinyon-juniper woodlands exist along the Hickman Bridge Trail and above the Scenic Drive. One morning in September, after the Neotropical migrants had already departed for their wintering grounds, I hiked up the gradual slope west from Slickrock Divide for about 2 miles (3.2 km), to experience this environment at that time of year. A few of the full-time residents were most obvious: plain titmice scolded me with their harsh "see-jert-jert" notes; Bewick's wrens, evident by their bold whitish eye lines, called their "screet" notes; raspy "shreep" calls of scrub jays were detected, but they kept their distance; a lone mourning dove flew overhead; and the mellow "cheet" flight-calls of house finches were also evident.

A number of fall wanderers were also identified. Most of these probably were searching for pinyon nuts: two flocks of pinyon jays were detected flying low over the woodlands, calling "jay" and "ja-ay" from a distance; a half-dozen Clark's nutcrackers, evident by their black-and-white flight pattern and drawn out "kra-a-a" calls, cruised over the ridge; a pair of common ravens soared overhead, checking out, no doubt, what I was up to in their territory; and a few rufous-sided towhees called "chee-ree" from the top of mountain mahogany shrubs. All of the other species found on my hike amounted to migrants heading south: red-breasted nuthatches, ruby-crowned kinglets, yellow-rumped warblers, lone Townsend's and Wilson's warblers, dark-eyed juncos, and pine siskins.

One of the most numerous fall birds, especially about the park's campground and picnic area, is the **red-naped sapsucker**. It was especially numerous in the orchards. And from the abundant sapsucker "wells" visible on the trunks of the apple trees, it was abundantly clear that it is a regular migrant and winter resident. Sapsuckers are quite different from the other members of the woodpecker clan, in that they drill for sap, not for insects. Sweet droplets of sap accumulate at the wounds and are literally lapped up by the birds with the aid of special brush-tipped tongues. They also feed on insects, fruit, berries, and "bast," the living tissue of woody plants located just under the bark.

Sapsuckers usually drill a series of ¼-inch-wide (.6 cm) "wells" into the growing tissue of the trees. According to ornithologist Jerome Jackson, "sap wells occur in two basic patterns. When searching for sweet sap, a sapsucker pecks a few small wells in a horizontal row. If the sap isn't particularly sweet, it moves on to another branch or tree. If, however, the sapsucker strikes a sweet "vein," it begins to excavate a vertical row of wells." The birds keep the wells open by constant attention. The flowing wells attract a number of other birds, such as hummingbirds, other woodpeckers, warblers, and orioles, as well as a variety of insects that attract yet another group of birds. Capitol Reef's red-naped sapsuckers may be considered important "keystone" species.

I also recorded two wrens that are numerous at various times of the year, canyon and rock wrens. The little, all-grayish-brown rock wrens are most common in summer; they called out thin, musical trills as I passed them by. Each individual bobbed up and down, with a downward jerk, preceding their musical calls. But the loveliest song of the day was that of the cinnamon and white **canyon wren**, a full-time resident. It sang only once, and in spite of trying to imitate its wonderful song, a technique I have used many other times successfully, it did not sing again. The memory of that one song, however, will remain with me forever. It was a long series of descending and decelerating "tew" notes, like "TE-EW, TE-EW, TE-EW, TE-EW, tew, tew, tew, tew, tew." See chapter 14 on Zion for further details about this bird. And see chapter 22 on Colorado National Monument for additional information about pinyon-juniper birds in general.

The high slickrock cliffs also provide nesting sites for some of the park's most dramatic birds: white-throated swifts, golden eagles, American kestrels, and prairie and peregrine falcons. White-throated swifts utilize high crevices, in which they build their nests of feathers and debris, "glued" together with their saliva. These black-and-white, cigar-shaped birds with narrow, swept-back wings, are most often seen flying along the high cliff face at a seemingly reckless speed, and emitting high-pitched, decelerating trills.

Golden eagles utilize some of the park's least accessible cliffs but are regularly seen from Fruita soaring over the high ridges. This is the park's largest bird, with a wingspan of 80 to 88 inches (2-2.2 m). Adults are all-dark-brown, except for faintly banded tails and heads that appear golden in the right light. Immature birds lack the golden head but possess distinctly white-banded tails.

Three falcons reside in the park during the spring and summer months. The smallest but most numerous of the three is the little reddish-backed American kestrel. These pointed-winged raptors can be reasonably common almost anywhere in the park. The larger falcon with all-gray plumage, except for its black "wingpits," is the prairie falcon. This species spends most of its time hunting the open sageflats and desert grasslands, and only rarely soars over the high cliffs. The most dynamic of the park's three falcons is the **peregrine falcon**. It is one of the world's fastest birds, having been clocked at over 200 miles (332 km) per hour in a dive. It is best identified by its slate gray back, bold moustachial stripes, and partially barred underparts.

Capitol Reef's peregrine population has increased considerably since it was assumed to have been wiped out by DDT during the 1950s and 1960s. Following the 1962 ban of DDT in the U.S. and Canada, peregrines have made a dramatic recovery in many of the Rocky Mountain parks, where essential habitat exists. Sandy

Borthwick told me that as many as four active aeries now exist in Capitol Reef National Park, and each of these have fledged young in recent years. This incredible bird can appear almost anywhere in the park from approximately March into September. After their prey base moves south for the winter, they also go south into Mexico or Central America. They then eat prey that may have consumed other prey or fed on insects contaminated with DDT; this deadly pesticide continues to be sold south of the border.

Wintertime at Capitol Reef is very different from the summer months. All the Neotropical migrants are long gone, migrants and transients have passed on by, and only the full-time residents and a few northern species that have found an adequate niche to keep them alive during this dormant time of year remain. Species that occur only in winter include common mergansers, bald eagles, northern pygmy-owls, black-capped and mountain chickadees, winter wrens, Bohemian waxwings, northern shrikes, evening grosbeaks, rosy finches, dark-eyed juncos, and Harris' and white-throated sparrows.

In summary, the park checklist includes 215 species, of which 128 are listed as permanent or summer residents, and assumed to nest. Of those 128 species, 7 are water birds, 17 are hawks and owls, and 9 are warblers.

Birds of Special Interest

Golden eagle. This large bird, which has an 80-inch (2-2.2 m) wingspan, is most often seen soaring high over the ridges in the evenings.

Peregrine falcon. One of the world's swiftest birds, it can be identified in flight by its large size, pointed wings, slate gray back, and heavy moustachial stripes (sideburns).

Chukar. It is most numerous at Fruita, where flocks of ten to 16 birds are common after nesting; adults possess black neck-markings and barred flanks, and pinkish-red bills, eye rings, and legs.

Red-naped sapsucker. This is a slender woodpecker with a yellowish belly and black, white, and red head. It is one of the park's important "keystone" species.

American dipper. Watch for this plump, all-gray-brown bird along Fremont Creek; it actually walks underwater in search of prey.

Canyon wren. Its loud descending and decelerating songs are commonplace; it can be identified by its snow white breast and cinnamon back and belly.

Yellow warbler. This is the little all-yellow bird of the riparian habitats; males possess chestnut breast-streaks.

Northern oriole. Watch for this orange-and-black bird among the cottonwoods near the campground and along the river.

Blue grosbeak. The male of this heavy-billed species is all-blue with a black face and cinnamon wing bars; females are dull brown.

House finch. This is the cheerful, lively songster in spring and summer; males possess bright red throats and eye lines and striped bellies.

13

Arches and Canyonlands National Parks, Utah

Words can't adequately describe the awesome beauty of the Canyonlands from Grand View Point Overlook. The scenery, spread out from horizon to horizon, is immense and lonesome, the essence of solitude. It embodies the true sense of wilderness, rarely so obvious elsewhere. The silence, the gentle breeze, the smell of juniper and cliffrose, all help to calm the soul and place one's self in perspective.

There was something very appropriate about the sudden appearance of a common raven, like a representative from another world that had come to enhance one's sense of peace. I watched it soar past the overlook, make a quick turn, and land on an ancient snag. The raven's coal black plumage, wedge-shaped tail, and huge bill were obvious. And then as if to break the spell, it called out a harsh, drawn-out croak. And again. It seemed totally in control. Then a second raven called behind me, and they both soared off toward the west, talking to one another, with deep "croo-croo" and "cur-ruk" notes. I watched them soar along the edge of the high cliff without moving their wings, in complete harmony with the environment.

I followed them as best I could, using the trail that runs west from the overlook along the edge of the great sky-island. The leaves of singleleaf ash were deep yellow with autumn, and snakeweed still contained yellow caps. A rufous-sided towhee flew across the trail and stopped briefly on a straggly squawbush. It was a male with an all-black hood, white underparts, except for its rufous flanks, and white edges on its black tail. Through binoculars I could see its blood-red eyes, gleaming in the morning sunshine like two bright rubies.

Common raven

Then at the base of the shrub, a small, all-gray-brown bird appeared, bobbed up and down, and called out a musical trill. It flew several feet to a jerky stop, spread its tail, and called out again.

This little rock wren of the open, rocky terrain had a stocky build and long bill. Although it was mostly gray to brown, it was finely speckled with black and white, and its flanks were a subtle buff color. I watched it search a tiny crevice and extract a small insect of some sort, which it immediately consumed. It then followed the crevice, almost crawling over the rocky surface, apparently searching for additional tidbits.

I couldn't help but admire this wonderfully adapted creature as it worked the rocky surface. It blended in so perfectly that, without binoculars, it would have been difficult to spot until it moved. Rock wrens are one of the dual park's most numerous birds and can be found wherever rocky terrain exists; that excludes only the open flats with deep soils. It is a common spring, summer, and fall resident, leaving its breeding territory in the parks for lower elevations only during winter. Along with the common raven, it is one of the area's most representative birds.

Suddenly, several white-throated swifts zoomed by my head, so close that I could actually feel wind movement. My attention riveted on these incredible birds as they shot straight upward for 100 feet (30 m) or more before plunging back past the cliff edge and disappearing into the great airshed below. Although I lost sight of these fast-flying creatures, I could hear their high-pitched twittering calls far below.

The pair of ravens had apparently circled back and now were riding the thermals just below me. They seemed to sense my admiration and remained almost motionless, giving me an opportunity to examine them from above. Their flight feathers were spread out like fingers, to help capture the rising air currents. Their feathered heads appeared much heavier from the side angle; the feathers on their foreheads and throats seemed almost shaggy.

I wondered if I was watching a mated pair, since this bird usually mates for life, building its stick nests on high, inaccessible cliffs. Then, as if they suddenly realized they were being scrutinized, they turned sharply to their left and rolled in unison, dropping 200 or 300 feet (61-91 m) before straightening out again. That brief glimpse of their acrobatic ability only enforced my admiration of this marvelous creature.

The Park Environment

Arches and Canyonlands together comprise an area of about 410,500 acres (166,127 ha) of magnificient geology in the "scenic heart" of the Colorado Plateau, in southeastern Utah. This vast area is dissected by innumerable canyons and washes that drain into either the Green or Colorado rivers, whose confluence is in about the center of Canyonlands. Elevations range from 3,600 feet (1,097 m) in Cataract Canyon on the Colorado River, to nearly 7,000 feet (2,134 m) at Cedar Mesa. Bill Ratcliffe was so impressed with Canyonlands that he wrote that this park contains "the best of Bryce Canyon, Zion, Mesa Verde, and Grand Canyon." But my favorite description of the canyonlands area was by Edward Abbey, who described the area as "the least inhabited, least inhibited, least developed, least improved, least civilized . . . most arid, most hostile, most lonesome, most grim bleak barren desolate and savage quarter of the state of Utah—the best part by far."

Much of these parks is still wilderness due to their inaccessibility. Canyonland's brochure states that, "To a large degree, Canyonlands remains untrammeled today. Its roads are mostly unpaved, its trails primitive, its rivers free-flowing." Canyonlands is breached by only two highways: from the north, Highway 313 crosses Island in the Sky and ends at Grand View Point Overlook; from the southeast, Highway 211 enters the Needles area and terminates at Big Spring Canyon Overlook. Arches is breached by a single 20-mile (32 km) long roadway through the center of the park that ends at Devil's Garden Trailhead. Numerous backcountry roads, many of which are negotiable only with four-wheel-drive vehicles, provide access to additional localities; the most popular of these routes is Canyonland's 100-mile (161 km) White Rim Trail. The two parks also contain more than 140 miles (225 km) of trails: 16 miles (26 km) in Arches, and 125 miles (201 km) in Canyonlands. F. A. Barnes' *Canyon Country Hiking* contains a good overview of the key trails.

There also is considerable river use in Canyonlands by both private and commercial river-runners. All trips below the confluence require a permit. Numerous commercial companies exist at Moab, Utah.

Visitor centers are located at Canyonland's north entrance, in the Islands in the Sky, and near the entrance to the Needles; Arches' visitor center is located at the park entrance, along Highway 191, 8 miles (13 km) north of Moab. Each of these centers has an information desk, orientation programs, exhibits, and sales outlet; bird field guides and a checklist are available. Interpretive activities in the parks vary with the season and include ranger-guided walks and evening programs. Schedules are available for the asking and are posted at the campground bulletin boards.

Both parks contain campgrounds: developed sites are located at Devil's Garden in Arches, and at Squaw Flat in the Needles section and at Willow Flat in the Islands of the Sky at Canyonlands. Primitive camping is permitted at numerous other locations along the rivers and along the parks' trails by permit only.

Vegetative zones in the two parks vary more by moisture and exposure than by elevations. Although much of the area seems to be bedrock and cliffs, this does not amount to a great deal of land mass because it is largely vertical. The vast majority of the acreage contains five rather distinct habitats: pinyon-juniper woodlands, snakeweed slopes, blackbrush-grass benches, sagebrush flats, and riparian riverbottoms.

The most widespread of these zones is the pinyon-juniper woodlands that are dominated by two-needle pinyon, Utah juniper, singleleaf ash, squawbush, and Mormon tea. The high rocky benches sometimes blend together with the woodlands, but they usually possess a community of blackbrush, four-winged saltbush, broom snakeweed, and grasses. The rather extensive flats are dominated by big sagebrush and four-winged saltbush, with various grasses. And the river flood plains and moist canyon bottoms contain riparian vegetation that is dominated by Fremont cottonwood, willows, and nonnative tamarisk.

Additional information can be obtained from the Superintendents at Arches National Park, P.O. Box 907, Moab, UT 84532; (801) 259-8161; or at Canyonlands National Park, 125 West 200 South, Moab, UT 84532; (801) 259-7164.

Bird Life

I followed the Grand View Overlook Trail for about 1 mile (1.6 km) to where it ended on a high point at the southwest corner of the great mesa. Far below was the White Rim, still several hundred feet above the Colorado River flood plain. Farther south I could see the Needles area of the park; farther still the La Sal Mountains formed a distant backdrop.

Several birds had flown ahead of me as I had progressed along the trail. I had identified a dozen or so northern (red-shafted) flickers; three ruby-crowned kinglets; a lone yellow-rumped warbler, green-tailed towhee, and hermit thrush; and small flocks of chipping sparrows and dark-eyed juncos. All of these were southbound migrants en route, no doubt, to their wintering grounds. But as I more or less herded the birds ahead of me, instead of "diving off" the high mesa top and continuing south, they seemed disoriented and doubled back. It was as if they were not yet ready to take the next step of their journey. I wondered if Grand View Point acted as a "migrant trap," discouraging migrants from continuing southward.

This was not the case, however, for the raptors. By mid-morning, I detected several hawks moving southward. From Buck Canyon Overlook, within less than an hour I identified 14 American kestrels, 3 Cooper's hawks, 2 sharp-shinned hawks, and a lone red-tailed hawk flying 200 to 300 feet (61-91 m) above the rim. A few of the kestrels circled a few times before continuing on, but the others passed by with little hesitency. Red-tails are full-time residents that occur throughout the parks. They are best identified by their large size, broad wings, and dull- to brick-red tails.

The pinyon-juniper woodlands of Canyonlands and Arches support a number of typical breeding birds. Most numerous of those are mourning doves, broad-tailed hummingbirds, ash-throated flycatchers, scrub jays, plain titmice, bushtits, Bewick's wrens, and house finches. Fewer numbers of gray flycatchers, pinyon jays, gray vireos, and black-throated gray warblers nest there as well.

The **ash-throated flycatcher**, an adaptable species that also utilizes riparian zones in washes and along the river, can be especially common within the park's short-tree woodlands. It is a slender bird with a grayish throat and yellowish belly, brown cap and gray-brown back, and reddish tail. Typical of flycatchers, it will perch on an open tree and every now and then dash out after a passing insect, usually returning to the same perch with a flip of the tail. Ash-throats are seldom quiet during the breeding season; their call is a rough "ka-brick," and their song is a rhythmic series of "ha-wheer" notes. And in places where rocky outcroppings or man-made structures exist, **Say's phoebes** can also be common. This fly-catcher may, at first glance, look like the ash-throated flycatcher, but Say's phoebes are very different from them; they lack the gray, yellow, and reddish colors but possess subtle brown, black, and buff colors. Their typical call, often heard throughout the day, is a plaintive "pee-ee" whistle. Say's phoebes often place their open nests, constructed of fine grasses and other plant materials, on ledges. Ash-throated flycatchers, on the other hand, are cavity-nesters, utilizing old woodpecker holes in trees and posts or natural cavities.

Arches' Devil's Garden Campground and Canyonland's Squaw Flat Campgrounds are located within sparse pinyon-juniper woodlands, and scrub jays and plain titmice can be fairly common. **Scrub jays** are particularly evident in late summer and fall when young birds are learning their skills. They often trail after their parents with loud squeals and scratchy "ike-ike-ike" calls. Young of the year have rather dull plumage compared with adults. This non-crested jay is all-blue above and grayish below, except for its white-streaked throat. It also possesses a white eye line and gray back. Scrub jays seem to enjoy an extremely wide range of food, plant and animal. When pinyon nuts and acorns are available in late summer they spend a great amount of time gathering these rich seeds, but they also eat grasshoppers, beetles, caterpillars, crickets, ants, ticks, mites, spiders, mice, lizards, frogs, and even small birds and their eggs. And if, in their rounds of the campground, they discover other more human-type foods, like spaghetti, bread, and cheese, they will not hesitate to help themselves.

The **plain titmouse** also consumes a variety of food, but it is so much smaller, only about half the size of a scrub jay, that its prey is limited. This little, all-gray, short-crested songbird spends a good part of its time foraging for food on smaller branches and foliage, often hanging upside-down. They also eat pinyon nuts, opening the hard shells with hard wacks of their rather short, blunt bills. It is not unusual to be first attracted to one of these tits by its woodpecker-like behavior. In fact, this little bird can go unobserved very near camp, until it is either discovered pounding food or by its clear whistle-songs, like "witt-y, witt-y, witt-y," or strange scolding noises that sound like "see-jert-jert," which they may repeat over and over again. See chapter 22 on Colorado National Monument and chapter 24 on Mesa Verde for additional information about pinyon-juniper birds.

The park's grasslands also possess a rather distinct bird life. Mourning doves, horned larks, sage thrashers, vesper and lark sparrows, western meadowlarks, and house finches inhabit this environment. **Horned larks** can be fairly common. They often sit on the roads, flying up and away in front of an approaching vehicle. In flight, their black tails and lighter underparts are most evident. But a closer view will reveal their yellowish faces with black chests, stripes below the eyes, and narrow black feathers that extend above their heads like tiny horns. They often are detected first by their high-pitched calls, like "tsee-ee." Another feature of this 7-inch (18 cm) bird is its habit of walking rather than hopping.

One of the area's most abundant birds, residing in every habitat from the river canyons to the highest mesas, is the gregarious, little **house finch**. Males are readily distinguished by their reddish throats and eye lines and streaked bellies; females lack the bright reddish colors. It is difficult to ignore this finch during most of the year, because as early as late winter, when the days are sunny, and throughout the summer months, their songs echo across the canyonlands and are unequalled. Their songs are one the most musical and cheerful in all the bird world, extended warblings that are rollicking and joyous. Arthur C. Bent, in his Life History series, includes a good description of this bird's vocalizations:

> The linnet [an earlier name] household furnishes an outstanding example of a "musical family." The male is an indefatigable songster, the female also sings on occasions, and the fledglings, lined up on a wire, literally "sing for their supper." To human ears, the keynote of all house finch utterances is cheerfulness. The song suggests happiness, and even the notes

House finch

that express anxiety over peril to the nest have a cheerfully rising inflection. Entirely absent from their vocabulary are the
strident bickering cries and harsh scolding notes that are so
freely used by many other species.

At lower elevations, the fields contain fewer grasses and a greater number of desert plants. These areas often support a few additional dry-land bird species, such as loggerhead shrikes and black-throated sparrows. The **loggerhead shrike** is one of the most interesting birds in the parks, in spite of its black-and-white plumage. Its stocky build and heavy, short bill are good clues to its odd behavior. Shrikes are predators, in spite of their small (about 9 in. or 23 cm) size, and are capable of taking surprisingly large mammals and birds, such as mice and mockingbirds. But their method of displaying their kills is most interesting. They actually carry their prey to pre-selected thorny shrubs or barbed wire and impale their prey, usually with their victim's head up and their body hanging down. Dozens of prey species have been found impaled on a single shrub or yucca, almost like ornaments on a Christmas tree. This practice of impaling their prey was first considered only as a method of storing their food until they were ready to eat, but recent studies have shown that males use this method of attracting females into their territories.

Less than 2 percent of the dual parks' plant life falls into the riparian zones along the rivers and in moist canyon bottoms. But these areas are often the richest areas for breeding birds, and they also are extremely valuable during migration. Nesting water birds, such as great blue herons, American coots, killdeer, and spotted sandpipers, occur there in spring and summer. The dense stream-side vegetation supports Cooper's hawks, western screech-owls, black-chinned hummingbirds, willow and ash-throated flycatchers, common yellowthroats, yellow-breasted chats, blue grosbeaks, northern orioles, and house finches. And dense brushy washes support lazuli buntings and rufous-sided towhees. See chapter 10 on Dinosaur National Monument for a discussion of birds that occur in the riparian zones.

Arches' Courthouse Wash also is lined with riparian vegetation, like an elongated oasis in an otherwise arid landscape. Over the years, Courthouse Wash has become recognized for its out-of-ordinary transients as well as its breeding birds.

The lower canyons also hold their own special appeal. Canyon wrens often serenade floaters from the cliffs and washes; their loud descending and decelerating whistle notes are some of the river-user's most cherished memories. White-throated swifts continuously fly overhead; their descending twitterings can be one of the most obvious sounds on the river. And at dusk, common nighthawks cruise over the grassy banks searching for insects; nesting birds can be identified by their territorial U-shaped dives and hollow booming sounds just before they pull out. And after dark, common poorwills sing their lonesome "poor-will" songs from the dry washes and slopes.

But of all the canyon birds, none is as exciting as the **peregrine falcon**. It is the fastest, the most dramatic, and the most charismatic. More than any other species, it represents the condition of our human environment. When human-use of DDT began to endanger our long-term existence, it was the peregrine that became the symbol of our endangered status. And when we acted to eliminate indiscriminate use of DDT by banning it within the U.S. and Canada, it was the peregrine that bounced back from near oblivion. According to Larry Thomas, Canyonland's resource specialist, at least six active aeries now exist within the inner canyons, and these birds produce eight to 12 youngsters (1.5 per aerie) each year.

According to G. H. Thayer, an ornithologist active in the 1910s and 1920s:

> The peregrine falcon is, perhaps, the most highly specialized and superlative well developed flying organism on our planet today, combining in a marvelous degree the highest powers of speed and aerial adroitness with massive, warlike strength. A powerful, wild, majestic, independent bird, living on the choicest of clean, carnal food, plucked fresh from the air or on the surface of the waters, rearing its young in the nooks of dangerous mountain cliffs, claiming all the atmosphere as its domain and fearing neither beast that walks nor bird that flies.

Canyonland's peregrine falcons spend only their spring and summer months on their breeding grounds; they go south to warmer climates for the winter. There, in Mexico or Central America, they may feed on birds that have ingested high levels of pesticides that are banned in the U.S. but sold south of the border. So, we must not relax our fight to eliminate the complete use of all toxic substances that will kill our birds.

Although peregrines and other Neotropical migrants go south for the winter, other birds from more northern latitudes join the full-time residents, and the pace of bird life continues. Bald eagles may be present along the rivers; northern harriers hunt the sagebrush flats; song sparrows and dark-eyed juncos feed in weedy areas; rosy finches flock on the open flats; and pine siskins fly overhead in small flocks, always en route elsewhere.

Christmas Bird Counts are taken annually at Moab and surroundings. These surveys provide the best perspective on the dual park's wintering avifauna. The 1991 count tallied 5,036 individuals of 68 species. The dozen most numerous species, in descending order of abundance, included European starling, dark-eyed junco, American robin, mallard, American crow, white-crowned sparrow, house sparrow, black-billed magpie, red-winged blackbird, house finch, song sparrow, and northern flicker.

In summary, the dual parks have recorded a total of 212 species, of which 63 are considered to breed. Of those, 4 are water birds, 10 are hawks and owls, and 3 are warblers. At least 9 species can be considered winter visitors only: Clark's nutcracker; black-capped and mountain chickadees; northern shrike; American tree, golden-crowned, and Harris' sparrows; rosy finches; and common redpoll.

Birds of Special Interest
Peregrine falcon. Watch for this marvelous creature along the riverway; it can be identified by its large size, slate gray back, heavy black moustachial stripes (sideburns), and pointed wings.

White-throated swift. Flocks of these cigar-shaped birds with white throats on black bodies are common along the cliffs.

Ash-throated flycatcher. This is a slim bird with a grayish throat, yellowish belly, and reddish tail; it has an obvious "ka-brick" call and sings "ha-wheer" in spring.

Say's phoebe. Watch for this little flycatcher near buildings and rocky outcroppings; it is all brownish with a buff belly.

Scrub jay. Common but shy within the pinyon-juniper woodlands, it has blue upperparts and grayish belly, and long tail.

Common raven. This is the large, all-black bird with a wedge-shaped tail and heavy bill; it is common almost everywhere in the dual parks.

Plain titmouse. Strictly found in the pinyon-juniper woodlands, it is all-gray-brown with a short crest and is usually detected first by its almost constant calls, thin "tsee" notes, or songs, like "witt-y, witt-y, witt-y."

Rock wren. This little all-gray-brown bird inhabits the barren, rocky slopes and canyons; it bobs up and down and sings a musical trill.

Loggerhead shrike. Watch for this mockingbird-sized, black-and-white bird that flies straight and fast; watch also for its decorated shrubs and yuccas.

House finch. Males possess reddish throats and eye lines, and streaked bellies; they usually occur in flocks and can be expected anywhere in the dual parks.

14

Zion National Park and Cedar Breaks National Monument, Utah

Zion's Gateway to the Narrows Trail begins at the Temple of Sinawava and follows the Virgin River past Watercress Spring and the hanging gardens for 1 mile (1.6 km). Looking upriver from the end of the paved trail, one can see the beginning of the narrowest portion of the gorge, where the 2,000-foot (610 m) cliffs become so narrow in places that two people standing at the base, holding hands with arms outspread, can touch both sides. Walking the Gateway to the Narrows Trail is like entering a different world after the warmer lower canyons. The plants and animals there are a fascinating blend of the canyon lowlands and the high, forested plateau.

Birdsong resounded from the streamside vegetation as I walked the trail one early morning in May. The bright greens of the new foliage contrasted against the red sandstone cliffs, and the rippling waters of the Virgin River added to the intimacy. Solitary vireo songs were the most obvious of the birdsongs; their loud whistles produced a rich, four-part melody. Across the river, among the willows and cottonwoods, I detected the rapid, robin-like song of a male black-headed grosbeak. Through binoculars, I located it and its mate feeding among the fresh foliage. There, too, was a brightly colored, male western tanager. Its canary yellow body, black wings, and red head looked like a Christmas ornament among the cottonwood leaves.

A rufous-sided towhee appeared atop a shrub at the water's edge and called a loud "chee-ee." Its coal black hood and blood-red eyes, spotted back, and rufous sides were obvious. It dived for cover with a flash of white tail-edges. A song sparrow was feeding along the river's edge; its buff body and striped chest, including its black breast-spot, gleamed in the morning light.

Canyon wren

Then a series of slowly descending whistle-notes of a **canyon wren** echoed from the base of the cliff just ahead of me. The song continued as I approached. It took me several minutes to find this little songster that suddenly popped into view from behind a fallen slab of reddish sandstone. I froze in place so as not to frighten it and slowly raised my binoculars into place. What a lovely bird it was! Its snow white throat and upper breast, rusty belly and back, with numerous black spots, and grayish head were most conspicuous. And its extremely long bill, for so small a bird, seemed almost out of proportion.

It suddenly sang again. I watched as its silvery notes descended down the scale like liquid "tews," ending with a mild "jeet." A second later it disappeared behind the rock, only to reappear a few seconds later at the side, where it searched a deep crack for food, creeping forward like a tiny rodent. Then it flew back to the top of the slab with a green caterpillar held tightly in its bill. And immediately on swallowing its prey, it sang again, an even louder and lovelier version of its long, descending and decelerating song: "TEW, TEW, TEW, TEW, tew tew tew tew tew tew."

The canyon wren is Zion's most charismatic and appealing bird. It not only occurs throughout the park in abundance, but its wonderful song has become part of the Zion mystique.

The Park Environment

Zion and nearby Cedar Breaks lie along the western edge of the greater Colorado Plateau and are situated on the smaller Markagunt Plateau of southwestern Utah. Geologically, these huge plateaus are being gradually pushed upward, and their abundant streams continue to cut through the relatively soft rock formation, resulting in steep, narrow canyons and majestic temples. The oldest rocks in the area are visible along the park entrance road; the middle-age Navajo Sandstone dominates Zion Canyon; and more recent formations are most evident at Cedar Breaks. Elevations range from 3,650 feet (1,113 m) in Zion's Coalpits Wash to 10,700 feet (3,261 m) along the rim of Cedar Breaks.

The lower portion of Zion Canyon is typical of the lush green streamsides of the American Southwest. Willows, Fremont cottonwoods, and nonnative tamarisk dominate the riparian habitats along the Virgin River. But desert conditions prevail in the nearby, open washes, where creosote bush and blackbrush are most abundant. Sand sagebrush, honey mesquite, and four-winged saltbush are also common. Riparian habitats at slightly higher streamsides, such as along Zion Canyon, are dominated by Fremont cottonwoods, velvet ash, and boxelder, with willows, seepwillow, and cattails common in scattered localities. The adjacent open flats often contain a varied environment of grasses, especially cheatgrass, and scattered oaks, junipers, and saltbushes.

Just above the canyon bottoms is the pinyon-juniper woodlands that dominate the slopes up to the edge of the plateaus and the start of the ponderosa pine forest. Utah juniper is most numerous in the lower areas and two-needle pinyon dominates higher elevations. Tracts of big sagebush occur throughout, and Mormon tea, mountain mahogany, cliffrose, squawbush, serviceberry, and scrub oak are of secondary importance. On a few southern slopes along the Kolob Canyons Road are chaparral-like stands of stunted Gambel's oak, mountain mahogany, and manzanita.

The high plateaus, generally above 7,000 feet (2,134 m) elevation, are dominated by ponderosa pine, Douglas fir, white fir, and aspen. Extensive stands of ponderosa occur along Zion's east entrance road and in numerous "hanging canyons," such as those along the Kolob Canyons Road. Big sagebrush grows on the high flats, and willows dominate the streamsides and washes that drain the highlands. Still higher at Cedar Breaks is a spruce-fir forest of Engelmann spruce and subalpine fir, with scattered stands of aspens and bristlecone pines, and subalpine meadows dot the landscape. Earl Jackson, in *Your National Park System in the Southwest in Words and Color*, reported that these meadows provide "lavish July and August flower displays" that include fringed gentians, lupines, columbines, penstemons, bluebells, and Indian paintbrush.

National park visitor centers are located near the entrance to Zion Canyon; Kolob Canyons, just off Highway 15 south of Cedar City; and at Point Supreme on the Cedar Breaks rim. Each has an information desk, exhibits, and sales counter. Field guides and a bird checklist are available. Ranger-guided walks and evening programs are presented throughout the summer seasons, and interpretive schedules are available for the asking.

Two campgrounds (side by side) are available inside Zion's South Entrance near Springdale: Watchman Campground is open all year, and South Campground is closed in winter. One Cedar Breaks campground is located just north of the visitor center. Other campgrounds and motels are available in the adjacent communities.

Additional information is available from the two superintendents: Cedar Breaks National Monument, P.O. Box 749, Cedar City, UT 84720; (801) 586-9451; and Zion National Park, Springdale, UT 84767; (801) 772-3256.

Bird Life

Canyon wrens are so much a part of Zion's massive cliffs and grottos that a visitor should never leave without experiencing this marvelous creature. Their wonderful songs are magic that cannot help but lift the spirit. I recall one occasion, during the almost four years that I worked at Zion, when a pair of canyon wrens had built a nest in the stone walls of the Zion Inn (now the park's Nature Center). Guests were able to watch adult wrens feeding their young along the walls and rafters; their songs rang out loud and clear across the gift shop on numerous occasions.

Zion Canyon is the heart of the park, although the Zion Canyon Scenic Drive is only 6 miles (9.6 km) in length and can be terribly busy in summer. Early mornings are the best time of day, not only because of less vehicular traffic, but also because that is when birds are most active.

One of the spring and summer residents of the deep canyons and adjacent cliffs is none other than the **peregrine falcon**. This is one of the world's swiftest and most dramatic birds, clocked at over 200 miles (322 km) per hour in a dive. The observation of courting birds is one of the most thrilling experiences in the natural world. Peregrines are large, powerful raptors, almost as large as red-tailed hawks, with long pointed wings, slate gray backs, and bold moustachial stripes offset by whitish cheeks and throat. They are powerful enough to prey on ducks, which are close to their same size, and fast enough to take the much smaller white-throated swifts. Swifts, black-and-white speedsters with narrow, swept back wings, can be common within the many canyons, where they fly with great speed and agility. These birds are often detected by their constant twittering calls.

Zion's peregrines have a long history of nesting within Zion Canyon, and there are good indications that at least a few birds continued to nest even when the the rest of the Rocky Mountain population was decimated by DDT. Although peregrine records in the park date back to 1939, the species was given greater attention after it was listed as endangered. Increases since the early 1980s, undoubtedly enhanced by restoration programs elsewhere in the Rocky Mountains, went from one active aerie in 1982, to 12 active aeries that produced 20 juveniles in 1991. Chapter 16 on Grand Canyon includes additional information about this endangered species.

Emerald Pools Trail, in Zion Canyon, has long been a favorite place of mine. There one can experience typical pinyon-juniper birds as well as those that prefer the cooler niches that exist in the little, moist side canyons. Common pinyon-juniper birds to be found along the trail include black-chinned and broad-tailed humming-birds, western wood-pewees, ash-throated flycatchers, scrub jays, mountain chickadees, plain titmice, bushtits, Bewick's wrens, blue-gray gnatcatchers, solitary vireos, black-throated gray warblers, chipping sparrows, and house finches. The all-gray, crested plain titmice; the skinny, long-tailed blue-gray gnatcatchers; and the black-throated gray warblers best represent this rather arid community.

Black-throated gray warbler

The **black-throated gray warbler** is one of the park's loveliest birds, although, except for the tiny yellow spot in front of each eye, it is all black-and-white. Its song is very different from other warbler songs and helps one to locate this little bird during the breeding season. Alexander Sprunt, Jr., in Griscom and Sprunt's *The Warblers of America*, described its song thusly: "A simple, pleasing song of four or more notes, the last syllable may ascend or descend: 'swee, swee, ker-swee, sick' or 'wee-zy, wee-zy, wee-zy, wee-zy, weet.'"

Black-throated grays are not so nervous as most warblers but go about their business in a methodical and deliberate manner, very much like vireos. I was able to watch a pair on the Emerald Pools Trail forage from only a few yards distance. They seemed to ignore me totally. I was reminded of another incident in Griscom and Sprunt's warbler book: W. L. Kinley, on discovering a nest, wrote:

> The moment the mother returned and found me at the nest she was scared almost out of her senses. She fell from the top of the tree in a fluttering fit. She caught quivering on the limb a foot from my hand. But unable to hold on, she slipped through the branches and clutched my shoe. I never saw such an exaggerated case of the chills. I stooped to see what ailed her. She wavered like an autumn leaf to the ground. I leaped down, but she had limped under a bush and suddenly got well. Of course I knew she was tricking me! But I never saw higher skill in a feathered artist.

Blue-gray gnatcatchers are often the most obvious birds of these woodlands because of their almost continuous, plaintive, thin, and buzzy "peeee" calls. Even in the warm afternoons this bird seems to remain busy. After the nesting season, when most of the summer residents flock with other songbirds, the gnatcatchers' continuous calls provide the best clues to locating the bird party. But for all its vocalizations, it is a diminutive bird with few distinguishing features. It is all gray and black with a long blackish tail, with obvious white outer feathers, and a sharp, white eye ring. Its behavior is rather distinct, and in spite of its small size, it often can be identified at a considerable distance by its method of flipping its tail up and down and sideways. Many people think that gnatcatchers look like miniature mockingbirds.

The **plain titmouse** is just that; it is little more than an "LGB," a little gray bird, with black eyes and bill and a stubby crest. But what this bird lacks in color it more than makes up for in personality. It is one of the most inquisitive of birds; it seems to look into every nook and cranny possible when searching for food. Its acrobatic behavior when foraging on the tree's outer twigs and foliage suggest that it is able to take advantage of a wide variety of foods. Arthur C. Bent, in his Life History series, reported that its diet consists of 57 percent plants and 43 percent animals. All the while it calls a loud "witt-y, witt-y, witt-y" or "ti-wee, ti-wee, ti-wee"; it also has a distinct "see-jert-jert" call.

Adjacent thickets of Gambel's oaks usually contain Virginia's warblers and rufous-sided towhees. Cordilleran flycatchers and canyon wrens occur along the base of the cliffs. Emerald Pools Canyon's moist streambeds and riparian vegetation support black phoebes, warbling vireos, western tanagers, black-headed grosbeaks, blue grosbeaks, and lazuli buntings.

The best place to find a variety of Zion's riparian birds is in the vicinity of the park campgrounds, below the visitor center. The adjacent cottonwoods, willows, and other streamside vegetation support all of the species mentioned for Emerald Pool Canyon, as well as several other species. These additional species include red-tailed hawks, hairy woodpeckers, ash-throated flycatchers, black-capped chickadees, yellow warblers, and northern (Bullock's) orioles.

Blue grosbeaks and lazuli buntings are two of the park's most attractive birds. Both are lowland nesters, preferring the thickets along the Virgin River and its side canyons up to about 4,500 feet (1,372 m) elevation. The blue grosbeak male is an all-blue bird, except for its chestnut wing bars and a heavy, silvery bill. The lazuli bunting male sports an all-turquoise hood, blue and black back, snow white belly, and chestnut breast and sides.

Black-headed grosbeaks are one of the park's most numerous summertime residents, occurring throughout the canyons as well as among the aspens and oaks in the highlands. Males possess black hoods, black and cinnamon mottled backs and wings, with three white wing-markings, orange-brown throats and breasts, and yellow wing linings. Females are duller versions of the males. Both possess a heavy bill, which is used for stripping the husks off fruit. There are times that black-headed grosbeak songs are the most numerous in the high country. Their notes are rich, rapid whistles that seem to rise and fall and possess minor trilling effects.

The riverway is also busy with a variety of birds. Violet-green, northern rough-winged, and cliff swallows hawk for insects. Dozens of songbirds come to drink at favorite waterholes along the water-way. An occasional belted kingfisher will visit the canyon, although this bird usually nests below the park. Various waterfowl are regular migrants but rare in summer. And an occasional great blue heron will wander upriver.

But none of these are more welcome than the plump, all-gray-brown **American dipper**. Wauer and Carter, in *Birds of Zion National Park and Vicinity*, reported it to be a "[c]ommon permanent resident along all of the rapid flowing streams in the Zion area; it probably utilizes side streams to the Virgin River more when the river is muddy." Sometimes known as "water ouzel" (an old name), it actually walks underwater in search of its prey and uses its wings to swim to depths of 20 feet (6 m) or more. It can forage on stream bottoms "in which the current is too fast and the water too deep for people to stand," according to Paul Ehrlich and colleagues. It nests at the water's edge on little overhangs on cliffs and among roots, even behind waterfalls, where it constructs a round to oval structure of soft green moss, seven or more inches (18 cm) in diameter (Headstrom), with an opening near the bottom, and lined with mosses and grass. See chapter 4 on Mount Revelstoke and Glacier and chapter 9 on Timpanogos Cave for additional information about this fascinating songbird.

In mid-summer, the desert lowlands, such as Coalpits and Huber washes, seem almost birdless. But in spring and fall, these areas can be alive with birds. Most obvious are the large, all-dark turkey vultures; black-plumed Gambel's quail; mourning doves with their sorrowful calls; greater roadrunners of cartoon fame; Say's phoebes, with their all-grayish-brown plumage; rock wrens that sing spirited trills; well-marked black-throated sparrows; and house finches.

Of all these desert birds, **house finches** are the most abundant, and also the most colorful. Males possess deep red throats, foreheads, eye lines, and rumps, whitish bellies with dark brown stripes, brown caps, and streaked backs. But their lively singing is what sets this species apart from all the other desert birds. In spring and summer, as well as on warmer winter days, this sparrow-sized bird can carry on for hours. Bent quoted Myron and Jane Swenk's description of its song:

The House Finch is a joyous bird, and it expresses its joy in its rollicking, warbling song. The song itself is not long, but it is rapidly repeated many times, producing a long-continued flow of singing. The song has many variations; in fact, but rarely do you hear two songs that are exactly alike. Different individuals will sing slightly differently, and the same bird will vary his song from time to time, but the song always has the same basic structure, is rather consistently given in 6/8 time, and all of the songs share the same general quality.

The Zion-Mt. Carmel Highway, the park's east entrance, and the Kolob Canyons, on the northwest, are generally dominated by ponderosa pine communities and are cooler than the lowlands in summer. Some of the best examples of this environment occur near the east entrance. Although many of the ponderosa pine birds are the same as those in the lower side canyons and on the high plateaus, there are two species that are generally limited to this forest type: pygmy nuthatch and Grace's warbler.

The tiny, short-tailed **pygmy nuthatch** can be abundant, and their high-pitched, peeping calls, like "pee-di pee-di-pee-di," often seem to radiate from every ponderosa pine tree. This is one of the park's most gregarious birds, always in small flocks. Even when nesting, helpers assist with all the chores. See chapter 11 on Rocky Mountain National Park and chapter 27 on Bandelier National Monument for further details about this little nuthatch.

Grace's warblers are less numerous and may require minor searching. I have usually found these lovely little birds by listening for their songs, which they will sing from among the high pine boughs every few minutes. The song is not loud; it is a series of melodic chips, accentuated at the end but stopping on a sudden note. Roger Tory Peterson, in *A Field Guide to Western Birds*, described the song as "Cheedle cheedle che che che che, etc. (ends in trill)." This is a fairly small warbler with a brilliant yellow throat and breast, a bold yellow streak over each eye, gray back, white belly and black streaks on each side, and two white wing bars. The Grace's warbler, named after the sister of ornithologist Elliot Coues, its discoverer, is one of Zion's best connection to the tropics. This bird is one of the park's Neotropical migrant that spends its winter in southern Mexico and Central America, inhabiting its breeding grounds only about four months, from late April through August. The long-term survival of this and all the other Neotropical migrants (about one-half of Zion's summertime birds) depends upon the health of both its nesting and wintering habitats.

The big sagebrush flats that occur throughout the ponderosa pine communities offer nesting sites for several additional birds. Lark sparrows frequent the open fields and flats just below the forests; the higher sageflats are utilized by vesper sparrows; and nesting among the sagebrush in the marginal areas are green-tailed towhees and chipping and Brewer's sparrows.

Potato Hollow, along the West Rim Trail, is a beautiful depression containing ponderosa pine, aspen, white fir, and Douglas fir. A walk through this little valley in early June will likely result in finding most of the typical breeding birds of Zion's high country. In the forest, watch for sharp-shinned and Cooper's hawks; band-tailed pigeons; broad-tailed hummingbirds; northern (red-shafted) flickers; hairy and downy woodpeckers; red-naped sapsuckers; western wood-pewees; violet-green swallows; Steller's jays; black-capped and mountain chickadees; white-breasted, red-breasted, and pygmy nuthatches; American robins; hermit thrushes; western and mountain bluebirds; Townsend's solitaires; ruby-crowned kinglets; solitary and warbling vireos; orange-crowned, Virginia's, and Grace's warblers; western tanagers; dark-eyed juncos; Cassin's finches; and pine siskins.

High-country ponds and streams, such as those along Little and Kolob Creeks, Blue Springs Lake, and the Kolob Reservoir, offer available nesting sites for a few additional birds. Mallards, green-winged and cinnamon teal, and spotted sandpipers occur at open water areas. Riparian thickets support dusky flycatchers, orange-crowned, yellow, and MacGillivray's warblers, and Lincoln's sparrows.

Of all the high-country birds, none is as appealing as the **western tanager**. The males are one of the West's most colorful species, possessing canary yellow bodies and rumps, offset with coal black backs and wings, except for two yellow wing bars, and bright red hoods. Females are nondescript versions with brownish heads. Wauer and Carter reported that it is one of the "most conspicuous birds in Zion Canyon during May. By the first week of June, most individuals have moved to the high country to nest, although it occasionally nests at lower elevations."

The spruce-fir forest community can best be experienced along Cedar Breaks' 5-mile (8 km) scenic drive and its two trails: the circular 2-mile (3.2 km) Alpine Pond Trail and the 4-mile (6.4 km) round-trip Wasatch Ramparts Trail. I spent a full day walking the trails and driving the roadway in early July; I located a total of 25 bird species.

The most obvious forest birds included broad-tailed hummingbirds, western wood-pewees, violet-green swallows, Steller's jays, mountain chickadees, ruby-crowned kinglets, yellow-rumped warblers, and dark-eyed juncos. Fewer numbers of blue grouse, northern flickers, olive-sided flycatchers, gray jays, Clark's nutcrackers, brown creepers, American robins, hermit thrushes, evening grosbeaks, pine grosbeaks, Cassin's finches, and red crossbills were detected.

Of these highland species, the **dark-eyed juncos** were most numerous and seemed to be present in and adjacent to each patch of forest. They sang their musical trills from the treetops or lower perches. All of the nesting juncos were of the gray-headed subspecies that earlier were called gray-headed junco. They possess all-gray bodies, except for their rufous backs, black lores (between the eyes and bill), and darker tails with white outer tail feathers. Other juncos, especially the Oregon subspecies, occur in the lower canyons and along the rims during migration.

The yellow-rumped warbler is another species that had its name changed in recent years. This bird, with an all-yellow throat, was previously known as Audubon's warbler; the eastern yellow-rumped warbler, earlier called "myrtle" warbler, has an all-white throat. The two forms were lumped when ornithologists discovered the two interbreeding where their ranges overlap in the north; see futher details in chapter 3 on Banff, Jasper, Kooetnay, and Yoho.

The extensive high-country grasslands east of the rim contained three very different songbirds. Most numerous were the **white-crowned sparrows**, singing from numerous shrubs scattered across the terrain. Their distinct black-and-white head patterns, plain breasts, and striped backs were readily apparent. Their songs were a series of clear whistles followed by a buzzy trill. I also found several Brewer's sparrows, singing their musical trills, and a few horned larks.

There, too, were two rufous hummingbirds. The date was July 7, and already these northern hummers were on their way south to where they will spend their winter months. They had stopped over to feed on the abundant flowers that covered the high meadows. Both were bright all-rufous males, and, as the air passed through their feathers, their loud wing whistles were quite audible.

The skies over Cedar Breaks' great amphitheater and high plateau also contained several birds of interest that day. Violet-green swallows were most numerous, and white-throated swifts were a close second. I also found a few cliff swallows, a family of common ravens soaring along the rim, and lone Cooper's and Swainson's hawks. Now and then Clark's nutcrackers flew by, going from one clump of conifers to the other, oftentimes calling their loud "kra-a-a" calls en route.

Some years golden eagles frequent the area, cruising over the meadows and soaring along the high rims. They are larger than all the other birds and fly with their great wings straight out, rather than in a shallow V-shape, like turkey vultures. Adults possess golden feathers on the heads that, in the right light, can be most obvious. Immature birds lack the golden plumage but show a broad white band on their tails.

One day in mid-September, the meadows were filled with mountain bluebirds, flycatching over the wilted flowers. Their bright blue plumage matched the deep blue sky. Dark-eyed juncos moved from one patch of dried flowers to another, searching for seeds. A half-dozen Brewer's blackbirds, en route to more southern climes, passed overhead. A pair of omnipresent common ravens called to one another near the rim. At the far edge was a pair of blue grouse, feeding on the juicy fruits of gooseberries.

By late fall, all the Neotropical songbirds and several other species are on their way to warmer climes to the south. A few of the hardier species, however, such as gray jays and Clark's nutcrackers, chickadees and nuthatches, and a few others remain all winter.

Christmas Bird Counts have been taken in Zion Canyon for several years and provide the best perspective on the wintering populations. The 1990 Zion National Park count tallied 4,134 individuals of 72 species. The dozen most numerous birds, in descending order of abundance, included dark-eyed junco, white-crowned sparrow, house finch, American robin, house sparrow, cedar waxwing, ring-necked duck, bushtit, mallard, European starling, pinyon jay, and northern flicker.

In summary, the combined bird checklists include 271 species, of which 129 are listed as permanent or summer residents and, therefore, assumed to nest. Of those 129 species, 10 are water birds, 17 are hawks and owls, and 9 are warblers. Six species are listed for winter only: ladder-backed woodpecker, winter and marsh wrens, golden-crowned kinglet, northern shrike, and golden-crowned sparrow.

Birds of Special Interest

Plain titmouse. This is the little, all-gray, crested bird of the pinyon-juniper woodlands that has a loud "witt-y, witt-y, witt-y" call.

Pygmy nuthatch. Common on ponderosa pines, it is distinguished by its tiny size, gray-brown plumage, short tail, and high-pitched, peeping calls.

Canyon wren. Its loud, descending and decelerating "tew" notes, heard throughout the canyons, is the signature of this little bird, which sports a cinnamon back and snow white belly.

Black-throated gray warbler. This pinyon-juniper species possesses all black-and-white plumage, except for a tiny yellow spot in front of each eye.

Grace's warbler. Limited to the ponderosa pines, it is best identified by its brilliant yellow throat and breast, white belly, and black streaks on its sides.

Western tanager. Males possess canary yellow plumage with black backs and wings, with two yellow wing bars, and red hoods.

Black-headed grosbeak. Common at all elevations, males sport black hoods, orange-brown throats and breasts, and yellow wing linings.

House finch. This desert finch usually occurs in flocks; males possess red heads and breasts and whitish bellies with dark brown stripes.

Dark-eyed junco. Summer birds possess all-gray plumage except for their reddish backs and black eyes and lores (between the eyes and bill).

15

Bryce Canyon National Park, Utah

The rosy dawn was beginning to lighten the eastern sky as I arrived at Bryce Canyon's Sunrise Point. Two dozen or more other travelers stood silently in the quiet but cool morning, eagerly waiting for the first shafts of sunlight to touch the rim of the great amphitheater spread out below us. We watched as the morning light touched the rim and gradually crawled downward over the vast assemblage of crags and spires. As if by magic, each layer of the pink cliffs seemed to change in texture and color as it was touched by the new day. Each of us claimed our own perspective on the changing scene before us.

My vision that morning included the greenery on the rim and scattered shrubs and pines within the vast amphitheater. That vision was also enhanced by the bird life that I either heard or observed while enjoying the sunrise. The most obvious was a pair of common ravens that soared overhead, perhaps to inspect the day's new crop of tourists, or as part of their normal dawn clean-up chores; they also check the roadways at dawn to claim any night-time casualities. When one raven landed on top of a tall snag near the parking lot, a quick glance through my binoculars revealed that it, indeed, had located a breakfast snack during its morning foray.

When that same raven called out several loud "auwk" notes, a few of the morning sunrise worshippers turned to find the source. When one person told a friend, "crow," that inaccuracy seemed to appease almost everyone. But I wanted to shout out that crows are farmland animals that do not occur at Bryce, that this was a raven, a very different bird. Common ravens are considerably larger than crows; they are not as sleek and they possess much larger heads and bills and long wedge-shaped tails. Crows' tails are short and squared. And what's more, common ravens, more than almost any other bird, represent environmental extremes. They occur in the lowest and hottest deserts, and also in the highest and most isolated highlands, places where crows do not live. The common raven, to many of us, is the symbol of wildness, a creature of solitude, the opposite of the closely related crow.

The combination of the innumerable shadows and sunlit caps of red, pink, and white, that were laid out before me in a dazzling sunrise display, and the domineering presence of a pair of common ravens, provided sanity to the new day. I recalled a Henry David Thoreau quote that I had read in the little shelter along Bryce Canyon's Bristlecone Loop Trail: "I need solitude. I have come forth to this hill . . . to see the forms of the mountains on the horizon—to behold and commune with something grander than man."

The Park Environment

Bryce Canyon is situated along the eastern flank of the Paunsaugunt Plateau, a portion of the greater Colorado Plateau. The intricate badlands formation contains innumerable pinnacles, spires, and ridges in layers of reds, pinks, and whites, together considered to be among the world's most outstanding examples of "headward" water erosion.

Elevations in the park range from 6,600 feet (2,012 m) in the Paria River Valley to 9,105 feet (2,775 m) at Rainbow Point, near the southern end of the park. Three rather distinct forest communities exist. Small areas of pinyon-juniper woodlands occur in the lowlands up to approximately 7,000 feet (2,134 m) elevation. Dominant woodland plants include two-needle pinyon and Utah juniper, fewer numbers of curl-leaf mountain mahogany and squawbush, and a variety of grasses and perennials.

Above the pinyon-juniper woodlands, to about 8,500 feet (2,591 m), is a ponderosa pine community that is dominated by ponderosa pine, with fewer numbers of Douglas fir, Rocky Mountain juniper, and squawbush. The understory contains significant amounts of manzanita and antelope bitterbrush. And in some protected locations, such as in canyons, stands of Gambel's oak are common. Open areas scattered throughout the ponderosa pine community produce an association of black sagebrush, rubber rabbitbrush, and grasses.

Above 8,500 feet (2,591 m) elevation is a fir-spruce-aspen community that is dominated by white fir, Douglas fir, blue spruce, and aspen. Common juniper and manzanita are common in the undergrowth. In a few isolated, windy locations, such as near Rainbow Point, stands of bristlecone pine persist.

The park encompasses an area of 35,835 acres (14,502 ha) that extends north to south for approximately 20 miles (72 km). The impressive badlands formations, locally called "hoodoos," lie along the eastern escarpment. The park's main road, which leads to a few side roads to scenic overlooks, two campgrounds, and a lodge and store complex, runs almost the entire length of the park, deadending at Rainbow Point.

The visitor center is located 1 mile (1.6 km) inside the park entrance. It has an information desk, an auditorium for daytime orientation and evening programs, exhibits, and a sales outlet. Bird field guides and a checklist are available. Interpretive activities include a wide range of nature walks and evening programs. Schedules are posted at pertinent locations and are available on request.

Additional information can be obtained from the Superintendent, Bryce Canyon National Park, UT 84717; (801) 834-5322.

Bird Life

Several other birds were present that morning at Sunrise Point. Dozens of pine siskins flew by in small flocks, calling out rising "tee-ee" notes in flight. A flock of American robins, their red breasts gleaming in the early morning light, passed overhead. A lone yellow-rumped warbler trailed after them, as if it had joined their flock for security. And then eight or ten **western bluebirds** approached our lookout, flying from snag to snag just elow the rim. I had detected their approach by their soft, flutelike "chew" notes. Although they detoured around the overlook, I was able to clearly see the males' bright blue backs and heads, chestnut breasts and flanks, and white bellies. The females and immature birds were duller versions of the brighter males. I couldn't help but wonder if these birds had nested within the park or were wanderers like ourselves.

Then the rather loud but dull "chink" call of a Townsend's solitaire on a surprisingly close snag attracted my attention. I focused my binoculars on this grayish, robin-sized bird. Its subtle gray-brown colors, offset by its bold white eye rings and outer tail feathers, were readily apparent. Solitaires are one of the Rocky Mountains' most romantic bird species, often nesting at treeline on steep, grassy slopes. They sing some of the sweetest songs in all the bird world. See chapter 7 on Yellowstone and chapter 9 on Timpanogos for descriptions of this bird and its behavior.

Mountain chickadee

The tall ponderosa pines along the high rim were in complete sunlight as I walked back to my vehicle; bird activity was in full swing. The most obvious of the half-dozen species detected was the little **mountain chickadee**; its rather loud "chick a-dee a-dee a-dee" songs and more subtle "fee-bee" and "fee-bee-bay" calls resounded among the high ponderosa foliage. The "fee-bee-bay" calls reminded me of the children's song, "Three blind mice." In spite of their singing it took me several seconds to locate one individual that was foraging among the long-needled foliage on a lower branch. I could clearly see its white eyeline between its black cap and cheeks, its black bib, and gray-brown body. I watched that bird as it explored the twigs and foliage, hanging upside-down part of the time, a truly arboreal acrobat.

Mountain chickadees, members of the Paridae or titmouse family, occur only in North America's western mountains. They are one of Bryce Canyon's most abundant full-time residents, residing in all three forest communities. They usually remain reasonably close to their nesting territories throughout the year, leaving the park only during the coldest winters. Although they are rather independent while nesting, utilizing a wide variety of cavities, they spend the rest of the year in bird parties. They usually form a nucleus to which other small birds are attracted. It is not unusual to find this bird in close association with brown creepers, white-breasted and red-breasted nuthatches, ruby-crowned kinglets, yellow-rumped warblers, and chipping sparrows.

A dark blue, high-crested bird suddenly flew up from the side of the trail just ahead of me; I immediately recognized it as a **Steller's jay.** There are few birds with the personality of this Rocky Mountain jay. It is a truly gorgeous bird, and one of the park's most abundant species. They can be especially numerous at North and Sunset Campgrounds, where they have learned to utilize human-foods as well as the vast variety of foods that nature provides them. Some places in the western mountains, this all-dark-blue jay is better known as "camp robber," for its habit of stealing food from campers. But feeding jays and other wildlife can lead to a dependency and diet deficiency that can have serious effects on their long-term survival.

I watched one individual "climb" a tall ponderosa pine, jumping or hopping from branch to branch around the tree trunk, as if it were climbing a spiral staircase. It stopped twice to cock its head, tall crest and all, and glare at me for interfering with its business.

Then it suddenly disappeared among the mass of green foliage. Once out of sight, it scolded me for several seconds with loud "shaack shaack shaack" notes. A few seconds later I located it again as it soared away through the pines.

In spring and summer, the ponderosa pine community supports a number of other breeding birds. The smallest, and one of the more numerous, of these is the **pygmy nuthatch**, a gregarious short-tailed bird with a gray-brown cap, white cheeks and throat, and buff underparts. It rarely strays far from ponderosa pines, where it will search every inch of a tree while foraging for insects and larvae. Its small size allows it to inspect every furrow of the trunk, every niche of the many branches, every group of pine needles, and every cone. The pygmy nuthatch will climb upside-down and up and down while foraging. It also will search the needle-strewn ground beneath the pines. If these birds are not readily located by their continuous and obvious activity, they can usually be detected by their high-pitched, rapid, peeping sounds. See chapter 27 on Bandelier for additional information about this little nuthatch.

In spring and summer, Bryce Canyon's ponderosa pines also provide nesting sites for the **Grace's warbler**, another species that rarely occurs in any other habitat. Although it is not as abundant as its pygmy nuthatch neighbor, it is more colorful and possesses a bright, cheerful song with a rapid musical trill. Grace's warblers are easily identified by their bright yellow throats, breasts, and bold eye lines, grayish-black backs, black-and-white wings, and white bellies with black stripes on the flanks. Grace's warblers are one of the park's Neotropical migrants that provide a connection to the tropics. They spend their winters in mountains south of the border, utilizing pine communities very similar to the ponderosa pine habitats. The long-term survival of the southern pines, from Mexico to Nicaragua, is just as important to Bryce Canyon's Grace's warblers as are their nesting communities in the park.

Other common spring and summer residents of the ponderosa pine community include broad-tailed hummingbirds, northern (red-shafted) flickers, western wood-pewees, violet-green swallows, white-breasted nuthatches, American robins, solitary vireos, chipping sparrows, western tanagers, brown-headed cowbirds, and house finches. One of the most attractive of these is the black, yellow, and red western tanager. Males are beautiful birds with yellow bodies, black wings with yellow wing bars, and red heads. Their songs are ringing whistles, somewhat like that of robins, and their calls, which usually continue throughout the daylight hours, are slurred "pit-er-ick" notes.

Scattered openings within the ponderosa pine community are usually dominated by black sagebrush and a number of perennials. The open sagebrush/grass meadow behind the visitor center is rather special because it contains a colony of Utah prairie dogs, reintroduced between the late 1970s and 1980s, according to the park's Chief of Interpretation, Susan Colclazer. A pair of red-tailed hawks have taken up residency nearby, probably due to this potential food source, and they can usually be found in the vicinity.

Higher elevations along the southern end of the main roadway support a forest community more representative of the northern Rocky Mountains. The fir-spruce-aspen communities support some of the same birds that breed within the ponderosa pine community: hairy woodpeckers, Steller's jays, mountain chickadees, white-breasted nuthatches, Townsend's solitaires, and yellow-rumped warblers. This ecosystem also supports several birds that nest only within the fir-spruce-aspen community, and a few of these are reasonably common at various times of year.

One of the best examples of the higher forest birds is the chickenlike **blue grouse**. It is usually found walking along the roadsides, searching for new leaves, buds, and insects. When approached, they often will freeze in place, and most travelers pass them by without an opportunity to admire this wonderful creature. When discovered, however, one can often approach surprisingly close before the bird realizes it has been located and walks away into the underbrush. Their general appearance is of a sooty gray bird with an all-black tail. However, in spring when the males are displaying, they can look very different. Then the males spread and cock their tails, inflate their necks to expose patches of reddish skin surrounded by snow white inner feathers, like a bull's-eye. And their yellow-orange combs above the eyes protrude over their caps. Courtship displays are a thing to behold. John Terres described the male's display thusly: they "flutter above the ground or make short circular flights, then strut in short hurried runs before females, with fanned tail tipped forward, head drawn in and back, wings dragging ground like small turkey gobbler."

Other birds found in the spruce-fir-aspen communities during summer include dusky flycatchers, brown creepers, red-breasted nuthatches, American robins, hermit thrushes, ruby-crowned kinglets, yellow-rumped warblers, and pine siskins. The most widespread of these is the **yellow-rumped warbler**, one of the few warblers that also winters in the U.S. Some individuals only move to lower elevations rather than migrate to the south. Therefore, except during mid-winter when its territory is snow-bound, at least a few of these showy songbirds can be found in the park. And they are easily identified by their black, white, and yellow features; they possess five yellow spots, on their cap, throat, sides, and rump. A brightly colored male can be gorgeous with its deep-yellow throat surrounded by its coal black chest and face, and showy yellow rump, which has earned it the nickname "butter-rump."

Another common summer resident of the highland forests is the **dark-eyed junco**. Nesting juncos represent the gray-headed race, with all-gray underparts and hoods, except for black patches between their eyes and bills, rufous backs, and distinct white feathers on the edges of their blackish tails. Their white "tail-flashes," as they disappear in the dense undergrowth, and their habit of hopping over the ground in search for seeds are helpful traits for identification. After nesting, this little junco can be expected along the entire Rim Trail. Most juncos move to lower elevations in winter when their food supply declines, although hardier individuals linger on their breeding grounds for as long as possible. During the most severe winters, when they are forced to migrate to warmer climes in the southern portion of their range, these are the little birds known as "snow birds."

Winter bird populations within the park have not been tallied for several years. But in the 1960s, Christmas Bird Counts were regularly undertaken. The 1965 count provides an example of the park's winter bird life. Counters tallied 571 individuals of 32 species. The dozen most numerous species, in declining order of abundance, included house sparrow, dark-eyed junco, pinyon jay, white-crowned sparrow, western meadowlark, pygmy nuthatch and red-winged blackbird (tied), bushtit, red crossbill, mountain chickadee, black-billed magpie, and scrub jay and Townsend's solitaire (tied).

In summary, the park's bird checklist includes 113 species, of which 107 are listed as either permanent resident or summer resident, and assumed to nest in the park. Of those, 8 are water birds, 11 are hawks and owls, and 4 are warblers. Four are listed as winter residents only: gray jay, white-crowned sparrow, rosy finch, and American goldfinch.

Birds of Special Interest

Blue grouse. This is the chicken-like bird occasionally found along the road or trails; it is bluish overall, with a black tail.

Steller's jay. It can be found anywhere in the park and is easily identified by its all-dark-blue body and tall crest.

Common raven. This is the all-black bird, with a large head and bill and wedge-shaped tail, that soars about the canyon overlooks; it has a variety of calls that are grunts and hoarse "caws."

Mountain chickadee. Their "chick a-dee a-dee a-dee" songs are commonplace about the campgrounds and rim; it is a tiny bird with black bib and head, with a white eyeline.

Western bluebird. This is the blue bird with a chestnut breast; its calls are soft, flutelike "chew" notes.

Yellow-rumped warbler. It can be found anywhere in the park and identified by its five yellow spots: on its rump, sides, throat, and cap.

Grace's warbler. This little bird occurs only among the ponderosa pines; it possesses an all-yellow throat and breast, and sings a musical trill song.

16

Grand Canyon National Park, Arizona

The view from the South Rim's Yavapai Point contains a vast and magnificient spectrum of the Grand Canyon of the Colorado River. The multiple layers of rock cliffs and terraces represent almost all the known ages of the earth, laid out within the canyon like the open pages of a great book. Geologists can point out each chapter of the earth's history, exposed in sequence, from the deepest inner canyon to the highest rimstone.

One day in May, I watched the morning light gradually crawl into the canyon, lighting each layer one by one, until it finally exposed the bright green vegetation fringing the mighty Colorado. Phantom Ranch, at the bottom of Bright Angel Canyon, glowed like a distant emerald. Just upriver was the Kaibab Bridge, one of two footbridges over the mud-red Colorado. Directly below my perch was the thread-like Bright Angel Trail, a connecting link from the South Rim.

My gaze into the depths was suddenly interrupted by a dozen or more white-throated swifts that careened along the cliffs so close to where I sat that I could actually feel air movement. Their expressive, high-pitched descending trill notes were almost explosive as they passed by. I turned my attention to a single pair of these black-and-white creatures that had veered away from the flock, almost straight up 200 to 300 feet (61-91 m) or more. I watched them clinging together in copulation as they fell hundreds of feet in mid-air, wings out to control their speed, but spinning them around like an airborne pinwheel. They were several hundred feet below the rim before they separated, immediately leveled off, and ascended again into the blue sky. Another time these flying cigar-shaped birds came so close that I could see their white throats, bellies, and flanks, which contrasted with their otherwise all-black plumage. They put on an incredible show. See chapter 22 on Colorado National Monument for details about this swift's nesting behavior.

Violet-green swallows were also present that morning, soaring along the cliff and over the pinyon-juniper woodlands behind me. These birds were flying much slower, without the all-out acceleration of the swifts. Through binoculars I could clearly see their snow white underparts, cheeks, and sides of their rumps, slightly forked tails, and violet-green backs. Each time one passed below me its back gleamed an almost velvety-green in the morning sunlight. Their calls were little more than high-pitched "chip" notes, far less exciting than the speedier swifts.

The much larger, all-black birds with wedge-shaped tails, soaring along the rim, were common ravens. There were five individuals in all. On closer inspection, through binoculars, I could see that three of the five were young of the year, already fledged and accompanying the adults on their morning foray. They undoubtedly had nested somewhere along the cliffs, building a stick nest lined with bark and hair, on some high, inaccessible ledge. They passed by with the customary swooshing sounds of their broad wings.

The loud decending and decelerating song of a **canyon wren** suddenly resounded from just below the rim. A moment later I was watching a cinnamon-colored bird with an all-white throat less than 30 feet (9 m) away. It moved with a jerky manner, probing a crack for food. I was totally ignored. Then it sang again, a loud, descending series of whistled notes: "TEW TEW TEW TEW tew tew tew tew tew." It gave a short metallic "jert" note and disappeared over the edge. What a lovely creature it was, and so fitting a bird at the Grand Canyon. All through the day, whenever I was close to the rim, I could hear their songs from the canyon below.

A melodic "flew" note attracted my attention to a brightly colored male **western bluebird**, perched on a pinyon snag only 50 to 60 feet (15-18 m) away. I had detected its stuttering "flew" notes earlier, but they had not registered until now. Less than a dozen feet away from the male was its mate, a faded version of the brighter male. He stood out in sharp contrast to the female: its hood and wings were a

Western bluebird

deep blue, almost a purple-blue color; its back, breast, and flanks were deep chestnut; and its belly was white, a truly gorgeous bird, and one of the most common residents at both the South and North Rim. This cavity nester utilizes deserted woodpecker nests as well as other tree cavities in pinyon and ponderosa pines.

The male bluebird suddenly shot out from its perch, flying almost directly upward, and I watched it snap its bill on a passing insect. But instead of returning to its original perch, it landed next to its lady and presented her with its insect catch. Her acceptance of it was an act of courtship that undoubtedly occurs often in spring but one few human beings are privileged to observe.

The Park Environment

Grand Canyon National Park is not only one of the world's most glamorous and photogenic canyons, but it truly is one of the greatest natural wonders on earth. Writer-historian John C. Van Dyke wrote that Grand Canyon is "[m]ore mysterious in its depth than the Himalayas in their height. The Grand Canyon remains not the eighth but the first wonder of the world. There is nothing like it." Theodore Roosevelt wrote that "[t]he Grand Canyon of Arizona fills me with awe. It is beyond comparison, beyond description, absolutely unparalleled throughout the wide world." And when commercial interests attempted to dam the canyon for profit, Roosevelt pleaded to Congress:

> I want to ask you to do one thing in connection with it in your own interest and in the interest of the country—to keep this great wonder of nature as it is now . . . Leave it as it is. You can not improve on it. The ages have been at work on it, and man can only mar it. What you can do is keep it for your children, your children's children, and for all who come after you, as the one great sight which every American . . . should see.

Congress established the Grand Canyon as a national park in 1919. The enlarged park now encompasses 1,218,376 acres (493,070 ha), an area larger than the state of Rhode Island. The Grand Canyon extends for 277 miles (446 km) along the Colorado River from Lees Ferry, at the southern end of Glen Canyon National Recreation Area, to Grand Wash Cliffs, the upper edge of Lake Mead National Recreation Area. The full length of the Grand Canyon is now protected within lands administered by the National Park Service. The canyon is approximately 1 mile deep (5,000-6,000 ft. or 1,524-1,829 m) and from slightly under 1 mile (1.6 km) to 18 miles (29 km) in width; the average width is 10 miles (16 km).

Grand Canyon National Park contains unparalleled scenery, a remarkable sequence of rock layers that records a significant part of North America's geologic history, one of the most spectacular examples of erosion anywhere in the world, more than 4,000 years of human history, and an assemblage of life zones that extends from arid desert lowlands to spruce-fir forests in the highlands.

These significant values were given special recognition when Grand Canyon National Park was granted World Heritage Site status by UNESCO (United Nations Educational, Scientific, and Cultural Organization) in 1979. World Heritage listing officially recognizes areas of "universal value" and "international respect."

Five distinct vegetation zones occur within the park: desert and its associated desertscrub and grasslands; pinyon-juniper woodlands and its associated mountain scrub and chaparral, sagebrush and blackbrush flats; ponderosa pine forests and associated meadows and oaks; spruce-fir forests and aspen groves; and riparian zones along the Colorado River and moist streamsides at a variety of elevations.

All these zones possess their own plant life, although there is considerable overlap due to the microenvironments created by the steep canyons and the resultant northern and southern exposures. For example, desertscrub occurs on exposed southern slopes remarkably high along the North Rim. Pockets of spruce and fir occur on shaded northern slopes at mid-elevations below the South Rim.

Typical desert plants found in the lower canyons, generally below 4,000 feet (1,219 m) elevation, include creosote bush, ocotillo, honey mesquite, acacias, and a variety of cacti. Typical desert birds found in this zone include greater roadrunners, Costa's hummingbirds, and black-throated sparrows. Desert grasslands and blackbrush flats occur on exposed benches between approximately 3,800 to 5,500 feet (1,158-1,676 m) and support nesting loggerhead shrikes, western meadowlarks, and black-throated sparrows.

Pinyon-juniper woodlands occur at elevations from approximately 4,000 to 7,500 feet (1,219-1,676 m). Two-needle pinyon and Utah juniper are dominant, but mountain mahogany, cliffrose, serviceberry, skunkbush, and snowberry are common as well. In some places, New Mexico locust, fendlerbush, fernbush, and Gambel's oak are present to form mountain scrub thickets. Elsewhere, manzanita, scrub oak, silktassel, cliffrose, and mountain mahogany form chaparral associations. Typical breeding birds of these areas include broad-tailed hummingbirds, scrub jays, plain titmice, blue-gray gnatcatchers, and black-throated gray warblers in the woodlands; rufous-sided towhees can be added in the scrub and chaparral areas.

The ponderosa pine forest areas, which occur from about 6,500 to 8,000 feet (1,981-2,438 m) elevation, are truly dominated by open stands of ponderosa pines, with a scattering of Douglas firs and white firs on the North Rim. The most typical birds of this zone are the pygmy and white-breasted nuthatches and Grace's warbler. And Virginia's warblers are associated with the groves of Gambel's oak.

Above 8,000 feet (2,438 m) can be found spruce-fir forest areas. These are diverse forests that can be dominated by a variety of boreal tree species: Engelmann and blue spruce, Douglas fir, and white fir; aspens occur throughout, often in dense stands. Typical spruce-fir forest birds include Steller's jays, red-breasted nuthatches, ruby-crowned kinglets, yellow-rumped warblers, and dark-eyed juncos; Williamson's sapsuckers and warbling vireos can be added in aspen stands. And a special characteristic of the North Rim is the rather extensive meadow environment that is filled with flowering perennials in summer. Typical birds of this meadow habitat include wild turkeys, broad-tailed hummingbirds, and mountain bluebirds.

At the bottom of the canyon flows the Colorado River. It and its lower tributaries support a riparian habitat that is dominated by Fremont cottonwoods, willows, tamarisks, and seepwillows. Typical riparian nesting birds include yellow warblers, yellow-breasted chats, and lazuli buntings.

Grand Canyon National Park is actually two distinct units; the South and North Rims are divided by the great chasm of the Grand Canyon, and by 200 miles (322 km) of highway from one entrance to the other. The more popular South Rim lies along the northern edge of the Coconino Plateau and is accessible via Highways 64 and 180 from Williams, Flagstaff, and Cameron, Arizona. The North Rim, which is closed in winter, lies along the southern edge of the Kaibab Plateau, and is accessible only via Highway 67 from Jacob Lake, Arizona. Campgrounds, overnight accommodations, and supplies are available on both sides.

National Park Service visitor centers or contact stations exist at Grand Canyon Village complex, Desert View, and Yavapai Museum on the South Rim, and near the Grand Lodge on the North Rim. Each has an information desk, orientation programs, exhibits, and sales outlet. Bird field guides, checklist, and the excellent book, *Grand Canyon Birds*, by Bryan Brown, Steve Carothers, and Roy Johnson, are available. The visitor center also is the heart of the South Rim's interpretive activities. Programs vary throughout the season and include evening programs, daily talks and walks, and special tours. Museums at Yavapai Point (geology) and Tusayan (Anasazi life) also contain exhibits and sales outlets. North Rim interpretive activities include most of the same type of programs. Interpretive schedules are printed in *The Guide*, available at park entrance stations or any of the park information desks.

Additional information can be obtained from the Superintendent, Grand Canyon National Park, P.O. Box 129, Grand Canyon, AZ 86023; (602) 638-7888.

Bird Life

Pinyon-juniper woodlands dominate the South Rim, although stands of ponderosa pine occur back from the rim on higher ridges and cooler slopes. But the South Rim's bird life is largely dominated by pinyon-juniper species. Besides western bluebirds, other common nesting birds include the mourning dove, with its well-known, mournful song; broad-tailed hummingbird, usually detected first by the male's loud wing-trill; northern flicker, with its red-shafted wings; hairy woodpecker, with its sharp, loud "keek" calls; ash-throated flycatcher, a slender, slightly crested bird that sings a "ka-brick" or "ka-wheer" song; the long-tailed scrub jay, with its bluish head, tail, and wings, and whitish underparts; the shorter-tailed pinyon jay, with its all-blue plumage and constant crowlike cries; mountain chickadee, with its black bib, cap, and mask, and white eyeline; plain titmouse, a little gray-brown bird with a short crest; the tiny bushtit, with its gray plumage and long, darker tail; white-breasted nuthatch, with its snow white breast and cheeks; American robin, with its red breast and cheery song; blue-gray gnatcatcher, looking like a miniature, long-tailed mockingbird; black-throated gray warbler, all black-and-white, except for a tiny patch of yellow in front of each eye; and chipping sparrow, with its reddish cap and song like a rapid, monotonous trill.

An early spring morning at Bow Lake, located on the Icefields Parkway in northern Banff National Park. (Photo by R. Wauer)

Cottonwood Slough, near Jasper townsite, Jasper National Park, is one of the best bird-finding areas in the four-park area. (Photo by R. Wauer)

Skunk Cabbage Marsh, in Mount Revelstoke National Park, is surrounded by the steep slope of the Columbia Mountains. (Photo by R. Wauer)

Maskinonge Lake, near the entrance to Waterton Lakes National Park, is one of the most productive wetland habitats in the dual parks. (Photo by R. Wauer)

St. Mary Lake, surrounded by impressive glacial peaks, lies along the east entrance to Glacier National Park, Montana. (Photo by R. Wauer)

Devil Canyon Overlook provides a spectacular view of the blue waters of the Bighorn River and 1,000-foot canyon walls of Bighorn Canyon. (Photo by R. Wauer)

Yellowstone Falls dominates the Grand Canyon of the Yellowstone in Yellowstone National Park. (Photo by R. Wauer)

The Pelican Creek wetlands in the foreground, with massive Yellowstone Lake in the background. (Photo by R. Wauer)

The Grand Tetons provide a spectacular backdrop to the Snake River and flood plain and the adjacent gray-green sagebrush flats. (Photo by R. Wauer)

In the fall, the Grand Tetons are highlighted by golden aspen foliage along the Snake River. (Photo by R. Wauer)

Wide open vistas, high cliffs, and sagebrush flats are visible from along Dinosaur's Harper's Corner Scenic Drive. (Photo by R. Wauer)

Trail Ridge Road passes over the "roof of the Rockies," at over 12,000 feet elevation, at Rocky Mountain National Park. (Photo by R. Wauer)

The multicolored cliffs of Capitol Reef National Park dominate the area that was called the "land of the sleeping rainbow" by the Navajos. (Photo by R. Wauer)

Arch's Courthouse Wash is lined with riparian vegetation, like an elongated oasis in an otherwise arid landscape. (Photo by R. Wauer)

Canyonlands National Park, as viewed from near Grand View Point, is immense and lonesome, the essence of solitude. (Photo by R. Wauer)

A ponderosa pine frames this view of Zion National Park, along the West Rim Trail. (Photo by R. Wauer)

Bryce Canyon's badlands formation, locally called "hoodoos," viewed from near Rainbow Point. (Photo by R. Wauer)

Looking across the Grand Canyon toward the North Rim and Bright Angel Canyon from the South Rim. (Photo by R. Wauer)

Sunset Crater rises above the black basalts and scattered ponderosa pines. (Photo by R. Wauer)

Walnut Canyon, best known for its prehistoric cliff dwellings, also contains lush riparian vegetation, including black walnuts. (Photo by R. Wauer)

The 20-room Montezuma Castle was built on a high limestone bluff overlooking Beaver Creek and its lush riparian vegetation. (Photo by R. Wauer)

The prehistoric Tonto ruins overlook a canyon dominated by Sonoran Desert vegetation that includes stately saguaro cacti, palo verde, jojoba, ocotillo, and acacias. (Photo by R. Wauer)

The Rincon Mountains, forested with conifers in the highlands, rise above the Sonoran Desert lowlands in Saguaro National Monument. (Photo by R. Wauer)

Chiricahua National Monument's Massai Point area is dominated by an amazing assortment of rock pinnacles and a lush chaparral environment. (Photo by R. Wauer)

The approximately 1,500-foot walls of the canyon rise over Crystal Lake on the Gunnison River in upper Curecanti National Recreation Area. (Photo by R. Wauer)

The northern edge of Mesa Verde (meaning "green table") and the distant San Juan Range are visible from Park Point. (Photo by R. Wauer)

The Great Sand Dunes, the tallest in North America, are situated at the base of a great arc of the Sangre de Cristo Mountains. (Photo by R. Wauer)

The prehistoric ruins of Tyuonyi, which contained 400 rooms, lie in the bottom of Frijoles Canyon in Bandelier National Monument. (Photo by R. Wauer)

El Morro's Inscription Rock cliffs, with its vast array of historic graffiti, juts out of the pinyon-juniper woodlands. (Photo by R. Wauer)

White Sands, the world's largest gypsum dune field with dunes to 60 feet high, is located at 4,000 feet elevation in New Mexico's Tularosa Basin. (Photo by R. Wauer)

The Guadalupe Mountains rise out of the Chihuahuan Desert lowlands; at mid-elevation is a pinyon-juniper woodland with sotol and numerous grasses. (Photo by R. Wauer)

Mexico's Sierra del Carmens provide a magnificent backdrop to the Rio Grande flood plain and Boquilla Canyon in Big Bend National Park. (Photo by R. Wauer)

Other less obvious pinyon-juniper birds include Cooper's hawks, western screech-owls, common nighthawks, common poor-wills, western and Cassin's kingbirds, gray flycatchers, and Bewick's wrens. Where Gambel's oaks or other deciduous vegetation are mixed into the woodlands, downy woodpeckers, Virginia's warblers, and black-headed grosbeaks also occur. See chapter 22 on Colorado National Monument for a more extensive description of typical pinyon-juniper bird life.

In the lower, open, and warmer canyons is a more sparse pinyon-juniper woodland area that contains many desert plant species. This environment supports a few additional breeding birds, including greater roadrunners, black-chinned hummingbirds, ladder-backed woodpeckers, northern mockingbirds, loggerhead shrikes, gray vireos, Scott's orioles, and rufous-crowned sparrows.

Grand Canyon's riparian environment has undergone a major change since the Colorado River was dammed in 1964. Prior to the Glen Canyon Dam, the flood plain experienced annual flooding that scoured out the canyons, leaving few patches of vegetation. Since 1963, however, the sediment load has declined by 80 percent and the flood plain has been colonized by a variety of plants. The new growth has led to an increased number of riparian birds. These include willow flycatchers, Bell's vireos, yellow and Lucy's warblers, yellow-breasted chats, hooded orioles, summer tanagers, blue grosbeaks, lazuli buntings, and house finches.

This increased foodbase in the lower canyons has had an effect on the park's predators. Riparian-nesters, like Cooper's and red-tailed hawks, and cliff nesters, like golden eagles, prairie and pere-grine falcons, and American kestrels, have undoubtedly increased. Of these key raptors, none has received as much attention as the **peregrine falcon**. This bird's dramatic decline during the 1950s and 1960s, due primarily to man's overuse of DDT, led to the eventual banning of DDT in the U.S. and Canada. The peregrine was placed on the endangered species list; and biologists, led by Dr. Tom J. Cade of Cornell University, developed an aggressive restoration pro-gram throughout the peregrine's range. Thanks to these efforts, this magnificient creature has made a remarkable recovery.

Peregrine falcon

Recent surveys by ornithologist Bryan Brown and colleagues have provided some startling numbers. A 21-day survey in 1989 located at least 58 pairs. The researchers wrote that the "[a]verage distances between pairs on the south rim, north rim, and Colorado

River were 3.7 miles [5.9 km], 5.0 miles [8 km], and 4.2 miles [6.8 km], respectively." Extrapolation from the 1989 data "indicates that approximately 100 pairs of peregrines could occur in those areas of the park." These data suggest that Grand Canyon's peregrine population, which, in a sense, represents the core of a much larger Colorado Plateau population, may be the densest ever reported.

With such a high population of peregrines scattered throughout the park, the likelihood of seeing one or a pair of these magnificent birds, from one of the many overlooks, is excellent, especially in spring when courting birds are most vocal and actively pursuing one another. Watch for a large, powerful, slate gray bird with long, pointed wings and wide, black moustachial markings against otherwise white cheeks. It may be detected first by thin "screeee" calls. If the opportunity arises to watch this falcon during courtship or hunting, you will not soon forget the experience. See chapter 6 on Bighorn Canyon for additional information about this bird's hunting prowess.

The North Rim is very different from the South Rim. It not only averages 1,500 feet (457 m) higher, but the greater rainfall and the southward-dipping strata feed almost twice as much runoff into the canyon. This results in deeply cut side canyons that set the North Rim back further from the Colorado River, and leaves spires, mesas, and plateaus standing. The higher Kaibab Plateau contains a variety of features that are unique, not the least of which is the Kaibab squirrel, a white-tailed, tassel-eared tree-squirrel that occurs nowhere else.

One morning in late September, when the aspen leaves were ripe with yellow and gold, I walked the 5-mile (8 km) Widforss Trail. In a sense, this trail is a microcosm of the North Rim. It begins at Harvey Meadow, just north of the North Rim Store complex, skirts Transept Canyon, and ends above Haunted Canyon at a magnificient overview. The morning was chilly; frost covered the top of the brochure box when I retrieved a Widforss Trail folder. Pygmy nuthatches called from all directions; their constant chirping calls resounded through the forest. Their only vocal competition came from mountain chickadees, another tiny but vociferous creature of the highland forest.

Widforss Trail climbs along a densely wooded canyon and onto the plateau where ponderosa pines fully dominate the scene. **Pygmy nuthatches** were obvious about the pines, crawling about the scaly trunks, all over the branches and foliage. A few were searching for breakfast on the foliage-strewn ground. It seemed to me that each and every individual was talking to another. I focused my binoculars on one of these stubby nuthatches, which was walking straight down a tree trunk searching every crack and cranny it came upon. Its short tail, buff underparts, white cheeks and throat, blackish cap, and grayish back were obvious. It was so involved with its morning foray that it seemed to totally ignore my presence. All the while, it continued its calls, which, from up-close, sounded like crisp "pee-di" notes.

A light hammering behind me attracted my attention to another pygmy nuthatch that had found a pine seed and was trying to open it the old-fashioned way. I watched it pound the nut more than a dozen times, with great blows from its stout bill, before the rich, meaty nut was exposed and consumed.

As I moved along the trail, it was readily apparent that the fall harvest was in full swing. During the next few hours among the ponderosa pines, Douglas firs, and white firs, I found a variety of creatures hard at work collecting seeds, undoubtedly preparing for the coming winter. Although pygmy nuhatches were most numerous, red-breasted and white-breasted nuthatches were also active. The little red-breasts seemed to prefer Douglas fir seeds that hung from the bract-covered cones. All three nuthatches nest on the North Rim; pygmy and white-breasted utilize cavities on ponderosa pines, and red-breasts prefer the denser spruce-fir associations.

Suddenly, a brown creeper, an even smaller bird, landed on the base of a Douglas fir less than a dozen feet (3.6 m) from me and began to move upward over the furrowed bark. Its brown back, with fine whitish spots, and buff rump were most obvious. Its behavior of creeping over the bark, with its fairly long tail pressed firmly against the trunk, was distinct. Then it called soft, high-pitched "see see" notes. I watched it continue up the trunk to the upper foliage, from where it suddenly flew to the base of another Douglas fir. It began its ascent again, foraging for insects over the furrowed bark.

Small flocks of red crossbills and pine siskins, and a lone Clark's nutcracker passed overhead as I continued along the trail. The ever-present **common ravens** soared along the edge of the high cliffs, with occasional "caugh" calls. And as the day progressed their communications expanded to a surprisingly varied repertoire of calls: "augh, augh, augh," "gruut," and a grating "r-r-r-r" sound, like it was trying to clear its throat. In spite of their abundance, I couldn't help but admire this large, gregarious species. From below, I could readily see its all-black body, wedge-shaped tail, and large head and bill. On one occasion, I was treated to an amazing display of aerial acrobatics.

A Cooper's hawk had appeared over the rim, soaring toward the south, when it suddenly turned back toward where I was standing enjoying the soaring antics of a pair of ravens. It was as if all three birds, the ravens and hawk, suddenly decided to get acquainted; they literally met in midair, closing to less than 10 feet (3 m) apart. There was a sudden loud "swoosh" as all three birds turn upward. The Cooper's hawk turned back toward the south and soared away, but both ravens rolled two or three times, veered downward for 70 to 100 feet (21-30 m), and then shot straight up again. It all happened in just a second or two.

Brown and colleagues wrote that "[b]y mid-winter, these flocks of ravens around the Canyon may contain over 200 birds each. A communal roost of ravens was found below Grandeur Point on the South Rim during the winter of 1982 and 1983 which contained an amazing 800 ravens."

Aspen stands are scattered along the trail, 100 feet (30 m) or so back from the rim. Most of their summer resident birds had already gone south, but I could well imagine those same groves ringing with songs: downy woodpeckers, western wood-pewees, violet-green swallows, mountain chickadees, red-breasted nuthatches, house wrens, American robins, western bluebirds, warbling vireos, orange-crowned warblers, and black-headed grosbeaks.

The few open areas in the ponderosa pine forest were mostly filled with drying perennials, but some grasses and a few of the late flowers remained. I identified a low-growing lupine, Indian paintbrush, a yellow-centered aster, and a thistle. In one meadow I encountered a mixed flock of chipping sparrows and dark-eyed juncos searching for seeds amid the sparse ground cover. The chippers consisted of many immature birds without their deep red caps, but they all possessed the fine, dark lines that ran from their bills through their eyes onto the back of their heads.

The **dark-eyed juncos** were all gray-headed forms, with reddish backs and black face-patches. I was able to approach to within a dozen feet or so before they took flight. They flew away into the adjacent vegetation with a flick of the white edges of their tail feathers. This little finch is another of the park's full-time residents; it nests in the high spruce-fir communities and moves into lower elevations below the snowline during winter. Juncos actually perform an altitudinal migration; those that remain close to their breeding ground move back and forth along the slopes in accordance with the snowline.

Other common summer residents of the spruce-fir forests of the North Rim include northern flickers, hairy woodpeckers, Steller's jays, Clark's nutcrackers, mountain chickadees, American robins, hermit thrushes, ruby-crowned kinglets, yellow-rumped warblers, western tanagers, and Cassin's finches. Fewer numbers of northern goshawks; Cooper's hawks; blue grouse; band-tailed pigeons; flammulated, northern pygmy-, and northern saw-whet owls; red-naped sapsuckers; olive-sided flycatchers; golden-crowned kinglets; and pine siskins also occur in this environment. In places where this habitat occurs on steep slopes, such as on northern slopes below the high rims, sharp-shinned hawks and Townsend's solitaires are also present.

In summer, the song of the **hermit thrush**, echoing from the conifer stands, can be one of the most appealing of all the highland birds. Its flutelike song was described by John Terres thusly: it "opens with clear flutelike note, followed by ethereal, bell-like tones, ascending and descending in no fixed order, rising until reach dizzying vocal heights and notes fade away in silvery tinkle." The hermit thrush is often heard but seldom seen, unless one visits the shadowy forest. Even then one must be quiet and patient and wait until it makes the first move. It often stays close to the forest floor, although it will sing its territorial songs from the very tips of the highest conifers. It may suddenly appear at the base of a tall conifer or among its heavy branches and sit like a sentinel until it is convinced you are not a threat. But even in the open, its colors are subtle: all brownish back, white eye ring, reddish rump and tail, and whitish underparts with black spots.

Of all the high-country birds to be found along Widforss Trail, none is as obvious as the **Steller's jay**, a fairly large, royal blue bird with a tall, blackish crest. This full-time resident can be shy and retiring, or it can be loud and obnoxious. Its mood seems to depend upon elements known only to jays. Most of my sightings were of lone birds at a distance flying from the top of one tree to another, usually quick flights with crests depressed. Now and again, I also detected jays scolding, nasal "screeech" or "skreek" calls from the forest. But I knew that they, too, were in tune to the season and busy with their fall harvest. Perhaps their aloofness was part of their seed-caching behavior. See chapter 4 on Mount Revelstoke and Glacier for additional information about this fascinating bird.

Widforss Trail ends at an open, southern bench covered with dense vegetation, most of which is more typical of lower elevations. Pinyons and junipers, cliffrose, Gambel's oak, New Mexico locust, and a few Utah agaves, banana yuccas, and cacti dominate the area. I sat on a sandstone bench admiring the grand view and watching for birds. Mountain chickadees and pygmy nuthatches were busy searching for pinyon nuts below me. A rufous-sided towhee called from the thicket. A lone blue-gray gnatcatcher flew up after a passing insect. An immature white-crowned sparrow, undoubtedly a migrant, responded to my low spishing calls, and came to within a few feet before retreating. My spishing also attracted a Townsend's warbler that landed on an adjacent pinyon before moving down the slope. Then, two violet-green swallows passed overhead, heading south across the canyon. I couldn't help but admire such creatures that can totally ignore such a chasm and continue, unabated, southward.

I was startled by a sudden "screeeee" call from along the rim to my right. A second later a **red-tailed hawk** soared into sight. It was a magnificent adult bird, and from my eye-to-eye perspective, its dark back and broad wings, whitish underparts, and brick-red tail provided outstanding contrast against the blue sky. This bird is by far the most common raptor in the park, residing from the lowest to the highest elevations and nesting in trees or on cliffs. According to Brown and colleagues, "Its nesting cycle is tied closely to the abundance of rainfall, which causes the preferred plant foods of the desert cottontail rabbit to grow in greater abundance. More winter rainfall means more rabbits in the spring. A high density of cottontail rabbits in spring results in higher red-tail nesting density and success rates."

Snow can arrive on the North Rim by October, closing that part of the park. The South Rim remains open all winter and, except during storms, the canyon is usually clear but cold. Some years, birders take a Christmas Bird Count to tally all the species present during one 24-hour period. In 1986, South Rim birders tallied 428 individuals of 27 species. The dozen most numerous species, in descending order of abundance, included common raven, western bluebird, dark-eyed junco, mountain chickadee, pine siskin, lesser goldfinch, ruby-crowned kinglet, black-chinned sparrow, pinyon jay, white-breasted and pygmy nuthatches (tied), and canyon wren.

In summary, the park checklist includes 287 bird species "known for the Grand Canyon region," of which 121 are known to breed. Of those 121 species, only 4 are water birds (snowy egret, mallard, killdeer, and spotted sandpiper), 15 are hawks and owls, and 8 are warblers. Five species are listed for winter only: Canada goose, bufflehead, ruddy duck, rough-legged hawk, and rosy finch.

Birds of Special Interest
Red-tailed hawk. This is the common broad-winged hawk with whitish underparts and a light- to brick-red tail.

Peregrine falcon. Watch for it along the rims or along the inner canyon; it is best identified by its powerful build, pointed wings, slate gray back, and black moustachial stripes (sideburns).

White-throated swift. This is the common black-and-white bird with swept-back wings and a loud descending trill that zooms past the overlooks.

Violet-green swallow. This common swallow occurs throughout the forested areas of the park; it has snow white underparts and cheeks and a violet-green back.

Steller's jay. The park's only all-blue, tall-crested bird, it is most numerous within the ponderosa and spruce-fir forests.

Scrub jay. This is the long-tailed, non-crested jay of the pinyon-juniper woodlands; it is blue above, except for a grayish back, with a whitish throat and grayish underparts.

Common raven. Its all-black plumage, wedge-shaped tail, and heavy head and bill are its most distinguishing features.

Plain titmouse. This is the little, all-grayish bird with a very short crest that is common throughout the park's pinyon-juniper woodlands.

Pygmy nuthatch. One of the park's smallest birds, it possesses a short tail, gray-brown back, darker cap, and white cheeks; it is seldom quiet, calling high, rapid piping notes.

Canyon wren. This is the bird of the canyons that sings a series of descending and decelerating "tew" notes; it is cinnamon above and has a snow white throat.

Western bluebird. Males possess bright blue hoods and backs, chestnut breasts and flanks, and white bellies.

Hermit thrush. This is a forest bird that is seldom seen, but its wonderful, clear, flutelike songs are commonplace along the forested rims.

Yellow-rumped warbler. It is best identified by five yellow spots: its cap, throat, sides, and rump; it nests in the high spruce-fir forests.

Dark-eyed junco. This is another spruce-fir nester but can be found almost anywhere in migration and winter; this little "snow bird" has obvious white edges on its blackish tail.

17

Wupatki, Sunset Crater Volcano, and Walnut Canyon National Monuments, Arizona

The Sinagua peoples lived in this region from about A.D. 600 until the mid-1200s, then departed, leaving behind only echoes of their past. The ruins at Wupatki and the cliff dwellings in Walnut Canyon provide stark evidence of their pre-Columbian settlements. Nature has since reclaimed the old farm plots and woodlands, but the stone walls remain, utilized only by a few of the native creatures for shelter, foraging, or as singing posts.

Rock wrens and canyon wrens, it appeared to me, had first claims on the deserted ruins. Rock wrens sang extended renditions of their trilling songs from each and every one of Wupatki's ruins. And at Walnut Canyon, canyon wren songs resounded from all the secret places below the rim. Their loud, descending and decelerating songs rocked the canyon, dominating the very essence of the prehistoric scene.

One can't visit either site without at least being aware of these two wrens. The rock wren is the plainer of the two, sporting gray-brown upperparts, with fine whitish spots, lighter underparts with buff flanks and tail, and a long, thin bill. It has a rather stocky build and a habit of bobbing up and down with quick jerking motions. When flying from one rocky perch to another, it will often spread its tail, bob up and down, and call sharp "tick-ear" notes from each new place. It will then commence its probing into various cracks, searching for insects among the ancient building stones. And in spring and summer, territorial birds will sing a complete song that John Terres described as "keree keree keree, chair chair chair, deedle deedle deedle, tur tur tur, keree keree trrrrrr."

Rock wren

Rock wren nests are constructed of grasses, other plant parts, and an assortment of other materials. They are located in holes or crevices. Unlike any other wren, the mated pair will actually decorate the nest entrance with small stones and a variety of other materials. Arthur C. Bent reported that "one passageway of a hole in earth to nest was lined with 1,665 items, of which 492 were small granite stones, 769 bones of rabbits, fishes, birds, and nesting materials."

The canyon wren is a handsome bird with a cinnamon back and belly, grayish-brown cap, snow white throat and breast, and an even longer bill. But its most distinguishing chacteristic is its wonderful, silvery song that consists of ten or more clear, "tew" notes, like "TEW TEW TEW TEW tew tew tew tew tew tew," each note slightly lower in pitch than the last. It sometimes ends its descending song with a short "jeet" note. It will often sing its full song time and time again in spring and summer, but by fall and in winter it will sing only occasionally during early mornings. The rest of the time it can be located by a metallic "tschee" call that it may also repeat many times.

Canyon wrens are full-time residents of the Southwest and are fairly well restricted to rocky canyons and outcroppings. They use deserted cliff dwellings for nesting whenever the occasion permits. Their nests are constructed of a twig base with a "cup of moss, spider web, leaves, catkins . . . lined with fine materials," according to Paul Ehrlich and colleagues. Rock wrens, on the other hand, prefer open rocky slopes and outcroppings, and they are summer residents only, migrating to lower, warmer regions to the west and south for the winter months.

The Park Environments

The three disjunct monuments are located along the southwestern corner of the greater Colorado Plateau, at altitudes that range from 4,800 feet (1,463 m) at Wupatki to 8,029 feet (2,447 m) at the summit of 1,000-foot-high (305 m) Sunset Crater. Wupatki is the largest (36,253 acres or 14,671 ha) of the three park units. It was established in 1924. Nearby Sunset Crater (3,040 acres or 1,230 ha), the remains of periodic eruptions during a 200-year period (starting about 1064), was established in 1930. The smallest of the three units is Walnut Canyon (2,249 acres or 910 ha), just south of Sunset Crater; it was established in 1915.

Vegetation zones range from a desertscrub habitat in the lower areas of Wupatki, pinyon-juniper woodlands at mid-elevations, ponderosa pine forests at higher elevations, and small but significant patches of Douglas fir and associated plants on the north-facing slopes of Walnut Canyon.

S. W. Carothers and H. H. Goldberg, in a 1976 *Plateau* article, refer to Wupatki's lowlands as "Great Basin desertscrub habitat," an area dominated by four-wing saltbush, sand sage, snakeweed, Russian thistle, and Mormon tea. This desert-like condition is undoubtedly due to many decades of grazing. Since the monument was fenced and cattle were eliminated in 1989, the lowlands have begun to recover. A greater abundance of grasses and perennials have begun to appear.

The pinyon-juniper woodlands, which dominate the higher areas of Wupatki as well as the rim of Walnut Canyon, include extensive stands of pinyon pine and Utah juniper; moderate numbers of mountain mahogany, fernbush, and cliffrose; and fewer numbers of banana yucca, squawbush, Gambel's oak, and prickly-pear cacti. Ponderosa pines increase with elevation and moisture. They are most abundant at the base of Sunset Crater and along the 3-mile (4.8 km) entrance road to Walnut Canyon.

The interior of Walnut Canyon contains Douglas fir dominated associations on the canyon walls and a riparian environment in the moist canyon bottoms. It was the black walnuts in the canyons that provided the name for this national monument. Other common plants of the canyon include New Mexico locust, boxelder, aspen, hop tree, narrowleaf cottonwood, and Gambel's oak.

One N.P.S. visitor center exists in each unit: at Wupatki Ruin in Wupatki, at the western entrance to Sunset Crater, and on the rim at Walnut Canyon. Each center has an information desk, exhibits, and sales desk; bird field guides are available at all three sites, but a bird checklist is available only for Sunset Crater and Walnut Canyon. Each area offers a number of picnicking sites, but camping is permitted only at the U.S. Forest Service campground adjacent to Sunset Crater. Interpretive activities are limited to self-guided trails, including two at Walnut Canyon that provide the visitor with an excellent understanding of humans' past and present use of the area's native plants and animals.

Additional information on the three monuments can be obtained from the Area Superintendent, Wupatki, Sunset Crater Volcano, and Walnut Canyon National Monuments; 2717 N. Steves Blvd. Suite #3, Flagstaff, AZ 86004; (602) 527-7134.

Bird Life

Sinagua comes from two Spanish words, *sin* and *agua*, meaning "without water," a term given to the early-day inhabitants of this arid land. The presence of water, at least during most of the year, is what made Walnut Canyon so valuable to the Sinagua peoples. Those same values enhance the bird life today. The moist soils and lush vegetation provide excellent birding opportunities. And the three-quarter-mile (1.2 km) Island Trail, which drops 185 feet (56 m) into the canyon and circles a high limestone ridge, provides superb close-up viewing of the canyon environment and its bird life.

In spring and summer, at least 16 bird species can be found with little effort: turkey vultures, with their black plumage, bare red heads, and V-shaped flight patterns; red-tailed hawks, evident by their broad wings and light- to brick-red tails; mourning doves, with their familiar, mournful calls; white-throated swifts, black-and-white speedsters that zip along the cliffs at about 110 miles (177 km) per hour; broad-tailed hummingbirds, best identified by the males' green backs and red throats; the red-shafted northern flickers; and acorn woodpeckers, black-and-white birds with bright red crowns and yellow throats.

Perching birds include the slender ash-throated flycatchers, with their vigorous "ka-brick" or "ka-wheer" calls; violet-green swallows, with their snow white underparts and cheeks, and violet-green backs; the royal blue Steller's jays, with their blackish crests; common ravens, with their all-black plumage, wedge-shaped tails, and large heads and bills; canyon wrens; American robins, with their bright red breasts and cheery songs; western tanagers, with the males' canary yellow and black bodies and red heads; black-headed grosbeaks, with their black heads, cinnamon to yellow underparts, and large bills; rufous-sided towhees, with the males' black hoods, blood-red eyes, and rufous sides; and little lesser goldfinches, with the males' black backs and bright yellow underparts.

Other canyon birds that are less numerous include Cooper's hawks, great horned owls, mountain chickadees, bushtits, solitary vireos, Virginia's and yellow-rumped warblers, and northern orioles.

The **acorn woodpecker** is one of the park's most obvious inhabitants because of its showy appearance and its habit of flying from snag to snag, constantly calling to its associates. Its call is a loud, raucous "ya-cup, ya-cup," often repeated numerous times. Its name comes from its use of acorns as a principal food, for when acorns are ripe this woodpecker will spend the majority of its time gathering those nuts and storing them in holes it has drilled in ponderosa pines or other tall woody structures. There are records of up to 50,000 acorns stuffed into one tree. They will also hoard other nuts, such as walnuts. And during the remainder of the year they will utilize their caches as well as taking large numbers of insects. It, therefore, is not unusual to see acorn woodpeckers flycatching from their high perches, dashing out after passing insects, grabbing them with a snap of their bills, and sailing back to a favorite snag. And all of this activity goes on with little concern about the hundreds of onlookers that might be present along Island Trail.

Another obvious bird of Walnut Canyon, as well as of Sunset Crater's ponderosa pine forest, is the **Steller's jay**. This is the crested jay of the West, very different from the blue jay of the East, although the two species hybridize in Colorado where their ranges overlap. Both can be belligerent and aggressive toward other birds. Steller's jay are fond of bird eggs and nestlings, and will also rob caches of other birds, such as acorns stored by the acorn woodpecker. See chapter 4 on Mount Revelstoke and Glacier about this bird's ability to cache its own food.

The pinyon-juniper woodlands support a different set of breeding birds, although there is some overlap with the canyon species. One of the most abundant of the "pygmy" forest species is the **plain titmouse**. True to its name, it possesses few distinguishing features, being all gray-brown, except for its short crest and black eyes and bill. But what it lacks in color, it more than makes up for in personality. Paul and Elsie Spangle wrote, in their out-of-print booklet *Birds of Walnut Canyon*, that it is "[o]ne of friendliest of the birds, the titmouse will closely examine anyone who will sit still long enough, and its cheery voice will accompany its sharp-eyed examination." Its song is a clear, whistled "witt-y, witt-y, witt-y," and its call notes, common throughout the year, are "see-jert-jert."

The plain titmouse is a cavity nester and one of the few songbirds that retains the same mate year after year. But they rarely live in flocks, staying mainly in pairs or family groups. Watching one or several of these tits searching for insects among the foliage and branches of a pinyon can provide enough amusement to retain one's interest for a considerable time. It is not unusual to see a titmouse "crawling" through the foliage or hanging upside-down from one leg. When one acquires a seed too large to swallow whole, it will hold the seed against a branch or rock with one foot and hammer away at it with powerful strokes of its short, stout bill until the nut is cracked and it can retrieve the meat.

Other typical pinyon-juniper birds include hairy woodpeckers, gray flycatchers, pinyon jays, mountain chickadees, white-breasted nuthatches, western bluebirds, black-throated gray warblers, and western tanagers. Other, less common, birds of this community include the common poorwills, black-chinned hummingbirds, western kingbirds, western wood-pewees, mountain bluebirds, solitary vireos, and hepatic tanagers. See chapter 22 on Colorado National Monument for a discussion of the pinyon-juniper bird life.

The **house finch** can be especially common in the arid lowlands, providing the rock wren company about Wupatki's ruins and rocky outcroppings. It is an active bird in spring, appearing in large flocks, and serenading anyone who will listen to its lively and melodious songs. Both sexes sing, and it is not uncommon to have mated birds singing at the same time, almost as if they were intent on out-singing the other. Males possess red foreheads, eyebrows, and throats; females lack the red color, and, except for heavy streaking on their underparts, which the males also have, are rather plain. But they are able to use a variety of environments for nesting, building nests in cracks or on ledges of the ruins or outcroppings, as well as on various plants, including cholla cacti.

Ponderosa pine birds include some of the same species that occur in the adjacent woodlands. But there are several additional birds that are limited, more or less, to the ponderosa pines, at least during the breeding season. The pygmy nuthatch and Grace's warbler are the best examples. The **pygmy nuthatch** is one of the most abundant and gregarious birds in any community. It constantly communicates with its neighbors and flits from tree to tree and from one feeding site to another. Not only is it one of the region's most active birds, it is one of the smallest. It is a short-tailed bird with a dark cap that contrasts with its white cheeks, bluish-gray back, and whitish to buff underparts. See chapter 27 on Bandelier for more details about this little bird.

Grace's warbler, on the other hand, may be difficult to find because of its more solitary personality and preference for the high ponderosa foliage. But this is a beautiful bird with a bright yellow throat and breast, streaked flanks, grayish back, and darker crown and cheeks with a bold yellow eyeline. It can best be located by the rather distinct song that it sings off and on throughout the day: a rapid, accelerating trill, like that of a chipping sparrow, but sweeter. See chapter 14 on Zion for further information about this warbler.

All of the conifer areas can be extremely busy during the fall when seeds are ripe. The pinyon-juniper, ponderosa, and Douglas fir communities experience a rush of seed-gathering that may attract birds from other habitats and from considerable distances. A late September visit to Walnut Canyon's mixed forest produced a strange assortment of species. Townsend's solitaires called high-pitched "eek" notes from high posts. I could see their slender, all-grayish-brown bodies with buff wing patches and white outer tail feathers in flight. Western bluebirds appeared in flocks of a few to a dozen or more individuals. Their mellow "flew" notes resounded from the forest, and their deep blue, chestnut, and white plumage was a lovely addition to the day.

Pygmy and white-breasted nuthatches were active among the pinyons and ponderosas. I watched one white-breast hammering away at a pinyon nut, holding it with one foot against a squared rock; I wondered if the rock had once been a building block for one of the many Sinagua dwellings. Mountain chickadees made themselves known by their constant "chick-adee-adee-adee" songs. And a bright male rufous-sided towhee called a loud "chreee" from atop a dense squawbush. Steller's jays, northern flickers, and a lone hairy woodpecker also were evident.

Flocks of American robins were present, as well. Many were only passing by, calling to one another while in flight. I located several among a brushy juniper, feeding on the ripe, purplish berries. And there, too, were three evening grosbeaks. I stopped to admire this lovely bird as they picked and ingested the ripe berries. All three were males; their bright yellow bodies and eyeline that crossed their foreheads provided wonderful contrast to their black-and-white wings and black-brown faces.

A flock of eight Brewer's blackbirds passed overhead, migrants no doubt en route to their wintering grounds to the south. A lone red crossbill, calling its harsh double-notes, passed over. The ascending "scree" calls of pine siskins were evident. I located a flock of eight or ten mountain bluebirds passing overhead. And yellow-rumped warblers were present among the ponderosa pine foliage; I watched one individual dash out after a passing insect. Its five yellow spots were evident through binoculars: on its cap, throat, sides, and rump.

Then suddenly a huge flock of American crows appeared from the west, calling out with loud "caws" and strange throaty grunts. There were at least 75 individuals. I watched as they circled and then descended into the pinyon-dominated woodland just behind the visitor center. They, too, had come to harvest the pinyon nuts. During the next half-hour I watched as they gathered nuts from the trees and on the ground. But even these large birds seemed unable to crack the nuts without a few sharp blows of their bills. They used the same technique as the smaller nuthatches, holding the nut against a stone or branch with one foot, and striking it with their bills. I imagine that the flock of crows visiting Walnut Canyon had come from the nearby fields and pastures, and that it was a typical wintering flock, which can number in the hundreds; flocks of up to 200,000 have been reported in the Midwest. And flocks regularly travel 50 miles (80 km) from their roosts to choice feeding sites. It was good evidence of the coming winter.

The best indications of the area's wintertime birds can be derived from the area's Christmas Bird Counts. These counts are taken annually in nearby Flagstaff, Arizona, and can provide a general picture of the monuments' wintering avifauna. The 1990 Flagstaff Christmas Count tallied 1,397 individuals of 51 species. The dozen most numerous birds, in descending order of abundance, included dark-eyed junco, common raven, European starling, house sparrow, white-crowned sparrow, pinyon jay, western meadowlark, Steller's jay, rock dove, American crow, western bluebird, and white-breasted nuthatch.

In summary, the combined checklists include 152 species, of which 45 are known to breed. Of those 45 species, none are water birds, 7 are hawks and owls, and 4 are warblers. Five are listed as winter residents only: Lewis' woodpecker, red-naped and Williamson's sapsuckers, dark-eyed junco, and evening grosbeak.

Birds of Special Interest

Acorn woodpecker. This black-and-white bird, with a red, white, and yellow head, is common at Walnut Canyon.

Steller's jay. This is the all-royal-blue crested jay that occurs throughout the ponderosa pine forests.

Plain titmouse. It is a pinyon-juniper species with all-grayish plumage and a short crest.

Pygmy nuthatch. This is the tiny, short-tailed nuthatch of the ponderosa pines; it has a dark cap and white cheeks.

Canyon wren. This cinnamon bird with all-white throat and breast is most often detected by its wonderful descending song at Walnut Canyon.

Rock wren. It is gray-brown with buff flanks and tail, and it can be common about Wupatki's ruins and on rock outcroppings.

Grace's warbler. This is the little, yellow-throated bird, with a melodic trill, that summers among the ponderosa pine foliage.

House finch. Males possess red breasts, throats, and eyebrows and heavily streaked bellies; they are most numerous in spring and summer at Wupatki.

18

Montezuma Castle National Monument, Arizona

I followed the self-guided trail beyond the visitor center to the "castle," a pre-Columbian cliff dwelling nestled in a shallow cave 100 feet (30 m) high on an imposing limestone bluff. The morning was bright and calm; birdsongs permeated the air. The loudest songs that morning were those of house finches singing from high points along the trail and from various outcroppings on the steep slope. Rock wrens, all-grayish birds with long bills, called "treiill" notes from the rocky slopes. One individual searched for insects along the trail in front of me. I was amused by its jerky motions and stop-and-go behavior. To my left, among the dense shrubbery of catclaw and willows, a Bewick's wren sang a rather complicated song of warbles, whistles, and trills. And further on, among the sycamores, I detected the sweet whistle song of a summer tanager.

Then, less than a dozen feet away, among the low foliage of a hackberry, a harsh "ti-she-she" call greeted me. It first sounded like a loud ruby-crowned kinglet call, but I knew that bird should be far away by now, on its breeding grounds in the spruce-fir forests to the north. It took me several seconds to locate the perpetrator: a trim little bridled titmouse. Through binoculars, I watched it forage among the new foliage, searching each group of leaves in a rather nervous fashion. It seemed extremely shy. I followed it from leaf to leaf as it moved about the foliage. But what a handsome bird it was. Its high crest and black-and-white face pattern, which reminds some folks of a horse-bridle, and thus earned it its name, gave it a special appeal. It possesses white cheeks crossed by a bold black line that runs from its bill through and beyond its eyes, and then turns downward to its all-black throat. Its overall plumage was a buff-gray color, but its back and wings are tinged with green.

Bridled titmouse

A second bird, probably the female, judging from its slightly faded features, suddenly appeared, and I tracked both individuals as they continued foraging. I followed them from eye-level into the high foliage of an adjacent sycamore, and then back down into the lower foliage and along the sycamore trunk. One individual poked into every crack and under every piece of loose bark imaginable, almost to ground level. Their nervous movements made them difficult to follow, but their constant vocalizations, which sounded more like chickadees than titmice, helped me to track their constant movements.

Suddenly, I realized that one of the birds was gathering nesting material, plant down and cobwebs. It soon disappeared into a crevice in a broken sycamore limb about 20 feet (6 m) high with a bill-full of nesting materials. Seconds later it reappeared without its load and immediately proceeded to search for more of the precious material.

Arthur C. Bent, in his *Life Histories of North American Jays, Crows and Titmice*, describes a bridled titmouse nest found in an oak stump: "The small entrance was six feet from the ground, and the cavity was a foot deep, and two and a half inches in diameter. It was lined on the bottom and well up on the sides with a mat composed of cottonwood down, shreds of decayed grasses, some hair from a rabbit, and many fragments of cotton-waste." My little bridled titmouse was right on target.

The Park Environment

Montezuma Castle and Montezuma Well are situated along Beaver Creek, a tributary of the Verde River, in the Verde Valley of north-central Arizona. The "castle" refers to a 20-room, five-story, twelfth century apartment house built by the Sinaguas in a cave on a high limestone bluff, overlooking Beaver Creek. The "well," a large limestone sink containing a small lake, is located 7 miles (11 km) northeast of the castle. The Sinaguas built houses along the walls and on the rim, and ditched water from the runoff to adjacent fields for their crops.

The combined 842 acres (341 ha), established as a national monument in 1906, includes a visitor center, picnic grounds at both units, and interpretive trails to the base of the castle and to the well and outlet, the starting point of the irrigation system. The park's visitor center, located at the entrance to the castle trail, has an information desk, exhibits, and sales outlet. Bird guides and an area checklist are available.

Beaver Creek flows south through a semi-desert environment that is dominated by creosote bush, honey mesquite, catclaw acacia, Fremont barberry, four-winged saltbush, winterfat, and broom snakeweed. A few Utah junipers and false paloverde occur on the higher northern slopes. A rather lush riparian habitat exists along the creek that is dominated by Arizona sycamore, Arizona walnut, netleaf hackberry, and willows. Common understory plants include catclaw acacia, velvet ash, Arizona baccharis, four-winged saltbush, and sacred datura.

Additional information can be obtained from the Superintendent, Montezuma Castle National Monument, P.O. Box 219, Camp Verde, AZ 86322; (602) 567-3322.

Bird Life

Bridled titmice, in spite of their diminutive size, are one of the area's most charismatic birds. In early spring, when the new, bright green leaves appear, this little full-time resident can be found everywhere within the riparian zone. But they have considerable competition, for several colorful breeding birds are also present and actively involved with defending territories and courtship.

One of the most abundant of the spring-summer residents, and also one of the most vocal, is the **western kingbird**. It will usually sing from a commanding perch among the high foliage or from the very top of a sycamore tree. Betty Jackson, a long-time resident at the monument, described one individual who "shrieked from the top of his tree, 'I'm the best man here! I'm the best man here!' Suddenly from three other trees came the answer, 'The hell you are! The hell you are!'" She continued, recalling that "they all flew up and met in the air a little way from the challenger's tree, and fought it out, violently and vociferously." Kingbirds can truly dominate the area. But they also can be confusing because two species—western and Cassin's—nest within the monument, and both possess gray chests and yellow bellies. Principal differences exist in their songs and plumage. Kevin Zimmer, in *The Western Bird Watcher*, points out that "[t]he Cassin's has a sharp 'chi-queer,' while the Western gives a 'whit' or series of the same, often strung together in an excited chatter." The western kingbird's gray chest "fades gradually" into its yellowish belly, and its black tail contains white outer feathers; it prefers the broadleaf vegetation along the creek. The Cassin's kingbird, on the other hand, is a darker bird that shows distinct color patterns, including a white throat, and its black tail has a whitish tip; it generally prefers the adjacent juniper slopes.

The **summer tanager** also nests within the riparian vegetation along Beaver Creek, although it usually is less conspicuous than the western kingbird. The male summer tanager, however, is difficult to ignore when it does come close enough to be seen. And during courtship it will often dash about the lower foliage in pursuit of its mate. Males are all-rosy-red birds with a blackish wash on their wings and large, pale bills. Females are dull yellow versions of the males. This 7-inch (18 cm) bird sings a song that sounds at first very much like a robin's song, but it is more hurried and includes a slight trill. During the breeding season it will sing all through the day, but it rarely sings after nesting. Then it can be located by its rather dry "kit-it-up" call notes.

Other riparian nesters to be expected include yellow-billed cuckoos, with their long, barred tails, reddish flight pattern, and "kuk-kuk-kuk" calls; Gila woodpeckers, with their black-and-white barred backs and rolling "churr" calls; little yellow warblers, with their all-yellow plumage, except for the male's chestnut chest-stripes; the larger yellow-breasted chats, with their variety of grunts, squeaks, chortles, and whistles; hooded orioles, with the male's orange-yellow head and coal black face and throat; and northern (Bullock's) orioles, larger than hooded, and with the male's black cap, back, and wings, and orange cheeks and underparts.

The thicket areas along the creekbed support an additional assortment of birds, although considerable overlap occurs throughout the flood plain. There can be found phainopeplas, all-dark birds with a tall crest and blood-red eyes, and the tiny Bell's vireos, which sing songs that ask and answer questions, such as "Wee cha

chu we chachui chee? Wee cha chu we chachui chew!" The equally
tiny Lucy's warblers can be common, as well, and identified by their
all-gray plumage, except for the male's rusty crown patch and
rump. There, too, are the bright red northern cardinals; blue grosbeaks, with the male's deep blue plumage, chestnut wing bars, black
face, and stout bill; lazuli buntings, with the male's bright turquoise
head, bluish back, cinnamon breast, and white belly; and Abert's
towhees.

The rather plain, brown **Abert's towhee** is surprisingly abundant along Beaver Creek, although it is more often heard than seen.
Like the very similar canyon towhee, which occurs on the drier
slopes above the riparian zone, it is a skulker that runs along the
ground and seldom exposes itself. Towhees are gregarious in their
behavior, however, and greet one another with loud and expressive
"peep, peep, peep" calls, especially when welcoming a mate. Males
sing a series of rapid notes, like "chip, chip, chee-chee-chee."
Ornithologist Allan Phillips, in *The Birds of Arizona*, described the
two species thusly: "Abert's towhee is a more cinnamon brown than
the canyon towhee; it lacks the chest spot, but shows a light-colored
bill framed in black feathers of the front part of the face."

I found this normally shy towhee to be extremely curious; I was
able to coax it into the open and to approach quite near by making
a series of squeaks with the back of my hand. One flew directly
toward me from a thicket, landing on a fallen log about 35 feet (11
m) away, but it stayed there only a second or two before flying to
the ground. Then it ran from one patch of grass to another with
jerky motions. However, I kept it close by with additional squeaks,
although it never did fully expose itself again.

Another bird of the riparian area, as well as the adjacent slopes,
is the **Gambel's quail.** This is the park's only quail, easily identified
by the male's black, teardrop-shaped plume, face, and belly, and
chestnut cap and sides. But like the towhees, it is more often heard
than seen. The Gambel's quail song, however, is well known, even if
the listener has never before seen this bird; it is the common birdsong of Western movies. Its typical song is an emphatic, four-note
"chi-CA-go-go," and its call notes are "wa-kuh," common among
conversing birds in a covey. John Terres wrote that "members of

covey utter low chuckles or grunt like young pigs—quoit, oit, woet."

The Gambel's quail is a true bird of the American Southwest, with a range that extends from southeastern California to southwestern Texas, north to the southwestern corner of Utah, and south into Sonora, Mexico. Paul Ehrlich and colleagues claim that it is the "most arid-adapted of quail"; they also point out that in summer it forages primarily early and late in the day, with "long quiet periods" in the middle of the day.

Beaver Creek has a history of high water after heavy summer storms, but shallow pools and a quiet flow are more typical. Two little flycatchers frequent the creekbed, the black phoebe and vermilion flycatcher. The **black phoebe** is a permanent resident that usually can be found flycatching off rocks in the creekbed. Its all-black body and contrasting white belly make identification easy. It usually can be located by its rather distinct song, a high-pitched "pi-tsee, pi-tsee." I located one especially active bird one day in October, and watched as it flew back and forth just inches over one area of the creek, snapping its bill time and again as it grabbed up flying insects. Black phoebes build nests of tiny mud pellets placed low on cliffs and rocky banks near the water.

In summer, the little vermilion flycatcher should be watched for, as it is one of the park's most beautiful creatures. Vermilion flycatcher males possess vermilion underparts and heads that contrast with their dark-brown backs, wings, and tails. In the sunlight, their vermilion plumage can appear velvety. Females are drab by comparison but have their own subtle beauty of light pink, white, and tan.

Beaver Creek also provides good hunting grounds for swifts and swallows. White-throated swifts and northern rough-winged and cliff swallows nest along the cliffs and banks, and violet-green and barn swallows either nest nearby or are late migrants. The swifts are easily identified by their swept-back wings, cigar shape, and black-and-white plumage; they also call loud twittering notes almost constantly. The rough-wing and cliff swallows nest on the bluff near the castle, and often are highly visible in their comings and goings. Rough-wings are rather drab, with brown upperparts and gray-brown underparts. They build twig nests in crevices along the bluff.

Cliff swallows are strongly patterned with dark chestnut and blackish throats, whitish foreheads, buff rumps, and light underparts. This is the bird that builds upside-down, gourd-like mud-pellet nests along the huge bluff in April and May. Like their black phoebe neighbors, they gather mud from the creek and paste hundreds of these tiny, round mud pellets together in shaping their nests. Henry Collins wrote, in a little out-of-print booklet, *Birds of Montezuma and Tuzigoot,* "Soon after nesting cares are over these swallows start their southward migration, often as early as July or August. One day they are here; the next they are gone—off on a flight that will take them as far as Brazil or Argentina—until the revolving seasons bring them back once more as heralds of another spring."

A number of other interesting birds are occasionally found within the riparian zone. Great blue herons come here to fish from a rookery on nearby Clear Creek, according to Babs Monroe, a park interpreter. Turkey vultures, identified by their all-dark plumage, bare red heads, and wings held in a shallow V-shape, are fairly common. Common ravens, with their broad, pointed wings, wedge-shaped tails, and heavy heads and bills, can be common among the heavy vegetation or soaring overhead. Common black-hawks, with their very broad wings and short, black-and-white banded tails, are less numerous. And smaller, reddish-backed American kestrels occur year-round but can be especially common in spring and summer.

Two larger raptors are also common, the great horned owl and red-tailed hawk. Babs Monroe told me that great horned owls occasionally nest on the walls of Montezuma Well, but they are most evident by their loud, hoarse calls, like "who who who-who." The red-tailed hawk, a broad-winged bird with a dull- to brick-red tail, can be especially obvious in early spring when courting; red-tails can put on quite a show. A pair will spend considerable time in flight, chasing one another and diving, spiraling, circling, and screaming loud "kreee-e-e-e" calls, like escaping steam. The smaller male will often dive at its mate from a considerable height, "whereupon she may turn over in the air and present her claws to his in mock combat," according to John Terres. He will also feed his lady during courtship, presenting her with a recently caught mouse or other prey species.

A red-tail's diet is extremely varied, one of the reasons that this bird is so common throughout its range from Alaska to Central America and the West Indies. Ehrlich and colleagues report that rodents make up as much as 85 percent of their diet, but it also is known to capture and eat cottontails, weasels, skunks, porcupines, a wide variety of birds, rattlesnakes, turtles, lizards, frogs, carp and catfish, numerous insects, spiders, and earthworms.

The Montezuma Well lake and wetlands contain a very different bird life. Although this habitat is small, and supports only a few resident species, it is visited by an amazing diversity of other birds at various times of the year. Resident species one is likely to find include pied-billed grebes, mallards, Virginia rails, soras, common gallinules, American coots, and common yellowthroats.

The adjacent desertscape, such as the area along the entrance roads to both park units, support a few additional nesting birds: greater roadrunners of cartoon fame; common poorwills, which are most vocal during the evenings and at dusk; little ladder-backed woodpeckers, with black-and-white barred backs; ash-throated fly-catchers, with their grayish throats, yellowish bellies, and reddish tails; tiny verdins, with yellow faces and rapid, high-pitched "chip" notes; northern mockingbirds, able to mimic other birdsongs; crissal thrashers, with their long bills and rufous crissums (under-tail coverts); loggerhead shrikes, with their large heads and black-and-white plumage; little black-throated sparrows, with coal black throats and tinkling songs; and in grassy areas, western mead-owlarks, evident by their yellow-and-black breasts and wonderful songs.

Wintertime welcomes many more northern species that come south and join flocks composed of full-time residents. Christmas Bird Counts provide one of the best indicators of these winter pop-ulations. The annual Camp Verde Christmas Counts include a por-tion of the monument. In 1990, counters tallied 13,729 individuals of 103 species. The dozen most numerous species, in descending order of abundance, included white-crowned sparrow, red-winged blackbird, European starling, dark-eyed junco, chipping sparrow, common raven, Cassin's finch, American robin, western mead-owlark, yellow-rumped warbler, house sparrow, and Brewer's black-bird.

In summary, the bird checklist, that includes Montezuma Castle, as well as Tuzigoot National Monument and adjacent Tavasci Marsh and Peck's Lake, includes 211 species. Of those 211 species, 40 are listed as permanent and an additional 37 species are summer residents and probably nest; 5 of the 77 summer residents are water birds, 5 are hawks and owls, and 5 are warblers.

Birds of Special Interest

Red-tailed hawk. This is the large, broad-winged hawk with a dull-to brick-red tail; it oftens soars over the well and creek.

Gambel's quail. The park's only quail, male's sport black teardrop plumes, faces, throats, and bellies, and chestnut sides.

Western kingbird. It is most often seen among the sycamores where it is noisy in spring; it has gray head, yellowish belly, and black tail with white outer edges.

Black phoebe. This little flycatcher hunts along the creek; it is identified by its coal black plumage and white belly.

Cliff swallow. This square-tailed swallow, with a chestnut throat and buff rump, builds mud-pellet nests on the bluff near the castle.

Bridled titmouse. One of the park's smallest and most charismatic species, it sports a tall crest and black-and-white head pattern.

Abert's towhee. This is the plump, dull-brown bird along the creek that has a black face and calls loud "peep" notes.

19

Tonto National Monument, Arizona

One can only imagine how the pre-Columbian Salado people, who occupied Tonto's cliff dwellings from about A.D. 1300 to 1450, perceived their natural environment. In order to survive in the arid landscape, they undoubtedly took advantage of every possible resource, plants and animals. But I couldn't help but wonder if those early inhabitants also had enjoyed the scenic splendor of their canyon, wondered at the soaring vultures and hawks, or been in awe of the myriad of birdsongs rising from the slope below.

I gazed down that same slope one early spring morning, tracing the ½-mile (.8 km) trail that zigzagged up the steep 350-foot (107 m) ascent from the visitor center, and identified the numerous birds around me. The most obvious were the large turkey vultures that soared along the slope and over the cliffs. Their all-dark plumage, bare red heads, long wings held in a shallow V-shape, and the slight rocking of their bodies were clearly evident. The other large black birds, although somewhat smaller than the vultures, were the common ravens, with their coal black plumage, wedge-shaped tails, and large heads and bills. One pair of these noisy creatures had constructed a stick nest in a crevice above the cliff dwelling. From the constant attention given the site, I could only assume that it contained nestlings. It wouldn't be long before these gregarious birds would be showing off their youngsters. The parents' teaching them about finding food, harassing their neighbors, and the secrets of aerial acrobatics would provide considerable amusement to the human visitors along the trail.

Two smaller groups of birds were diving and soaring along the cliffs, sometimes in wild plunges from high overhead, past hikers, and into the valley below. The fastest of the two were white-throated swifts, identified by their swept-back wings and black-and-white bodies. These speedsters have been clocked at more than 100 miles (160 km) an hour in a dive; I could feel air movement when they passed nearby. The other small birds of the cliffs were cliff swallows, easily separated from the swifts by their flat glides and normal wingbeats, white bellies, dark wings, blackish throats, buff to cinnamon collars and rumps, and square tails.

Both of these birds nest along Tonto's cliffs, but they utilize very different methods. Cliff swallows build mud nests with tubular entrances, constructed of hundreds of tiny mud pellets glued together with the bird's saliva, and placed high on the cliffs. These colonial nesters can number in the hundreds, and their feeding activities help control flies and other flying insects, which they consume by the millions. Swifts, on the other hand, build their nests of feathers, also glued together with their saliva but placed inside crevices on the high cliffs. While each swallow compartment is limited to one pair and their nestlings, a dozen or more swifts may utilize a single crevice.

Tonto's swallows and swifts are summer residents only. The swift is one of the earliest birds to return in the spring, a sure sign of the new season. They winter to the south, from the southern border of the United States (see chapter 21 on Chiricahua and chapter 31 on Big Bend) to Central America, utilizing crevices in cliffs like those at Tonto. Cliff swallows travel all the way to South America for the winter. They are true Neotropical migrants, and one of Tonto's best connections to the tropics. The health of their South American habitats is just as important to the cliff swallows' long-term survival as are those environments in which they spend their summers.

The Park Environment

Tonto National Monument encompasses 1,120 acres (453 ha) of rugged canyonlands just above Roosevelt Lake in the Sierra Ancha Mountains of south-central Arizona. The monument was established in 1907 to protect the remains of Salado cliff dwellings, built in natural caves. The Lower Ruin consists of 16 ground floor rooms, 3 of which had a second story, and a 12-room annex; the Upper Ruin contains 32 ground floor rooms; 8 had a second story. The cave dwellings are situated on southeastern-facing slopes approximately 700 and 1,100 feet (213-335 m) above Salt River (or Roosevelt Lake). Park elevations range from 2,300 feet in the north to 3,900 feet (701-1,189 m) in the southwest corner.

The area lies within the upper edge of the Sonoran Desert, where tall, stately saguaro cacti dominate the slopes and ridges. Other common plants include catclaw acacia, honey mesquite, palo verde, jojoba, and ocotillo. Less numerous are the century plant, four-winged saltbush, sotol, tomatillo, broom snakeweed, and a variety of cacti. Tonto Creek supports a riparian zone where Arizona sycamore, Arizona walnut, net-leaf hackberry, and mesquite are most numerous.

The park visitor center lies at the end of a 1-mile (1.6 km) entrance road off Highway 88. There can be found an information desk, exhibits, a 12-minute slide program, and a sales outlet; bird field guides are available, and a checklist is available for the asking. Interpretive activities include the self-guided Lower Ruin Trail, and guided tours to the Upper Ruin in fall, winter, and spring, on a reservation-only basis. There is a small picnic area along the entrance road, but there is no camping inside the park.

Additional information can be obtained from the Superintendent, Tonto National Monument, HC 02, Box 4602, Roosevelt, AZ 85545; (602) 467-2241.

Bird Life

Songbirds were active along the slope, chasing one another about the abundant shrubs or singing from the top of saguaros or other high posts. The rolling songs of **cactus wrens** were most obvious, like a deep, throaty "chuh, chuh, chuh, chuh," with a number of variations. Their football-sized, grass nests were abundantly evident along the slope, built on chollas and spiny shrubs. These birds keep even their old nests in repair, raising new families in the newer one and using the older nests for roosting sites. One especially vocal cactus wren was perched at the very top of a tall saguaro to the right of the cave dwelling. I could clearly see its rust-brown cap, bold white eyebrow, streaked back, and whitish underparts with black spots. See chapter 29 on White Sands for additional details about this large wren.

The smaller, red-breasted bird, perched on another saguaro, just down the slope, was a male **house finch**. Its song was far more melodious than the cactus wren, and it seemed to continue indefinitely. It was a long series of scrambled phrases, like "swing, swing, swing, sweem, sweem, te swee," sung over and over again. Its mate, all brownish with a heavily streaked breast and belly, was perched on a nearby catclaw, also singing the same song. I couldn't help wonder if they were purposely dueting, like so many tropical wrens. They suddenly took flight, passing overhead toward the top of the cliff; they were calling sweet "cheet" notes as they passed.

A **Gila woodpecker** suddenly appeared out of a hole in a saguaro further down the slope, flying up to one of the massive arms, and called out a loud "churr" note. I focused my binoculars on this medium-sized bird and could see it was a female, without the male's bright red cap, but with fawn-colored underparts and a black back, heavily barred with white lines. In flight, its bright-white wing patches were most evident. The smaller ladder-backed woodpecker, another resident of the park and greater Southwest, also possesses a black-and-white back, as well as a black-and-white head. But the Gila woodpecker is restricted to the saguaro cactus forest of Arizona and adjacent Mexico. It and the saguaros reach the northeastern edge of their ranges near Tonto. This woodpecker bores nest holes in saguaros that provide nest sites for a large number of other cavity-nesters. See chapter 20 on Saguaro for further details about this unique species.

One of these cavity-nesters is the tiny **elf owl**, the world's smallest owl at less than 2 ounces (57 g). It is fairly common at Tonto, in spite of being rarely seen because of its nocturnal habits. Elf owls have a loud voice, "which consists of chucklings and yips like a puppy dog," according to Allan Phillips and colleagues, who wrote in *The Birds of Arizona* that "most of their calling is done at dusk from the entrance to the hole, and again at dawn, following the Cassin's kingbird chorus. Also they call incessantly during moonlit nights in spring, after which they are hard to detect."

Elf owl

Most elf owl sightings are limited to flashlight observations of their heads at the entrance of a nest-hole high in a saguaro. Their dark bills, whitish eyebrows, and bright yellow eyes give them a truly ferocious appearance. Indeed, they are a deadly predator that takes a wide variety of creatures, including insects caught on the wing or on the ground, such as moths, grasshoppers, and crickets, as well as scorpions, lizards, and snakes.

Several loud "ka-brick" calls of **ash-throated flycatchers** resounded around me, but it took several minutes to locate one of these rather plain, slender birds, perched on a palo verde down the slope. Through binoculars, its grayish throat and breast, yellowish belly, and brownish cap and rufous tail were obvious. It suddenly shot almost straight up for 20 feet (6 m) or so, grabbed a passing insect with a snap of its bill, and returned to the same perch with a quick flip of its tail. Insects and spiders make up about 92 percent of its diet, with fleshy fruits accounting for the remainder, according to Arthur C. Bent.

Other birds were present that morning. I spotted a red-tailed hawk, with its brick-red tail; white-winged doves were calling "who cooks for who, who cooks for you-all;" mourning doves were singing low, mournful songs; the equally sorrowful song of a Say's phoebe came from below the visitor center area, where I later found it nesting under the roof edge; rock wrens, all-grayish birds with their jerky motions, were calling loud trills; a curve-billed thrasher produced its loud snapping calls from the little wash to the right; the mellow whistles of a Scott's oriole floated across the canyon; and a pair of canyon towhees greeted one another with loud screeching calls.

I located the **canyon towhees** on a rock outcropping 100 feet (30 m) below me. I watched them through binoculars as they went about their strange behavior, which I attributed to courtship: one individual, I assumed the male, was standing before the other with its wings drooped and quivering all over, like a leaf in a breeze. Both birds called loud and continuous "pink" notes. Their rufous caps glowed in the morning light, contrasting with the rest of their rather drab, all-brown bodies, except for their cinnamon-colored crissums. This bird nests on the ground or on low shrubs amid grasses, where they utilize "mouse-runs" through the grass for escape routes. The male suddenly put its head back and sang a song that sounded like "chili-chili-chili-chili."

The canyon towhee was once lumped with the California towhee under the generic name of "brown towhee" until it was split into two species by the American Orithologists' Union. Its range extends from eastern Arizona to the Texas Big Bend Country, north only to southeastern Colorado.

Two additional birds were encountered on my walk back to the visitor center that morning, Gambel's quail and black-throated sparrow. I had detected distant calls of **Gambel's quail** from the ruins, but their four-note "chi-CA-go-go" calls, the sounds of Western movies, were most common near the canyon bottom. Then I discovered a lone male perched on a catclaw at the far corner of the visitor center parking lot. It was standing erect with its all-black plume and face, rufous cap, grayish chest and nape, and rusty wing patch highlighted by the bright sunlight. We watched each other for several minutes before it flew to the ground, where I could hear low clucking calls, probably from its mate.

Black-throated sparrows were common in the lower canyon, and even more numerous near the picnic area later in the day. This lovely little sparrow is one of the park's common full-time residents, distinguised by its coal black throat and face, bold white eyebrows and a slash between the throat and cheeks, grayish underparts, and gray-brown wings and tail. During the spring months, when birds are most active, its tinkling bell-like songs are abundant throughout the desert. It also seems to be one of the area's most curious birds, responding almost immediately to low spishing notes.

Greater roadrunners also occur in the park but are more common below the canyon in the open desert, according to Dessamae Lorrain, one of the park's interpreters. She told me that this long-legged bird, made famous by its cartoon character, is one of the park's most asked-about birds.

A few other desert species are more likely to be found in the lower canyon: little common ground-doves, with their ascending "wah-up" calls; lesser nighthawks, flying during the evenings and at dusk;

northern mockingbirds, with their aptitude for mimicking other bird-songs; and blunt-headed, black-and-white loggerhead shrikes.

Tonto Creek's riparian habitat supports a very different assortment of birds, although there is some overlap with the adjacent desert environment. Many of the desert birds visit the creekbed for water, and many of the riparian species sing from high points or search for food in the adjacent desert. Common riparian species include the little black-chinned hummingbirds; western wood-pewees, which sing descending "pe-eer" songs; tiny Bell's vireos, with their distinct question and answer songs, described by Phillips and colleagues as, "Wee cha chu we chachui chee? Wee cha chu we chachui chew!"; equally tiny Lucy's warblers, with their all-grayish bodies, except for rufous rumps and nondescript crown patches; rosy-red summer tanager males, with their yellowish bills; all-red, crested northern cardinals; and the dark-backed lesser goldfinches, with their canary yellow underparts.

Other birds found in the Cave Creek riparian zone and adjacent thickets include western screech-owls with their "bouncing ball" songs; black-tailed gnatcatchers with their distinct scratching calls; the black-and-white, crested bridled titmice; western kingbirds, with their yellow bellies and black tails with white edges on their outer feathers; white-bellied black phoebes, which frequent the creekbed; Bewick's wrens, with their long tails and white eyebrows; crissal thrashers, a long-tailed bird named for its rufous crissum; the pert phainopepla; the large-billed, black-headed grosbeak; and hooded and northern orioles, both with orange-yellow and black markings.

Phainopeplas are fascinating birds for several reasons. They are North America's only representative of the silky-flycatcher family. They have two breeding seasons; April and May breeders apparently move northward and nest again in June and July. And they are one of the handsomest of birds. Both sexes possess a tall, somewhat shaggy crest and slightly fanned tails. The males are coal black, except for blood red eyes and snow white wing patches visible in flight. Females are duller versions of the charismatic males.

The scattering of junipers and pinyons that occurs along the cooler north-facing slopes supports a few additional birds, including Cassin's kingbirds, scrub jays, mountain chickadees, plain titmice, western bluebirds, black-throated gray warblers, and western tanagers.

In winter, surprisingly large populations of birds occur within Tonto's riparian habitats. Most numerous are blue-gray gnatcatchers; tiny ruby-crowned kinglets, with their constant movement, white eye rings, and bright red (partially hidden) crown patches; nondescript, long-tailed house wrens; secretive hermit thrushes; tiny, reddish-capped chipping sparrows; larger lark sparrows, with their boldly marked chestnut- and white-striped heads; Lincoln's sparrows of the thickets, which possess buff chest bands; white-crowned sparrows, with the adults' distinctly marked black-and-white head stripes; and bright yellow-and-black American goldfinches.

Other less common wintering birds include sharp-shinned hawks, northern harriers, American kestrels, red-naped sapsuckers, mountain bluebirds, yellow-rumped warblers, song sparrows, dark-eyed juncos, and Lawrence's goldfinches.

In summary, the monument's bird checklist includes 143 species, of which 89 are listed as permanent or summer residents, and assumed to nest. Of those 89 species, none are water birds, 10 are hawks and owls, and 6 are warblers.

Birds of Special Interest

Turkey vulture. This is the large soaring bird, with bare all-red head, that holds its wings in a shallow V-shaped position and rocks slightly from side to side.

Gambel's quail. The park's only quail, it is easily identified by its plump body, black plume and throat, and loud calls, "chi-CA-go-go."

Greater roadrunner. Watch for this long-legged cuckoo in the desert areas below the canyon.

Elf owl. This tiny, yellow-eyed owl nests in unused woodpecker holes in saguaros; it is active only after dark.

White-throated swift. From early spring through fall, these speedy black-and-white birds are common along the high cliffs.

Gila woodpecker. This is the large woodpecker of the saguaros with a black-and-white barred back and loud "chuuur" calls.

Ash-throated flycatcher. Often detected first by its loud "ka-brick" calls, it is a slender bird with a grayish throat, yellowish belly, and reddish tail.

Common raven. It can be common over the cliffs or visiting the picnic area and parking lots; it is all-black with a wedge-shaped tail and large head and bill.

Cactus wren. This is the large wren that builds grass nests on the chollas and sings loud, hoarse "chuh chuh chuh chuh" songs.

Black-throated sparrow. It is a true desert bird of the open slopes that sports a coal black throat, two white face stripes, and a whitish belly.

House finch. Males possess bright red throats and foreheads and heavily streaked bellies; it is one of the park's most common and gregarious species.

20

Saguaro National Monument, Arizona

Early mornings in a saguaro forest are one-of-a-kind adventures that everyone, even those only remotely appreciative of nature, should experience. The tall cactus forest produces a certain calming effect that we all need in today's technological world. The dawn chorus of birds starts each morning with a vigor and excitement that makes one keenly aware of the new day. The avian chorus reverberates among the saguaros; it can be difficult to differentiate species amid the din. Only after the initial uproar can one begin to identify individuals.

Cactus wrens, northern mockingbirds, curve-billed thrashers, Gambel's quail, white-winged doves, and house finches are most evident. Cactus wrens, for example, sing a loud, rollicking "chuh chuh chuh" song that truly can overpower most of the other species. In spring, it is not unusual to find several individuals singing their songs from the very top of the saguaros. To me, their voices are synonymous with the bass in a choir. And if the large number of unruly grass nests on chollas and various thorny shrubs are any indication, they also are one of the park's most abundant species. However, cactus wrens build several nests annually, utilizing only one for raising a family and the others as dummy nests or for roosting; they therefore maintain numerous nests throughout the year.

Curve-billed thrashers also nest on chollas and thorny shrubs but build a stick nest well-hidden within the protective spines of their hosts. And curve-bills sing a song with loud, clear caroling, very similar to that of a mockingbird. And their even louder, sharp "whit-wheer" calls, given throughout the year, are enough to overpower any of the other desert sounds. This is a reasonably large bird with a mottled breast, heavy, long and curved bill, and yellow and black eyes.

The addition of northern mockingbird voices to the morning chorus tends to add melody to the cacophony. And these black-and-white songsters are likely to continue singing even after the rest of the choir has retreated to attend to family chores. John Terres reported that northern mockingbirds sing 39 different "species songs and 50 call notes, has imitated cackling of hen, barking of dog, postman's whistle, and even notes of piano." And anyone who has lived in a mockingbird's territory is well aware of their all-night serenades during the breeding season.

Gambel's quail provide a very different perspective to the morning din, as their emphatic "chi-CA-go-go" calls ring out across the terrain. Males, with their black teardrop-shaped plumes, faces, throats, and bellies, and chestnut sides and caps, often perch on taller shrubs to sing their territorial songs.

Other singers in the dawn chorus are the white-winged doves, usually perched at the top of saguaros so that they can be adequately heard. Their part in the chorus, although somewhat redundant, is a drawled but loud cooing rendition of "who cooks for you? who cooks for you all?" Every now and then these large doves will make swift courtship flights, wide circles on stiff wings, before settling on the same or an adjacent saguaro, where they resume their part in the chorus.

Every choir must have its lead singer, and the saguaro chorus leader is none other than the house finch, the smallest of the group but one of the most melodious. Their part consists of a joyous and warbling melody with many variations. Males possess bright red breasts, throats, and bold eye lines, and heavily striped bellies. Their spirited songs ring out even above the cactus wrens, thrashers, quail, and white-wings.

The Park Environment
Saguaro National Monument is comprised of 87,114 acres (35,255 ha) of desert valley, foothill, and mountain terrain, within two separate units, approximately 30 miles (48 km) apart. The eastern

Rincon Mountain section, of which 57,930 acres (23,444 ha) were designated wilderness in 1976, ranges in elevations from 2,700 feet (823 m) near the visitor center to 8,666 feet (2,641 m) at the summit of Mica Mountain in the Rincons. The much smaller western Tucson Mountains section, adjacent to the Tucson Mountain County Park and Arizona-Sonoran Desert Museum, is situated between 2,200 and 4,687 feet (671-1,429 m) elevation. Both units offer a visitor center that has an information desk, exhibits, orientation programs, and sales outlet; bird field guides and a checklist are available.

Interpretive activities vary by unit and season; they include naturalist-guided walks and self-guided trails and drives, as well as environmental education programs for school children. Activity schedules are posted at each center. The park also contains over 200 miles (321 km) of backcountry trails.

The Rincon Mountain unit of the monument was established in 1933, and the Tuscon Mountain unit was established much later, in 1961, to protect a healthy stand of saguaros. Although there has been considerable concern and research on the long-term decline of the Rincon Mountain saguaros, many of the theories about their decline could not be proven. Chief Park Interpreter Tom Danton explained that the National Park Service believes that the saguaro decline relates to two key factors. First, cattle were common within the Rincon Mountain unit until 1978, when they were finally excluded. These nonnative creatures stepped on immature plants indiscriminately, and they fed on most of the nursery shrubs that were essential for shading young saguaros. On the other hand, cattle had been excluded in the western unit since about the turn of the century. Second, the Rincon Mountain unit is subject to lower winter temperatures, and the severe freeze of 1938 affected many plants; it often takes several years before bacterial necrosis (epidermal browning) appears and the entire plant slowly succumbs. Since 1978, nursery plants in the Rincon Mountain unit have begun to recover and it appears that the saguaros are staging a slow but steady increase.

The park's vegetation zones vary from desertscrub habitats in the lowlands, from the base of the mountains to about 5,200 feet

(1,585 m) elevation; desert grasslands from 4,000 to 5,000 feet (1,219-1,524 m); pine-oak-juniper woodlands and forest in the Rincon Mountains from 4,400 to 8,600 feet (1,341-2,621 m); and a mixed conifer forest on northern slopes and in canyons from 7,000 to 8,000 feet (2,134-2,438 m) elevation. Riparian areas occur at all elevations.

The mixed conifer forest is dominated by Douglas fir with fewer numbers of ponderosa and southwestern white pines, Gambel's oak, New Mexico locust, and white fir. The pine-oak forest contains many of the same species as well as Chihuahua pine, numerous oaks, alligator juniper, and Arizona madrone. The slightly lower pine-oak-juniper woodlands, often forming a chaparral environment, are dominated by various oaks, manzanitas, Wright silktassel, Schotts yucca, and sacahuista.

Desert grasslands are dominated by a variety of grasses with widely scattered trees and shrubs; most common are velvet mesquite, ocotillo, Mexican blue oak, junipers, sotol, sacahuista, agaves, and Torrey vauquelinia. And below this zone is the desertscrub that is dominated by saguaro, ironwood, palo verde, catclaw acacia, velvet mesquite, and ocotillo. Common understory plants include creosote bush, desert broom, graythorn, and numerous chollas, pricklypears, and smaller cacti.

Additional information can be obtained from the Superintendent, Saguaro National Monument, 3693 So. Old Spanish Trail, Tucson, AZ 85730-5699; (602) 296-8576.

Bird Life

Few birds of the saguaro forest are as important as the Gila and ladder-backed woodpeckers and northern (gilded) flicker. These three species excavate cavities within the saguaros that are utilized by an amazing variety of wildlife. The most numerous of the three excavators is the **Gila woodpecker**, a middle-sized woodpecker whose total range is analogous to saguaros and the larger cardons, a tree-cactus south of the border. It is next to impossible to drive or walk among the saguaros without seeing and hearing this bird. Gila woodpeckers are easily identified by their black-and-white barred backs, rumps, and central tail feathers. Their underparts and heads

Gila woodpecker

are gray-tan, except for the yellowish wash on their bellies, and the male's red caps. In flight they show small but bright white wing patches. And their call is loud "chuur" notes.

The larger **"gilded" flicker** has been lumped with the western "red-shafted" and eastern "yellow-shafted" flickers under the single title of northern flicker. And like the Gila woodpecker, this bird's range also coincides with that of the large tree-cacti. It can readily be identified as a flicker with yellow-shafted wings, a bold, black chest marking over whitish underparts that are spotted with black, brown barred back, and a distinct white rump.

The much smaller **ladder-backed woodpecker** has a much broader range from central Texas to southeastern California and south into Central America. True to its name, this 7-inch (18 cm) woodpecker sports a black-and-white barred back and tail, spotted sides, and black-and-white face pattern that is not unlike that of the bridled titmouse. Males possess a bright red crown.

Nature has effectively provided a three-species construction crew to build apartment complexes for three distinctly different-sized groups of wildlife. The builders use the cavity for only one year, pecking out a new one annually. The construction, however, is normally done in summer or fall, after the nesting season. This allows the cactus to form a callus over the soft tissue inside the cavity by the following season. Saguaro cavity-nesters, therefore, rarely utilize nest-lining.

Saguaro cavities, which are used for both nesting and roosting, have the additional feature of being cool in summer and warm in winter, varying from outside temperatures by as much as 10 to 15 degrees. They also have the advantage of holding relative humidity that is 5 to 10 percent higher than the outside air. Ruth Kirk points out, in an excellent *Audubon* article titled "Life on a Tall Cactus," that "[t]his significantly lessens the drain on birds' body moisture and is a particular advantage for nestlings."

At least 20 species of birds are known to utilize saguaro cavities for nesting. Besides the three woodpeckers, they include the American kestrel; western screech-, ferruginous pygmy-, and elf owls; ash-throated and brown-crested flycatchers; western kingbird; purple martin; violet-green swallow; cactus and Bewick's wrens;

Bendire's thrasher; western bluebird; European starling; Lucy's warbler; house finch; and house sparrow.

The largest of these is the **American kestrel**, a small falcon with a reddish back and tail, blue-gray pointed wings, and with double black stripes on its face. It flies with fast wingbeats and also hovers in the air while searching for prey. Allan Phillips and colleagues point out that this is Arizona's commonest hawk, and that "principally they feed on grasshoppers and other insects." And John Terres mentions an early study on desert wildlife that documented the kestrel's tolerance to great heat and the ability to get all of its moisture from a carnivorous diet, freeing it from the need for drinking water.

The smallest of the cavity-nesters is the 4-inch (10 cm), tiny even by warbler standards, **Lucy's warbler**. It is pale gray above and whitish below, with the male's red-brown rump and partially concealed cap. But in spite of its rather dull appearance, it is fiesty and aggressively defends its breeding territory. It is one of the earliest non-wintering warblers to appear in the spring. Throughout its nesting cycle, it will sing all day through. Its song is a lively melody that has been described as "wee-tee wee-tee wee-tee wee-tee che." No other warbler is known to nest in the desert. By late summer this mite is en route south to its wintering ground in western Mexico.

There also are a few birds that nest on the saguaros but do not use cavities: Harris hawks, with their dark plumage, chestnut wing patches, and white tails with a broad black band; the common red-tailed hawks, which also nest on cliffs; white-winged doves, with their large white wing patches, most obvious in flight; mourning doves, which sing sorrowful songs throughout the day; great horned owls, which often build huge stick nests among the saguaro's protective arms; and the all-black common ravens, with their wedge-shaped tails and large heads and bills.

All the other desertscrub birds nest on shrubs, cacti, or on the ground. Most common are the greater roadrunners, lesser nighthawks, common poorwills, black-chinned and Costa's hummingbirds, verdins, northern mockingbirds, curve-billed thrashers, black-tailed gnatcatchers, phainopeplas, Bell's vireos, northern cardinals, pyrrhuloxias, canyon towhees, black-throated sparrows, hooded orioles, house finches, and lesser goldfinches.

The tiny **verdin** is one of the busiest and noisiest of the desert birds. They usually can be located by their almost constant "chip" notes. Verdins are dull gray birds with an all-yellow face and chestnut shoulder patches. They build softball-sized nests of interlaced thorny twigs, leaves, and grass, bound together with spider webs, and lined with feathers and soft down from various plants, and placed among the branches of thorny shrubs or desert mistletoe. Ehrlich and colleagues describe these nests as being "well protected and insulated, may last several seasons, giving the appearance of greater nesting density than is actually the case. Early season nests oriented so entrances protected from prevailing winds (to avoid cooling), late season nests oriented to face winds (to facilitate cooling)." A male builds several nests from which its mate selects her favorite in which to raise a brood. The remaining nests are maintained as dummy nests and for roosting.

Phainopepla

The **phainopepla** is most charismatic, a pert and lively bird with a tall crest that has a liking for brush containing mistletoe. Males are real charmers, glossy black with blood-red eyes, and bright white wing patches that are obvious only in flight. Appropriately, phainopepla is Greek for "shining robe." Females are all-grayish. Courting males perform fascinating displays, circlings and zigzagging above their territories, sometimes to 300 feet (91 m) in the air. Nests often are built in mistletoe. But what makes this bird so fascinating is its very different behavior of nesting early in spring and then moving northward to more moist habitats and nesting again. Wintering birds usually occur in small flocks, but individuals maintain separate feeding territories.

Eastern visitors to the Southwest are often surprised to find **northern cardinals** within Saguaro's forest and riparian habitats. Cardinals often visit the watering area behind the Rincon Mountain Visitor Center. But, nonetheless, it is the same species that is so common at home feeders in the East. The all-red male with a black bib is unmistakable. The nondescript female, however, can, at first glance, be mistaken for the similar pyrrhuloxia. This desert bird also is crested, but male and female adults possess yellowish rather than reddish bills. Male pyrrhuloxias have red instead of black faces, gray backs, and red crests, wings, and tails.

The desert grasslands contain about the same bird species as can be found in the desertscrub, with a few additions. Montezuma quail are true grassland birds, identified by their small, rounded appearance and the male's black-and-white, harlequin-like head. Canyon towhees are all-brown, robin-sized birds with a single breast spots, buff throats, and rusty caps and undertail coverts. Rufous-crowned sparrows prefer rocky areas and are distinguished by their rufous crowns, whitish eye rings, black whisker stripes, and clear underparts. Scott's orioles are yellow-and-black birds with lovely, rich songs, and a preference for nesting on yuccas.

The mountain woodlands and forests support a very different assortment of breeding birds. Common pine-oak-juniper birds include common poorwills, nocturnal species that are most evident by their melancholy "poor-will" calls; broad-tailed hummingbirds, with their green backs and the males' red gorgets; colorful acorn woodpeckers, with their red, black, and yellow head patterns; brown-backed Strickland's woodpeckers; Cassin's kingbirds, with their black tails tipped with white; Mexican jays, large, non-crested jays with all-gray underparts; bridled titmice, with their black-and-white heads and tall crests; bushtits, tiny, all-brown-gray birds; white-breasted nuthatches; long-tailed Bewick's wrens, with their bold whitish eyebrows; blue-gray gnatcatchers, mainly black-and-white, with long, loose tails; shy little Hutton's vireos, with their characteristic "sweeeet" songs; red-faced warblers, with their red, black, and white head patterns; painted redstarts, with their black, red, and white plumages; large-billed black-headed grosbeaks; rufous-sided towhees, with the males' black hoods and blood-red eyes; and little lesser goldfinches, with the males' blackish backs and bright yellow underparts.

Of all these birds, the **Mexican jay** is the most obvious during most of the year, although it can be surprisingly quiet and illusive when nesting. At other times, flocks of five to 18 of these loud and aggressive birds can be expected. They are extremely curious and will investigate any unusual noise or incident. They may approach stealthily without a sound, but when discovered they will fly off with a great clamoring. These jays are all-blue above, except for their black bills and dark eye patches, and all-gray underneath. See chapter 21 on Chiricahua for more information about this Mexican species.

The Rincon Mountains' mixed conifer forest contains a few additional species, although many of the woodland birds can also be found there. Additional species include band-tailed pigeons, whiskered screech-owls, northern pygmy-owls, whip-poor-wills, hairy woodpeckers, greater pewees, western wood-pewees, cordilleran flycatchers, violet-green swallows, Steller's jays, mountain chickadees, red-breasted nuthatches, house wrens, hermit thrushes, American robins, solitary and warbling vireos, yellow-rumped and olive warblers, western tanagers, and yellow-eyed juncos.

The majority of the highland birds either migrate south for the winter months or move down-slope as soon as their food supply declines. A number of additional northern species arrive in late fall or early winter and stay until spring. National Park Service biologists Roy Johnson and Lois Haight surveyed lowland areas in the monument during December and January 1990-1991, and recorded 27 species at five sites. The dozen most numerous species, in descending order of abundance, included Brewer's sparrow; white-crowned sparrow; verdin; black-throated sparrow; Gambel's quail, chipping and vesper sparrows (tied); mourning dove; ruby-crowned kinglet; Gila woodpecker and cactus wren (tied); and Bewick's wren.

In summary, the monument checklist includes 187 species, of which 123 are listed as either permanent or summer residents (and assumed to nest). Of those, none are water birds, 16 are hawks and owls, and 8 are warblers. Twenty-two species are listed for winter only: black vulture; northern harrier; ferruginous hawk; killdeer; long-eared owl; Anna's hummingbird; red-naped and Williamson's sapsuckers; sage thrasher; Brewer's, vesper, sage, fox, song, Lincoln's, white-throated, and white-crowned sparrows; dark-eyed junco; red-winged and Brewer's blackbirds; Cassin's finch; and Lawrence's goldfinch. Most of these are undoubtedly also transients.

Birds of Special Interest

American kestrel. This little falcon can occur anywhere in the park; it possesses a reddish back, blue-gray wings, and two black stripes on its white face.

Gambel's quail. Watch for it in the lowlands; males have a tall, teardrop-shaped plume, black face and throat, and chestnut cap and sides.

White-winged dove. Common in spring and summer about the saguaros, this large dove has bold white patches on its wings.

Gila woodpecker. This, the park's most common woodpecker, is identified by its black-and-white barred back and tan-gray underparts.

"Gilded" flicker. This cactus woodpecker has yellow-shafted wings, barred back, black chest stripe, and spotted underparts.

Mexican jay. It normally occurs only in the Rincon Mountains; it is non-crested, all-blue above, and grayish below.

Verdin. This is the tiny desert bird with a yellow face, chestnut shoulder patches, and loud "chip" call.

Cactus wren. Its loud, harsh "chuh chuh chuh chuh" calls, constant activity, and large size help identify this very common desert wren.

Curve-billed thrasher. This is the large, dull-gray-brown bird with a mottled breast, long, curved bill, and distinct "whit-wheet" calls.

Phainopepla. Males are glossy black with a tall crest and blood-red eyes; females are dull versions of the males.

Lucy's warbler. This is a tiny all-gray bird of the sagauro forest and riparian zones; males possess a rusty rump and concealed cap.

Northern cardinal. Males are all-red with a black bib; females are duller versions.

21

Chiricahua National Monument, Arizona

Chiricahua's dominant bird is undoubtedly the Mexican jay. One can't spend any amount of time within the park without getting acquainted with this charismatic creature. It usually is a bold and aggressive bird that will approach a camper or hiker with great curiosity. But at other times, especially during the nesting season, it can be shy and elusive. It usually occurs in active and noisy flocks of five to 18 individuals, moving through the forest with little heed for human beings. At other times it can approach with great stealth, silently closing in on a point of interest. But when discovered, it and its companions may suddenly erupt out of the trees with great clamoring and verbosity.

One morning in fall, after many of the summer resident birds had already departed for warmer climates, and ripe acorns hung from the oaks, I visited Chiricahua's Faraway Ranch. Harvest-time was in full swing. The cacophony of Mexican jays, acorn woodpeckers, northern flickers, white-breasted nuthatches, and bridled titmice was audible from as far away as the parking area. And as I approached the ranch buildings I realized that the majority of birds were centered around the tall oak trees. The drum of acorns falling on the tin roofs added to the uproar.

Mexican jays were everywhere. Two to three dozen individuals had laid claim to the oak trees and seemed intent on harvesting the entire crop for themselves. They were actively searching the foliage for viable acorns, going about their investigations in a seemingly haphazard fashion, jumping from limb to limb and knocking more acorns loose than they gathered. Those were the acorns that drummed the tin roofs. Standing beneath the trees I watched one

Mexican jay

individual collect an acorn and hammer it with its large, heavy bill until it was able to retrieve the rich meat. Other jays found acorns below the oaks, either on the bare ground or among the weedy surroundings. Perhaps their roughshod movement among the foliage was intentional.

At one point in my observations I noticed that many of the Faraway jays were youngsters, evident by their yellowish bills rather than the solid black bills of adults. Nor were the young birds as brightly colored as their parents. In sunlight, the adults' deep blue upperparts contrasted with their all-gray underparts, and their blackish ear coverts were also readily apparent. But all the jays that morning seemed intent on the acorn harvest. I was reminded of Herbert Brandt's writings about this bird's relationship to oaks in *Arizona and Its Bird Life*:

> The jay is so closely confined to the live oak belt that it may be considered obligated to that strangly dominant tree. The latter furnishes the wily bird with acorns for a major food, twigs for the foundation of the nest, rootlets to line the cradle, . . . a form fork offers a proper site in which to anchor the nest. When the jaylet first opens its eyes it sees only the features and foliage of the live oak; yet evidently it is so well satisfied with its sturdy birth tree that it never leaves those evergreen mansions, but lives its whole obligate life bound to a natural economy of acorns.

The Park Environment

Arizona's Chiricahua National Monument is analogous to Big Bend National Park in Texas in that both areas represent northern extensions of Mexico's mountain provinces. The affinity for much of Chiricahua's flora and fauna lies below the border within the evergreen Madrean forest and woodland of the Sierra Madre Occidental. Chiricahua's Apache and Chihuahua pines, Apache fox squirrel, and mountain (Yarrow's) spiny lizards are Mexican species that barely enter the United States.

A total of 12,120 acres (4,905 ha) of the Chiricahua Mountains is included within Chiricahua National Monument (established in 1924), and 95 percent of that area is designated wilderness. "Chiricahua" is said to be an Opata Indian term for "mountain of the wild turkeys." Vehicular access is limited to an 8-mile (13 km) scenic drive to Massai Point (6,870 ft or 2,094 m elevation) and trailhead. The park contains 17 miles (27 km) of designated trails, two of which are self-guided: Massai Point and Rhyolite Canyon nature trails. Access to the monument is from the west, via state Highways 186 or 181. The larger portion of the Chiricahua Mountains, including Cave Creek Canyon and Rustler Park, falls under the administration of the Coronado National Forest. Access in these areas is via the Pinery Canyon gravelled road that crosses the mountains between the monument entrance road and Portal, Arizona, and the Turkey Creek and Rucker Lake roads south of the monument.

The park's visitor center is located near the west entrance at the start of the Bonita Canyon Scenic Drive and Rhyolite Canyon Trail. There can be found an information desk, orientation program, exhibits, and a sales outlet; bird field guides and a checklist are available. A park campground is located beyond the visitor center. Picnicking sites are available at Bonita Creek Trail, Faraway Ranch, Massai Point, and Sugarloaf parking area.

The visitor center also is the centerpiece for the area's interpretive program, which includes guided walks, talks, and evening programs, some of which address the park's rich bird life. Programs vary, and a schedule of interpretive activities is available for the asking.

Chiricahua National Monument is comprised primarily (90 percent) of a mixed oak-conifer woodland. Dominant oaks include Arizona white, Emory, silverleaf, and netleaf oaks. Dominant conifers include Arizona cypress, alligator juniper, two-needle pinyon, Chihuahua and ponderosa pines, and Douglas fir. Other common trees and shrubs of this environment include Schotts yucca, Wheeler sotol, bear-grass, Arizona walnut, Arizona sycamore, mountain mahogany, New Mexico locust, poison ivy, skunkbush sumac, birchleaf buckthorn, Arizona madrone, and manzanita. The park's higher and more open slopes often contain chaparral vegetation that is dominated by manzanita, Toumey oak, mountain mahogany, and buckbrush.

The lower, western edge (entrance) of the park contains a riparian habitat that is dominated by Fremont cottonwood, willows, Arizona sycamore, Arizona cypress, pines, netleaf hackberry, and desert willow. The adjacent arid grasslands are dominated by numerous grasses and scattered soaptree yuccas, agaves, white-ball acacia, velvet mesquite, ocotillo, and various cacti.

Additional information can be obtained from the Superintendent, Chiricahua National Monument, Dos Cabezas Route, Box 6500, Willcox, AZ 85643; (602) 824-3560.

Bird Life

The Mexican jay is one of the Mexican species that enter the United States only in a few ranges that connect to Mexico's more massive Sierra Madre Occidental and Oriental. This bird was earlier known as "gray-breasted" jay, but it is now known, appropriately, as "Mexican" jay.

Chiricahua supports several other reasonably common Mexican songbirds, although none are as abundant as the Mexican jay. The other species include the heavily streaked sulphur-bellied flycatchers, with their yellowish underparts and rusty tails; Mexican chickadees, with their coal black caps and bibs and dark gray flanks; active bridled titmice, with their tall crests and black-and-white heads; red-faced warblers, with their red, black, and white heads and white rumps; painted redstarts, with their all-black plumage, except for bright red bellies and snow white wing patches and outer tail feathers; and yellow-eyed juncos, with their rufous backs and wing coverts, black tails with white outer tail feathers, and gray heads with bright yellow eyes offset by black lores. Less common birds of Mexican affinity include whiskered screech-owls, blue-throated and magnificient hummingbirds, Strickland's woodpeckers, greater pewees, dusky-capped flycatchers, and olive warblers. Thick-billed parrots have recently been reintroduced in the Chiricahuas and may become a resident once again.

Of all these tropical birds, none possesses the appeal of the little **red-faced warbler**. Gale Monson described this species, in Griscom and Sprunt's *The Warblers of America*, as "small and quick. . . . It feeds through the outer portion of the coniferous trees, with constant small jerks of the tail. Also like many other warblers, it is adept at flycatching. Close examination will show the bill to be stout at the base, the upper mandible arched like a Titmouse's." Red-faced warblers may return from their wintering grounds in western Mexico to Central America by early April. Soon after, males can be heard singing clear and penetrating whistled notes, like "a tink a tink, tsee, tsee, tsee, tswee, tsweep." By May, paired birds are constructing nests of pine needles, fine bark, and soft plant materials in depressions on the ground, concealed in grasses or sheltered by rocks or logs. And by early September, adults and their fledglings depart for their winter homes. It is a true Neotropical migrant whose existence depends upon the long-term survival of both its breeding and wintering grounds.

The Rhyolite Canyon Trail, including the popular ¼-mile (.4 km) nature trail, provides easy access into the heart of the oak-pine woodlands. One morning in May I followed this trail up-canyon to Echo Canyon. Birdsong, from the full-time residents as well as the summer-only residents, was all around me. Mexican jays were heard now and again, but their general lack of dominance that day suggested that they still were involved with nesting chores. **Acorn woodpeckers**, however, adequately filled in for the usually noisy

Acorn woodpecker

jays. These woodpeckers were, in fact, not only vocally active but easily observed flying here and there and paying little attention to the hiker. Their loud calls, usually described as "ja-cob" or "whack-up," never ceased. I discovered a pair of these gregarious birds on a tall snag just off the trail, and I was able to examine them at my leisure. Acorn woodpeckers are middle-sized woodpeckers with all-black backs, tails, and wings, except in flight, when white wing patches and their snow white rumps are obvious. Their most conspicuous feature is their contrasting black, white, red, and yellow heads, almost clownlike in appearance.

The tall snag, on which these woodpeckers rested when they were not cavorting about or chasing after flying insects, contained several dozen acorns that had been wedged into holes the previous year. Acorn woodpeckers hoard acorns each fall, jamming them into holes drilled for that purpose for use during the remainder of the year. There are records of old trees elsewhere in the West with 50,000 or more storage holes, but none of the various trees located along the Rhyolite Canyon Trail contained more than a few dozen.

The common flycatcher that morning was the **ash-throated flycatcher**, most evident by its occasional "ka-brick" calls. It took me several minutes to locate one of these rather nondescript flycatchers. When I finally did find one it was carrying a bill-full of nesting material into a cavity in an oak snag. Its grayish throat and breast above a yellowish belly and crissum contrasted with its reddish tail and dark wings and head, which was slightly crested.

Bridled titmice were present as well, and although their vocalizations were common, very chickadee-like versions of rapid "chick-a-dee-dee" notes, they were not so easily observed. After several minutes of seeing only pieces of these birds disappearing among the foliage, I made thin squeaking notes with my lips against the back of my hand. Almost instantly one individual approached to within 15 to 20 feet (4.5-6 m), to where I was able to observe it for several minutes, calling it back each time it seemed to lose interest. It truly was a lovely little bird; its bridle-like, black-and-white face pattern, tall, loose crest, and gray-green back were most appealing. In winter, this species leads the bird parties, and anyone searching for birds at that time of year can locate the flock by listening for these active little tits.

My squeaking had also attracted two other avian members of the oak-pine community, the white-breasted nuthatch and black-headed grosbeak. The white-breasted nuthatch was walking straight down the scaly trunk of a sycamore, probing under the loose bark for insects. Its all-white underparts and face, black cap and nape, and grayish back and tail were most obvious. So were the nasal "yank" notes it made every few seconds.

The **black-headed grosbeak** was a beautiful male, probably nesting among the adjacent oaks. It glared at me from among the green sycamore foliage. Its deep cinnamon, almost rose-red, throat, flanks, and chest gleamed in the morning light, contrasting with its coal black cap, face, and tail. It was close enough that, through binoculars, I could see its very large, triangular bill very well. It suddenly gave a loud "pik" call and flew away up the drainage. Its bright yellow underwing coverts were obvious in flight. And a few seconds later I detected its distinct song, a series of rich robinlike whistles. One of the best descriptions of its voice comes from Joseph Grinnell and Robert Storer's writings in Arthur C. Bent's Life History series:

> The black-headed grosbeak possesses a rich voluble song that forces itself upon the attention of everyone in the neighborhood. In fact at the height of the song season this is the noisiest of all the birds. The song resembles in some respect that of a robin, and novices sometimes confuse the two. The grosbeak's song is much fuller and more varied, contains many little trills, and is given in more rapid time. Now and then it bursts forth fortissimo and after several rounds of burbling, winds up with a number of "squeals," the last one attenuated and dying out slowly.

Bent adds a description of the length of one grosbeak's song that began 15 minutes before sunrise, and the bird "sang from the time it began, almost without any intermission, for a period of 3 hours, each rendition of its song being followed by another with scarcely a pause between."

Rufous-sided towhees were also common along the Rhyolite Canyon Trail, preferring the dense thickets along the edge of the drainage. Rufous-sided males are one of the park's most distinguished birds, readily identified by their coal black hoods with contrasting blood-red eyes, black backs with many white spots, whiter underparts, and rufous sides. Territorial males were extremely active along the canyon, singing songs that consisted of two sharp notes followed by a trill, such as "clip-clip-cheeee." Several other towhees were detected by their foraging activities among the leaves. Like their eastern cousins, this towhee scratches backward with both feet, raking aside the litter in its search for insects and seeds underneath. How they are able to remain upright is a complex operation that includes excellent balance and considerable skill. The unique sound of a towhee's foraging activities can be most helpful in locating this thicket-dweller.

Other resident birds found within the oak-pine woodlands during my May hike included broad-tailed hummingbirds, northern flickers, Mexican chickadees, bushtits, canyon wrens (in the rocky drainage), American robins, Hutton's vireos, Grace's warblers, western and hepatic tanagers, brown-headed cowbirds, yellow-eyed juncos, and lesser goldfinches.

Mexican chickadees and yellow-eyed juncos were only present in the higher and deeper canyons where Douglas fir was reasonably common. Mexican chickadees called out their rather distinct husky, buzzing "kabree, kabree, kabree, kabree" notes from the high pines and Douglas fir. Brandt referred to this little chickadee as a "fur bird" because of the great amount of mammal hair utilized in their nests.

Yellow-eyed juncos were present at all elevations, from ground level to the very tip of the taller trees, from where they sang melodic three-part songs, with contrasting pitch and rhythm, described by John Terres as "chi chip chip, wheedle, wheedle, wheedle, che che che che che." I located several individuals foraging over the pine needle-clad ground with a strange gait that Allan Phillips and colleagues described as "a peculiar shuffle, between a hop and a walk." This junco is very different from the wintering dark-eyed juncos that nest in the mountains of central Arizona and northward. Yellow-eyed juncos, earlier known as "Mexican juncos," possess a quiet and calm demeanor, moving over the terrain with leisure, seldom in a hurry. Wintering dark-eyes move in a jerky fashion and always seem to be in a rush.

Lower Bonita Canyon, near Faraway Ranch and below, contains riparian vegetation along the creekbed and desert grasslands on the northern slope and southern flats. Common riparian birds include black-chinned hummingbirds, acorn woodpeckers, northern flickers, western wood-pewees, ash-throated and brown-crested flycatchers, Cassin's kingbirds, violet-green swallows, American robins, black-headed and blue grosbeaks, and hooded and northern (Bullock's) orioles. The most obvious of these birds is the Cassin's kingbird, a dynamic 9-inch (23 cm) bird that is difficult to ignore in spring and summer. Its aggressive and blustery manner, gray and yellow plumage pattern, and loud and ringing "chibew" calls help to identify this hardy flycatcher.

Desert grassland birds are most common along the entrance road. These include American kestrels; Gambel's quail; greater roadrunners; common poorwills; Say's phoebes; crissal thrashers; phainopeplas; loggerhead shrikes; canyon towhees; Cassin's (during wet years), rufous-crowned, black-chinned, and black-throated sparrows; and Scott's orioles. The Scott's oriole can often be found along the entrance road, flying across the valley from yucca to yucca; they are especially common when yuccas and century plants are in flower. Males are gorgeous birds with coal black hoods, backs, wings (with yellow shoulder patches), and tails, and bright yellow underparts and rumps. Females are yellow-olive and heavily streaked with black. Their songs are lovely renditions of rich whistled phrases, somewhat like that of a western meadowlark.

From any viewpoint where the open sky can be seen, one is certain to find **turkey vultures**, with their bare red heads, great wingspan and wings held in a shallow V-pattern, and slight tilting from side to side. These scavengers utilize thermals from the warm lowlands, riding these drafts for hours on end, rarely flapping their wings. They may begin their soaring in the lower canyons and ride thousands of feet upward as the day progresses, to a point where they can no longer be seen with the naked eye. Nesting vultures utilize the abundant rock and dirt ledges of the monument, laying two or three brownish-blotched white eggs directly on the ground; young are fledged and able to fly in 70 to 80 days.

Chiricahua also is within the breeding range of the zone-tailed hawk, a turkey vulture look-alike that often soars with vultures. Zone-tails possess feathered heads and black-and-white banded tails, but they otherwise look very much like turkey vultures. They have the same bi-color wings that are held in a shallow V-pattern in flight, and they fly with a slight tilting from side to side. Their ability to mimic turkey vultures provides them with a good cover-up so that they can prey upon lizards that frequent the high cliffs.

Other soaring birds found in the park include Cooper's hawks, with their short, rounded wings and long tails; red-tailed hawks with light- to brick-red tails; the huge golden eagle, best identified by its size, flat wingspan, and the adult's golden head; prairie falcons, with pale plumage and black wingpits; and the much smaller, black-and-white white-throated swift.

White-throated swifts are most common within the canyons, where they nest in crevices on the cliffs and chase down their insect prey with swift flights. They have cigar-shaped bodies with swept-back wings. They often are detected first by their loud, descending twittering calls high overhead. Swifts should not be confused with the summering violet-green swallows, with their snow white under-parts and violet-green backs.

Chiricahua is far enough south for white-throated swifts, which summer as far north as Alberta, Canada, to spend their winters here. They are able to congregate overnight in large overhangs and crevices on south-facing cliffs, actually hanging together like bees in a hive. They are able to withstand occasional below-freezing temperatures; semi-hibernation allows them to conserve their energy for several days until warmer temperatures prevail and insects are again available. See chapter 22 on Colorado National Monument for additional details about this fascinating bird.

Most of Chiricahua's other birds either go south for the winter months or are able to withstand the cooler temperatures. Although no winter bird surveys have been undertaken within the park, Christmas Bird Counts at Portal, Arizona, provide some perspective on the bird life at that time of year. The 1990 Portal Christmas Count tallied 12,517 individuals of 122 species. The dozen most numerous of those birds, in descending order of abundance, included red-winged blackbird, white-crowned sparrow, dark-eyed junco, Brewer's blackbird, Brewer's sparrow, mourning dove, vesper sparrow, Mexican jay, savannah sparrow, house finch, bushtit, and canyon towhee.

In summary, the park checklist includes 179 species, of which 112 are listed as either permanent or summer residents and, therefore, are assumed to nest. Of those 112 species, none are water birds, 19 are hawks and owls, and 8 are warblers. Twenty-five of the 179 species are listed only as winter visitors: northern harrier; ferruginous hawk; red-naped and Williamson's sapsuckers; red-breasted nuthatch; ruby-crowned kinglet; western and mountain bluebirds; Townsend's solitaire; hermit thrush; American pipit; cedar waxwing; northern cardinal; pyrrhuloxia; green-tailed towhee; chipping, vesper, savannah, grasshopper, song, Lincoln's, and white-crowned sparrows; lark bunting; dark-eyed junco; and pine siskin. Several of these most certainly also occur in migration.

Birds of Special Interest
Turkey vulture. This is the common, long-winged bird that soars with a shallow V-shaped pattern and slight tilting from side to side; it has an all-dark plumage and bare red head.

White-throated swift. Its great speed, black-and-white plumage, swept-back wings, and constant twittering calls help identify this cliff-loving species.

Acorn woodpecker. This gregarious woodpecker frequents snags and is rarely silent; it can be identified by its black, white, red, and yellow head pattern.

Ash-throated flycatcher. It occurs throughout the lower, open woodlands in spring and summer, and sports a grayish throat and chest, yellowish belly, and reddish tail.

Mexican jay. One of the park's most common full-time residents, it is easily identified by its blue upperparts, dark bill and ear coverts, and all-gray underparts.

Red-faced warbler. This beautiful bird with a red, black, and white head pattern, frequents the cooler canyons and uplands in spring and summer.

Black-headed grosbeak. Males possess black heads, wings with white wing bars, and tails with contrasting cinnamon underparts and large, heavy bills.

Rufous-sided towhee. This bird of the thickets sports an all-black head and back, red eyes, white underparts, and chestnut sides.

Yellow-eyed junco. It prefers the cooler canyons and uplands, and is identified by its rufous back, gray head with bright yellow eyes, and black tail with white outer feathers.

SOUTHEASTERN ROCKY MOUNTAINS

Sight is a faculty; seeing an art.

—George Perkins Marsh

22

Colorado National Monument, Colorado

The high-pitched twittering of white-throated swifts echoed from the canyon below. Seconds later a dozen or more black-and-white birds zoomed by me and ascended several hundred more feet before they dived back into the canyon depths. One or two of the swifts passed so close that for a brief moment I could clearly see their cigar-shaped bodies and narrow, swept-back wings. Above me, their all-white breasts gleamed in the sunlight, contrasting against their black bodies. With binoculars I could also see the distinct white patches on their flanks. And then they twisted and dove, almost as if they were completely out of control, all the while emitting a drawn-out twittering, a loud, descending "skee-e-e-e-e" sound. Seconds later they again seemed in full control, flying along the red rock cliffs at a speed that has been estimated at more than 100 miles (160 km) per hour.

What an incredible bird is the white-throated swift. It is too often taken for granted because of its abundance within the southern mountains, but at Colorado National Monument it is impossible to ignore. Swifts occur everywhere along the Rim Rock Drive, from the deep canyons and chasms to several hundred feet overhead. Standing at one of the numerous overlooks anytime during the daylight hours, except in winter, they are impossible to ignore. They may pass by so close that you can feel the air movement created by their swift passage. Daily, they put on an unbelievable show of agility and grace in flight. In spring, their wild flights become part of their courtship. And a careful observer may even see two birds clinging together in copulation as they drop and spin downward several hundred feet, wings out to control their speed. They always

White-throated swift

recover before reaching the ground, and seconds later are zooming
upward again into the bright blue Colorado sky.

White-throated swifts are cliff-nesters, utilizing cracks and
crevices on the high canyon walls where they use their own saliva to

glue feathers together to build a tiny platform of sorts on which they lay their tiny eggs. A colonial species, up to a dozen pairs may utilize the same crevice. After nesting, as many as 200 individuals may roost together in larger crevices.

Swifts are so adapted to flight that their tiny feet serve only as hooks to cling to the rock surface. If a bird were to land on the ground, it would be unable to push itself off the ground to resume flight; its entire survival depends upon its wings. Swifts feed on flying insects that they capture in flight. Although they possess tiny bills, they are able to open their mouths extremely wide to capture prey. This ability, combined with their incredible agility in flight, makes them formidable predators.

They have yet another characteristic that makes them special. Like the closely related hummingbirds (both are members of the order Apodiformes) and common poorwills, swifts are able to become torpid during periods of very cool temperatures. This semi-hibernation allows them to conserve their energy when insects are unavailable. During these times they gather together in a protected crevice and hang together like bees in a hive. But as soon as the day is warm enough and insects are flying again, the swifts are back in the air, providing an aerial show to whomever is present along the Rim Rock Drive.

The Park Environment

Colorado's Rim Rock Drive provides access to one of North America's most picturesque and rugged landscapes. The 23-mile (37 km) park drive winds up the escarpment onto Black Ridge and skirts the high canyon rims, providing breath-taking views into a number of spectacular red-walled canyons. Each possesses intermittent streams that flow northeast into the Grand Valley of the Colorado River. The monument (20,500 acres or 8,296 ha) is but a tiny part of the greater Colorado Plateau, which encompasses 130,000 square miles (50,193 sq km) of the Four Corners region of Colorado, Utah, Arizona, and New Mexico. But Colorado National Monument "is where the plateau begins," according to Rose Houk, the author of a beautifully illustrated booklet, *A Guide to the Rim Rock Drive, Colorado National Monument.*

Ecologically, the monument is dominated by pinyon-juniper woodlands, an environment not necessarily endowed with a high diversity of plant life. The flora is relatively simple, with two-needle pinyon and Utah juniper being most abundant, and yucca, mountain mahogany, rabbitbrush, Mormon tea, big sagebrush, and single-leaf ash being of secondary importance.

In drainages below the rim, where the soils are moist for a good part of the year, are riparian habitats that are dominated by cotton-woods. And in places disturbed by human uses, nonnative Russian olive and tamarisk trees abound.

The park's only visitor center is located along the northern portion of Rim Rock Drive, 4 miles (6.4 km) from the West (Fruita) Entrance and 19 miles (30 km) from the East (Grand Junction) Entrance. There can be found an information desk, exhibits, a short orientation program, and a sales outlet. Bird guides and a checklist are available. Interpretive activities are scheduled throughout the summer months, including evening talks at the campground near the visitor center. Nearby is the self-guided Alcove Nature Trail.

Additional information can be obtained from the Superintendent, Colorado National Monument, Fruita, CO 81521; (303) 858-3617.

Bird Life

Soaring birds are a significant part of the park's natural environment. The deep canyons and high rims provide thermals that are tailor-made for large soaring birds. On almost any summer day, from any one of the numerous overlooks, one is likely to find soaring turkey vultures, red-tailed hawks, golden eagles, American kestrels, and common ravens. Less numerous are Cooper's and sharp-shinned hawks, northern harriers, and prairie and peregrine falcons.

Most common of the soaring birds is the **turkey vulture**, easily recognized by its all-dark plumage, bare, red head, and shallow V-shaped flight pattern (its wings are held at a slight angle), and their manner of tipping from side to side. Turkey vultures provide house-cleaning services to the environment because of their preference for rotting carrion, which they find from the air by both sight and scent. Which sense is more important to them in locating food has not yet been determined, but low-flying turkey vultures definitely use their sense of smell in locating carrion. These vultures nest within the monument, utilizing the bare floors of ledges or overhangs, where they deposit two blotched or unmarked eggs in spring. Both sexes incubate the eggs and feed the young by regurgitation. The youngsters fly when they are 70 to 80 days old and soon become members of the park's aerial circus.

The **golden eagle** is the largest of the park's soaring birds, with a wingspan of up to 90 inches (229 cm); a turkey vulture's wingspan is only about 72 inches (183 cm). Park Ranger Bill Row told me that three pairs of golden eagles reside in the park, and the Fruita Canyon pair is spotted by sharp-eyed visitors on a regular basis. In spite of their large size, soaring eagles can rarely be identified by size alone; it is extremely difficult to determine size at a distance. However, their flat profile in flight, resulting from their wings being held nearly horizontally, is a good first clue to their identity. Pete Dunne and colleagues, in *Hawks in Flight*, point out that, "Viewed as a whole, a golden eagle, with its long, broad, shapely wings, its small head, and its longer tail, greatly resembles an overgrown, dark buteo."

When sitting, the eagle's obvious bulk and heavy bill help in identification. Adults appear all-dark-brown, except for their golden nape and crown, which vary in color "from straw yellow to deep orange-brown," according to Bill Clark, in *A Field Guide to Hawks of North America*. Their head color can appear so much lighter than the rest of their bodies that from some angles they may seem almost white; this has led to their misidentification as bald eagles.

Although golden eagles feed on carrion, most often they hunt and kill their own prey, utilizing jackrabbits, prairie dogs, ground squirrels, and quail. But they also have been known to take deer fawns, skunks, snakes, turtles, and even insects.

But of all the park's soaring birds, peregrine falcons receive the greatest amount of attention because of their endangered status and the fact that the park is the summer home of two nesting pairs. The area between Monument Canyon and Book Cliff View along the Rim Rock Drive is the best place to see these magnificent creatures. A lucky observer may even be fortunate enough to see a peregrine

hunting. This magnificent bird can actually chase down and cap-
ture white-throated swifts in midair. See chapter 16 on Grand
Canyon for additional details about the status of this bird in the
Rocky Mountains.

One spring morning I walked the Liberty Cap Trail, starting from
the Rim Rock Drive trailhead, and followed it for a couple of miles
through the pinyon-juniper woodlands. It had rained the night before
and the normally dry red soil was still wet, even sticky in places. The
crystal clear, sunny morning was full of birdsong. Mourning doves,
solitary vireos, blue-gray gnatcatchers, Bewick's wrens, and scrub jays
were calling near the start of the trail. Almost immediately I discovered a pair of **bushtits** constructing a nest in a pinyon just off the trail.
I watched these tiny, all-grayish birds with brown cheek patches, as
they brought fragments of grasses, leaves, lichens, and moss to their
woven basket-nest, which resembled a hanging gourd. At one point at
least three individuals were actively involved with nest-building.
Bushtit nests are rather unique because of their construction. They
are built with an entrance on one side near the top with a horizontal
passage into the bowl where the eggs are laid. A pair will usually roost
in the nest once the clutch is complete.

Bushtits are highly gregarious and usually occur in large family
groups. Birds from previous clutches, known as "helpers," usually
help build the nests, feed the nestlings, and forage together. After
the nestlings are fledged, it is not unusual to find 30 to 40 birds
flocking together. John Ehrlich and colleagues reported flocks of up
to 70 individuals. They also wrote that, during cold weather,
"[g]roups roost huddled in tight mass, saving energy from reduced
heat loss."

The two-syllabled song of a **gray flycatcher** attracted me away
from the bushtits. The sharp "tu-weet" songs, uttered every few seconds, helped me to zero in on this little gray-brown bird with a faint,
but complete, white eye ring and two indistinct wing bars. It if were
not for its song, however, this little *Empidonax* flycatcher would be
difficult to identify with certainty. On the other hand, a careful
inspection with binoculars will usually reveal two additional features
that help with identification: its lower mandible is bi-colored,
whitish at the base with a black tip; and its tail movement consists of

a slow downward movement first and then an upward jerk back to the original position. All the other *Empidonax* flycatchers jerk their tails upward first and then back to their normal positions.

I found several other birds during my walk through the short-tree woodlands. A hairy woodpecker called a sharp "peek" call some distance ahead of me. A pair of northern flickers, with red-shafted wings, flew across the near horizon. A Say's phoebe sailed out from an adjacent rock outcropping to the top of a pinyon and sang a drawn-out and plaintive "pee-eeee" song. I found a pair of mountain bluebirds perched atop a pinyon in a small sagebrush flat; the female was carrying a large, fat caterpillar, and I wondered if she was already feeding young. A pair of black-throated gray warblers were busy foraging for insects on a brushy pinyon. Every so often the brighter male threw its head back and sang. And a rufous-sided towhee sang a buzzing trill from the edge of the sagebrush flat.

The **black-throated gray warbler** is a trim, black-and-white bird with a wonderful song, a drawling "wee-zy, wee-zy, wee-zy, weezy, weet" or "swee, swee, ker-swee, sick." The last syllable may either ascend or descend. This warbler's range includes all of the pinyon-juniper woodlands of the western mountains and extends into the manzanita thickets in the south and fir forests in the uplands. Its head pattern is rather unique with a black cap, broad, black cheeks bordered by bold white stripes, and a black throat. It also possesses a tiny yellow spot in front of each eye. See chapter 14 on Zion for a discussion of this bird's elusive behavior.

The most accessible of the riparian habitats are located near the two park entrances. These areas possess a different assortment of birds and are well worth a visit. Riparian species that may not be found elsewhere in the monument include the Gambel's quail, black-chinned hummingbirds, western kingbirds, black-billed magpies, northern (Bullock's) orioles, lazuli buntings, house finches, and lesser goldfinches.

The most colorful of these birds is the **lazuli bunting**, a sparrow-sized bird that is easily identified (at least the male is). No other bird possesses a bright turquoise (lazuli-colored) head, bluish back, white belly, and chestnut sides. The female is brownish, darker on the back and with lighter underparts, and a bluish rump. Both sexes are curious and usually can be attracted close-up by spishing. They will chip loudly and can be rather aggressive when nesting. See chapter 10 on Dinosaur for additional details on this bird's behavior and song.

One morning I visited the rather small riparian area at the Fruita Entrance, where I walked along the upper slope, with my back to the sun, and identified the various species encountered. At one point I must have approached too close to the cottonwoods, because suddenly I was attacked by a Cooper's hawk. It sounded only a brief warning, a series of loud "keek, keek, keek" calls, before it zoomed out of the canopy directly toward me, barely missing my head. If I hadn't ducked at the last second I am sure it would have hit my cap. It made several more attacks before I backed away. It then flew to an open perch, approximately 25 feet (8 m) high among the cottonwoods, where it seemed to dare me to approach.

The sitting hawk provided me an excellent view. It was a male with bright reddish bars on its chest, a long, rounded tail with heavy dark bars, a blackish cap, and fierce red eyes. It was a magnificent bird, and seemed more than willing to contest my presence. So, I continued down the little drainage and made a wide circle, coming back to the same location from below where I could scan the cottonwoods for a nest. It took me a considerable time, but I located two nests; one was probably from the previous year, but the other one held a sitting bird that peered at me over the edge. I couldn't find the male again, but I was sure that he was nearby, ready for another attack if I ventured too close to his domain. Instead, I retreated, leaving them in peace, knowing that Cooper's hawks already have been threatened by human development much too often. It is important that parks, such as Colorado National Monument, provide the long-term security required for the continued survival of all raptors, as well as the perpetuation of their essential habitats.

In summary, the park's checklist of birds includes 127 species, of which 44 occur throughout the year; 77 are present in spring and summer and apparently nest. Of those, only one (killdeer) is a water bird, 10 are hawks and owls, and 4 are warblers. Four species are listed only for winter: blue grouse, red-breasted nuthatch, brown creeper, and American tree sparrow.

Birds of Special Interest

Turkey vulture. This is the park's most abundant soaring bird and easily identified by its dark plumage, bare red head, and V-shaped flight pattern; it also tilts slightly from side to side.

Golden eagle. Larger than a turkey vulture, it flies with its wings held horizontally, and its head shows a golden tinge in the right light.

White-throated swift. Dozens of these black-and-white birds can usually be seen at any of the overlooks. Its long, swept-back wings and constant twittering calls help to identify this swiftly flying species.

Gray flycatcher. This is the little, nondescript flycatcher of the pinyon-juniper woodlands. Listen for its distinct "tu-weet" songs and see if you can detect its unique tail movement.

Bushtit. The smallest of the park's birds, it is gray with brownish cheek patches; it usually occurs in flocks of a few to many individuals.

Black-throated gray warbler. A resident of the park's pinyon-juniper woodlands, it is easily identified by its black-and-white plumage and a tiny yellow spot in front of each eye.

Lazuli bunting. Watch for it at brushy areas; males have a turquoise-colored head, bluish back, white belly, and chestnut sides.

23

Black Canyon of the Gunnison National Monument and Curecanti National Recreation Area, Colorado

A male mountain bluebird hovered in midair, like a giant blue butterfly, and then fluttered to the ground. A second later it reappeared with a wasp or bee held tightly in its rather small, black bill. I watched as it flew to the top of a pinyon pine and immediately consumed its catch. The sunlight gleamed from its sky-blue plumage, giving it a majestic countenance. From another angle its back appeared almost turquoise color; its underparts a paler blue. It had no rust color as do the western and eastern bluebirds, its closest relatives. Except for its very black bill, legs, and eyes, it was all blue.

Suddenly, it sang a short but melodic song, almost like that of the eastern bluebird but slightly higher in pitch, a sweet and clear "trually, trually, trually." I couldn't remember ever hearing a song from a mountain bluebird; usually they are silent except for their mellow "terr" calls. It was then that I noticed the female mountain bluebird, a grayer version of the male, sitting just below and to the left. Then both birds took flight, flying over the gray sagebrush to another pinyon. Through my binoculars I watched as they sat side by side, seemingly to enjoy each other and the cool morning as much as I.

By May they will be preparing a nest in some cavity of a tree or post. Most often they utilize old woodpecker nests, which they line with grasses, weeds, feathers, and animal hair. And within four weeks, four to eight youngsters are fledged and being taught the art of flycatching. Although insects make up the bulk of their diet, mountain bluebirds feed on other things as well: earthworms, snails, and berries.

Mountain bluebird

As the season progresses, several family groups may gather together, and by the time cold weather arrives flocks of a few dozen to several hundred individuals can be expected. The high, open flats and pinyon-juniper woodlands of the two parks can then be alive with bluebirds. But during mid-winter they usually move to somewhat lower elevations. And during the most severe winters they may wander far distances into the warmer deserts.

But just as soon as slightly warmer weather arrives, as early as late-February or early March, they reappear as if by magic. And once again the woodlands are filled with the sky blue birds of spring.

The Park Environments

The dual parks stretch approximately 45 miles (72 km) along the Gunnison River, which has been dammed to form three reservoirs, and include one of America's most outstanding canyons. Beginning near Gunnison, Colorado, the river enters the broad expanse of Blue Mesa Lake; surface elevation is 7,519 feet (2,292 m). Below Blue Mesa Dam is the long, narrow Morrow Point Lake (surface elevation is 7,160 feet or 2,183 m), and below Morrow Point Dam is Crystal Lake, situated at 6,755 feet (2,059 m) elevation within Black Canyon. Below Crystal Dam the river flows freely through all the rest of Black Canyon. The latter two sections are restricted by the 1,200- to 2,300-foot (366-700 m) canyon walls. The northwestern section of the canyon was recognized for its scenic beauty and established as Black Canyon of the Gunnison National Monument in 1933.

Today, the combined units encompass a total of 55,786 acres (22,576 ha), possess outstanding scenery and wildlife, and offer a wide variety of recreational and educational opportunities. Park visitor centers are located at Elk Creek; Lake Fork, at Blue Mesa Dam; at Cinnamon, near Morrow Point Dam; and at Gunnison Point, along Black Canyon's South Rim Road. All four centers have information desks, exhibits, and sales outlets, where field guides and a bird checklist can be acquired. National Park Service interpretive activities include evening programs and a variety of ranger-guided walks during the summer season. Schedules are available at the park information stations for the asking.

Curecanti contains numerous campgrounds, scattered along the full length of the reservoirs and canyon rims. Black Canyon of the Gunnison National Monument has only two, one on each rim.

The topographic relief of the two units is as dramatic as any of the national parks in the Rocky Mountains. Geologist Wallace Hansen wrote that "[s]everal western canyons exceed the Black Canyon in overall size. Some are longer, some are deeper, some are narrower, and a few have walls as steep. But no other canyon in North America combines the depth, narrowness, sheerness, and somber countenance."

The area's vegetation exhibits similar diversity, ranging from lush riparian streamsides dominated by cottonwoods and willows, to high, cool, and steep north slopes dominated by Douglas fir and white fir, with scattered patches of aspens. In between are four rather distinct plant communities: broad sage flats where big sagebrush is the most abundant plant species; mountain brush that is predominantly Gambel's oak, serviceberry, squaw current, and mountain mahogany; pinyon-juniper woodlands of two-needle pinyon and Utah juniper; and a few ponderosa pine stands.

Additional information can be obtained from the superintendents of Black Canyon of the Gunnison National Monument, Suite A, 2233 East Main, Montrose, CO 81401; (303) 249-7036; and Curecanti National Recreation Area, 102 Elk Creek, Gunnison, CO 81230; (303) 641-2337.

Bird Life

The canyon birds, those that nest on the inner canyon walls and associated vegetation, are some of the most exciting and interesting of the 226 species that have been reported for the two areas. None is as dynamic as the **peregrine falcon**, a raptor that entirely disappeared from the area for almost three decades, due to eggshell thinning caused by consuming pesticide-contaminated prey. Many of their prey species, such as insect-eating swifts and bats and grain-eating waterfowl, had obtained high pesticide concentrations from DDT-sprayed fields. However, after peregrines were declared endangered and DDT was barred in 1972, wildlife agencies and private organizations mounted a concerted restoration effort, and peregrine populations began to recover. There are now three active aeries within the Gunnison River canyons, and park visitors can once again enjoy this most exciting of all birds of prey.

Peregrines are not the largest of the parks' birds; the golden and bald eagles and great blue herons are considerably larger. But peregrines are the swiftest and most dramatic. Watching a peregrine stoop at more than 200 miles (322 km) per hour, perform aerial acrobatics over the canyon rim, or strike a white-throated swift that might be flying at more than 100 miles (160 km) per hour and catch it in midair before it reaches the ground, can be an experience not soon forgotten.

The two most likely locations for watching this magnificent falcon are Pioneer Point and Dragon Point. Watch for a hawk-sized bird with a slate-colored back (young birds are brownish), whitish underparts, a broad black moustachial stripe on each cheek (like sideburns), and long, pointed wings. In early spring it may be detected by its high-pitched whistles, often produced high above the cliff on which its mate is perched. And when the young are fledged, they may call to one another as the adults teach the youngsters to hunt. Watching a wild peregrine can be the most remarkable wildlife experience of your lifetime.

The much smaller but more numerous birds with swept-back wings and black-and-white underparts are **white-throated swifts**. They can look all the world like flying cigars. And if their wing motion reminds you of a hummingbird, it is because they belong to the same taxonomic order, Apodiformes; both can become torpid during cold weather. Their wild flights often come so close to human beings enjoying the canyon view that a rush of air is felt. Swifts nest in crevices on cliffs and copulate in flight, sometimes tumbling several hundred feet in the air, wings out to slow their descent, before recovering. See chapter 22 on Colorado National Monument for additional details about this fascinating bird.

The other bird commonly seen flying over the cliffs is the violet-green swallow, identified by its violet-green back, white underparts and rump. It, too, nests on cliffs as well as in cavities in conifers and aspens. They usually occur in colonies of 12 to 20 individuals.

The clear, descending whistle-song of the canyons is that of the canyon wren, a little bird with a snow white breast and cinnamon back. The rock wren also lives on the cliffs and rocky outcroppings. Its gray-to-buff plumage and habit of bobbing up and down when alarmed help to identify this little bird.

As the day warms and thermals begin to rise, watch for the soaring birds. Most common are the common ravens, coal black birds with pointed wings, large bills, and wedge-shaped tails. Red-tailed hawks are usually distinguished by their broad wings and relatively short, light- to brick-red tail; immature red-tails may even possess slightly barred tails with only a hint of red. The all-dark birds with bare red heads, which hold their wings at a shallow V-shape and tip slightly from side to side, are turkey vultures. And the larger all-dark bird that flies with its wings straight out, is none other than the golden eagle. The head of adult birds often show a golden tinge, from which their name was derived. Although this magnificent raptor is never common, it is seen from Pioneer Point and Gunnison Point with surprising regularity.

Waterfowl and other water birds are most abundant on Curecanti's lakes during the spring and fall migration. Twenty-one species of ducks, geese, and swans, and 33 species of shorebirds, waders, and other water birds have been reported. However, only a few of those are present during the summer months. The most obvious of these is the **great blue heron**, a huge bird that can be expected almost anywhere along the lakes and riverway. They are most numerous along the Gunnison River above Blue Mesa Lake. According to Superintendent John Chapman, a nesting colony of 50 to 60 birds exists just outside the park.

Great blues are superlative fishermen and possess great patience. They will stand perfectly still along the shore or in shallow water and wait for a fish or other prey species to come within striking range of their lethal bills. Suddenly, so fast their movement is barely visible, they will strike down and come up with a fish, frog, or even a small mammal held (usually) crosswise in their very long, strong bill. Larger fish will be speared. They will then work their prey into position and swallow it whole.

Great blue herons stand almost 4 feet (1.2 m) tall. The blue or gray-blue color is most evident on their backs and wings while in flight. Their heads are black-and-white with a long black plume on breeding adults. They possess long yellow-green legs that are often held in a trailing position while in flight. Their long necks are usually folded in an S-shape when flying, a characteristic that helps to separate this huge bird from the similarly sized sandhill cranes that are spring and fall visitors only. Sandhills fly with their necks stretched out in front.

Only two species of waterfowl can be expected in the parks at all times of the year, the mallard and common merganser. **Mallard** drakes are easily identified by their bright green heads, yellow bills,

narrow white collars, and chestnut breasts. In flight they show a
bright blue speculum bordered with white. Mallard hens, on the
other hand, are mottled with overall brown color, and lack the yellow bill and green head. Only the blue speculum can match the colorful males. Mallards spend most of their spring months along the
river and tributaries, nesting on grassy banks. By June, the mallard
hen may appear at pools with a brood of up to 18 chicks. Mallards
spend most of their free time in shallow, ponded waters where they
feed on stems and leaves of various water plants. They find much of
their food underwater by tipping, placing their heads underwater
with only their tails sticking above the surface.

Common merganser

The **common merganser** is a very different duck with very different habits. Although it is only slightly larger than the mallard,
and the drakes also possess bright green heads, it is a predator that
dives completely underwater and swims down its catch. Mergansers
are able to catch and hold on to slippery fish with their hooked bills
that possess serrated margins. Their bills are usually bright red, and
both sexes possess white breasts. Drakes are quite distinguished
with their black-and-white bodies; hens possess chestnut heads and
grayish bodies.

Mergansers are true opportunists when it comes to nesting. They are known to utilize tree cavities or deserted hawk and owl nests, sometimes 50 feet (15 m) or more high. They also nest on the ground, in earthen banks, or on cliff ledges. John Terres reported that a New Hampshire common merganser attempted to nest in a house chimney but could not get out, and so starved. And Betty Jackson reported nesting in Montezuma Castle cliff dwelling. Clutch sizes range from six to 17 eggs and fledglings are escorted into open water by the hen. There they may join other family groups. It is not unusual to find 20 or more youngsters being tended by one hen while the other hens are elsewhere.

During the summer, between Memorial Day and Labor Day, Black Canyon Boat Tours offers 90-minute trips three times daily on Morrow Point Lake, starting from Pine Creek Trail. This trip provides an opportunity to see the canyon up close, and waterfowl, herons, turkey vultures, hawks, eagles, and falcons can often be seen. National Park Service interpreters provide a narration about the geology, ecology, and wildlife encountered.

One morning in May I walked the Neversink Trail, near Curecanti's east entrance; I recorded 38 bird species in two hours. Most of those birds were actively courting and nest-building. The tall cottonwoods near the trailhead were filled with birdsong. American robins sang their "cheerily, cheer-up, cheerio" songs, and I watched one individual gather billfuls of grass and tiny twigs off the ground and carry those loads into the cottonwoods. A male northern (Bullock's) oriole sang its rich disjointed song from the high foliage. It appeared to be examining some of last year's grass-woven nests. And a pair of black-headed grosbeaks were also feeding together, sampling the numerous cottonwood buds.

The more persistent songs that morning were being delivered by one of the smallest of the songsters, the **yellow warbler**. Their songs emanated from the cottonwoods as well as the fresh willows and shrubs along the river. While walking the mile-long (1.6 km) trail, I found more than two dozen of these bright yellow birds. Each male seemed to be trying to out-sing the next. And several curious individuals approached very close to me when I spished. The male's reddish breast streaks were obvious, and both sexes possessed faint wing bars and piercing black eyes. The yellow warbler's song is a lively, cheerful melody that Peter Vickery, in *The Audubon Society Master Guide to Birding*, described as "3-4 well-spaced tseet-tseet-tseet notes followed by more rapid sitta-sitta-see."

This little yellow-tailed bird has a number of local names, including "wild canary" and "summer warbler." It is the most widely known of all North America's wood warblers, but it is present along the Gunnison River only from early May through September. It then migrates south to Mexico, Central America, and northern South America. It is a true Neotropical migrant whose survival depends upon the health of both its breeding territory in Colorado and its wintering grounds in the tropics.

Suddenly, I detected a soft, fluttering sound ahead of me, similar to the whinny song of a distant eastern screech-owl. Almost instantly I recognized it as the sound of a territorial flight of the **common snipe**. It took me several minutes to locate the bird that was flying high over the river and adjacent pasture, covering several acres in a wide circle. Every 10 to 20 seconds it made a slight dive to gain airspeed, then spread its outer tail feathers so that the rushing air would vibrate the distended feathers and produce a hollow whistling sound. It made seven circles before it settled back into the wetlands, where it undoubtedly was nesting.

Terres explained the snipe's territorial flight as "primarily a sexual display over the home, or nesting, range to warn other males against intruding into established male's territory, but is also directed toward female mate on ground, later toward the nest; it is most frequent when bird is flying at 300-360 ft. [90-119 m] above ground and may be performed by either sex during early part of breeding or occasionally by both at once; sound reverberating over home bog or swamp can carry for half a mile."

Killdeers, European starlings, western meadowlarks, red-winged blackbirds, and Brewer's blackbirds were present in the adjacent pasture. An American kestrel was hovering overhead, waiting for some prey to appear. The cottonwoods at the far end of the pasture contained a red-tailed hawk and a pair of black-billed magpies. A lone great blue heron and a pair of northern rough-winged swallows flew over.

The swift but shallow river had attracted an additional set of birds that day: two dozen or more violet-green swallows flew back and forth in search of insects; two spotted sandpipers were bobbing up and down as they rushed here and there for insects along the shoreline; a pair of mallards were visible at the far bend; further away I detected the honking calls of Canada geese; and then a plump, gray bird appeared in the center of the riverway, bobbing up a moment before diving underwater once again. This was an American dipper, a high mountain bird that feeds on aquatic life by searching the stream bottoms.

The Neversink Trail follows the river, crossing little tributaries, and passing below the bright green cottonwood canopy. Black-capped chickadees sang "chick-a-dee-dee-dee" songs in the high foliage; all the individuals that I observed possessed all-black caps and bibs and white shading over much of their wings. Other birds observed within the cottonwood grove included a lone downy woodpecker and western wood-pewee, red-naped sapsuckers, white-breasted nuthatches, yellow-rumped and Wilson's warblers, and a flock of pine siskins. Several house wrens sang their bubbling songs from among the undergrowth. And two broad-tailed hummingbirds were busy gleaning insects from spider webs. Common yellowthroats and song sparrows were present among the streamside shrubbery.

The park's upland habitats are most readily accessible along the South Rim Drive at Black Canyon. The South Rim Campground is located in the heart of the mountain brush community. An early morning visit there turned up all of the typical birds of that environment. Most abundant were **rufous-sided towhees**, pert songsters with all-black hoods, except for the male's blood-red eyes, tails with white edges, white underparts, and rufous sides. It seemed to me that every serviceberry shrub in the campground possessed a towhee, each singing a buzzing trill or a song that Paul Lehman, in *The Audubon Society Master Guide to Birding*, interpreted as "chup-shup-zeee."

Virginia's and orange-crowned warblers were singing from the various clusters of Gambel's oaks. American robins songs were plentiful. And several green-tailed towhees sang their songs and meowed at me from the dense shrubbery. Other songbirds present included a dusky flycatcher, chipping sparrows, brown-headed cowbirds, and dark-eyed (gray-headed) juncos.

Betty and I drove slowly along the South Rim, watching for whatever might appear. Mountain bluebirds were plentiful along the roadsides. A Cooper's hawk flapped off a perch and soared away as we approached. And then at the edge of the roadway was a **blue grouse**, a chicken-sized bird with mottled brown and sooty-blue plumage. It froze in place; perhaps it thought it had not been discovered. We were able to stop the vehicle, open the side window, and Betty took several minutes of videotape before it finally walked away. Our bird was a male that exhibited none of the elaborate behavior that would occur during courtship.

On their strutting grounds, called leks, males show off their finery and perform unique dances and flights to entice mating. Terres reports that they "strut in short hurried runs before females, with fanned tail flipped forward, head drawn in and back, wings dragging ground like small turkey gobbler; also takes stand on rock, stump, log, or treetop; inflate purplish-red or yellow air sacs to make hooting or groaning sounds sometimes heard 500 ft. away." See chapter 7 on Yellowstone for an additional description of this bird's courtship display.

The Warner Point Nature Trail starts at the end of the South Rim Drive and follows a ridge between a pinyon-juniper-covered south-facing slope and a north-facing slope dominated by Douglas fir. The south-facing slope contained an assortment of pinyon-juniper and Gambel's oak birds: mourning doves, blue-gray gnatcatchers, black-throated gray and Virginia's warblers, western tanagers, chipping sparrows, and rufous-sided towhees. The northern side contained an assortment of conifer species: house wrens, hermit thrushes, Townsend's solitaires, solitary vireos, yellow-rumped warblers, dark-eyed juncos, and pine siskins. Numerous white-throated swifts and violet-green swallows soared overhead.

At Warner Point, I searched the sky and along the canyon walls for peregrines that I knew were present; their aerie was in use, and the female may already have been incubating eggs. The peregrine tercel was probably sitting nearby, guarding the aerie from unwanted visitors. Or he may still have been out hunting and could have returned at any time with food for the incubating female. We waited for an hour or more, but the peregrines were no-shows. But I knew that the Black Canyon of the Gunnison contained the home territories of two pairs of peregrines. What greater value can a park serve?

When peregrines and the other Neotropical migrants go south for the winter months, a different assortment of species occur in the parks. Christmas Bird Counts are taken at five locations along the Gunnison River. Two of those counts, at Curecanti National Recreation Area and Hotchkiss, provide the best perspective on the wintering birds. The 1990 Christmas Counts tallied 988 individuals of 27 species at Curecanti and 3,361 individuals of 70 species at Hotchkiss. The dozen most numerous birds reported on the combined counts, in descending order of abundance, included European starling, mallard, dark-eyed junco, rosy finches, red-winged blackbird, black-billed magpie, Canada goose, house finch, common raven, house sparrow, pinyon jay, and horned lark.

In summary, the combined bird checklists for Black Canyon and Curecanti include 226 species, of which 39 are full-time residents and 70 are known to nest. Of those 70 species, 8 are water birds, 13 are hawks and owls, and 7 are warblers. Eleven species are listed only in winter: common goldeneye, rough-legged hawk, short-eared owl, Bohemian waxwing, northern shrike, rosy finches, common redpoll, American tree sparrow, Harris' sparrow, Lapland longspur, and snow bunting. A few of these may also be migrants.

Birds of Special Interest
Great blue heron. Watch for this large, long-legged wader along the river and reservoirs; it is generally blue with a black-and-white head.

Mallard. The area's most common duck, males possess bright-green heads, white collars, and yellow bills; females are duller.

Common merganser. This is the fish-duck of the reservoirs, identified by the male's green head, red bill and feet, and white underparts; females have cinnamon heads.

Peregrine falcon. It can occur anywhere in the parks but is most common along the high cliffs of the canyons. It is identified by its pointed wings, slate gray back, whitish underparts, and broad black sideburns.

Blue grouse. Chicken-sized, it is mottled brown and sooty blue in summer and is most likely to be found in the conifer forests.

White-throated swift. This black-and-white bird frequents cliffs and is distinguished by its swept-back wings and continuous, twittering calls in flight.

Rufous-sided towhee. Most numerous in brushy areas, it sports an all-black hood, blood-red eyes, white underparts, and rufous sides.

24

Mesa Verde National Park, Colorado

Mesa Verde's pinyon pine seeds were ripe and ready for harvest. The mature, rounded cones had opened to expose the abundant seeds, and resident birds and mammals were taking advantage of the fall crop. The rich pinyon seeds were once harvested by early-day Indians, but now the bounty is left to the wildlife.

Clark's nutcrackers and Steller's and scrub jays were the most obvious gatherers. While the jays retrieved many of their pinyon seeds from the ground, Clark's nutcrackers gathered theirs directly from the open cones. I watched one aggressive nutcracker from about 40 feet (12 m) as it extracted a dozen or more seeds from a single cone, prying them out with its crowbar-like bill. Through binoculars I could actually see the shapes of the seeds inside its special throat pouch, where it was holding the seeds until it could cache them for later use. Their sublingual pouch, located under the tongue, can temporarily store up to 95 seeds. The seeds will later be buried for use during the winter. Clark's nutcrackers are known to "store more than 30,000 pinyon pine seeds during a single season, placing them in caches with 4-to-5 seeds each," according to Paul Ehrlich and colleagues. What's more, they are able to locate up to 1,000 caches of seeds for months afterwards. See chapter 3 on Banff, Jasper, Kootenay, and Yoho for additional information about this fascinating bird.

Jays also cache seeds underground, but their caches are less numerous than nutcrackers, and their ability to carry seeds is limited. Steller's and pinyon jays can carry only a few seeds at a time within their expanded esophagus, and scrub jays normally carry only one seed at a time. Both birds and trees benefit from this arrangement because many of the seeds that are not recovered generate and grow into new pinyons.

Rock squirrels and chipmunks were also taking advantage of the pinyon pine harvest. Both of these mammals had climbed high in the trees to reach the cones. And like the nutcrackers, these squirrels were able to carry several seeds in their pouches at a time. One especially belligerent rock squirrel, sitting at the very top of the pinyon, scolded me with loud "keept" calls when I got too close.

The pervasive use of pinyon seeds can easily be understood when one learns that a single pound of the nuts "provides 2,880 calories, more than the food energy in a pound of chocolate, and nearly as much as in a pound of butter," according to Ronald Lanner. Indians ate pine nuts in "various ways—raw, roasted, or boiled." Lanner wrote, in *The Piñon Pine: A Natural and Cultural History*, that "Navahos mashed their oil-rich *edulis* kernels to a rich tasty butter, like peanut butter, which was spread on hot corncakes. The Northern Paiutes ate whole *monophylla* nuts boiled in water, or they washed them and prepared a soup or mush to be sucked from the fingers."

The fall harvest was not limited to pinyons. Douglas fir cones were also mature, and ripe seeds hung from many of the scaly cones. And as might be expected with these much smaller seeds, they had attracted a number of smaller birds. Red-breasted, pygmy, and white-breasted nuthatches, mountain chickadees, and pine siskins were actively gathering Douglas fir seeds. I watched a pair of red-breasted nuthatches working the cones on one stately Douglas fir. Every few seconds one would fly to an adjacent juniper to store its seeds. Through binoculars I watched them cache their seeds under loose juniper bark. I couldn't help but wonder how often other birds or mammals robbed their caches. But during the 15 minutes or so that I watched them gathering and hiding seeds, they never used the same place twice.

The Park Environment

The very essence of Mesa Verde (Spanish for "green table") is the Anasazi. One can almost feel their presence within the park, from the high mesas and promontories to the narrow canyons. And no wonder! These ancient peoples walked every inch of the area during the almost 1,000 years (from about A.D. 550 to almost 1300) in which they lived there. Archeologists report ruins on the mesa top and canyons at a density of about 100 per square mile.

Congress established Mesa Verde as a national park in 1906, to protect the thousands of fragile and irreplaceable prehistoric Indian sites. The park was enlarged to 52,074 acres (21,074 ha) in 1963; 8,100 acres (3,278 ha) was designated as wilderness in 1976; and in 1978, the park was selected for World Heritage Cultural Site status by UNESCO (United Nations Educational, Scientific and Cultural Organization), because of its world-renowned archeological sites.

Access to Mesa Verde is available off Highway 160, 10 miles (16 km) east of Cortez, Colorado, and park roads extend onto Chapin and Wetherill mesas. The park's visitor center is located at Fair View, and an excellent park museum is located on Chapin Mesa near Spruce Tree House. Both sites have information desks, exhibits, and sales outlets where bird field guides and a checklist are available. A variety of ranger- and self-guided tours of the principle ruins are available during the season. A schedule is available for the asking.

The park contains one campground (open from May to mid-October), located at Morefield Village, along the entrance road, and overnight accommodations (also open from May to mid-October) are available at Fair View. Hiking within the park is limited. Permits are required for the 2.8-mile (4.5 km) Petroglyph Trail, and the 2.1-mile (3.4 km) Spruce Canyon Trail. Three unrestricted trails are available in the Morefield area: 2.3-mile (3.7 km) Point Lookout Trail; 1.5-mile (2.4 km) Knife Edge Trail; and 7.8-mile (12.5 km) Prater Ridge Trail.

The high plateau of Mesa Verde averages about 7,000 feet (2,134 m) in elevation, is approximately 15 miles long and 9 miles wide (24x14 km), tilts toward the south, and contains more than a dozen deep canyons. Park Point (8,572 ft or 2,613 m), at the northern edge of the mesa, is the park's highest point, while the lowest canyon bottom is 6,040 feet (1,841 m) elevation.

Vegetation zones vary with altitude and exposure, from the cooler northern ridges and canyons to the warmer, more open mesa tops. Mountain shrub habitats occur on the highest mesas, such as along the Prater Ridge Trail and at Park Point. Dominant mountain shrub plants include Gambel's oak, serviceberry, Fendlerbush, ante-

lope bitterbrush, and snowberry. Pinyon-juniper woodlands cover
the slightly lower mesa top, although mountain shrub is common
in the cooler side canyons. Principal pinyon-juniper plants include
two-needle pinyon, Utah juniper, mountain mahogany, and antelope bitterbrush. A scattering of ponderosa pines and Douglas fir
also occurs on the mesas; these trees are more abundant along the
northern slopes and side canyons. A few stands of aspens can also
be found in these cooler locations. Open flatlands in the lower
canyons often are dominated by big sagebrush, rubber rabbitbrush,
four-winged saltbush, and greasewood.

Additional information can be obtained from the
Superintendent, Mesa Verde National Park, CO 81330; (303) 529-
4566.

Bird Life

All during my September hike along the Prater Ridge Trail, I walked
in and out of various habitats that, during the nesting season,
would contain rather distinct groups of birds. But in the fall, most
of the area's breeding songbirds had already departed for their wintering grounds. The full-time residents and a few migrants and
wintering birds were utilizing whichever habitat might provide the
greatest abundance of food.

Townsend's solitaires, for instance, were surprisingly common
among the pinyon-juniper stands. Breeding birds prefer the higher
slopes, nesting on the ground under shrubs or clumps of grass. But
in fall and winter they frequent the lower slopes to feed on the abundant juniper and mistletoe berries. Because of the extremely large
numbers of solitaires that day, I imagined that many of them had
recently come from the higher San Juan Range visible to the northeast. And in the early morning they were singing their loud whistles
and rambling squeaks, and calling loud, flutelike "clenk" notes. In
flight, they are trim, grayish birds with double, brown wing bars,
and long tails with white edges. Perched on a treetop, their bold,
white eye rings and rather small black bills were most obvious.

Other birds found in numbers that day included northern (red-
shafted) flickers, hermit thrushes, American robins, solitary vireos,
rufous-sided towhees, chipping sparrows, and dark-eyed (gray-

headed) juncos. There were smaller numbers of turkey vultures; sharp-shinned, Cooper's, and red-tailed hawks; Williamson's sapsuckers; hairy woodpeckers; *Empidonax* flycatchers, including one cordilleran flycatcher; common ravens; white-breasted and pygmy nuthatches; house and rock wrens; blue-gray gnatcatchers; orange-crowned, yellow-rumped, and Wilson's warblers; green-tailed towhees; and evening grosbeaks. And high overhead I detected white-throated swifts and violet-green swallows on a number of occasions.

None of these birds represents Mesa Verde so well as **common ravens**, the large, all-black birds with broad, pointed wings, wedge-shaped tails, and large heads and bills. This is the bird depicted on the park's checklist. There was never a time during my hike that at least one of these vociferous birds could not be detected by their gravely calls or strange creaking noises. Marilyn Colyer, the park's natural resource ranger, told me that "ravens have 48 identified calls—one mimics a turkey very well." Ravens are cliff-nesters, and Mesa Verde offers a host of sites. It is not unusual to find family groups soaring over the canyons or exploring the ruins. And one or two individuals can usually be found in the early mornings patrolling the park roads for road kills from the previous night. In winter, up to 80 ravens flock together and can often be seen flying to a common roost about a half-hour before sunset. Ravens are extremely adaptable birds, able to eat almost anything, from a variety of live creatures, such as birds and their eggs, rodents, snakes, and lizards, to carrion.

As I was returning from my hike, starting down the incline to the campground, a pair of **golden eagles** soared over the northern cliffs just below eye-level. I had a magnificent view of one adult and one immature eagle: their large bodies and flat wings were most obvious, and the adult's golden head and the black-and-white tail of the immature bird were also evident. This magnificent bird nests along the East Rim each year, according to Colyer, and I wondered if these birds were from that aerie. It is the park's largest bird, and a full-time resident. Adults usually mate for life, nesting on remote cliffs very early in the spring. They are most often seen soaring over the high ridges, but they also spend considerable time hunting the sagebrush flats. Their preferred food is jackrabbit.

I had searched the sky all during my hike for peregrine falcons, but without success. Colyer had told me about two active park aeries that had produced young in 1992. Although Mesa Verde's original peregrine population had been totally eliminated by pesticides, along with most of the other Rocky Mountain peregrines, they have been nesting on Mesa Verde's remote cliffs since the mid-1980s.

Morefield Campground is situated in an open valley that is dominated by clumps of Gambel's oaks and open fields with grasses and rabbitbrush. Morefield's Gambel's oaks provide one of the best places in the park to find black-capped chickadees and Virginia's warblers. Black-capped chickadees, at first glance, look very much like their mountain chickadee cousins that prefer the conifers, but a careful examination will reveal an all-black cap and throat, without the white eye line of the mountain chickadee, and a distinct whitish wash over the wings. This bird also has a different song, a distinct "chick-a-dee" or "chick-a-dee-dee-dee." It also has a slurred "chureee" call. Mountain chickadees sing "chick a-dee a-dee a-dee."

Virginia's warblers, perhaps more than any other bird, nest only among Gambel's oak, and so their entire range coincides with that of the Gambel's oaks in the southern Intermountain West. They are most easily located by their rather distinct songs, a long series of musical one- or two-syllable notes on the same pitch that descend slightly at the very end. They are often difficult to find among the thick oak foliage, but low spishing noises will usually attract a territorial bird into view. Then one can see their gray to brownish plumage with yellow throats, undertail coverts, and rumps, and bold, white eye rings. Occasionally one can also see a reddish crown patch, but that is usually concealed.

Another bird I found surprisingly common at Morefield Campground in September was the wild turkey. At least two dozen of these large birds, mostly sub-adults, wandered along the roadway and among the clumps of oaks searching for acorns and other seeds and almost any small creature they might discover. I watched one youngster, carrying a small snake about, being chased by an adult who eventually forced the smaller bird to drop its prey and then immediately grabbed it up and swallowed it. Why the smaller bird itself did not swallow it immediately I'll never know.

Turkeys are native to the Mesa Verde area and were prominent in Anasazi culture. Turkeys were eaten, bones were used for tools, and turkey petroglyphs occur in various places within the canyons. The species was eliminated from the area, probably by disease contracted from domestic poultry, according to Colyer, but the National Park Service and Colorado Department of Fish and Game have recently (1990) reintroduced it to the park. The birds at Morefield Campground are the result.

The park's pinyon-juniper woodlands, most evident on the lower mesas and along the southwest-facing slope above the Morefield Amphitheatre, support a number of typical pinyon-juniper birds in spring and summer: mourning doves, common poorwills, broad-tailed hummingbirds, hairy woodpeckers, ash-throated and gray flycatchers, violet-green swallows, scrub jays, plain titmice, bushtits, white-breasted nuthatches, Bewick's wrens, blue-gray gnatcatchers, solitary vireos, black-throated gray warblers, chipping sparrows, and house finches.

Broad-tailed hummingbirds can be abundant at flowering shrubs and perennials. They often are detected first by the male's distinct trilling whistle in flight. This sound is created by air rushing through slots in the tapered tips of their outer wing feathers. It can be especially evident when the male is courting; he will often make spectacular U-shaped dives over his lady friend. Breeding territories are maintained by the female, but males service several females and do little to help with nest-building, incubation, and feeding of the young. The males are truly promiscuous rakes!

Scrub jays are the non-crested jays with blue bodies, expect for grayish backs and bellies, white throats with grayish streaks, and black bills and lines through the eyes. And like all jays, they can be loud and boisterous. Scott Terrill, in *The Audubon Society Master Guide to Birding*, provides the best description of this bird's songs and calls: "A very harsh, often-repeated ike-ike-ike, with slight upward inflection; long, rough, slightly metallic, sharply rising iennk; rough, rapidly repeated quick-quick-quick; also several usually raucous variations."

Scrub jays usually occur in flocks of a few to a dozen individuals, and they are one of the most curious of birds, investigating almost any unusual noise or activity. They may sneak up on a perpetrator, but they themselves can raise a great ruckus when disturbed. If they discover a predator, such as a coyote, fox, or snake, their loud clamoring can be heard for half a mile and will cease only when the predator moves away. Even then, they may follow it from tree to tree, or with long undulating flights, for a considerable distance.

Pinyon jays can also be common. These gregarious birds usually occur in flocks of 30 to 80 individuals. Most sightings are of extended flocks flying low over the pinyon-juniper woodlands with rapid wingbeats in a rather direct flight. But more often than not, they are detected first by their shrill cawing calls. Adults are all-blue jays, except for whitish streaks on their throats, and noticeably short tails.

Plain titmouse

Another common pinyon-juniper bird is the little, all-gray, slightly crested **plain titmouse**. But what it lacks in appearance, it more than makes up for in personality. Although it is barely five inches (13 cm) in length, it can be ferocious and persistent, scolding any intruders to its territory with harsh "tsick-a-der-der" calls. It also sings a clear "whit-y, whit-y, whit-y" song in spring. I watched a family of these birds among the pinyons along the parking lot at the park museum. Their acrobatic behavior was fascinating as they climbed about the pinyon foliage and cones in search of food. One individual disappeared inside a cavity and emerged with a spider, which it beat against a branch before swallowing it whole. Another individual held a pinyon nut against a branch and beat it with several severe whacks of its bill. It apparently cracked the nut sufficiently to pry out the rich meat, which it swallowed a little at a time.

My favorite pinyon-juniper bird is the little black-and-white **black-throated gray warbler**. Males possess an all-black head, except for two bold white stripes above and below the eyes and a tiny yellow spot in front of each eye. Females are duller birds, without the coal black throats. These are active birds that are usually detected first by their very distinct, but rather quiet, songs: a buzzy "weezy, weezy, weezy, weezy-weet." They seem to sing most adamantly during the warm, dry afternoons. Black-throated grays are typical Neotropical migrants that nest in the United States and spend their winters in warmer climates from southern California and Arizona south to southwestern Mexico. The long-term survival of all the Neotropical migrants depends upon the continued existence of their essential habitats in both the U.S. and in the tropical forests. See chapter 14 on Zion for additional details about this bird's behavior.

Mesa Verde's multitude of ruins are the high point of any visit to this magnificent park. But whether one is walking through Cliff Palace or Badger House Community, or hiking the Spruce Canyon Trail, the surrounding bird life is similar. Many of the species are attracted to the cliffs and nooks and crannies of the ruins. Common ravens, croaking about the ruins or soaring low along the canyon walls, are hard to ignore. And the loud descending and decelerating whistle-songs of **canyon wrens** are also commonplace about the ruins. Although their wonderful songs are most memorable, seeing these little cinnamon-colored birds with snow white breasts and long bills creeping about the ruins adds immeasurably to the Mesa Verde experience.

The high-pitched chattering songs of **white-throated swifts**, as they swoop along the canyon after insects or chase one another in hair-raising dashes, also is commonplace. They are famous for freefalling for a hundred feet or more during copulation. A careful observer can usually locate their nest site, high overhead along a deep crack in the cliff face. There they actually construct feather nests, cemented together with their saliva, in which they deposit their tiny eggs. This swift may never touch the ground, because it spends its entire life in flight or on high cliffs; their tiny, weak feet are not adapted for perching, only for grasping onto the cliffs.

Wintertime birds at Mesa Verde are limited to the full-time residents and a few northern species that have moved south or to lower elevations where there is a greater amount of food. For instance, flocks of 20 to 100 rosy finches can usually be found along south-facing slopes on the North Rim from October through March.

In summary, the park checklist includes 186 species, of which 106 are known or assumed to breed in the park. Of the 106 nesting birds, only 4 are water birds (Canada goose, mallard, killdeer, and spotted sandpiper), 14 are hawks and owls, and 6 are warblers. Eight species have been observed in the park only during the winter: Williamson's sapsucker, horned lark, American crow, western bluebird, cedar waxwing, dark-eyed junco, and pine and evening grosbeaks; a few are undoubtedly also migrants.

Birds of Special Interest
Golden eagle. This large raptor can best be seen soaring over the northern cliffs; adults possess all-dark plumage with a golden color on their head.

Broad-tailed hummingbird. Common in spring and summer, it is best identified by its all-green back and the male's red gorget and high-pitched flight.

White-throated swift. Watch for this black-and-white bird, with swept-back wings, flying along the cliffs; it often has a high-pitched twittering call.

Scrub jay. This non-crested blue jay is one of the park's most common birds; it is most often found in the pinyon-juniper woodlands.

Pinyon jay. It is usually found in large flocks, flying low over the pinyon-juniper woodlands; adults are all-blue with short tails.

Clark's nutcracker. It is especially common in the fall when it is gathering pinyon seeds; it is black-and-white and crow-sized.

Common raven. This all-black bird with pointed wings, wedge-shaped tail, and heavy bill is common throughout the park year-round.

Plain titmouse. Watch for this rather plain, all-gray bird with a short crest among the pinyons and junipers.

Townsend's solitaire. This is the slender, all-gray bird with brown wing bars that can be abundant on the mesas in fall.

Virginia's warbler. It nests in stands of Gambel's oak and is best identified by its grayish plumage, bold white eye ring, and yellowish breast, rump, and undertail coverts.

Black-throated gray warbler. This is the little black-and-gray warbler of the pinyon-juniper woodlands that sings a weak, wheezy song.

25

Great Sand Dunes National Monument, Colorado

The high-pitched "chaeck, chaeck" call of a black-billed magpie erupted from the cottonwood foliage behind me. I turned just as it flew to the adjacent cottonwood, where it landed among the bright green leaves and announced its arrival with another emphatic "chaeck" call. A moment later it hopped to a higher branch in full sunlight, so that its entire black-and-white plumage shined like a bright jewel. Its snow white belly and wing patches contrasted with its all-black back, head, and tail. With binoculars I could see the greenish sheen on its long black tail and the blue gloss on its wings. A remarkably beautiful bird!

A moment later, it again took flight, flapping and soaring up Medano Creek to a larger clump of cottonwoods. In flight, its long, wedge-shaped tail streamed out behind it, more than half the bird's total length, and the white markings on its wings and rump formed an obvious V-shape. "Chaeck," it called again on landing. I wondered if it had a nest among the dense foliage. Magpies build large, bulky stick nests, 2 to 4 feet (61-122 cm) high with an opening on one side. They usually place their nests close to the tree trunks and are known to use the same nest for several years. They may also mate for life. In winter, magpies usually flock with several family groups and may move to lower elevations.

The black-billed magpie is an opportunist that will take advantage of almost any food source encountered. Although Paul Ehrlich and colleagues consider it the "most insectivorous" of any North American Corvid (crow family), John Terres reports that although it "eats insects throughout the year, including flies and their larvae and pupae from carrion," it also "cleans up roadside carcasses of

Black-billed magpie

dead animals; picks and eats ticks from backs of elk, mule deer,
bighorns; eats remains of animals killed by coyotes and other carni-
vores; sometimes pecks flesh at sores or cuts on backs of horses,
cows, sheep; takes some eggs and young of small birds in spring;
also eats mice, snakes, some grain and fruit."

At Great Sand Dunes it is one of the most showy and most common of the park's bird life. It occurs in all the park's habitats from the lower, open flats to the mixed conifers in the surrounding mountains.

The Park Environment

The Great Sand Dunes are situated at the base of a great arc of the Sangre de Cristo Mountains that rise to more than 14,000 feet (4,267 m) elevation and serve as a magnificent backdrop to the national monument. The dunes cover an area of about 24,986 acres (10,112 ha) and are the tallest in North America, reaching a height of almost 700 feet (213 m). The sand was derived from eroded rock materials in the San Juan Mountains, visible far across the valley to the west, and deposited at the foot of the Sangre de Cristo Mountains by prevailing southwest winds. Today, the dunes are considered a dynamically stable system, primarily due to the great amount of moisture within the dunes that prevents extensive movement. Only the drier exterior sands shift with the winds, forming remarkable shapes and patterns.

The upper edge of the dune field encroaches on the adjacent forest in a number of locations, sometimes smothering trees and shrubs. The lower edge of the dunes is fringed by broad, open flats that are dominated by rubber rabbitbrush and a few less numerous low-growing shrubs, succulents, and grasses: trumpet gooseberry, wax current, Apache plume, fringed sage, horsebrush, blue grama, Indian rice grass, yucca, and plains pricklypear cactus. Pinyon-juniper woodlands occur at slightly higher elevations on several gentle slopes. Narrowleaf cottonwoods are common in the lower drainages, and aspen, Rocky Mountain juniper, Douglas fir, and white fir dominate the drainages at slightly higher elevations. The mountain slopes above, like those of Ptarmigan Peak to the east and Herard to the north of the park, are part of the Rio Grande National Forest.

Monument roads are limited to the park extension of Highway 150, which runs only four miles (6.4 km) into the park's southeast corner, ending at the Pinyon Flats Campground and the Medano Pass Primitive Road. The visitor center, Montville trailhead, and a side road to Mosca (picnic area and trails to the dunes) are located just beyond the visitor center. The visitor center has an information desk, exhibits, sales area for books and videos, including bird guides and a park checklist of birds. A 15-minute slide program on the park is also available for viewing on request. Interpretive activities include evening talks and nature walks in summer, and the self-guided Montville Nature Trail. A schedule is posted at the visitor center.

Additional information can be obtained from the Superintendent, Great Sand Dunes National Monument, 11500 Highway 150, Mosca, CO 81146; (719) 378-2312.

Bird Life

Another member of the crow family, common along the entrance road or soaring over the forested slopes, is the **common raven**. It may be alone or in a flock of a dozen or more individuals, oftentimes chasing one another in wild displays of aerial acrobatics. Sometimes they will soar to great heights, utilizing the warm thermals that rise above the dunes or over the high ridges. Other times they take advantage of the same winds that shape the dunes, moving across the open flats with great speed, rarely flapping their wings.

The common raven may be considered the monument's most effective predator. It can be very aggressive, preying on a wide variety of smaller creatures: rodents, reptiles and amphibians, and a variety of invertebrates. And it also feeds on carrion; it has learned to patrol the entrance road in the early mornings to locate casualties that may still be present from the previous night, unclaimed by another scavenger.

Four additional members of the crow family are regular visitors to the lowlands, as well: the Steller's, scrub, and pinyon jays, and Clark's nutcracker. All of these birds forage among the pines, picking seeds from the open cones. Steller's jays can be especially common after nesting in the forests at higher elevations.

Pinyon jays often occur in huge flocks, traveling through the pinyon-juniper woodlands in search of mature cones. It is not unusual to see a hundred or even a thousand pinyon jays, flying in groups or stretched out over a mile or more, and calling to one another to retain communications so they can let the others know about their findings. That many large, highly vocal birds can cause quite a stir. Their call, as described by Scott Terrill in *The Audubon Society Master Guide to Birding*, is "a high, descending, nasal, crow-like 'caw-ah,'" and they also produce various mewing, chattering, and cawing calls.

Even during the nesting season, these jays can be found in large numbers. That is because they often nest in colonies, where they may build a hundred or more nests on a few acres of pinyon-juniper woodlands. They usually nest in late winter or in late summer, depending on the availability of pinyon seeds, which they either consume or cache underground for the winter. They also are noted for their complex social organization. Terres points out that feeding flocks maintain "4 to 12 sentries posted at some high points, motionless and silent until an intruder appears. Then the sentries give low, rhythmic krawk-krawk-krawk warning."

Pinyon jays are stout, uniformly grayish-blue birds with short, rounded wings, and short tails. If seen up close, instead of from the usual distance, their whitish throats, dark lores (feathers in front of the eyes), and long, stout bills are obvious.

Clark's nutcrackers nest high in the surrounding mountains and visit the park during the nonbreeding season. Some birds may take advantage of the bison herds on the nearby Zapata Ranch. Nutcrackers have been found feeding on insects, which they find under bison droppings during cold winters.

In spite of the extent of the rabbitbrush flats, that habitat supports only a minimum bird population. And only one species—**vesper sparrow**—can be found in numbers. This is the rather large, plain, light-colored sparrow with only one obvious distinction, its white outer tail feathers. This feature is best seen in flight. But with binoculars, one can also see its white eye rings, dark cheeks, streaked breast, and chestnut-colored shoulder patches. And in spring and summer, vesper sparrow songs echo across the flatlands, emanating from the tops of shrubs as well as pinyons at the edge of the grasslands. Their songs are sweet and musical, two long notes followed by two higher ones, and a descending trill. Peter Vickery, in *The Audubon Society Master Guide to Birding,* interpreted their songs as "here-here-where-where all together down the hill."

Of the park's various habitats, the aspen community possesses the highest species diversity. One morning in early May, I followed the little stream, across the highway from the visitor center, upward past the cottonwoods into a rather extensive aspen grove. At one place I found about 20 aspens that had been felled by beavers in an apparent attempt to dam a little watercourse that flowed from a hillside seep.

Overhead were violet-green swallows, soaring here and there in search of insects. Their snow white underparts and rumps were in direct contrast to their dark, violet-green backs. Occasionally, a **yellow-rumped warbler** dashed out for an insect and then coasted back to the protective canopy of the aspens. Yellow-rumps were the most abundant songbird that morning, and their variable songs, "tsit tsit tsit," followed by an energetic trill at a lower pitch, were commonplace along the drainage; two or three different birds could be heard from any one location. Several times I was able to watch these songsters near the very tops of the trees, with their heads thrown back in full song, and their bright yellow throats gleaming in the morning light.

The yellow-rumped warbler is fairly easy to identify because of its very distinct pattern. It possesses five yellow patches: on its throat, cap, both sides, and rump. Males sport a black chest, face, and back, and white wing bars. Females possess a similar but duller pattern. This yellow-throated bird was once known as "Audubon's" warbler, but when it was lumped with the white-throated "myrtle" warbler of the east, their names were changed to yellow-rumped warbler since both birds possess bright yellow rumps. Some birders refer to this warbler as "butter-rump."

The higher-pitched songs from the aspen canopy were those of orange-crowned warblers. It took me several minutes to find one of these nondescript birds with their overall yellowish plumage. Except for its somewhat brighter eyebrows and undertail coverts, and tiny yellow marking at the bend of its wings, it has no distinct markings.

I watched a pair of **mountain chickadees** carrying nesting material to a cavity in a tall, broken aspen limb. Both birds were participating in nest-building chores, and every now and then they uttered a hoarse "chick a-dee a-dee a-dee" song. And several times they whistled "fee-bee" or "fee-be-bay," down scale like the children's song, "Three Blind Mice." The white eye lines that separate their black caps from their black masks were evident through binoculars. I couldn't help but admire these little songsters as they carried load after load of nesting materials into the dense foliage. I knew that they had found a deep cavity in the trunk or branch in which they would soon be feeding eight to nine youngsters.

Chickadees are undoubtedly one of our most popular birds, and their caricatures are commonplace as numerous household designs. But most of these caricatures are representative of the all-black-capped Carolina chickadee of the eastern forests or the black-capped chickadee of the northern states, not the mountain chickadee, with the white eye line, of the western mountains.

The toy-horn-like songs of red-breasted nuthatches attracted my attention, and it took me several minutes to find this little boreal species. Unlike the larger, white-breasted nuthatch, which occurs within the cottonwood communities, red-breasted nuthatches sport buff to reddish underparts, slate gray backs, and black-and-white head patterns: black caps, white eye lines, and black streaks from their bills, through their eyes to the backs of their heads. But its behavior is what makes it special. It not only walks up and down and upside-down on tree trunks and branches, but much of the time while it is prying into tiny cracks and crevices in search of insects, it is uttering its very distinct call, more like a toy horn than any other bird's call I know.

I found three species of woodpeckers within the aspen grove: the little downy woodpecker, the larger red-naped sapsucker, and the still-larger northern (red-shafted) flicker. All three nest in aspens, where they construct interior cavities in the tree's relatively soft heartwood. Their presence is a great boon to other cavity-nesters that do not construct their own nests but take advantage of deserted woodpecker nests. In fact, of 21 species of birds found in the aspen community that morning, eight were cavity-nesters: the three woodpeckers, violet-green swallow, mountain chickadee, red-breasted nuthatch, house wren, and mountain bluebird.

The **American robins** were in full song during my visit. On two occasions I watched birds gather billfuls of nesting materials on the ground—grasses, tiny twigs, and unidentified things—that they carried away into the aspens. Males were obvious because of their brighter breasts and contrasting black heads. But their spirited songs were most evident, like a springtime message to the listener that all is well. I listened carefully to their cheery songs and discovered that it changes pitch in mid-song. Terres translated their caroling as "cheer-up, cheer, cheer, cheer-up."

Other birds detected that morning included a pair of red-tailed hawks that screamed overhead; mourning doves, with their sorrowful calls; numerous broad-tailed hummingbirds; several dusky flycatchers, singing "clip te-wee" songs; a pair of warbling vireos that scolded me at one point; at least five brown-headed cowbirds, calling squeaky whistles from the treetops; both rufous-sided and green-tailed towhees, their songs emanating from the adjacent shrubbery; a pair of dark-eyed juncos (once called gray-headed junco), chasing one another about a jumble of fallen branches; and five pine siskins flying through the canopy.

The dominating pinyon-juniper woodlands are well-represented at the Pinyon Flats Campground. A walk through this area in spring and summer will more than likely result in finding most of the typical birds of this community. The most numerous species include the mourning dove, broad-tailed hummingbird, Say's phoebe, violet-green swallow, pinyon jay, black-billed magpie, common raven, mountain chickadee, plain titmouse, bushtit, mountain bluebird, American robin, brown-headed cowbird, western tanager, black-headed grosbeak, and chipping sparrow.

The trumpet gooseberry bushes near the registration station were filled with sweet-smelling flowers during my May visit. A male **broad-tailed hummingbird** was guarding one particular bush and performing its territorial display by making headlong dives from 50 or more feet (15 m) above the shrubbery, and then flying right back up to the same height in a great U-shape flight. Its wingbeats produced a loud, trilling whistle, loudest at the bottom of each dive. I never did see its mate, although this species is known for its U-shaped courtship displays.

After six or seven dives it landed on the top of a nearby pinyon pine and gave me a clear frontal view. Its rose-red gorget, extending only slightly beyond its throat, gleamed in the sunlight like a bright ruby. It was otherwise all-emerald-green except for its white underparts and blackish tail and bill. It stayed only a few minutes before it flew down into the gooseberries and began to feed on the sweet trumpet-like flowers.

Then, suddenly, another creature appeared nearby, hovering among the gooseberries and feeding in a similar fashion. It took me a second or two to realize that it was not another hummingbird but a moth. Its two-inch wingspan and spindle-shaped body with buff bands could easily fool the uninformed. But this was a sphinx moth, known to scientists as *Hyles lineata*, which exhibits very similar behavior while feeding. At one time I was watching both the hummingbird and moth through my binoculars at the same time. I was reminded that some people incorrectly believe that the sphinx moth, sometimes known as hummingbird moth, metamorphoses into a hummingbird. Henry Walter Bates discusses native beliefs about these creatures in *The Naturalist on the River Amazons*, a fascinating book about his South American adventures.

In summary, the park's 1989 checklist of birds includes 155 species, of which 60 are considered year-round residents and 86 are summer residents or visitors. Of the more than 140 summertime residents, 4 are water birds, 18 are hawks and owls, and 11 are warblers. Nine species are listed only for winter: bald eagle, rough-legged hawk, merlin, Bohemian and cedar waxwings, northern shrike, rosy finches, American tree sparrow, and Harris' sparrow.

Birds of Special Interest

Broad-tailed hummingbird. It is common in all habitats throughout the summer months. Its rose-red throat patch, bright green back, and the male's trilling flight are obvious.

Pinyon jay. Huge flocks of this blue-gray, non-crested jay, can be expected any time of year. It is most numerous in the pinyon-juniper woodlands where it feeds on pinyon nuts.

Black-billed magpie. This is the long-tailed, black-and-white bird common near the dunes. Its call is an emphatic "chaeck" note.

Common raven. Watch for this large, all-black bird with a large bill and wedge-shaped tail along the entrance road or soaring over the dunes.

Mountain chickadee. This is the park's most common chickadee. It has a white eye line and sings "chick a-dee a-dee a-dee."

American robin. It can be found almost anyplace in the park and is easily identified by its red breast, dark back, and blackish head. It sings a cheery song in spring and summer.

Yellow-rumped warbler. This common summer resident is marked by five bright yellow patches: on its cap, throat, sides, and rump.

Vesper sparrow. It can be common on the open sage flats along the entrance road; it is nondescript except for its white outer tail feathers.

26

Capulin Volcano National Monument, New Mexico

The view from the Crater Rim Trail provides a wonderful perspective of the high plains country of northeastern New Mexico and adjacent states. The morning was clear and bright, and I imagined that I could see far into Colorado, Kansas, Oklahoma, and Texas. To the west were the snow-capped peaks of the Sangre de Cristo Mountains. And the prairie grasslands below encircled Capulin Mountain like a great green cape. My immediate environment was dominated by a pinyon-juniper woodland, rising out of the black soils of the old volcanic cone.

Birdsong surrounded me that early June morning. The plaintive calls of mourning doves resounded across the slope. A western wood-pewee sang its emphatic "phreee" song from a nearby snag. A pair of Cassin's kingbirds were actively courting beyond. Scrub jays called further down the slope. The wheezy song of a blue-gray gnatcatcher emanated from the nearby pinyon foliage. Three brown-headed cowbirds flew overhead, calling out squeaky, high-pitched notes. And the robin-like song of a black-headed grosbeak was evident just ahead of me.

But the most numerous songs of the morning were those of rufous-sided towhees. From any one place along the trail, I could detect three or four "chup-chup-zeeeee" songs below me. Several "zreee" calls were also evident. It took very little effort to coax one or two of these black, white, and rufous songsters into view. One especially bright male sat at the very top of a mountain mahogany shrub and scolded me. Its all-black hood, except for its blood-red eye, black-and-white back and wings, and rufous sides gleamed in the morning light. It dropped into the shrubbery as I approached;

Rufous-sided towhee

the white corners of its dark tail seemed to bid me farewell as it ducked for cover.

Rufous-sided towhees are one of America's most familiar birds. They occur throughout the country but are especially numerous in the Rocky Mountain states in summer. Although a few remain on their breeding grounds through the winter months, most migrate to lower elevations, sometimes as far south as Mexico. They can then be common in gardens and brushy fields, as well as at feeders.

I watched a pair of birds feeding on the ground under a Gambel's oak. They were clearing away the dead leaves and other debris by jumping backward, throwing the loose materials behind them in their search for insects, spiders, and seeds. They would then jump forward and peck at the various food items that had been uncovered. Once berries ripen in late summer, they take advantage of that readily available food source, as well.

During the almost three hours that I spent along the Crater Rim Trail that morning, I must have seen or heard two dozen rufous-sided towhees. They undoubtedly are the park's most abundant and also one of the park's most colorful and personable birds.

The Park Environment

Capulin Volcano has long been a conspicuous landmark, rising over 1,500 feet (457 m) above the surrounding plains, 8,182 feet (2,494 m) at the rim. Approximately four miles (6.4 km) around the base, Capulin Volcano is a remnant of the final stage of volcanic activity that occurred between 4,500 and 10,000 years ago. Today, it is a lone, dormant cone with a 415-foot-deep (126 m) crater at the top. The 792-acre (320 ha) national monument was established in 1916 to protect the symmetrical cinder cone from human exploitation.

Vegetation near the base of the cone represents the short grass prairie of the high plains. Predominant plant species include blue and sideoats gramas, big and little bluestems, and various species of sage. The cone itself is covered with a high density of pinyon pines and oneseed junipers on the north, east, and southern exposures. The western slope is composed of scattered pinyons and junipers with occasional stands of Gambel's oaks, mountain mahoganies, skunkbushes, currents, gooseberries, and thimbleberries. A small stand of ponderosa pines occurs along the lower, northwestern slope.

The park's visitor center is located near the entrance, off State Highway 325, just north of Capulin, New Mexico. It houses an information desk, exhibits, orientation program, and sales outlet that includes bird field guides and a bird checklist. Interpretive activities are limited to a short nature trail near the visitor center and the Crater Rim Nature Trail.

The park does not have a campground, although one is available at nearby Capulin. A picnic area is located along the Rim Drive at the base of the mountain.

Additional information can be obtained from the Superintendent, Capulin Mountain National Monument, Capulin, NM 88414; (505) 278-2201.

Bird Life

Each of the park's three rather distinct habitats supports its own set of bird species, although there is considerable overlap. The prairie grasslands along the entrance road are dominated by the green-tailed, rufous-sided, and canyon towhees; western meadowlarks; and three sparrows: vesper, lark, and chipping. **Lark sparrows** are most numerous, readily identified by their striking chestnut, white, and black head patterns, clear underparts with a black spot in the center of their breasts, and rounded tails with large, white corners. In addition, their songs are one of the finest of the sparrows'. Arthur C. Bent, in *Life Histories of North American Cardinals, Grosbeaks, Buntings, Towhees, Finches, Sparrows, and Allies*, quotes T. S. Robert's description, thusly:

> This song is composed of a series of chants, each syllable rich, loud, and clear, interspersed with emotional trills. Though seemingly hurried, it is one continuous gush of sprightly music; now gay, now melodious, and then tender beyond description, the very expression of emotion. At intervals the singer falters, as if exhausted by exertion, and his voice becomes scarcely audible; but suddenly reviving in his joy, it is resumed in all its vigor, until he appears to be really overcome by the effort.

Lark sparrows were named after the Old World larks, which are excellent singers and sing in flight. Flight songs of lark sparrows are delivered during courtship as the males display before their ladies. Males sing from the ground, low shrubs, tree foliage, or while flying from one perch to another. A territorial male will also challenge other males when approached too closely. It will first raise its head and elevate its bill, but if that posture doesn't send its challenger away it will fly at the intruder, actually striking it. At times the two competitors will fly at one another and fly high in the air, striking one another with their wings. This may occur several times before one or the other retires from the field of combat.

The scrub oak woodlands lie just above the prairie, serving as a transition zone between the prairie grasslands and pinyon-juniper woodlands. Three bird species breed within the scrub oak habitat that are not known to nest in the prairie or pinyon-juniper woodlands: wild turkey, hairy woodpecker, and northern oriole. More common species in summer include house and rock wrens, American robin, mountain bluebird, blue-gray gnatcatcher, brown-headed cowbird, black-headed grosbeak, green-tailed and rufous-sided towhees, and lark and chipping sparrows.

Chipping sparrows are usually most evident because of their continuous singing, a long, unmusical, dry chipping, from whence their name was derived. Their single-pitched trills are often delivered from near the top of a tree or shrub for several minutes at a time. These tiny sparrows are easily identified by their rufous caps, black line through the eyes, gray collars, and clear breasts. But in spite of their size, they are one of the feistiest of sparrows. They seem to be continuously battling with their neighbors. But they are most gregarious, and even during the nesting season continue to feed in small flocks. And in winter they will join much larger flocks that move south to warmer climes where seeds are more readily available. There they become common feeder birds.

Capulin Volcano's chipping sparrows are often parasitized by brown-headed cowbirds that lay their eggs in the nests of the smaller birds. Cowbirds actually remove sparrow eggs or youngsters to benefit their own, which are raised by the foster parents, usually to the detriment of the chipping sparrows' smaller and less aggressive nestlings. See chapter 31 on Big Bend for additional details on cowbird parasitism.

The **American robin** is another obvious resident of the scrub oak woodlands, and its bright red breast and cheery songs are difficult to ignore on a bright, sunny morning. Except for rufous-sided towhees and chipping sparrows, it was the most numerous bird present. Nests were located at 2 to 5 feet (.6-1.5 m) above the ground on brushy Gambel's oaks in May. Many robins were still busy building their rather sloppy, cup-shaped structures, usually on branches near the trunks. I watched one female, identifiable by her duller color, carrying a huge billful of grasses and small twigs. She was so loaded down, she looked more like a huge pile of grasses flying across the terrain than a bird.

Robins usually produce two clutches during a single season. Both sexes build the nests and incubate the eggs. However, once the first clutch is fledged, their care is left to the male while the female often spends her time incubating the second clutch.

I also watched a lone male searching for earthworms along the roadside. It would run a short distance, then stop and cock its head as if it were listening intently for any movement. On several occasions it would walk a few feet further, then stop, cock its head again, and then stab the ground to retrieve a fat, juicy worm. Early ornithologists believed that robins found worms by hearing, but more recent research has suggested that they locate their prey by sight instead.

Another bird that occurs within the scrub oak community, probably due to the rocky outcroppings, is the little, gray-brown **rock wren**. It can be difficult to find amid the ashy soils, but its constant singing often gives it away. It "sings sprightly songs" that sounds like "keree keree keree, chair chair chair, deedle deedle deedle, turturtur, keree keree trrrrr," according to Bent. It also has a loud "tick-ear" call that is sometime interspersed between songs.

This bird is an extremely adaptable species that occurs throughout the arid West, at almost all elevations. It was the only species that I found to be nesting from below sea-level to over 11,000 feet (3,353 m) elevation in Death Valley National Monument. At Capulin Volcano, it seemed to prefer the dry slopes of the crater, undoubtedly nesting in rocky crevices and under loose rock. John Terres paraphrased Bent's description of this bird's use of stones and other material: "Places stones near opening to nests, sometimes for 8-10 in. (20-25 cm) out from hidden nest built of grasses, horsehair, feathers; one passageway of a hole in earth to nest was lined with 1,665 items of which 492 were small granite stones, 769 bones of rabbits, fishes, birds, and nesting materials."

Rock wrens are also present within the pinyon-juniper woodlands and can sometimes be found about the parking area at the summit. It can best be identified by its distinct bobbing behavior and indistinct plumage; whitish underparts, gray-brown back, and a tint of cinnamon on the rump and tail. When disturbed, it will bob up and down, run a few feet, bob again, and call "tick-ear, tick-ear."

The **black-headed grosbeak** can be numerous among the pinyons and junipers. But its songs can be confused with those of the American robin, which is also present in this short-tree community. The grosbeak's song is a number of clear, rapid whistles that often includes trills. The grosbeak's song is more rapid, rich, and varied than the robin's, and contains many little trills.

Male black-headed grosbeaks are black and orange-brown birds: they possess all-black heads, except for their silvery bills, black wings with white patches, and orange-brown underparts, backs, and collars. Females possess a similar pattern but are much lighter in color with a whitish head stripe above each eye. As expected from their heavy bills, grosbeaks feed on a variety of hard foods, such as beetles. A study of 225 stomachs revealed that 190 contained beetles. Vegetable matter also constituted a large percentage, especially cherries; no evidence of strawberries, apricots, or prunes was found. Weed and other seeds were found in about 15 percent of the stomachs examined.

Other summer residents of the pinyon-juniper woodlands, not already mentioned, include turkey vultures, red-tailed hawks, American kestrels, and common ravens, often found soaring overhead by mid-mornings. Woodland birds include broad-tailed hummingbirds, northern flickers, Lewis' woodpeckers, ash-throated flycatchers, black phoebes, mountain chickadees, pygmy nuthatches, house wrens, northern mockingbirds, solitary vireos, Virginia, yellow-rumped, and black-throated gray warblers; western and hepatic tanagers; house finches, and lesser goldfinches. Nighttime birds include large great horned owls and the much smaller common poorwills, that are sometimes found perched on the roadway early in the mornings.

Turkey vultures can be numerous over the crater once the thermals develop from the warm air rising over the dark landscape. They often soar for hours on end with few if any wingbeats, sometimes making tight circles, but at other times soaring considerable distances from thermal to thermal. They are easily recognized by their all-black plumages (although the lighter flight feathers are a dark silver-gray color), bare red heads, and distinct flight pattern; their wings are dihedral or held in a shallow V-shaped angle, and they tip slightly from side to side in flight. The turkey vulture's unique flight usually can identify this bird even at a considerable distance.

The presence of the two western species of tanagers in the monument is rather unusual, because it represents the eastern edge of the range for both species. The male western tanager sports bright yellow underparts and collar, black wings, and red head; females lack the red head but possess similar, but duller, bodies. The male hepatic tanager is liver-red color overall, except for grayish cheeks, flanks, and back; females possess yellow underparts and brownish backs and wings. These birds are members of a large family that is mostly of tropical affinity; they and the eastern scarlet tanager are the only three of 236 members of the tanager family, restricted to the Western Hemisphere, that regularly occur in the United States. They therefore are true Neotropical migrants that spend their winters in the tropical climes of Mexico and Central and South America. Their long-term survival depends as much upon the health of their winter homes as it does on the viability of their breeding grounds.

In summary, the park's bird checklist includes 115 species, of which 43 are known to nest. None of those are water birds, 5 are hawks and owls, and 3 are warblers.

Birds of Special Interest

Turkey vulture. Watch for this large, all-dark bird soaring over the crater; it has a bare red head and wings held in a shallow V-shaped angle in flight.

Rock wren. This little gray-brown bird of the rocky slopes bobs up and down when disturbed. It sings a variable song of trills and calls "tick-ear."

American robin. One of the park's most common birds, it is easily recognized by its reddish breast and lively caroling.

Black-headed grosbeak. Chunky, robin-sized birds, males are orange-brown with black heads and wings with white markings.

Rufous-sided towhee. This bird prefers shrubbery areas; it has an all-black hood with blood-red eyes, black back and wings with white spots, and rufous sides.

Chipping sparrow. These are tiny sparrows with all-reddish caps, black lines through the eyes, and whitish underparts.

Lark sparrow. Its head pattern contains chestnut and white stripes edged with black, clear underparts with a solid black breast spot, and a rounded tail with conspicuous white corners.

27

Bandelier National Monument, New Mexico

Early mornings in Frijoles Canyon are like being in a great cathedral. The high canyon walls, stately trees that guard the banks of Frijoles Creek, and reverberant birdsong create an atmosphere of peace and contentment. The sounds echo back and forth from one side of the canyon to the other, producing a mantra-like aura. The loud, descending songs of canyon wrens, twittering calls of white-throated swifts, clear whistles of solitary vireos, loud caroling of American robins, and flutelike renderings of hermit thrushes, all blended together and amplified by the canyon walls, are more wondrous than a great choir at its very best.

I crossed the stone bridge by the visitor center and walked up-canyon, through the picnic area and beyond to where the path hugs the creek. The lush riparian vegetation was filled with fresh, bright green leaves. The taller ponderosa pines also were sprouting new foliage. Abundant violet-green swallows soared up and down the canyon in search for insects. Western wood-pewees, Hammond's flycatchers, warbling vireos, Virginia's warblers, western tanagers, and black-headed grosbeaks were all present in numbers. But none were as busy as the tiny pygmy nuthatches; every ponderosa pine seemed to possess its own group. I focused my binoculars on one pair of these short-tailed birds that were feeding, almost crawling, upside-down on the tree trunk. Three additional individuals were circling the outer branches beyond, searching the foliage for food. Their whitish underparts, uniform dark backs and wings, and brown caps gleamed in the morning sunlight. All the while, they called to one another never-ending peeping sounds, like "pee-di pee-di pee-di."

Pygmy nuthatches are not only one of Bandelier's most vocal full-time residents, but they are one of the best representatives of the ponderosa and pinyon pine forests of the Rocky Mountains.

Pygmy nuthatch

They are one of the smallest of all songbirds, barely larger than a hummingbird, and they can be one of the most numerous. They possess some fascinating traits. They are extremely gregarious birds, almost always in flocks of a few to many individuals. Even while nesting they are assisted by a small cadre of helpers; unmated birds and siblings help with all the family chores from nest-building to feeding the youngsters. Paired birds usually form full-time bonds and remain together for life. Research has shown that "pairs with helpers fledge more young than do unaided pairs," according to Paul Ehrlich and colleagues. Additionally, pygmy nuthatches hide extra food, usually conifer seeds, throughout their territories for leaner times of the year. They also utilize a wide variety of insects, which they capture by probing the tree trunks, smaller branches, and even among the cones on the outer branches. Their hoarding habits can keep them extremely busy throughout the spring and summer months.

Hoarding contributes to their ability to remain on their breeding grounds even during cold and snowy weather. Although there may be some altitudinal movement during severe winters, Bandelier's pygmy nuthatches can usually be found in the same places, such as in Frijoles Canyon, year-round.

The Park Environment
Bandelier National Monument lies along the eastern slope of the Jemez Mountains of north-central New Mexico. It includes a series of mesas separated by steep-walled canyons cut into the ancient volcanics of the Pajarito Plateau. These mesas provide a series of steps between the semi-desert Rio Grande lowlands and the boreal zones of the Jemez Mountain highlands. The park was originally established in 1916 to protect the widely scattered Indian ruins that were inhabited from the early 1200s until about 1550. These include "small compact dwellings, large circular pueblos with central plazas, cavate dwellings, isolated kivas, seasonal farm sites, ceremonial caves, and shrines," as summarized by Earl Jackson in *Your National Park System in the Southwest*. The best of these ruins include Tyuonyi (400 rooms) in Frijoles Canyon, and Tsankawi, a disjunct unit to the east.

The park was enlarged to 32,727 acres (13,244 ha) in 1976 to incorporate additional high forests and a portion of Cerro Grande, of which 23,267 acres (9,416 ha) were designated as wilderness. Elevations range from 5,300 feet (1,615 m) at the southeastern corner of the park along Cochiti Reservoir (a section of the flooded Rio Grande) to the 10,199-foot (3,109 m) Cerro Grande, on the northwestern corner. Most of the park is accessible only by trails. State Highway 4 largely follows the park's northern boundary and cuts across the Valle Grande, a huge, collapsed volcanic crater.

Vegetation zones vary with elevations. Extensive pinyon-juniper woodlands exist on the lower mesas, dominated by two-needle pinyon and oneseed juniper, with lesser numbers of wavyleaf oak, mountain mahogany, squawbush, and yuccas. The lower edge of this zone contains big sagebrush, Mormon tea, and cane cholla. A ponderosa pine zone occurs just above the pinyon-juniper woodlands, although much of this environment was converted to grassland by a 1977 fire. Gambel's oak is common throughout, with Douglas fir, white fir, limber pine, aspen, and New Mexico locust present on cooler slopes. In the uplands is a spruce-fir community, dominated by Engelman spruce and white fir, with scattered stands of aspens. And near the summit of Cerro Grande is a grassland environment that is slowly being invaded by Douglas fir and ponderosa pines.

The many canyons, especially those at lower elevations, such as Frijoles Canyon, contain a lush riparian formation. Dominant woody plants include cottonwood, box elder, and ponderosa pine, with fewer numbers of willows, junipers, water birch, chokecherry, and western mountain maple. Further up-canyon, Gambel's oak and New Mexico locust are also common. And at the mouth of the lower canyons, floodwaters of Cochiti Reservoir have changed the shorelines in recent years so that marshy habitats are evolving.

The park's visitor center lies at the end of the paved roadway to Frijoles Canyon. It houses an information desk, exhibits, and sales outlet that includes field guides and a checklist of park birds. Ranger-guided walks leave from the visitor center and nightly campfire talks are held at Juniper Campground, near the park entrance, during the summer season.

Additional information can be obtained from the Superintendent, Bandelier National Monument, Box 1, Suite 15, Los Alamos, NM 87544; (505) 672-3861.

Bird Life

Frijoles Canyon is the most productive bird-finding area in the entire monument. In spring, resident birds as well as migrants, species en route to higher elevations in the park or elsewhere in the Rocky Mountains, are present. And by July, a few northern nesters, such as the rufous hummingbird, already en route to their wintering grounds south of the border, are present. Frijoles Canyon truly provides a smorgasbord of the area's bird life.

One late-May visit there produced 43 species within a 1-mile (1.6 km) walk above the stone bridge. **Violet-green swallows** were most abundant. Their velvety-green backs and snow white underparts were practically everywhere among the treetops and over the open areas, such as Tyuonyi ruins. I watched one pair nest-building in a vacant woodpecker hole in a tall cottonwood, and several others were utilizing tiny crevices in the adjacent cliff face. Their constant twittering, like "tsip, tseet, tsip," was repeated over and over again.

There was never a time when I could not detect the harsh, nasal, songs of **western wood-pewees**. Their loud "pee-er" or "zheer" songs emanated from the trees along the streamsides as well as from the upper slopes. I located one of these 6.5-inch (16.5 cm) birds singing from near the top of a box elder; I was able to watch it for several minutes. It, undoubtedly, was one of the plainest of songbirds, having few distinguishing features. It was almost all-gray-brown color; the exceptions were its white belly, like an inverted "V," two dirty-white wing bars, and blackish bill and eyes. It does not have whitish eye rings, as do the very similar *Empidonax* flycatchers. Once, it dashed out after a passing insect, which it captured with a snap of its bill, and then returned to the same perch and pumped its tail twice before consuming its catch.

A solitary vireo suddenly appeared nearby, and I shifted my attention to this more brightly marked songster. It was a clearly marked male with a bluish-gray back, whitish underparts, two distinct wing bars, snow white throat, and bold, white eye rings and lines from the eyes to the stout, black bill, giving it an appearance of wearing eyeglasses. Then it sang a surprisingly loud, but sweet, series of whistle notes, like "chu-wee, cheerio."

Solitary vireos are very adaptable birds that nest throughout the park, from the riparian habitats near the Rio Grande to the spruce-fir communities on Cerro Grande. They build a loose, hanging nest of grasses, bark, and other materials, bound together with webbing from spiders or tent caterpillars, usually in a fork of a horizontal branch on the utter edge. Incubating birds often will allow an extremely close approach, at times permitting themselves to be touched.

The other vireo of the riparian habitats is the very plain warbling vireo that sings a loud, melodious warble, more like that of warblers than the defined whistle-songs of vireos. Several other songbirds, not already mentioned, were also found along Frijoles Canyon that morning: ash-throated flycatchers, white-breasted nuthatches, house wrens, hermit thrushes, yellow-rumped and Grace's warblers, rufous-sided towhees, and chipping sparrows. Fewer numbers of Say's phoebes, Steller's jays, western bluebirds, rock wrens, mountain chickadees, plain titmice, yellow, MacGillivray's, and Wilson's warblers, hepatic tanagers, Cassin's finches, lesser goldfinches, and evening grosbeaks, were observed.

Hairy woodpeckers and northern flickers were also common along the canyon, as were broad-tailed hummingbirds and mourning doves. And along the canyon rims, turkey vultures were numerous, soaring from rim to rim, or flapping up-canyon to find thermals that they might use for soaring. A family of common ravens were already out cruising the canyon rims in search of food. Their all-black plumage, heavy bills, and wedge-shaped tails helped to identify these large birds.

Two additional raptors occasionally are seen along Frijoles Canyon. Zone-tailed hawks hunt lizards along the high rims, mimicking turkey vultures in both appearance and flight so well that they can easily fool an unaware observer. They differ from turkey vultures by possessing all-feathered heads and banded tails. Peregrine falcons are less common but do occur over Frijoles Canyon on rare occasions.

Broad-tailed hummingbird

Broad-tailed hummingbirds were extremely active along the trail. Several individuals were feeding on the numerous flowering plants of the undergrowth. A number of males were displaying before their ladies, making great U-shaped dives with loud, trilling whistle sounds. The whistle is produced form air rushing through slots of the first two outer primaries of the tapered wings; the female's are not tapered. I watched one male hover at the bottom of its dive, directly over a cowering female that seemed more fearful than submissive.

Broad-tailed hummingbirds are also common within the pinyon-juniper woodlands of the mesa just above Frijoles Canyon. They readily come to feeders hung by campers at Juniper Campground. The somewhat smaller black-chinned hummingbird, with white underparts and a velvet-black instead of rose-red throat, can also be common. When the all-rufous male rufous humming-birds put in their appearance later in the summer, they can be extremely aggressive, claiming a territory and successfully keeping the other hummers away.

The Juniper Campground area supports a typical population of pinyon-juniper birds. Although many of these birds also occur in Frijoles Canyon, the composition is very different. The most numerous resident of the pinyon-juniper woodlands is the **plain titmouse**, a little, all-gray, crested bird with a loud, harsh "witt-e, witt-e, witt-e" song. In spite of its rather drab appearance, it is one of the most personable birds imaginable. Curious, it will often approach very close to campers, although it is constantly on the move from one tree to another. It usually occurs alone or with its mate, rarely in flocks, as chickadees do. Titmice feed primarily on insects in summer, climbing about tree limbs, often hanging upside-down at odd angles. Later in the summer they will feed on seeds, including pinyon nuts, which they pry from the cones and then crack the shells by hammering them with their heavy bills.

Rufous-sided towhees are also numerous in the pinyon-juniper woodland, especially at scattered thickets of mountain mahogany and oaks. The male's coal black hood with blood-red eyes, black backs with numerous white spots, black tail with distinct white corners, white belly, and rufous sides help to identify this robin-sized songster. Females are duller versions of the males. This bird will often sing loud "chup-chup-zeeee" songs from the top of a shrub or tree, especially at dawn and dusk. The all-brown canyon towhee occurs on the lower slopes.

Two flycatchers reside among the pinyons and junipers in summer, but, in spite of being reasonably common, they are more often heard than seen. The ash-throated flycatcher is the largest of the two, about 8.5 inches (22 cm) in length, and sports a reddish tail, yellowish belly, grayish-brown back and head, and ash-colored throat. When excited it will show its distinct crest. Its typical call is "ka-brick" or "ha-wheer." The smaller gray flycatcher, distinguished only by its whitish belly, grayish back, darker wings with two faint wing bars, and whitish eye rings, can best be identified by its song: a vigorous "chuwip" or "chi-bit."

The characteristic warbler of Bandelier's pinyon-juniper woodlands is the little black-throated gray warbler. The male's black-and-white pattern, except for a tiny yellow spot in front of each eye, includes a black cap, bold black cheeks bordered with white, and a completely black throat; females are duller versions.

They are best detected by their strange, buzzy songs, like a drawling "wee-zy, wee-zy, wee-zy, wee-zy-weet" or "swee, swee, ker-swee, sick," either ascending or descending on the last syllable. See chapter 14 on Zion National Park for a description of this bird's fascinating behavior.

One of the most obvious birds of this environment is the **western bluebird**, best identified by the male's deep blue hood, wings, and tail, and chestnut back, breast, and flanks. Bluebirds are cavity-nesters, utilizing vacant woodpecker nests and crevices in trees and posts. Although a member of the thrush family, known for their wonderful, flutelike songs, western bluebird songs usually are little more than mellow warbles. However, during courtship they sing a more extended song that Arthur C. Bent included in his extensive description of the species: "Tempo much like that of Robin's song. K-few, f-few, f-few, f-few, eh-eh, few, few, eh-eh, few, eh-eh, few, f-few."

One day in May I watched a pair of western bluebirds nest-building in a ponderosa pine in the upper section of Juniper Campground. Both birds carried so many billfuls of grass, weeds, bark, and other materials into an old woodpecker nest, I began to wonder how they could still maneuver inside. Most of the material was collected from the ground, but the male also spent considerable time tearing off some bark fragments from an adjacent juniper. Occasionally, they would be distracted by passing insects and fly out in pursuit. Their long wings and wide gape contributed greatly to their success.

Other typical birds of Bandelier's pinyon-juniper woodlands include mourning doves, with their sorrowful calls; white-backed hairy woodpeckers; violet-green swallows; scrub jays, with their blue backs and whitish underparts; pinyon jays, which wander throughout, sometimes in huge flocks; tiny, long-tailed bushtits; black-and-white blue-gray gnatcatchers with long tails and wheezy calls; solitary vireos; Virginia's warblers from the adjacent Gambel's oaks; liver-red hepatic tanagers; black-headed grosbeaks; lesser goldfinches with their yellow bodies and green-black backs; and chipping sparrows.

Of all those bird species, the tiny chipping sparrows may be the most abundant. Their loud, monotonous trills, all on one pitch, can continue throughout the day. They are distinguished by their all-rufous caps, black lines that run from their bills through their eyes, to their gray collars, whitish underparts, and streaked backs. They can be feisty birds when defending a territory or when feeding together, often in small flocks.

Many of the pinyon-juniper birds range into the ponderosa pine forest on the higher mesas. And conversely, the ponderosa pine species are regular visitors to the lower woodlands. The best examples include American kestrels, which also nest on the cliffs, red-shafted northern flickers, white-breasted nuthatches, and western tanagers.

Of the more than three dozen species that nest within the park's ponderosa pine forest, the Steller's jay, pygmy nuthatch, western bluebird, solitary vireo, and Grace's warbler might be the best representatives. The best known of these is probably the dark blue, crested, Steller's jay. It was once called "long-crested jay," because of its very tall, blackish-blue crest, depressed in flight and not evident. But on landing, its crest is most obvious. So is its loud, raucous call, a harsh "kwesh, kwesh, kwesh." See chapter 3 on Banff, Kootenay, Jasper, and Yoho for additional comments on this bird's behavior.

The **Grace's warbler**, a lovely yellow-throated warbler that sports white underparts, gray back with black streaks, and a bold yellow line above eyes, is the most characteristic warbler of the ponderosa pine forest. Its song is a rapid, musical trill, like "chee-chee-che-che," with numerous variations. Unlike the other nesting warblers, this bird seems to stay high in the foliage, rarely coming to the ground or feeding among the adjacent oaks. Its diet apparently consists solely of the insects that it gleans from the foliage and twigs of ponderosa pines. This bird also is Bandelier's best example of a Neotropical migrant that spends winters in southern Mexico and northern Central America. Its survival depends upon the health of the forests in both regions of the Western Hemisphere.

Scattered patches of Gambel's oak occur throughout the mid-elevations of the park, extending from cooler niches in the lower canyons to the open, southern slopes to almost 9,000 feet (2,743 m) elevation. Although a number of birds frequent these areas, such as solitary vireo, black-headed grosbeak, and rufous-sided towhee, only the Virginia's warbler is totally dependent upon Gambel's oaks. This little yellow-and-gray bird can be surprisingly common, and its lovely songs can often be heard from every stand of Gambel's oak. Ludlow Griscom and Alexander Sprunt, Jr., in *The Warblers of North America*, described this bird's songs thusly: "In a voice full for so small a bird, they pour forth a variety of animated verses. Che-we-che-we-che-we, che-a-che-a-che, the song sounded to one observer, while another wrote it as zdl-zdl-zdl-zdl, zt, zt, zt, zt." The bird's name comes from the name of the wife of the first collector (S. F. Baird); it was not named after the state. It breeds only in the Intermountain West, and winters in western Mexico.

The spruce-fir vegetation in Bandelier's highlands supports many of the same bird species that occur in the northern Rocky Mountains. Of the 30 or more species known to nest, the most abundant include northern flicker, western wood-pewee, Steller's jay, mountain chickadee, house wren, American robin, warbling vireo, yellow-rumped warbler, western tanager, and dark-eyed junco.

The **dark-eyed junco** is most numerous. This little gray-headed bird with distinct white edges to its long tail was earlier called gray-headed junco. But the western Oregon junco and the eastern slate-colored junco were lumped with gray-headed juncos of the Intermountain West and called dark-eyed junco. It is a ground-nester that spends most of its time in the low shrubbery and on the ground. It will, however, sing from the treetops during the breeding season. Then its musical trill, a rapid twittering that often changes pitch half-way through, can be commonplace. In winter it moves to lower elevations, and during especially cold winters it will migrate far south into warmer climes; there it often is referred to as "snow bird."

Some of the other summer residents of the spruce-fir community include ruffed grouse, wild turkeys, red-naped and Williamson's sapsuckers, gray jays, Clark's nutcrackers, red-breasted nuthatches, hermit thrushes, mountain bluebirds, ruby-crowned kinglets, orange-crowned warblers, red crossbills, and pine siskins. Green-tailed towhees and white-crowned sparrows frequent the shrubby vegetation near the summit of Cerro Grande.

The vast majority of the park's songbirds move out of the highlands during the winter months. Those that do not migrate south frequent the warmer, lower slopes, such as Frijoles and Burnt mesas. Although there have not been any Christmas Bird Counts done within the park, I conducted bi-weekly surveys on these mesas during the winters of 1977-1978 and 1978-1979. The dozen most numerous birds recorded, in descending order of abundance, included American robin, dark-eyed junco, western bluebird, Cassin's finch, rufous-sided towhee, evening grosbeak, pine siskin, Townsend's solitaire, Lewis' woodpecker, northern flicker, pygmy nuthatch, and common raven.

In summary, the park's bird checklist includes 160 species, of which 110 are listed as either permanent or summer residents, and assumed to nest. Of these, 3 are water birds (mallard, great blue heron, and killdeer), 13 are hawks and owls, and 7 are warblers. Two species are listed for winter only: evening grosbeak and Cassin's finch.

Birds of Special Interest

Broad-tailed hummingbird. Common at all elevations in summer, it is best identified by its all-green back and rose-red throat.

Western wood-pewee. This little, nondescript flycatcher is best distinguished by its descending "pee-er" songs.

Violet-green swallow. Its violet-green back and snow white underparts help identify this common swallow.

Plain titmouse. This is the little, all-gray, crested bird of the pinyon-juniper woodlands that sings a harsh "witt-e, witt-e, witt-e" song.

Pygmy nuthatch. Possible the park's most abundant bird, it is a tiny, short-tailed bird that is most numerous on ponderosa pines.

Western bluebird. This is the lovely deep-blue and cinnamon-colored bird of the park-like areas of the monument.

Grace's warbler. This ponderosa pine warbler possesses a bright yellow throat, white underparts, gray back, and bold yellow eye line over dark gray cheeks.

Dark-eyed junco. Its generally gray underparts and head are a sharp contrast to its rufous back, black lores, and white edges of its dark tail.

28

El Morro National Monument, New Mexico

The pool at the base of Inscription Rock had attracted numerous birds, residents as well as a wide variety of migrants. I stood in the shade of a ponderosa pine and watched their comings and goings. The bravest of the lot were some of the migrants, mostly sparrows and warblers that had recently passed through the arid countryside before discovering this tiny oasis. The patch of flowers below the pool, dominated by snakeweed, desert groundsel, and evening primrose, was literally crawling with birds. I watched chipping sparrows; orange-crowned, Nashville, and Wilson's warblers; green-tailed towhees; and pine siskins search for food among the yellow blossoms.

The adjacent ponderosa pines, pinyons, and junipers were also filled with birds. Most of these were full-time park residents: scrub jays, mountain chickadees, plain titmice, white-breasted nuthatches, Bewick's wrens, American robins, and rufous-sided towhees. The loudest of the group were the scrub jays that called to one another continuously. They seemed less concerned with my presence than just plain curious about anyone paying more attention to birds than to the historical graffiti that decorated the sandstone cliff behind me.

Although scrub jays are common throughout the pinyon-juniper woodlands of the West, I never tire of their appearance and antics. Almost a foot long, including their long, seemingly loose tails, they possess grayish underparts with streaked throats, darker gray triangular patches on their backs, and all-blue heads, wings, backs, and tails. Adults also possess heavy black bills and black eye patches that run from the bill through the eyes. They often appear shy, but are seldom quiet. Their loud, raspy calls vary from a

Scrub jay

"shreeep" to a sharp "iennk," and often include hurried "quick, quick, quick" notes. They can also be extraordinarily sly, approaching campers or picnickers without making a sound. But if frightened they will race off with a great deal of emotion, calling and flapping their wings with louder than normal beats.

Scrub jays usually occur in family groups of a few to 10-to-15 individuals, and pairs usually establish long-term bonds. They are almost always on the go, rarely staying long in one place—unless, that is, they have discovered a predator, such as an owl, fox, or snake. Then they will create great havoc, which will continue until the intruder leaves their territory.

I was suddenly attracted to the aerial acrobatics above me. A mixed flock of white-throated swifts and violet-green swallows were circling along the cliff, the swifts emitting loud, descending twittering calls. Although both these species nest in cracks and crevices in the sandstone cliffs, sometimes reasonably close to each other, they are very different birds. **White-throated swifts** are more closely related to hummingbirds than to swallows and other songbirds. They fly with stiff and very rapid wingbeats, and look like flying cigars with white throats and flanks. They have been clocked at more than 100 miles (160 km) per hour in flight. Swifts are so adapted to flight that their tiny, weak feet are able only to hold on to the cliffs; they are unable to perch. See chapter 22 on Colorado National Monument for additional details about this fascinating bird.

Violet-green swallows also are cliff-nesters, but they nest in tree cavities, as well. They display a very different flight than the neighboring swifts, one that is truly swallow-like. They also can perch on trees and wires. And instead of emitting drawn-out twittering calls, they produce high-pitched "tweet" and "chip" sounds in flight. They also are more colorful than the black-and-white swifts, possessing snow white underparts, cheeks, and flanks, blackish wings, and violet-green backs. In the right light their backs can be a beautiful velvet-like violet-green color.

Cliff swallows also nest on the El Morro cliffs but construct mud pellet nests at suitable sites rather than utilizing cracks and crevices. Arthur C. Bent pointed out in *Life Histories of North American Flycatchers, Larks, Swallows, and Their Allies*, that cliff swallow nests "are cleverly constructed of pellets of mud or clay, are roofed over, and generally assume a flask, retort, or bottle shape with a narrow entrance leading into an enlarged chamber." Bent also includes a description of their activities in New Mexico by Alexander Wetmore: "The birds came down to the lake shore in little bands of ten or a dozen and alighted close together with trembling wings extended at an angle from their backs, standing high on their legs to avoid soiling their feathers. After alighting they leaned over, filled the mouth with mud with one or two sharp digs and then rose to fly back up the steep slopes to the colony." This species sports blackish backs, caps, and squared tails, white bellies, and chestnut rumps, cheeks, and throats.

Between the scrub jays, with their aggressive behavior, and the aerial antics of white-throated swifts and the two swallows, a visit to El Morro is rarely without the presence of bird life.

The Park Environment

El Morro, Spanish for "the headland," refers to a sandstone monolith that rises 200 feet (61 m) above the open flats; it has a long history of human visitation. Inscription Rock, at the east end of the cliff face, contains petroglyphs and carvings left by a long series of visitors, dating from pre-Columbian times to the present. Historian Charles F. Lummis wrote in the park's visitor register in 1926: "No other cliff on earth records a tithe as much of romance, adventure, heroism. Certainly all the other rocks in America do not, all together, hold so much of American history. Oñate here carved with his dagger two years before an English-speaking person built a hut anywhere in the New World, and 15 years before Plymouth Rock." The historic monolith and adjacent landscape (total of 1,279 acres or 113 ha) were established as a national monument in 1906, America's second-oldest national monument (after Devil's Tower, Wyoming).

At 7,200 feet (2,195 m) elevation, the area's vegetation is dominated by a pinyon-juniper woodland of two-needle pinyon and oneseed juniper, and fields of big sagebrush, rabbitbrush, four-wing saltbush, and grasses. Ponderosa pines occur along the base of the cliffs and Gambel's oaks thrive on the cooler north face.

The park's visitor center is situated at the end of a 1.2-mile (1.9 km) entrance road, off State Highway 53, that crosses the northern portion of the monument. The visitor center has an information desk, exhibits, and sales outlet; field guides and a bird checklist are available. Interpretive activities are limited to evening programs on weekends and a self-guided Inscription Rock/Mesa Top Trail that begins behind the visitor center and follows a 2-mile (3.2 km) loop-route. A small campground also exists along the entrance road.

Additional information can be obtained from the Superintendent, El Morro National Monument, Route 2, Box 43, Ramah, NM 87321; (505) 783-4226.

Bird Life

Another of the monument's aerial acrobats that is almost always in evidence is the **common raven**. Except for occasional turkey vultures and the resident red-tailed hawks, ravens are the largest of the park's soaring birds. They, too, nest on the El Morro cliffs and can compete in soaring with any of the broad-winged birds. The common raven can be identified by either its drawn-out croaking calls or hoarse "croo-croo" or "cur-ruk" notes, or by its large size, all-black plumage, and distinct silhouette: broad pointed wings, wedge-shaped tail, and large head and bill.

The smaller American kestrel, with its reddish back, pointed wings, and moustachial stripes, can sometimes be found over the cliffs, as well. But it spends most of its time hunting the adjacent flats.

The pinyon-juniper woodlands of the park support a rather distinct bird life, fairly typical of this community throughout the American Southwest. The monument campground was built within this environment. Most common of the pinyon-juniper birds are the broad-tailed hummingbirds, ash-throated flycatchers, scrub and pinyon jays, plain titmice, bushtits, white-breasted nuthatches, Bewick's wrens, western bluebirds, blue-gray gnatcatchers, hepatic tanagers, chipping sparrows, and house finches. Less common are the western screech-owls, hairy woodpeckers, Cassin's kingbirds, gray flycatchers, American robins, solitary vireos, black-throated gray warblers, and black-headed grosbeaks. See chapter 22 on Colorado National Monument for additional details on pinyon-juniper birds.

The ponderosa pine and Gambel's oak communities provide additional nesting habitats for birds. **Pygmy nuthatches**, for example, rarely stray far from ponderosas. These tiny, short-tailed, brown, gray, and buff birds are most often detected first by their almost constant and rapid, high-pitched "peep" calls. They are able to extract seeds from ponderosa pine cones, and they also forage for insects over the entire tree, from the furrowed trunks to the small branches and outer foliage. Seeing these nuthatches walking up and down the trunks or completely upside-down on the branches is commonplace. Other nesting birds of the ponderosa pine stands include northern (red-shafted) flickers, Lewis' woodpeckers, western wood-pewees, mountain chickadees, solitary vireos, and western tanagers.

Stands of Gambel's oaks provide nesting habitats for black-chinned hummingbirds, warbling vireos, orange-crowned and Virginia's warblers, black-headed grosbeaks, and rufous-sided towhees. The most widespread of these birds is the **rufous-sided towhee.** This is one of America's better-known songbirds and is easily recognized by the male's coal black hood and blood-red eyes, black back and tail, whitish belly, and chestnut sides; females are duller versions of the males. This large sparrow spends most of its time on the ground, searching for food by jumping backwards to clear the shallow ground-cover. During its breeding season it can be one of the park's most conspicuous birds; it will sing from dawn till dusk, often from the top of the oaks and adjacent shrubs. Its song has provided its name: a slurred "tow-whee" or whining "chee-ee" calls.

The top of El Morro's sandstone monolith provides an excellent overview of the surrounding landscape. The Mesa Top (loop) Trail passes through all of the park's habitats and provides a good perspective on the area's bird life. There is no better place to hear the cascading songs of **canyon wrens,** a loud descending and decelerating series of "tews" that end abruptly, or with an added "jeet." The bird itself is not shy but, because of its habit of creeping in and out of rocky holes and crevices, it is not readily visible. Suddenly it will pop up on a rocky outcrop in full view. Its snow white throat, grayish cap, and cinnamon body, flecked with black and white, and long blackish bill, give it an almost exotic appearance.

Rock wrens are also present along the trail, but these all-grayish birds, with buff rumps, lack the charisma and song of the canyon wrens. Rock wren songs are a variety of buzzes and trills; see chapter 7 on Yellowstone for more information on this bird's singing ability. However, they are one of the most common songbirds on the Mesa Top Trail. I found one individual, crouched in the shade of a wax current shrub, with a huge, squirming grasshopper held

EL MORRO NATIONAL MONUMENT

tightly in its long bill. The grasshopper was almost half as long as the rock wren. Through binoculars, I watched for almost four minutes before it finally consumed the entire grasshopper. It first beat its prey against the rocky ground, until it could no longer attempt escape. It then proceeded to tear the insect apart by hacking it with deft thrusts, rearing back and chopping down with its lethal bill. It took a dozen or more blows before the grasshopper's legs and wings were separated. Then it cut the body into pieces with additional blows, consuming the smaller pieces one at a time. When it departed, I checked the ground and found nothing left of the grasshopper but one tarsus and pieces of torn wings.

When I finally completed my rock wren study, I discovered an Abert's squirrel, less than 40 feet (12 m) away, studying me just as carefully. It surprised me to find this beautiful tassel-eared squirrel at El Morro. This species is normally a resident of much more extensive ponderosa pine forests. I couldn't help but wonder how secure many of the wildland species are with so much of their essential habitats being eliminated or subtly changed by the hand of man. Most of the national park units, such as tiny El Morro, still support reasonably intact habitats, but even these areas are being changed by external influences. It is imperative that the few intact habitats that still remain be given greater protection than they currently have.

In summary, El Morro's checklist of birds includes 151 species, of which 54 are known to have nested within the monument. Of those, there are no water birds, four are hawks and owls, and Virginia's warbler is the only warbler. Six species are listed for winter only: bufflehead, rough-legged hawk, cedar waxwing, northern shrike, and American tree and white-throated sparrows.

Birds of Special Interest
White-throated swift. This is the bird flying swiftly along the cliffs, with a cigar-like body, white throat, and swept-back wings.

Violet-green swallow. It is often found with the swifts, but it possesses snow white underparts and velvety violet-green backs.

Cliff swallow. This is the swallow that builds mud nests on the cliffs; it has a whitish belly and cinnamon rump and throat.

Scrub jay. One of the park's most common birds, it is blue with a gray back, whitish underparts, blackish cheeks, and a long tail.

Common raven. This is the large, all-black bird with a wedge-shaped tail, pointed wings, and large bill, that often soars over El Morro.

Rock wren. It is common on the rocky slopes of El Morro, identified by its all-grayish body and buff rump, and jerky behavior.

Canyon wren. This is the little white-and-cinnamon bird that sings a wonderful descending and decelerating song.

Rufous-sided towhee. Watch for this large sparrow in brushy areas; males possess an all-black hood and blood red eyes.

29

White Sands National Monument, New Mexico

The loud, obnoxious songs and rasping "creeek" calls of cactus wrens can hardly be ignored—especially when they are the very first creatures to greet you on your arrival at White Sands National Monument. Few species of wildlife are as dependable as White Sand's cactus wrens. And if at least one of these robin-sized birds is not already present when you arrive, a few squeaks or spishing sounds will immediately attract one or more from wherever they might be to investigate the disturbance. The visitor center parking lot, at the entrance to the park's Heart of Sands Loop Drive, is lined with cane chollas, yuccas, and a few other native plant species. And almost every cholla and yucca contains an active cactus wren nest or the grassy remnants of earlier nests.

Cactus wren nests are flask-shaped, football-sized structures of grasses, small sticks, strips of bark, and other debris, built among the plant's protective spines and sharp leaves. Although the nests often appear messy and poorly constructed, a second look will reveal a rather intricate pattern. Each nest is fully enclosed and waterproof; the insulated inner chamber, lined with feathers, is reached through a narrow passage built at one end near the top. A pair of wrens will build two or more nests, one of which they utilize for raising a family and the others as dummy nests in which one of the adults or (later) the fledged birds will roost. Two or occasionally three broods are produced annually.

Cactus wrens are one of the bird world's most fascinating creatures. They often will sit for long periods of time at the very tip of a yucca stalk or other tall structure, surveying their domain, and every now and then sing their unique songs: "a low, rough choo-choo-choo-choo to chug-chug-chug-chug, cora-cora-cora-cora,

Cactus wren

and other variations; all sound like a car refusing to start," according to Scott Terrill in *The Audubon Society Master Guide to Birding*. Then, after proclaiming their territories, they will glide down to their mates and greet one another with peculiar "growls" and posturing, crouching with tails and wings extended.

I watched one individual in the parking lot searching the grills of several newly arrived vehicles for insects. It would fly up and extract a butterfly, grasshopper, or some other insect, and then fly back a few feet to consume its meal. After six or seven successful insect snacks, it flew to the ground in the adjacent planter and began to sort through the debris. I watched it lift several pieces of yucca leaves and peer underneath for prey. If nothing was found it left the material undisturbed, but on two occasions it threw the material aside with a quick twist of the head and grabbed up the prey found underneath. It seemed especially adept at this method of hunting.

Cactus wren diets vary. John Terres reported that it eats "beetles, ants, wasps, grasshoppers, bugs, some spiders and an occasional lizard and tree frog; also some cactus fruit, elderberries, cascara berries, some seeds, sometimes visits bird feeders for bread, pieces of raw apple, fried potatoes."

The Park Environment

The monument includes the world's largest gypsum dune field, including dunes to 60 feet (18 m) high, numerous plants and animals that have adapted to the arid conditions, and scenery that consists of snow white dunes that contrast with the surrounding mountains and blue sky. Located at 4,000 feet (1,219 m) elevation within the Tularosa Basin of south-central New Mexico, at the eastern base of the San Andres Mountains, the monument encompasses a total of 144,420 acres (58,446 ha), of which about one-half is dominated by the graceful dunes.

Dune vegetation is limited to scattered sand verbenas, soaptree yuccas, skunkbush sumacs, and rosemary-mint on the slopes, and patches of Rio Grande cottonwoods, yuccas, and grasses in depressions and along the edges. Saltbush flats, such as that along the first half of the dunes drive, are dominated by four-winged saltbush, yuccas, chollas, and a number of grasses. Pickleweed is common on the alkali flats and dry Lake Lucero. Honey mesquite, four-winged saltbush, and creosote bush occur on the lower mountain slopes. The Tularosa Basin is considered the northern edge of the Chihuahuan Desert.

White Sands National Monument is situated along Highway 70, between Las Cruces and Alamogordo, New Mexico, and is best viewed from the 8-mile (13 km) self-guided Heart of Sands Loop

Drive. The monument visitor center, located along Highway 70, has an information desk, orientation program, exhibits, and a sales outlet; field guides and a bird checklist are available. Interpretive activities include walks, evening programs, and the self-guided Big Dune Nature Trail. Camping is not available within the park but is available at nearby Alamogordo.

Additional information can be obtained from the Superintendent, White Sands National Monument, P.O. Box 1086, Holloman AFB, NM 88330-1086; (505) 479-6124.

Bird Life

The visitor center grounds are the park's most productive bird-viewing area. Mourning doves, Say's phoebes, western kingbirds, northern mockingbirds, northern and Scott's orioles, house finches, and house sparrows can usually be found there in spring and summer with little effort. And a dozen or more additional species can be found with a little more time.

Say's phoebes are the slender, brownish-gray birds with buff-colored bellies and black tails. They possess a graceful flight and usually remain close to the buildings on which they build their nests. They often are found sitting at the edge of a building or at the tip of a tall adjacent plant, from where they search for passing insects. They fly swiftly out to snatch up their prey with a snap of their bills, and often return to the same perch, settling down with a flip of their tails. Their calls are a mournful "pee-ur" sound that can usually be heard throughout the day.

Western kingbirds frequent the cottonwood trees behind the visitor center and usually can be located by their distinct "whit" calls or a drawn-out and harsh, metallic "ker-er-ip, ker-er-ip" or "pkit-pkit-pkeetle-dot" song. Kingbirds are exquisite birds with an upright stance and pale to bright yellow underparts, grayish throats, and a black tail with white outer edges. Unlike their Say's phoebe cousins, which are full-time residents in the monument, kingbirds spend their winters elsewhere. By September, however, the kingbird population will increase substantially as southbound migrants stop over to enjoy the oasis-like environment. But they soon leave for warmer climates to the south.

Scott's and northern orioles also go south for the winter months. Northern (Bullock's) orioles nest among the cottonwood foliage, while the **Scott's oriole** is a grassland species that builds suspended basket-nests of grasses on yuccas. It occurs about the visitor center as well as among the dunes. Males are extremely attractive birds with coal black hoods, backs, chests, and tips of their tails, and yellow underparts and rumps; they also have a bright yellow patch at the bend of each wing. Females are gray-green with whitish wing bars. But what is most attractive about this bird is its loud, clear whistle song with numerous variations, which sounds superficially like the western meadowlark's song. A Scott's oriole song, echoing across the dunes, can be ventriloquistic and almost haunting in character.

The song of the **northern mockingbird** is one of the finest in the bird world. It can include renditions that are exact duplications of oriole songs one minute, cactus wren songs the next minute, and of several other local species after that. Mockers can carry on for hours, changing their songs continuously. And if you whistle a short, catchy phrase several times, a mocker will often repeat that same phrase. They too are dune birds and can be expected within their rather restricted territories all 12 months of the year.

Besides the birds already mentioned, there are a few other residents of the visitor center grounds: mourning doves are common and their mournful songs can be heard throughout the year; greater roadrunners can sometimes be found about the parking areas running down lizards; black-chinned hummingbirds feed at flowering shrubs; Chihuahuan ravens soar overhead or search the parking lot and roads for food; brown-headed cowbirds are social parasites that watch for opportunities to lay their eggs in other bird's nests; house finches, with the male's reddish heads and streaked bellies, sing spirited songs; and house sparrows are almost always searching for seeds and insects along the edge of the parking areas.

Chihuahuan ravens are all-black birds slightly larger than crows but smaller than the more heavyset common ravens. These birds were earlier called "white-necked ravens," because their neck feathers are white at the base, a feature evident only on a windy day. Their calls are low, drawn-out croaks, like a hoarse "quark, quark."

Scaled quail also occur about the visitor center grounds but are more numerous on the saltbush flats. Early morning is the best time of day to see this elusive bird. Then it often walks along the roadsides; with binoculars one can see it well enough from a distance and not frighten it away. Scaled quail are blue-gray birds with breast feathers that appear scaly; they also have top-notches with white tips that have given them the name "cottontops." Their calls are loud and repetitive, emphatic "chuk chuk" or "pe-cos" sounds. Gambel's quail are also present on occasions but are very different: males possess black throats, faces, and teardrop-shaped plumes, chestnut caps and sides, and their call is a querulous "chi-CA-go-go," the call so often heard in Western movies.

Another bird found along the roadway, as well as on the alkali flats, is the **horned lark**, a sparrow-sized bird with a black, white, and yellow head and black crescent on its chest. Oftentimes, the initial sightings are of birds flying up from the roadway and away with only their blackish tail and high pitched "tsee-ee" notes in evidence.

But of the monument's various dune birds, none are as fascinating as the **loggerhead shrike**. This is the black-masked, white, gray, and black bird that is sometimes called "butcher-bird," due to its predatory habit. Male shrikes capture insects, small rodents, birds, and reptiles, and actually impale them on thorns or sharp yucca leaves; it will even use barbed wire. Its cache of prey decorates various plants in its territory and serves as an attractant to female shrikes.

Loggerhead shrikes look at first glance like a mockingbird, because they are both black-and-white with white wing patches. But shrikes are stockier birds with shorter and more powerful bills, and they fly in a straight line with faster wingbeats. Shrikes lack the singing ability of mockingbirds, producing loud, harsh, almost rattling screech calls.

Watch, too, for the little black-throated sparrow on the saltbrush and alkali flats. It is readily identified by its coal black throat and two white facial stripes. It is a pert and charismatic bird that is a true desert species. It often is detected first by its faint tinkling notes. Other saltbush flat and desert slope birds include lesser and common nighthawks, ladder-backed woodpecker, Chihuahuan and common ravens, verdin, Bewick's wren, crissal thrasher, pyrrhuloxia, and rufous-sided and canyon towhees. Park naturalist John Mangimeli told me that pyrrhuloxias are common all winter around the visitor center.

Open water is extremely rare within the monument since Garton Pond, located across the highway from the visitor center, dried up. Little more than a tenth of an acre of open water and cattails remain. Only occasional marsh wrens and common yellowthroats still use their old haunts.

Migration time, however, can be something special in the monument, when thousands of birds stream southward across the saltbush flats. One early September morning I recorded 46 bird species in about two hours by walking the roadway for about two miles. The most abundant species was the little chipping sparrow, with its reddish cap, gray underparts, and black-and-brown striped back. Other migrants found in numbers included western wood-pewees; orange-crowned, yellow-rumped, MacGillivray's, and Wilson's warblers; blue grosbeaks; green-tailed towhees; Brewer's, clay-colored, vesper, lark, and white-crowned sparrows; lark buntings; red-winged, yellow-headed, and Brewer's blackbirds; and lesser goldfinches. Smaller numbers of house wrens, sage thrashers, one American redstart, common yellowthroats, western tanagers, black-headed grosbeaks, Lincoln's sparrows, and pine siskins were recorded.

I also watched a lone northern harrier hunting for prey over the flats. It slowly quartered back and forth at less than a dozen feet high as if it had sectioned off certain portions of the flats to hunt one at a time. Every now and then it would suddenly twist in the air and drop onto the ground, as if pouncing on a prey species. This hawk remains throughout the winter months and, according to Mangimeli, can usually be found hunting these fields.

Heavy rains, which can occur during the spring and fall migration, create temporary pools between the dunes and at Lake Lucero that can attract significant numbers of wading birds and shorebirds. White-faced ibis, American avocets, and willets can usually be found among the dunes. And grebes, ducks, and shorebirds stop-off at Luke Lucero.

In summary, the park's bird checklist includes 196 species, of which 70 are listed as permanent or summer residents and "breeder."

Of those 70 species, only 2 are water birds (American coot and killdeer), 9 are hawks and owls, and 2 are warblers (Lucy's warbler and common yellowthroat). Twenty-six species are listed only as winter residents, but several of those must also be migrants.

Birds of Special Interest

Scaled quail. This is the park's only common quail and is easily identified by its blue-gray plumage and white-tipped crest.

Say's phoebe. It is especially common near the visitor center; it possesses gray-brown plumage with a buff-colored belly.

Western kingbird. Watch for this flycatcher about the cottonwoods near the visitor center; its yellow belly and black tail with white outer edges are its most distinguishing features.

Chihuahuan raven. This all-black bird is best identified by the white base of its neck feathers, seen only on windy days, and hoarse "quark" calls.

Horned lark. This sparrow-sized bird is often found walking along the roadway and flats about the dunes; it is best identified by its black chest, yellowish throat, and black lines on its head.

Cactus wren. The park's most obvious bird, its nests are common on chollas and yuccas, and its harsh, rasping songs can be heard year-round.

Northern mockingbird. This is the black-and-white songbird with a long tail and diversity of songs; it is a full-time resident in the park.

Loggerhead shrike. It is like a mockingbird but heavier-bodied and a more direct flight. Sometimes it is called "butcher-bird" because of its predatory nature.

Scott's oriole. This is the black-and-yellow bird that frequents the dunes and builds its pendulous nests on yuccas.

30

Carlsbad Caverns and Guadalupe Mountains National Parks, New Mexico and Texas

The cave mouth was a huge gaping hole in the layered limestone terrain. The entrance trail snaked back and forth across the steep slope and disappeared into the cave's rocky gullet. Lines of visitors, enticed by the cool breeze, followed the trail and disappeared into the cavern. The only living things I detected emerging from the deep hole were cave swallows. Only they seemed to have conquered both the darkened cavern mouth and the brilliance of day, moving freely back and forth between the two environments.

Cave swallow

I sat near the cave entrance on a weathered block of gray limestone, observing the swallows' activities. There were at least a dozen individuals visible at any one time. Their high-pitched "weet" notes echoed from the steep slopes and from inside the cave's shadowy entrance. Six or seven individuals suddenly plummeted from the sky and dashed into the cave, close to the ceiling, en route no doubt to their mud nests and the gaping bills of their nestlings. It was impossible to distinguish individual swallows in their comings and goings, but their intent was obvious.

A cactus wren sang a harsh, rollicking "chuh chuh chuh chuh" song from a tall sotol stalk above the cave entrance. Through binoculars I could see its streaked breast, banded tail, bold white eye line, and heavy bill, which firmly grasped a large insect of some sort. Then it flew to a cane cholla that held a football-sized, grass nest, well-protected by the numerous cactus spines. A second cactus wren suddenly emerged from the nest opening at the side, and the first individual, insect and all, disappeared inside. I could only imagine the eager responses of the nestlings.

Two plump, all-brown birds suddenly moved to the right of the cholla, and I immediately recognized them as canyon towhees. It took me several minutes to see their rusty crowns and crissums and dark chest spots. I had already seen this bird at the cavern's parking lot, where one pair had been searching for insects brought in on vehicle grills. They had also been common along the cave entrance trail, chasing one another among the desert plants, calling out loud chips, and singing songs that sounded like "chili chili chili."

The loudest songs detected, however, were those of the northern mockingbirds. At least three mockers were within hearing distance; each seemed intent on out-singing the others. Their repertoire of melodies, including whistles and squeals, chucks and churrs, far surpassed all the other songbirds that day. One individual alighted on a green-leafed ocotillo, and I was able to clearly see its black-and-white plumage and yellowish eyes.

It suddenly flew up after a passing insect. But just inches before it could capture its prey, a cave swallow, flying much faster than the mockingbird, swooped down and snatched its meal away from the gaping mockingbird. The mocker glided away to another perch, seemingly unperturbed, while the swallow continued on into the cave and a waiting family.

The Park Environment

The Guadalupe Mountains are the southwestern portion of a huge horseshoe-shaped formation of Permian limestone that rises to 8,749 feet (2,666 m) elevation at Guadalupe Peak. The majority of the ancient reef lies below the surface of the ground but is exposed at three locations: for approximately 30 miles (48 km) of the Guadalupe Mountains escarpment from near Carlsbad, New Mexico, to Guadalupe Peak, in Texas; the Apache Mountains, northeast of Van Horn, Texas; and the Glass Mountains, east of Alpine, Texas.

Guadalupe Mountains National Park, Texas, encompasses 86,416 acres (34,972 ha) of Guadalupe Peak and its adjacent ridges, canyons, and desertscape. The northeastern portion of the range declines gradually in elevation and simply disappears into a matrix of rocks and gravels. Carlsbad Caverns National Park, New Mexico, with its more than 70 caves, including famous Carlsbad Caverns, covers an area of 46,755 acres (18,921 ha) at the northern end of the escarpment, directly northeast of Guadalupe Mountains National Park.

Vegetation within the dual parks is primarily Chihuahuan Desert, although the deep, cool canyons and uplands of Guadalupe Mountains contain representatives of Rocky Mountain flora. Chihuahuan Desert plants form two rather distinct associations, desertscrub and succulent desert. Creosote bush dominates the open flats and bajadas of the desertscrub, although honey mesquite, blackbrush, white-thorn acacia, ocotillo, and snakeweed are also abundant. Succulent desert vegetation forms a transition zone on the escarpment and extends from the mid-elevation slopes to near the summit. Dominant plants within this area include creosote bush, lechuguilla, sotol, bear-grass, oneseed juniper, mariola, slim-leaf goldeneye, Faxon yucca, and New Mexico agave.

An evergreen woodland occurs on the cooler northern slopes and in canyonheads between approximately 4,500 and 7,000 feet (1,372-2,134 m) elevation. Characteristic plants include two-needle pinyon, alligator juniper, gray oak, Texas madrone, and fragrant sumac. Redberry juniper is also common at Carlsbad Caverns. And above 6,000 feet (1,829 m) is a coniferous forest that is dominated by limber and ponderosa pines, Douglas fir, and Gambel's oak. A "semi-virgin forest" occurs on about 100 acres (247 ha) in the Bowl, a relict area representative of cooler times.

And in moist canyons, such as Guadalupe's McKittrick Canyon, are riparian habitats where canyon maple, chinkapin oak, and Knowlton hornbeam are most abundant. Alligator juniper, Texas madrone, chokecherry, velvet ash, Texas walnut, desert-willow, littleleaf sumac, netleaf hackberry, and Apache-plume are dominant in the open portions of the canyon.

National park visitor centers are located at Carlsbad Caverns, at the end of a 7-mile (11 km) road beyond White City, and at Guadalupe Mountains Pine Springs, off Highway 62/180, the main route between El Paso, Texas, and Carlsbad, New Mexico. Both centers have information desks, orientation programs, exhibits, and sales outlets; field guides and area bird checklists are available. Camping is permitted only at Pine Springs, although backcountry camping is also available by permit.

Interpretive activities include all-year cave tours and a variety of nature walks and evening talks, including the famous bat flight talk at the cave entrance at dusk from early spring through October. Interpretive schedules are available for the asking and are posted at various bulletin boards.

Both parks possess considerable backcountry that, except for Carlsbad's Walnut Canyon Desert Drive, is accessible only by hiking trails; these include 80 miles (129 km) in Guadalupe Mountains and 40 miles (64 km) in Carlsbad Caverns National Park. More than half of Guadalupe Mountains park (46,850 acres or 18,960 ha) is official "wilderness." *Trails of the Guadalupes*, a hiker's guide by Don Kurtz and William Green, contains a good overview of Guadalupe's backcountry.

Additional information can be obtained from the superintendents at Carlsbad Caverns National Park, 3225 National Parks Highway, Carlsbad, NM 88220; (505) 785-2232; and Guadalupe Mountains National Park, HC 60, Box 400, Salt Flat, TX 79847; (915) 828-3251.

Bird Life

Cave swallows and Carlsbad Caverns are synonymous. These swallows are one of the park's most common birds and can readily be seen at the cave entrance from late February through October. But this was not always the case. Prior to the mid-1950s, cave swallows were a Mexican breeder only and rarely seen north of the border. Cave swallows first appeared in the park at undeveloped caves in Slaughter Canyon in the 1950s, and two pairs finally nested just inside Carlsbad Caverns in 1966. That colony increased annually after that and, although their numbers vary from year to year, as many as 4,000 birds are present some years, representing the largest colony north of Mexico. Their range has also expanded eastward into southern Texas as far the Gulf of Mexico; they also occur in Florida.

Cave swallows are often confused with the closely related and more widespread cliff swallows. Both are square-tailed swallows with dark backs, whitish underparts, and buff rumps. Cliff swallows possess dark chestnut and blackish throats and pale foreheads, while cave swallows possess chestnut foreheads and only a tinge of buff on their throats. Cliff swallows build enclosed mud-pellet nests on cliffs and walls of buildings, while cave swallows build open-topped mud-pellet nests attached to the ceilings of limestone caves and sinkholes, culverts, and similar twilight sites.

At Carlsbad Caverns, cave swallows are sometimes misidentified as a species of bats because both live in or near the cave. Bats, however, are nocturnal mammals that normally spend their daylight hours far underground. Cave swallows, on the other hand, are birds that are active during the daylight hours and roost in their nests or on adjacent ledges just inside the mouth of the cave at night.

Since 1980, local school teacher Steve West and a cadre of volunteers have captured and banded more than 8,500 cave swallows at Carlsbad Caverns in an attempt to learn more about their life history and migration. Steve told me that their data have shown that "males are primarily responsible for nest construction although females are the only ones that incubate the eggs." And for the first time, a band recovered in Mexico may provide some clue to their winter range.

The entire surface of Carlsbad Caverns National Park is dominated by Chihuahuan Desert vegetation, and so the resident birds evident near the cave and along Walnut Canyon Desert Drive and the various trails are desert species. Most obvious are those already mentioned, which dwell at the cave entrance, and a handful of other species. One of the most widespread is the little **black-throated sparrow,** usually found in flocks of a few to a dozen individuals and often detected first by its musical tinkling songs. It is easily identified by its pert manner, coal black throat, white belly, and dark cheeks that are bordered by two bold, white stripes. Its scientific name is *bilineata,* Latin for "two-striped." It was earlier called "desert" sparrow; it resides in the hottest of North America's deserts, where it is able to obtain its daily supply of water from desert seeds that it eats. They also are curious birds and can often be enticed into the open by low spishing sounds.

The common woodpecker of the desert is the little **ladder-backed woodpecker,** named for its black-and-white barred back. This is the only true Chihuahuan Desert woodpecker; the other woodpeckers found in the dual parks prefer riparian habitats or forested areas. Ladder-backs are small enough to actually nest in century plant stalks. And their nest chambers are utilized by several other cavity-nesters, such as ash-throated flycatchers, plain titmice, Bewick's wrens, and western bluebirds. Males possess red crowns; females have all-black crowns.

The Chihuahuan Desert quail is the **scaled quail**, a blue-gray bird with a conspicuous white-tipped crest and breast feathers that look scalloped or scaled. It is also known as "blue quail" and "cottontop," for obvious reasons. One cannot spend very much time in the desert without at least hearing this bird. Their calls consist of loud barking "kuck-yur" notes or a low whistled "pe-cos," and the sound can carry for a considerable distance in the desert. Harry Oberholser, in the monumental *The Bird Life of Texas*, reported that "[b]order Mexicans translate this quail's most frequent call as 'toston' (tos-TONE), which name they apply to the species." Flocks of a few to two dozen individuals are sometimes found running ahead of a visitor on the trail or roadway. It is considered one of the "running quail," fleeing to safety on its powerful legs and flying only when hard-pressed.

Scaled quail

Scaled quail have a broad range from southern Arizona to northern New Mexico and southwest Kansas, south to the Mexican states of Jalisco, Guanajuarto, and Mexico. They seem to have a preference for desert grasslands, although they can also be found in extremely arid areas. At night, they roost on the ground, employing "a clever precautionary means of self-defense against night-prowling enemies by forming a circle, tails together, head outward," according to J. Stokley Ligon, author of *New Mexico Birds*, who adds, "thus every bird represents a night sentinel on guard against surprise attack."

Other common desert birds include the greater roadrunner, great horned owl, lesser nighthawk, common poorwill, Say's phoebe, verdin, loggerhead shrike, pyrrhuloxia, and house finch.

Chihuahuan Desert communities along the Williams Ranch road, at Guadalupe Mountains park, contain all the same species. But in places where grasses are common, a few additional birds can be found: curve-billed and crissal thrashers, Cassin's and rufous-crowned sparrows, eastern and western meadowlarks, and Scott's orioles.

Rufous-crowned sparrows are the most numerous of these, although they have a habit of flying into the shrubbery just when one is trying to get a good look. However, patience will prevail, and they are best identified by their rufous crowns, single black whisker stripes, and clear, grayish breasts. This sparrow seems to frequent rocky places, and they are one of the most vocal of all birds, continuously calling to one another, even after the nesting season and in winter. They often perform a squealing duet upon greeting their mate. Their calls are clear, thin, descending notes, like "tew-tew-tew-tew." And their songs are a "staccato chittering, which changes in pitch, somewhat like a softened house wren's song," according to John Terres.

Rattlesnake Springs is an outstanding desert oasis located below the escarpment southeast of Carlsbad Caverns. This area of huge Fremont cottonwoods, willows, tamarisk, cattails, and other water-loving plants, is considered the single best bird-finding site in the two parks. West reports that Rattlesnake Springs also "is a well-known vagrant trap for birds passing through the area," and that "almost 90 percent of all the species recorded in the park have been found" there.

Cave swallows utilize the lush grounds in spring and summer for gathering insects. The cottonwoods ring with the calls of mourning doves, ash-throated flycatchers, western kingbirds, summer tanagers, orchard and northern (Bullock's) orioles, and lesser goldfinches. And the dense undergrowth and swampy areas reverberate with the songs of Bell's vireos, common yellowthroats, yellow-breasted chats, northern cardinals, blue grosbeaks, painted buntings, and red-winged blackbirds.

The orioles can be especially evident in spring when they are actively defending territories and courting. They seem to spend an inordinate amount of time pursuing one another among the foliage. The little orchard orioles, with the males' black hoods, breasts, and tails, and chestnut backs and bellies, call sharp "chuck" notes at one another. Their occasional songs are loud, rapid bursts of melody that Arthur Bent described as "Look here, what cheer, what cheer, whip yo, what cheer, wee-yo." Rattlesnake Springs marks the western edge of the breeding range of this eastern oriole.

The larger **northern oriole**, distinguished by the male's black crown, orange cheeks, underparts, and rump, and large white wing patches, sings a slower song with rich, whistled notes, interspersed with guttural notes and rattles. Oriole nests are easily identified, because of their pendant character, although they are usually well-hidden among the foliage. Typical northern oriole nests are attached to twigs near the end of branches, 10 to 40 feet (3-12 m) above the ground. They consist of oval-shaped woven bags, of vegetable fibers, inner bark, and horsehair, approximately 6 inches (15 cm) deep. The nests are usually lined with wool, down, hair, and mosses. See chapter 12 on Capitol Reef for additional details about this lovely bird.

One early spring day park naturalist Brent Wauer (my brother) and I drove the Williams Ranch road, watching for wildlife along the way. Winter birds were still present. Black-throated sparrows were most numerous; curve-billed and crissal thrashers were fairly numerous; and sage sparrows were scattered among the open desertscrub environment along the first couple miles of the roadway. This little sparrow, with its brown-gray back, bold white whisker stripe, and black breast spot, ran here and there among the shrubbery, pausing only in response to loud chipping sounds made with my lips on the back of my hand.

Brushy areas in desert drainages and along the lower edge of the pinyon-juniper woodlands are the best places to find the smaller **black-chinned sparrow**. One September day I watched a pair of these desert shrub sparrows foraging near Pine Springs Campground; Brent informed me that this area is the best place in the park to see this species. Both individuals were climbing about the four-winged saltbush at the edge of the parking lot. They seemed extremely active, going up and down the stems but spending equal time on the ground. Males possess a coal black chin that contrasts with their all-gray underparts, rump, and collar, and rusty wings; females are duller versions of the males.

Black-chins were also present at the mouth of McKittrick Canyon, singing their very distinct songs that reminded me of field sparrow songs, their closest relatives. Black-chin songs begin with a series of "sweet" notes that are followed by a rapid descending trill, like a bouncing ping-pong ball.

McKittrick Canyon cuts into the heart of the Guadalupes, providing access to the high cliffs and some choice riparian habitats along the way. In early spring the area can be alive with birds. Although the lower slopes are dominated by desert species, the scene changes dramatically after about one mile. Black-chinned and rufous-crowned sparrows, canyon towhees, rock wrens, and ash-throated flycatchers are most numerous near the mouth. And gray vireos are also present; singing males seem to claim territories about one-quarter mile in length.

The cascading songs of **canyon wrens** welcome visitors to the inner canyon. Their unique, descending and decelerating whistles echo across the canyon, but it takes a sharp eye to find the perpetrator. Canyon wrens are lovely little birds with snow white throats, cinnamon backs and bellies with numerous black-and-white flecks, and long black bills. The bill length provides a good clue to their habit of searching for food in every crack and cranny among the rocky terrain. And every now and then they will sing their wonderful songs.

Hummingbirds can be also common along the canyon, and once century plants begin to flower they provide a showplace for these brightly colored Lilliputians. One June morning I sat in the shade of a Gambel's oak and, through my binoculars, watched hummingbirds feeding on the flowers of a nearby New Mexico agave. Black-chinned hummingbirds were most numerous, distinguished by their purple-black chins, which contrasted with their white chests. Broad-tailed hummingbirds were common as well, easy to identify by the males' trilling wingbeats and rosy-red throats. But two larger hummers also put in their appearance during my hour-long vigil: blue-throated and magnificent.

Magnificent hummingbird

I detected the presence of the blue-throated hummingbird before I actually observed it because of its loud "seep" calls made in flight. When it finally approached the yellow flowers, its size, in comparison with the smaller black-chins hovering nearby, was striking. The male's bright blue throat and the white corners of its tail were also evident. But the hummingbird of the day was the equally large **magnificent hummingbird** that suddenly appeared, as if by magic. Its deep green back and throat patch, shiny black belly, and purple crown gleamed in the bright morning sunlight like a bright jewel. It stayed only a few seconds before flying off with rather loud heavy wingbeats, almost directly over where I stood in admiration. Although I had seen this bird several times before in the Chisos Mountains of Big Bend National Park, the McKittrick Canyon sighting was one of the most memorable. I have seen it in

McKittrick several times since then, and in spite of being at the northern edge of its breeding range, it is the best place I know to find this tropical species.

The chinkapin oak groves scattered along the canyon often contain their own assortment of birds. Although several species feed among the foliage, at least one bird nests there, the Virginia's warbler. This rather drab bird is mostly gray with yellow on its breast, rump, and crissum, and a bold white eye ring. Other birds that frequent riparian woodlands include blue-gray gnatcatchers, solitary vireos, black-headed grosbeaks, and rufous-sided towhees.

McKittrick Creek is an intermittent stream that forms lush pockets of saw-grass and sedges in protected places but disappears into the gravels elsewhere. The surface flow provides water for hundreds of birds throughout the year and is especially important during the warm summer months. Even those birds that nest on the high cliffs, such as white-throated swifts and swallows, utilize the waterway to catch insects or gather nesting materials.

The little **cordilleran flycatcher** is one of the species that hawks insects along the creek, often from perches over the waterway, but it builds its nest at the base of the cliffs in protected niches. This bird was known as western flycatcher until it was split from the west coast form. It sings a very distinct two-syllabled song, with the second note higher: "pit-peet!" Kenn Kaufman gives the best description of these flycatchers in his book, *Advanced Birding*. It also is identified by its yellowish underparts, greenish-brown back, and almond-shaped eye ring.

Peregrine falcons also occur in upper McKittrick Canyon but sometimes visit the lower canyon. Its continued survival, even during the years when DDT had eliminated all northern populations, attests to the canyon's relative isolation. Peregrines are one of the world's most exciting birds, stooping at more than 200 miles (332 km) per hour. The watchful visitor to McKittrick Canyon may be fortunate to observe this dynamic falcon as it courts high above or hunts along the canyon. Such an observation can provide memories that will last a lifetime.

A rather extensive woodland of pinyons and junipers exists above the desert, at the base of the escarpment, as well as on the open ridges at higher elevations. Much of the pinyon-juniper bird life is similar to that which exists throughout the American Southwest, but the plain titmouse is at the southeastern edge of its range in the Guadalupes. This little gray-brown bird with a short crest can best be found along the Smith Spring Trail or at Dog Canyon.

Other rather typical pinyon-juniper birds at Guadalupe Mountains include common poorwills, broad-tailed humming-birds, ladder-backed woodpeckers, scrub jays, bushtits, Bewick's wrens, blue-gray gnatcatchers, western bluebirds, hepatic tanagers, canyon towhees, chipping sparrows, brown-headed cowbirds, Scott's orioles, house finches, and lesser goldfinches.

One week in June I hiked the Bear Canyon Trail to the highlands and camped overnight in the Bowl. The relict forest in this high depression contains a few mountain birds that do not occur with regularity elsewhere in the park. I found several of the highland spe-cialties reasonably common: common nighthawks; whip-poor-wills; acorn woodpeckers; western wood-pewees; Steller's jays; mountain chickadees; pygmy and white-breasted nuthatches; house wrens; hermit thrushes; warbling vireos; orange-crowned, yellow-rumped, and Grace's warblers; western tanagers; and dark-eyed (gray-headed) juncos. A few other species were less numerous: band-tailed pigeons, western screech-owls, flammulated owls, olive-sided flycatchers, brown creepers, pine siskins, and evening grosbeaks.

The most obvious of these was the **Steller's jay**, an all-blue jay with a blackish-blue crest. A pair of these birds spent considerable time watching me as I prepared my camp, and their loud, grating calls were evident throughout my stay. See chapter 4 on Mount Revelstoke and Glacier for further details about this bird's fascinat-ing behavior.

A survey of Guadalupe Mountain birds undertaken during the 1970s by George Newman of Texas Christian University revealed that a few other high-country species also occur there at least occa-sionally. These include wild turkeys (common now), spotted owls, red-naped sapsuckers, and Clark's nutcrackers.

Wintering species within the dual parks include full-time resi-dents as well as a number of more northern visitors. Christmas Bird

Counts have been taken in both parks for several years, and these counts provide the best perspective on the wintertime populations. In 1991, 3,322 individuals of 85 species were tallied at Carlsbad, and 2,737 individuals of 81 species were tallied at Guadalupe Mountains. The combined counts included 113 species; the dozen most numerous species, in descending order of abundance, included dark-eyed junco, meadowlarks (most were not specifically identified), chipping sparrow, mourning dove, rufous-crowned sparrow, white-crowned sparrow, western bluebird, eastern bluebird, black-throated sparrow, American robin, rufous-sided towhee, and canyon towhee.

In summary, the two parks' checklists account for a total of 347 species, of which 94 are known to nest. Of those 94 species, only 1 (killdeer) is a water bird, 12 are hawks and owls, and 4 are warblers. Fourteen species are listed for winter only.

Birds of Special Interest

Scaled quail. This is the bluish quail with a white top-notch that is most often found along the desert roadways; its call is a loud barking "kuck-yur" or "pe-cos."

Magnificent hummingbird. One of the largest of hummingbirds, males possess a metallic green throat and purple crown; it is best found about century plants in McKittrick Canyon.

Cordilleran flycatcher. This is the little, yellowish *Empidonax* flycatcher that nests under ledges along Guadalupe's many canyon bottoms.

Cave swallow. It is common at Carlsbad Caverns, where it nests in the twilight area near the cave entrance and forages over the surrounding desert.

Steller's jay. It occurs only in the Guadalupe highlands in Texas and is recognized by its all-blue body and tall, blackish crest.

Canyon wren. This is the little cinnamon bird with a snow white throat and a beautiful descending and decelerating song.

Canyon towhee. It is common throughout the parks' desertscrub environments; it is all-brown with a rusty crown and crissum, and a dark breast spot.

Rufous-crowned sparrow. It is a little sparrow of the rocky slopes that sports a rufous crown, black whisker stripes, and grayish breast.

Black-chinned sparrow. This tiny sparrow is especially common at Pine Springs Campground; it has a black chin that contrasts with its all-gray underparts, rump, and collar.

Black-throated sparrow. It is best identified by its coal black throat, white belly, and dark cheeks that are bordered by two bold white stripes.

Northern oriole. Males possess orange underparts, rumps, and cheeks; black caps, throats, tails, and wings with large white patches; it is common at Rattlesnake Springs in spring and summer.

31

Big Bend National Park, Texas

I could hear the song ahead of me, to the right of the trail. There was silence for a few minutes, broken only by the almost ubiquitous calls of Bewick's wrens and the hoarser notes of Mexican jays. And then I heard the song again, closer now and coming from the little arroyo along the trail. I stopped and waited for the little yellow-and-gray bird that I expected would soon move into the higher branches of an oak that grew above the surrounding brush. Suddenly, there it was! My first Colima warbler! I watched it work its way up and around the Emory oak, gleaning the branches and leaves for insects. It captured a long, green caterpillar, and for just a second or two seemed to examine its breakfast before swallowing it. The Colima warbler fed there in the sunlight for several minutes, and every 30 seconds or so it would put its head back and sing, a song a little like that of a yellow warbler, but shorter and faster and not so melodic.

I fell in love with Big Bend National Park on that first visit and later had the opportunity to spend six years there as Chief Park Naturalist.

To birders, Big Bend National Park in West Texas is America's number one national park. More species of birds have been recorded there (447) than in any other of North America's "crown jewels." And several of Big Bend's 447 species are Mexican residents that barely range north of the border. The most important of these is the diminutive Colima warbler that occurs nowhere else north of Mexico.

Several other Mexican birds, including the zone-tailed hawk, white-eared and Lucifer hummingbirds, and varied bunting can be found more easily in Big Bend than anywhere else. And no other national park has reported so many species of hummingbirds (15). In addition, the area is home to the endangered peregrine falcon.

The Park Environment

One of the largest and wildest of the U.S. national parks, Big Bend's 801,163 acres (324,226 ha) of Rio Grande flood plain, desert, and mountain habitats represent the best example anywhere of the Chihuahuan Desert ecosystem. The Rio Grande forms the southern boundary of the park and is contiguous with Mexico for 118 miles (225 km). This vital river, which originates in the Colorado Rockies, is usually only a trickle by the time it reaches El Paso, Texas. Most of the flow that passes through Big Bend National Park comes out of Mexico via the Rio Conchos, which enters the Rio Bravo del Norte (the Mexican name for the Rio Grande) at Presidio, Texas, southeast of El Paso. Within the park, the lush, green flood plains are scattered between three magnificent canyons: Santa Elena, Mariscal, and Boquillas. All contain cliffs that tower to about 1,500 feet (457 m) above the waterway. The Rio Grande provides a popular recreational rafting route, especially within the three canyons, and also serves as an important route for migrating birds during both spring and fall.

Below the park, an additional 127 miles (204 km) of the Rio Grande was established as the Rio Grande Wild and Scenic River in 1978. The canyons along this stretch of the river are every bit as dramatic as those in the park.

The Chisos Mountains serve as a magnificent centerpiece for the park. These are the southernmost mountains in the United States and the only contiguous mountain range contained entirely within a national park. Although only about 16,000 acres (6,475 ha) are above 3,700 feet (1,128 m) elevation, the lower edge of the woodlands, the Chisos comprise an island of greenery that is surrounded by the arid Chihuahuan Desert. The summit of Emory Peak is 7,835 feet (2,388 m) in elevation. On a clear day it affords views of most of West Texas and far into Coahuila, Mexico. The high escarpment approximately 50 miles (80 km) southeast of the Chisos, the western edge of Mexico's Maderas del Carmen, rises to about 9,000 feet (2,744 m) elevation. That area and its bird life are further discussed by this author in *Naturalist's Mexico*.

The Chisos Basin, located at 5,300 feet (1,615 m) elevation in the heart of the mountains, contains a visitor center, campground, trailhead, motel, lodge/dining room, and gift shop. Most people who go to the park, especially during the summer months, visit the Chisos Basin, but obtaining overnight accommodations in the motel often requires reservations far in advance, especially during holidays and weekends. The Basin's high elevation gives it pleasant temperatures in summer. The Chisos trails, which originate from the Basin, provide excellent walking and hiking routes into the higher mountains and to The Window toward the west, the setting for superb sunset views.

The best time to visit Big Bend National Park is during the cooler winter months, November through March. The majority of the park's winter visitors prefer to camp in the lowlands, especially at the park's principal campground, Rio Grande Village. Situated on the eastern edge of the park along the Rio Grande, the location allows for easy day-trips across the river to Boquillas, Coahuila. Boquillas Canyon and the magnificent limestone cliffs of the Sierra del Carmens provide the backdrop for Rio Grande Village. At dusk the cliffs can be a deep rose color, reflecting the sun as it sets behind the Chisos Mountains far to the west.

Cottonwood Campground, on the park's western edge, has a similar setting. Its backdrop is the 1,500-foot (457 m) cliffs of the Sierra Ponce, which catch the early morning light. The tiny Mexican village of Santa Elena can be reached by fording the Rio Grande near Castolon, the historic U.S. Army compound and trading post.

Above the flood plain are six distinct vegetative zones I referred to as "ecological associations" in a 1971 *Southwestern Naturalist* article. The six areas and their dominant plants include: (1) arroyo-mesquite-acacia association, dominated by lanceleaf cottonwood, honey and screwbean mesquites, catclaw and mescat acacias, and desert-willow; (2) lechuguilla-creosote bush-cactus association, dominated by creosote bush, lechuguilla, ocotillo, blind prickly pear, and clavellina; (3) sotol-grass association, dominated by tobosa and chinograma in the warmer areas and sotol, bear-grass, blue three-awn, and various grama grasses in cooler areas; (4) deciduous woodland association, dominated by Graves and Emory oaks, evergreen and littleleaf sumacs, Texas madrone, canyon maple, mountain sage, and scarlet bouvardia; (5) pinyon-juniper association, dominated by Mexican pinyon; drooping, alligator and redberry junipers; gray, Emory and Graves oaks; evergreen and littleleaf sumacs; and several grasses; and (6) cypress-pine-oak association, dominated by Arizona cypress, Douglas fir, ponderosa pine, Mexican pinyon, junipers, Texas madrone, birchleaf buckthorn, silk-tassel, mountain sage, Emory and Graves oaks, and canyon maple.

The park's principal visitor center is located at Panther Junction, and houses an information desk, exhibits, and excellent sales areas where general field guides, as well as a park-specific bird guide, *A Field Guide to Birds of the Big Bend* (by this author), and a bird checklist are available.

Regularly scheduled talks, bird walks, and special bird seminars are available. Park interpreters give evening talks and bird walks at Rio Grande Village and the Basin Campgrounds. Schedules are available on request. In addition, the Big Bend Natural History Association sponsors the "Big Bend Seminar" program, which includes a variety of sessions on bird identification and ecology. Further details are available from the Big Bend Natural History Association, P.O. Box 86, Big Bend National Park, TX 79834.

Additional information on the park can be obtained from the Superintendent, Big Bend National Park, TX 79834; (915) 477-2251.

Bird Life

The Colima warbler is the park's most renowned songbird, in spite of the fact that it is resident only from mid-April through September. It spends the rest of the year in Mexico's western mountains from Sinaloa to northern Oaxaca. Seeing the Colima warbler on its U.S. breeding grounds in the Chisos Mountains is not easy, however, and normally requires at least a 6-mile (9.6 km) round-trip hike to Laguna Meadows, its most accessible habitat. The most reliable place to find this warbler is in Boot Canyon, which requires a 9-mile (14.5 km) round-trip.

Lucifer hummingbird

The **Lucifer hummingbird** is another of Big Bend's Mexican specialties. Although sightings of this species are possible in a few other localities north of the border, it occurs regularly and in numbers only at Big Bend National Park. Like the Colima warbler, it is present only during the spring and summer months. Lucifers seem to appear mysteriously in early March with the first flowering acacias in the lowlands. But by late May, when century plants (Havard agave) begin to bloom on the slopes of the Chisos, it practically abandons the desert for the mountains. Blue Creek Canyon and along the Window Trail are good places to find Lucifers then. And in summer, when the brilliant red flowers of the mountain sage appear, they feed almost exclusively at these beautiful shrubs, which grow in abundance above approximately 6,500 feet (1,980 m).

Big Bend's Chisos Mountains hold the record for the greatest number of hummingbird species recorded in any of the national parks, 15. Besides the Lucifer, four other hummers that occur there—broad-billed, blue-throated, magnificent, and white-eared—are more common in Mexico than within the United States. Although the two large hummers, magnificent and blue-throated, are present all summer, the white-eared and broad-billed hum-mingbirds usually visit the park only for brief periods when the mountain sage is in bloom. Two species—plain-capped starthroat and berylline—are listed by the park as hypotheticals, according to park naturalist Jeff Selleck.

The common hummingbird of the Big Bend lowlands is the little black-chinned hummingbird, while the broad-tailed hummingbird is the common species in the Chisos woodlands. Broad-tails frequent the pinyon-juniper woodlands as well as the cypress-pine-oak associations in the upper canyons. Ruby-throated, Costa's, Anna's, rufous, Allen's, and calliope hummingbirds occur only as migrants or as occasional visitors. The rufous humming-bird can be the single most numerous hummer above the desert after mid-summer when these northern nesters, already on their southbound migration, reach the Chisos Mountains. There they feed on the sweet nectar of mountain sage and several other Chisos plants in preparation for their journeys to their winter homes in southern Mexico and Central America.

Although the Rio Grande serves as the most important route for northbound migrants in spring, the Chisos provide an extremely valuable feeding and resting site for southbound travelers. By early August, when the desert lowlands are at their lowest ecological ebb, the flowering slopes of the Chisos often are teeming with bird life.

Along the roadway to Santa Elena Canyon, on the western flank of the Chisos Mountains, there is a small, quiet place called the Old Ranch, or Sam Nail Ranch. A small working windmill pumps water into a little trough that overflows onto the parched ground. A bench has been placed in the shade of the native black walnut trees where one can sit in the cool stillness. It is a wonderful place to watch and listen. Sitting there one morning in early summer, I became com-pletely mesmerized by the abundant activity around me.

It did not begin immediately. I must have sat there for three or four minutes. Then I was attracted to the movement of a red blotch just above me to the right. A male summer tanager was searching for food in the walnut foliage. There, too, was a black-chinned hummingbird, busy inspecting a spider web. It darted in and retrieved a tiny insect that had been detained in the web.

From the lower vegetation beyond came the short, rapid song of a **Bell's vireo**, a nonmusical chattering, "chu-che-chu-che-chu-che-chu," ending with an upward inflection. But when it immediately repeated its song, it ended with a downward inflection. It is said that this little songster asks a question and immediately responds. I watched this little yellow-tinged bird, with its rather stubby bill and whitish eye rings and eyebrows, work its way to within a few feet of me, then gradually disappear into the shadows of the underbrush. But its song continued, and I heard it throughout the two hours I spent there at the Old Ranch. Its song was joined by that of a yellow-breasted chat, which came close enough to see only briefly before moving away into the denser vegetation.

Suddenly a **painted bunting** appeared at the water. I had not seen it approach in spite of its bright colors. It drank its fill and then flew into the adjacent shrubbery. It sat there a moment wiping its bill, and then, as I watched through my binoculars, it sang a song of incredible sweetness. It was clear and musical, a song that Paul Sykes, in *The Audubon Society Master Guide to Birding*, described as "pew-eate, pew-eate, j-eaty-you-too." As it flew away, I was attracted to a long-tailed bird just arriving at the water. It was a crissal thrasher, named for its reddish crissum (the area under the rump).

There were other birds there that morning: ladder-backed woodpecker, cactus wren, northern mockingbird, verdin, both northern cardinal and the look-alike pyrrhuloxia, house finch, and lesser goldfinch. I had briefly entered the birds' world, and they had ignored my presence. It was a wonderful sensation and a memory that is everlasting. Visitors to Big Bend National Park are given opportunities of this nature that few other places provide.

Pyrrhuloxias are one of Big Bend's most appealing birds, although at first they very much look like the closely related cardinals. They differ in having yellow, snubby, down-curved bills, rather than straight-edged reddish bills, and they lack the all-red plumage of male cardinals. Instead, male pyrrhuloxias are grayish with red faces and throats, tips of their crests, wings, tails, and bellies. They are true desert birds, while cardinals prefer the heavier growth of the flood plain. Their songs are similar but can be separated with practice. Roger Tory Peterson described its voice thusly: "Song, a clear quink quink quink quink quink, on one pitch; also a slurred, whistled what-cheer, what-cheer, etc. thinner and shorter than cardinal's song."

In the summer, after the nesting season is past, it is not unusual to find 10 to 12 species of warblers among the Chisos' pines and oaks. Most numerous of these are the black-and-white, orange-crowned, Nashville, Virginia's, Colima, yellow, yellow-rumped, black-throated gray, Townsend's, black-throated green, Grace's, and Wilson's warblers. This group includes species that nest in both the western and eastern forests but converge in the Chisos afterwards.

The **varied bunting** is a contender for the park's most beautiful bird. Although its beauty is subtle, compared with some warblers and the closely related painted bunting of the Rio Grande flood plain, the varied bunting's purplish body, red nape and throat, and bluish rump make it truly spectacular in good light. An earlier name for this bird, and well-deserved, was "beautiful" bunting. It is another Mexican species that visits the southern border area of the United States only in summer. It frequents the brushy grasslands that occur between the desert and the Chisos woodlands. During years with heavy or average rainfall, this bird can be found in surprising abundance, but it can be uncommon during dry years. The best locations to find this bird include Blue Creek Canyon above the old ranch buildings, lower Green Gulch, and along the Window Trail.

Several of its summertime neighbors are also of interest to bird enthusiasts. They include the ash-throated flycatcher, crissal thrasher, phainopepla, and rufous-crowned and black-chinned sparrows.

The steep, wooded side canyons to the north of the Window Trail provide habitat for gray and black-capped vireos, two birds that are becoming increasingly difficult to find. Researchers have discovered that increased numbers of brown-headed cowbirds have seriously affected these two vireos. Cowbirds are obligate brood parasites, species that cannot build their own nests and must take advantage of other nests and host species. Female cowbirds lay their eggs in the nests of other (usually smaller) birds and may remove the host bird's eggs. Or the young cowbirds, which hatch (in 11 or 12 days) ahead of their nest-mates, may force out the natural young, either physically shoving the smaller birds from the nest or out-competing them for food. The foster parents feed whichever nestling is the most aggressive.

Female brown-headed cowbirds have extremely long reproductive periods and the ability to "take advantage of a continuous supply of host nests for about a two-month period. An average female lays about 80 eggs; 40 per year for two years," according to John Ehrlich and colleagues. They can be characterized as "passerine chickens." Ehrlich added that "circumstantial evidence indicates that in some areas, at least some female cowbirds specialize in particularly vulnerable host species, to the apparent exclusion of other species nesting nearby that serve as common hosts in other parts of the cowbird's range." This may be the case for the black-capped vireo.

The black-capped vireo was listed as endangered following a 1985 assessment of the status of this species in Texas and Oklahoma by ornithologists Joe Marshall and Roger Clapp. They reported that the horse corral in the Chisos Basin had created an artificial environment that greatly increased cowbird populations. The cowbirds in turn have probably reduced populations of the smaller nesting birds within the Chisos Mountains. The vulnerable black-capped vireo is especially threatened. Marshall and Clapp recommended cowbird control at the centrally located corral, although other developments, such as roadways, campgrounds, and other open areas around buildings, also attract cowbirds. Numerous other species, including gray vireos, Colima warblers, and hepatic tanagers, would also benefit.

The black-capped vireo is a dynamic little songbird with a coal black cap, white eye rings and lines in front of the eyes (like bold, white spectacles), greenish-gray back, snow white belly, and yellowish flanks. Its song sounds a little like that of the white-eyed vireo but is more musical. John Terres describes it as "there now, wait-a-bit," or "come here, right-now-quick." The rather plain gray vireo sings a song that is always in three parts, like "chu-weet, chee," with various inflections.

Since about 1970, the larger, bronzed (red-eyed) cowbird has moved into the park's lowlands and begun to impact the orchard and hooded orioles. Declines in both populations have occurred.

Similar encroachment apparently affected yellow warblers during the first half of the 1900s, when early naturalists reported the yellow warbler to be a common nesting bird along the Rio Grande. Populations of brown-headed cowbirds were low at the time, but when cowbird numbers increased during the 1940s and 1950s, there was a sharp decline in yellow warblers, and by the 1960s, nesting yellow warblers were non-existent within the flood plain.

As many as six to ten pairs of **peregrine falcons** annually nest on the high cliffs of the major canyons, especially in Santa Elena and Boquillas canyons, and an additional two or three pairs nest in the Chisos Mountains. For many years the Big Bend area was considered one of the "last strongholds" of the peregrine, south of Alaska.

All of these magnificent falcons were threatened with extinction because of ingesting prey that had fed on DDT-affected prey or grain. The persistent compound causes eggshell thinning and collapse, resulting in non-reproduction of the species, and eventual extinction. The peregrine was placed on the endangered species list in 1969. Since 1972, when DDT was officially banned from use in the United States and Canada, peregrine populations have begun to recover. Restoration projects have helped in many areas, but the fact that a few wild, protected places with relatively unaffected populations still existed, such as Big Bend's canyon country, undoubtedly played a vital role in providing a recruitment base. The Big Bend peregrines were less affected than birds in other areas because they depend on a resident prey base that does not move in and out of the area, and so does not in contact with DDT. The Big Bend peregrines, as well as those of the adjacent Sierra del Carmens in Mexico, primarily feed on white-winged doves, band-tailed pigeons, and Mexican jays.

The **zone-tailed hawk** is another bird of Mexican affinity that frequents open cliffs throughout the park. These hawks are most often found along the Rio Grande where they fly just above the cliff tops and make short dives to capture lizards off the high, open cliffs. They actually mimic the look-alike turkey vultures that utilize the same habitats, a behavior that ornithologist David Ellis and colleagues term "predaceous mimicry." Both species have bi-colored flight patterns of black and gray, fly with their wings held in a shallow V-position, and rock slightly side to side in flight. However, zone-tails have banded tails and feathered heads, unlike the all-dark tails and bare, reddish heads of turkey vultures. The zone-tail's similarity to turkey vultures is extremely useful in fooling their lizard prey.

Other hawks that nest in the park include the common red-tailed hawks and American kestrels at all elevations, Swainson's and Harris' hawks and prairie falcons in the desert lowlands, Cooper's gray hawks on the Rio Grande flood plain, and sharp-shinned hawks and golden eagles in the mountains. Swallow-tailed and Mississippi kites; red-shouldered, broad-winged, white-tailed, rough-legged, and ferruginous hawks; northern harriers; ospreys; crested caracaras; and merlins all occur as migrants or casual visitors.

Ten species of owls are found in the park. Barn, burrowing, long-eared, short-eared, and northern saw-whet owls are visitors only. Five species nest. The most numerous of these is the great horned owl, which can be found at all elevations and at all times of the year. Its lonesome, hooting calls, like "whooo, whoo, who-who," can be heard throughout the lowlands, most often during its breeding season from early winter through April and May.

The eastern screech-owl's range overlaps with that of the look-alike western screech-owl at Big Bend National Park. It is not unusual to hear the songs of both species during the same evening along the flood plain or in the Chisos woodlands. The western screech-owl's song is described as a "bouncing ball" sound, while the eastern screech-owl's song is a quavering whistle; it also sings a high whinny song on occasions. Upper Green Gulch is an easy-to-reach area to listen for the two songs. Ornithologist Joe Marshall studied these birds in the park and discovered some hybridization of the two species.

Throughout the lowlands, the tiny **elf owl** can be seen after dark. It is particularly common at Rio Grande Village, where it nests in trees and utility poles in and adjacent to the campground, utilizing deserted sites originally excavated by ladder-backed woodpeckers. Elf owls are under 6 inches (15 cm) in length, possess yellow eyes, and lack ear tufts. They feed on insects and other arthropods, usually captured in flight.

Big Bend's other small owl, the flammulated owl, occurs only in the higher canyons of the Chisos Mountains, but it is difficult to find. Once found, however, it is easy to identify; it is the only small owl with all-brown eyes. The yellow eyes and white eyebrows of the smaller elf owl gives it a fierce countenance. The large, brown eyes and tawny-brown coloration of the flammulated owl make it appear more mellow than ferocious.

The **Bewick's wren** is the most abundant bird in the park above approximately 4,000 feet (1,219 m) elevation; it is especially abundant within the pinyon-juniper woodlands. It has an incredible variety of songs and seems to imitate several other songbirds, including the Colima warbler. Arthur C. Bent uses several quotes in describing its song: "the song is sweet and exquisitely tender—one of the sweetest and tenderest strains I know"; "not a voluble gobble, like the house wren's merry roundelay, but a fine, clear, bold song, uttered as the singer sits with head thrown back and long tail pendent, a song which may be heard a quarter of a mile or more"; and "in imitative ability the Bewick's wren has, apparently, no rival . . . other than the mockingbird." Its song also can be ventriloquistic in nature, making it difficult to accurately pinpoint its location. Bewick's wrens can be secretive but are readily identified by their brownish backs, long tails, and bold white eye lines. Its cousin, the canyon wren, has only one song but often sings only pieces of the melody. However, its resonance makes up for its lack of variety. Its clear, descending whistle song cannot be mistaken for any other. This little wren is at home in the upper canyons of the Chisos as well as in the massive canyons along the Rio Grande.

The blue jay of the Chisos is the **Mexican jay**, once called gray-breasted jay. These large, non-crested jays frequent the woodlands, traveling in troops of five to 18 birds and, like jays everywhere, can be quite aggressive and loud. Other common woodland birds, not already mentioned, include the "sweeet"-singing Hutton's vireo, liver-red hepatic tanager, and rufous-sided towhee.

Vermilion flycatcher

Winter visitors to the park usually get their introduction to Big Bend's varied bird life at the lowland campgrounds. Although many of the Mexican specialties are far south of the border at that time of year, many northern species mix with the full-time residents to delight the nature enthusiast. Probably no better example is the gorgeous **vermilion flycatcher**. The male's brilliant red underparts and crown and contrasting brown-black back and tail are a familiar sight around Rio Grande Village and Cottonwood campgrounds. Their sharp "peet" or "peent" calls can be heard throughout the winter, and males begin to display as early as February. Terres described this behavior thusly: "uttering ecstatic notes of pit-a-see! pit-a-see! or pu-reet!, mounts upward vertically in air, red crest erected, breast feathers swollen, tail lifted; with wings vibrating rapidly, hovers in butterfly-like flight, then slowly flutters down to female."

The male house finch also has a reddish breast, but it cannot compare with the vivid plumage of the vermilion flycatcher. House finches usually appear in flocks during the winter, as do the white-crowned sparrows that feed on the ground at the campground edges.

The tiny, nondescript bird with white eye rings, which usually is seen darting around in the trees and shrubs, constantly flitting its wings, is the ruby-crowned kinglet. A summer resident in the high Rocky Mountains, it over-winters in the warmer southern states. And the yellow, black, and white birds seen feeding on insects among the foliage are yellow-rumped warblers, also visiting from the summer homes among the coniferous forests in the north. Both the western "Audubon's" subspecies, with yellow throats, and the eastern "myrtle" subspecies, with white throats, occur together in winter and during migration.

Everyone's favorite avian clown, the **greater roadrunner**, is another common sight in the Big Bend lowlands. One can watch for hours as this bird of cartoons and posters, and a real-life character, runs about on its long legs, feeding on lizards, spiders, and other creatures. Its ability to hunt down and kill rattlesnakes is probably exaggerated, though possibly true. A member of the cuckoo family, the roadrunner would be difficult to confuse with any other species. It is a strange-looking bird! Its tail seems too long and loose, its bill too large for its head, its body too skinny, and its long legs give it a gawky, off-balance appearance. Yet few birds are more perfectly adapted to desert conditions. It can chase down the fastest lizard, dodge the swiftest snake, and it nests among the long, protective spines of cholla cactuses and other thorny shrubs. As a year-round resident, it is an appropriate symbol of Big Bend's desert landscape. No visitor to this great national park should be satisfied to leave without seeing the roadrunner in its desert abode and the Colima warbler in its Chisos highlands.

Christmas Bird Counts have been taken annually in the park for many years and provide the best perspective on the winter bird populations. The 1990 count, in the Rio Grande Village area, tallied 415 individuals of 56 species. The dozen most numerous birds, in descending order of abundance, included black-throated sparrow, white-crowned sparrow, yellow-rumped warbler (both Audubon's and myrtle forms), pyrrhuloxia, scaled quail, verdin, American pipit, western bluebird, northern mockingbird, rock wren, spotted sandpiper and (equal numbers) common raven and house finch.

In summary, the 1988 revision of Big Bend's checklist of birds includes 434 species. Seventy-four of those are present throughout the year, and 110 species are known to nest; 7 of those are water birds, 16 are hawks and owls, and 5 are warblers. Twenty-four species occur only in winter.

Birds of Special Interest
Zone-tailed hawk. A migrant and summer resident in the Chisos Mountains and along the Rio Grande canyons, it looks very much like the common turkey vulture.

Peregrine falcon. It is present all year and nests on cliffs in the Chisos and along the river. It is most numerous in migration from early March to early May along the Rio Grande.

Greater roadrunner. This is the long-legged bird of cartoon fame; it is most common in the lowlands, along the roadways and in the campgrounds.

Elf owl. Fairly common in summer below the mountain woodlands; it can best be found at nest-sites in cottonwoods and utility poles at Rio Grande Village.

Lucifer hummingbird. Present in the park from March through September, it utilizes flowering acacias in spring, century plants in early summer, and mountain sage in late summer.

Vermilion flycatcher. Common at Rio Grande Village and Cottonwood Campgrounds all year, the male's brilliant red plumage is unmistakable.

Mexican jay. Troops of five to 18 of these non-crested blue and gray jays are fairly common within the Chisos woodlands.

Bewick's wren. The most numerous summer resident in the mountains, its vast repertoire of songs can be confusing.

Bell's vireo. This tiny bird is common in summer along the flood plain at scattered wet areas below the woodlands. It is best located by its rapid songs.

Colima warbler. Big Bend's most famous bird, it nests in the Chisos Mountains and can best be found at Laguna Meadow and Boot Canyon.

Pyrrhuloxia. This desert bird looks a little like a cardinal but has a red stripe down its chest, on its wings and tail, and a yellowish rather than reddish bill.

Painted bunting. This is the almost gaudy rose-red, blue, and greenish bunting of the flood plain; females are greenish.

Varied bunting. This bunting is purplish with a red nape and throat and bluish throat; it summers in brushy areas between the desert and pinyon-juniper woodlands.

Checklist of Birds Occurring Regularly in the Rocky Mountain Parks

LOONS

__ Pacific loon
__ Common loon

GREBES

__ Least grebe
__ Pied-billed grebe
__ Horned grebe
__ Red-necked grebe
__ Eared grebe
__ Western grebe
__ Clark's grebe

PELICANS

__ American white pelican

CORMORANTS

__ Double-crested cormorant

BITTERNS AND HERONS

__ American bittern
__ Least bittern
__ Great blue heron
__ Great egret
__ Snowy egret
__ Little blue heron
__ Tricolored heron
__ Cattle egret
__ Green heron
__ Black-crowned night-heron
__ Yellow-crowned night-heron

IBIS

__ White-faced ibis

SWANS, GEESE, AND DUCKS

__ Tundra swan
__ Trumpeter swan
__ Greater white-fronted goose
__ Snow goose
__ Ross' goose
__ Canada goose
__ Wood duck
__ Green-winged teal
__ Mallard
__ Northern pintail
__ Blue-winged teal
__ Cinnamon teal
__ Northern shoveler
__ Gadwall
__ American wigeon
__ Canvasback
__ Redhead
__ Ring-necked duck
__ Greater scaup
__ Lesser scaup
__ Harlequin duck
__ Oldsquaw
__ Surf scoter
__ White-winged scoter
__ Common goldeneye
__ Barrow's goldeneye
__ Bufflehead
__ Hooded merganser
__ Common merganser
__ Ruddy duck

VULTURES

__ Black vulture
__ Turkey vulture

HAWKS AND EAGLES

__ Osprey
__ Bald eagle
__ Northern harrier
__ Sharp-shinned hawk
__ Cooper's hawk
__ Northern goshawk
__ Common black-hawk
__ Harris' hawk
__ Gray hawk
__ Broad-winged hawk
__ Swainson's hawk
__ Zone-tailed hawk
__ Red-tailed hawk
__ Ferruginous hawk
__ Rough-legged hawk
__ Golden eagle

FALCONS

__ Crested caracara
__ American kestrel
__ Merlin
__ Peregrine falcon
__ Gyrafalcon
__ Prairie falcon

GROUSE, TURKEY, AND QUAIL

__ Gray partridge
__ Chukar
__ Ring-necked pheasant
__ Spruce grouse
__ Blue grouse
__ Willow ptarmigan
__ Rock ptarmigan
__ White-tailed ptarmigan
__ Ruffed grouse
__ Sage grouse
__ Sharp-tailed grouse
__ Wild turkey
__ Montezuma quail
__ Scaled quail
__ Gambel's quail
__ Northern bobwhite

RAILS, GALLINULES, AND COOTS

__ Virginia rail
__ Sora
__ Common moorhen
__ American coot

CRANES

__ Sandhill crane
__ Whooping crane

PLOVERS, STILTS, AND AVOCETS

__ Black-bellied plover
__ Lesser golden-plover
__ Snowy plover
__ Semipalmated plover
__ Killdeer
__ Mountain plover
__ Black-necked stilt
__ American avocet

SANDPIPERS, PHALAROPES, AND ALLIES

__ Greater yellowlegs
__ Lesser yellowlegs
__ Solitary sandpiper
__ Willet
__ Spotted sandpiper
__ Upland sandpiper
__ Long-billed curlew
__ Marbled godwit
__ Ruddy turnstone
__ Sanderling
__ Semipalmated sandpiper
__ Western sandpiper
__ Least sandpiper
__ White-rumped sandpiper
__ Baird's sandpiper
__ Pectoral sandpiper
__ Dunlin
__ Stilt sandpiper

__ Buff-breasted sandpiper
__ Short-billed dowitcher
__ Long-billed dowitcher
__ Common snipe
__ Wilson's phalarope
__ Red-necked phalarope

SKUAS, GULLS AND TERNS

__ Pomarine jaeger
__ Parasitic jaeger
__ Franklin's gull
__ Bonaparte's gull
__ Mew gull
__ Ring-billed gull
__ California gull
__ Herring gull
__ Sabine's gull
__ Gull-billed tern
__ Caspian tern
__ Common tern
__ Forster's tern
__ Black tern

PIGEONS AND DOVES

__ Rock dove
__ Band-tailed pigeon
__ White-winged dove
__ Mourning dove
__ Inca dove
__ Common ground-dove

CUCKOOS

__ Yellow-billed cuckoo
__ Greater roadrunner
__ Groove-billed ani

OWLS

__ Barn owl
__ Flammulated owl
__ Eastern screech-owl
__ Western screech-owl
__ Whiskered screech-owl

__ Great horned owl
__ Snowy owl
__ Northern hawk-owl
__ Northern pygmy-owl
__ Elf owl
__ Burrowing owl
__ Spotted owl
__ Barred owl
__ Great gray owl
__ Long-eared owl
__ Short-eared owl
__ Boreal owl
__ Northern saw-whet owl

NIGHTJARS

__ Lesser nighthawk
__ Common nighthawk
__ Common poorwill
__ Whip-poor-will

SWIFTS

__ Black swift
__ Chimney swift
__ Vaux's swift
__ White-throated swift

HUMMINGBIRDS

__ Broad-billed hummingbird
__ White-eared hummingbird
__ Blue-throated hummingbird
__ Magnificent hummingbird
__ Lucifer hummingbird
__ Ruby-throated hummingbird
__ Black-chinned hummingbird
__ Anna's hummingbird
__ Costa's hummingbird
__ Calliope hummingbird
__ Broad-tailed hummingbird
__ Rufous hummingbird
__ Allen's hummingbird

KINGFISHERS

__ Belted kingfisher
__ Green kingfisher

WOODPECKERS

__ Lewis' woodpecker
__ Red-headed woodpecker
__ Acorn woodpecker
__ Gila woodpecker
__ Golden-fronted woodpecker
__ Yellow-bellied sapsucker
__ Red-naped sapsucker
__ Williamson's sapsucker
__ Ladder-backed woodpecker
__ Downy woodpecker
__ Hairy woodpecker
__ Strickland's woodpecker
__ Three-toed woodpecker
__ Black-backed woodpecker
__ Northern flicker
__ Pileated woodpecker

FLYCATCHERS

__ Olive-sided flycatcher
__ Greater pewee
__ Western wood-pewee
__ Yellow-bellied flycatcher
__ Alder flycatcher
__ Willow flycatcher
__ Least flycatcher
__ Hammond's flycatcher
__ Dusky flycatcher
__ Gray flycatcher
__ Cordilleran flycatcher
__ Buff-breasted flycatcher
__ Black phoebe
__ Eastern phoebe
__ Say's phoebe
__ Vermilion flycatcher
__ Dusky-capped flycatcher
__ Ash-throated flycatcher
__ Great crested flycatcher
__ Brown-crested flycatcher
__ Sulphur-bellied flycatcher
__ Couch's kingbird
__ Cassin's kingbird
__ Thick-billed kingbird
__ Western kingbird
__ Eastern kingbird
__ Scissor-tailed flycatcher

LARKS

__ Horned lark

SWALLOWS

__ Purple martin
__ Tree swallow
__ Violet-green swallow
__ Northern rough-winged swallow
__ Bank swallow
__ Cliff swallow
__ Cave swallow
__ Barn swallow

JAYS, MAGPIES, AND CROWS

__ Gray jay
__ Steller's jay
__ Blue jay
__ Scrub jay
__ Mexican jay
__ Pinyon jay
__ Clark's nutcracker
__ Black-billed magpie
__ American crow
__ Chihuahuan raven
__ Common raven

TITMICE

__ Black-capped chickadee
__ Mexican chickadee
__ Mountain chickadee
__ Boreal chickadee
__ Chestnut-backed chickadee
__ Bridled titmouse
__ Plain titmouse
__ Tufted titmouse

VERDINS

__ Verdin

BUSHTITS

__ Bushtit

NUTHATCHES

__ Red-breasted nuthatch
__ White-breasted nuthatch
__ Pygmy nuthatch

CREEPERS

__ Brown creeper

WRENS

__ Cactus wren
__ Rock wren
__ Canyon wren
__ Bewick's wren
__ House wren
__ Winter wren
__ Sedge wren
__ Marsh wren

DIPPERS

__ American dipper

KINGLETS AND GNATCATCHERS

__ Golden-crowned kinglet
__ Ruby-crowned kinglet
__ Blue-gray gnatcatcher
__ Black-tailed gnatcatcher

SOLITAIRES, THRUSHES, AND ALLIES

__ Eastern bluebird
__ Western bluebird
__ Mountain bluebird
__ Townsend's solitaire
__ Veery

__ Gray-cheeked thrush
__ Swainson's thrush
__ Hermit thrush
__ Wood thrush
__ American robin
__ Varied thrush

MOCKINGBIRDS, THRASHERS, AND ALLIES

__ Gray catbird
__ Northern mockingbird
__ Sage thrasher
__ Brown thrasher
__ Bendire's thrasher
__ Curve-billed thrasher
__ Crissal thrasher

PIPITS

__ American pipit
__ Sprague's pipit

WAXWINGS

__ Bohemian waxwing
__ Cedar waxwing

SILKY-FLYCATCHERS

__ Phainopepla

SHRIKES

__ Northern shrike
__ Loggerhead shrike

STARLINGS

__ European starling

VIREOS

__ Bell's vireo
__ Black-capped vireo
__ Gray vireo
__ Solitary vireo
__ Yellow-throated vireo

__ Hutton's vireo
__ Warbling vireo
__ Philadelphia vireo
__ Red-eyed vireo

WOOD WARBLERS

__ Tennessee warbler
__ Orange-crowned warbler
__ Nashville's warbler
__ Virginia's warbler
__ Colima warbler
__ Lucy's warbler
__ Parula warbler
__ Yellow warbler
__ Chestnut-sided warbler
__ Magnolia warbler
__ Black-throated blue warbler
__ Yellow-rumped warbler
__ Black-throated gray warbler
__ Townsend's warbler
__ Hermit warbler
__ Black-throated green warbler
__ Grace's warbler
__ Palm warbler
__ Bay-breasted warbler
__ Blackpoll warbler
__ Black-and-white warbler
__ American redstart
__ Prothonotary warbler
__ Worm-eating warbler
__ Ovenbird
__ Northern waterthrush
__ Louisiana waterthrush
__ Connecticut warbler
__ MacGillvray's warbler
__ Common yellowthroat
__ Hooded warbler
__ Wilson's warbler
__ Red-faced warbler
__ Painted redstart
__ Yellow-breasted chat
__ Olive warbler

TANAGERS

__ Hepatic tanager
__ Summer tanager
__ Western tanager

GROSBEAKS, CARDINALS, AND ALLIES

__ Northern cardinal
__ Pyrrhuloxia
__ Rose-breasted grosbeak
__ Black-headed grosbeak
__ Blue grosbeak
__ Lazuli bunting
__ Indigo bunting
__ Varied bunting
__ Painted bunting
__ Dickcissel

TOWHEES, SPARROWS, AND ALLIES

__ Green-tailed towhee
__ Rufous-sided towhee
__ Canyon towhee
__ Abert's towhee
__ Cassin's sparrow
__ Rufous-crowned sparrow
__ Rufous-winged sparrow
__ American tree sparrow
__ Chipping sparrow
__ Clay-colored sparrow
__ Brewer's sparrow
__ Field sparrow
__ Black-chinned sparrow
__ Vesper sparrow
__ Lark sparrow
__ Black-throated sparrow
__ Sage sparrow
__ Lark bunting
__ Savannah sparrow
__ Baird's sparrow
__ Grasshopper sparrow
__ LeConte's sparrow

__ Sharp-tailed sparrow
__ Fox sparrow
__ Song sparrow
__ Lincoln's sparrow
__ Swamp sparrow
__ White-throated sparrow
__ Golden-crowned sparrow
__ White-crowned sparrow
__ Harris' sparrow
__ Dark-eyed junco
__ Yellow-eyed junco
__ McCown's longspur
__ Lapland longspur
__ Chestnut-collared longspur
__ Snow bunting

BLACKBIRDS AND ORIOLES

__ Bobolink
__ Red-winged blackbird
__ Eastern meadowlark
__ Western meadowlark
__ Yellow-headed blackbird
__ Rusty blackbird
__ Brewer's blackbird
__ Great-tailed grackle
__ Common grackle
__ Bronzed cowbird
__ Brown-headed cowbird
__ Orchard oriole
__ Hooded oriole
__ Northern oriole
__ Scott's oriole

FINCHES

__ Black rosy finch
__ Brown-capped rosy finch
__ Gray-crowned rosy finch
__ Pine grosbeak
__ Purple finch
__ Cassin's finch
__ House finch
__ Red crossbill
__ White-winged crossbill
__ Common redpoll
__ Hoary redpoll
__ Pine siskin
__ Lesser goldfinch
__ American goldfinch
__ Evening grosbeak

OLD WORLD SPARROWS

__ House sparrow

Common and Scientific Plant Names

Acacia, catclaw. *Acacia greggii*
Acacia, mescat. *Acacia constricta*
Agave, Havard. *Agave havardiana*
Agave, New Mexico. *Agave neomexicana*
Agave, Utah. *Agave utahensis*
Alder. *Alnus*
Alder, green. *Alnus crispa*
Alder, mountain. *Alnus tenuifolia*
Alder, thinleaf. *Alnus tenuifolia*
Antelopebrush. *Purshia tridentata*
Apache-plume. *Fallugia paradoxa*
Arnica, heartleaf. *Arnica cordifolia*
Ash, desert. *Fraxinus velutina*
Ash, fragrant. *Fraxinus cuspidata*
Ash, mountain. *Sorbus scopulina*
Ash, singleleaf. *Fraxinus anomala*
Ash, velvet. *Fraxinus velutina*
Aspen. *Populus tremuloides*
Aster, golden. *Chrysopsis villoso*
Avens, yellow. *Dryas drummondii*
Azalea, false. *Menziesia ferruginea*
Baccharis, Arizona. *Baccharis thesioides*
Balsamroot, arrowleaf. *Balsamorhiza sagittata*
Barberry, Fremont. *Berberis fremontii*
Bearberry. *Arctostaphylos uva-ursi*
Beargrass. *Xerophyllum tenax*
Bear-grass. *Nolina erumpens*
Birch, water. *Betula papyrifera*
Bitterbrush, antelope. *Purshia tridentata*
Blackbrush. *Coleogyne ramosissima*
Bluebell. *Mertensia*
Blueberry. *Vaccinium*
Bluestem, big. *Andropogon gerardi*
Bluestem, little. *Schizachyrium scoparium*
Bouvardia, scarlet. *Bouvardia ternifolia*
Box, false. *Pachistima myrsinites*
Boxelder. *Acer negundo*
Buckbrush. *Symphoricarpos occidentalis*
Buckthorn, birchleaf. *Rhamnus betulaefolia*
Buffaloberry. *Shepherdia*

Buffaloberry, Canada. *Shepherdia canadensis*
Buffaloberry, silver. *Shepherdia argentea*
Buttercup, snow. *Ranunculus adoneus*
Bunchberry. *Cornus canadensis*
Campion, moss. *Silene acaulis*
Cattail. *Typha latifolia*
Century plant. *Agave*
Cercocarpus, curlleaf. *Cercocarpus ledifolius*
Cheatgrass. *Bromus tectorum*
Chinograss. *Bouteloua breviseta*
Chokecherry. *Prunus melanocarpa*
Cholla, cane. *Opuntia imbricata*
Cinquefoil, alpine. *Potentilla gracilis*
Cinquefoil, shrubby. *Potentilla fruticosa*
Clavellina. *Opuntia schotti*
Cliffrose. *Cowania mexicana*
Cliffrose. *Pursia tridentata*
Columbine. *Aquilegia*
Cottonwood. *Populus*
Cottonwood, black. *Populus trichocarpa*
Cottonwood, eastern. *Populus deltoides*
Cottonwood, Fremont. *Populus fremontii*
Cottonwood, lanceleaf. *Populus acuminata*
Cottonwood, narrowleaf. *Populus angustifolia*
Creosote bush. *Larrea diverticata*
Current, golden. *Ribes aureum*
Current, gooseberry. *Ribes montigenum*
Current, squaw. *Ribes aureum*
Current, wax. *Ribes cereum*
Cypress, Arizona. *Cupressus arizonica*
Desert-willow. *Chilopsis linearis*
Devil's-club. *Oplopanax horridum*
Dogwood. *Cornus*
Dogwood, Red-osier. *Cornus stolonifera*
Douglas-fir. *Pseudotsuga menziesii*
Dryad. *Dryas hookeriana*
Elderberry. *Sambucus*

Elm. *Ulmus pumila*
Fairy bells. *Disporum trachycarpum*
Fernbush. *Chamaebatiaria millefolium*
Fendlerbush. *Fendlera rupicola*
Fern, lady. *Athyrium felix-femina*
Fir, subalpine. *Abies lasiocarpa*
Fir, white. *Abies concolor*
Fireweed. *Epilobium angustifolium*
Forestiera, New Mexico. *Forestiera neomexicana*
Gentian, fringed. *Gentiana thermalis*
Golden-aster. *Chrysopsis villosa*
Gooseberry, currant. *Ribes montigenum*
Gooseberry, trumpet. *Ribes leptanthum*
Grama, blue. *Bouteloua gracilis*
Grama, chino. *Bouteloua ramosa*
Grama, hairy. *Bouteloua hirsuta*
Grama, sideoats. *Bouteloua curtidendula*
Grape. *Vitis*
Grass, threeawn. *Aristida purpurea*
Greasewood. *Sarcobatus vermiculatus*
Hackberry, globe. *Vaccinium globulare*
Hackberry, netleaf. *Celtis reticulata*
Hawthorn. *Crataegus rotundifolia*
Hemlock, mountain. *Tsuga mertensiana*
Hemlock, western. *Tsuga heterophylla*
Holly-grape. *Mahonia repens*
Honeysuckle. *Lonicera*
Hoptree, common. *Ptelea angustifolia*
Horsebrush. *Tetradymia canescens*
Horsetail, swamp. *Equisetum hyemale*
Juniper, alligator. *Juniperus deppeana*
Juniper, common. *Juniperus communis*
Juniper, creeping. *Juniperus horizontalis*
Juniper, drooping. *Juniperus flaccida*
Juniper, oneseed. *Juniperus monosperma*
Juniper, redberry. *Juniperus pinchoti*
Juniper, Rocky Mountain. *Juniperus scopulorum*
Juniper, Utah. *Juniperus osteosperma*
Kochia. *Kochia scoparia*
Labrador tea. *Ledum groenlandicum*
Larch, alpine. *Larix lyallii*
Lechuguilla. *Agave lecheguilla*
Lily, wood. *Lilium umbellatum*
Locust, New Mexico. *Robinia neomexicana*
Lupine. *Lupinus*

Madrone, Texas. *Arbutus texana*
Mahonia, Fremont. *Mahonia fremontii*
Manzanita, green leaf. *Arctostaphylos patula*
Maple, ashleaf. *Acer negundo*
Maple, canyon. *Acer grandidentatum*
Maple, western mountain. *Acer glabrum*
Meadowrue, western. *Thalictrum fendleri*
Menziesia, rusty. *Menziesia ferruginea*
Mesquite, honey. *Prosopis glandulosa*
Mesquite, screwbean. *Prosopis pubescens*
Mistletoe. *Phoradendron*
Mormon tea. *Ephedra viridis*
Moss, feather. *Hypnum imponens*
Mountain-ash, Cascade. *Sorbus scopulina*
Mountain mahogany. *Cercocarpus montanus*
Mountain mahogany, birchleaf. *Cercocarpus betuloides*
Mountain mahogany, curl-leaf. *Cercoparpus ledifolius*
Mountain-sorrel. *Oxyria digyna*
Mulberry. *Morus microphylla*
Ninebark, mallow. *Opulaster malvaceus*
Oak, Chinquapin. *Quercus muhlenbergi*
Oak, Emory. *Quercus emoryi*
Oak, Gambel's. *Quercus gambelii*
Oak, Graves. *Quercus gravesei*
Oak, gray. *Quercus grisei*
Oak, scrub. *Quercus pungens*
Ocotillo. *Fouquieria splendons*
Olive, Russian. *Eleagnus angustifolia*
Paintbrush, Indian. *Castilleja*
Penstemon. *Penstemon*
Penstemon, Eaton. *Penstemon eatoni*
Phlox, moss. *Phlox*
Pine, bristlecone. *Pinus aristata*
Pine, Chihuahua. *Pinus leiophylla*
Pine, limber. *Pinus flexilis*
Pine, lodgepole. *Pinus contorta*
Pine, pinyon. *Pinus edulis*
Pine, ponderosa. *Pinus ponderosa*
Pine, white-bark. *Pinus albicaulis*
Pinyon. *Pinus edulis*
Pinyon, Mexican. *Pinus cembroides*
Pinyon, two-needle. *Pinus edulis*
Poison-ivy. *Rhus radicans*
Prickly pear, blind. *Opuntia rufida*

Prickly pear, plains. *Opuntia polycantha*
Rabbitbrush, rubber. *Chrysothamnus nauseosus*
Rasberry. *Rubus idaeus*
Redcedar, western. *Thuja plicata*
Rhododendron, Rocky Mountain. *Rhododendron albiflorum*
Ricegrass, Indian. *Oryzopsis hymenoides*
Rose, prairie. *Rose arkansana*
Rose, wild. *Rose woodsi*
Russian-olive. *Eleagnus angustifolia*
Sagebrush, big. *Artemisia tridentata*
Sagebrush, black. *Artemesia nova*
Sagebrush, sand. *Artemesia filifolia*
Sage, fringed. *Artemisia frigida*
Sage, mountain. *Salvia regla*
Saltbush, four-winged. *Atriplex canescens*
Sandwort, arctic. *Arenaria obtusiloba*
Saskatoon. *Amelanchier alnifolia*
Saw-grass. *Cladium jamaicense*
Saxifrage, purple. *Saxifraga oppositifolia*
Sedge, elk. *Carex*
Seepwillow. *Baccharis glutinosa*
Serviceberry. *Amelanchier alnifolia*
Shadscale. *Atriplex confertifolia*
Silk-tassel. *Garrya lindheimeri*
Silktassel bush. *Garrya flavescens*
Skunkbush. *Rhus trilobata*
Skunk cabbage. *Lysichitum americanum*
Snakeweed, broom. *Gutierrezia sarothrae*
Snowberry. *Symphoricarpos*
Sorrel, mountain. *Oxyria digyna*
Sotol. *Dasylirion leiphyllum*
Springbeauty. *Claytonia lanceolata*
Spruce, black. *Picea mariana*
Spruce, blue. *Picea pungens*
Spruce, Engelmann. *Picea engelmannii*
Spruce, white. *Picea glauca*
Squawbush. *Rhus trilobata*
Stonecrop, lanceleaf. *Sedum stenopetalum*
Sumac, evergreen. *Rhus virens*
Sumac, littleleaf. *Rhus trilobata*
Sycamore. *Platanus occidentalis*
Sycamore, Arizona. *Platanus wrightii*
Tamarisk. *Tamarix*
Thimbleberry. *Rubus parviflorus*
Thistle. *Cirsium*
Thistle, Russian. *Salsola iberica*

Tobosa. *Hilaria mutica*
Tomatillo. *Lycium pallidum*
Twinberry, black. *Lonicera involucrata*
Twinberry, red. *Lonicera utahensis*
Twinflower. *Linnaea borealis*
Walnut, Arizona. *Juglans major*
Walnut, black. *Juglans niger*
Willow. *Salix*
Willow, coyote. *Salix exigua*
Willow, creeping. *Salix arctica*
Willow, goodding. *Salix gooddingii*
Willow, pussy. *Salix discolor*
Winter-fat. *Eurotia lanata*
Wintergreen. *Chimaphila*
Wolfberry. *Lycium andersonii*
Wolf-willow. *Elaeagnus commutata*
Wortleberry, grouse. *Vaccinium scoparium*
Yew, Pacific. *Taxus brevifolia*
Yucca. *Yucca*
Yucca, banana. *Yucca baccata*
Yucca, datil. *Yucca baccata*
Yucca, Faxon. *Yucca faxoniana*
Yucca, soaptree. *Yucca elata*

BIBLIOGRAPHY

Abbey, Edward. 1971. *Desert Solitaire*. New York: Random House, Ballantine Books.

Able, Kenneth P. 1991. Migration biology for birders. *Birding*. April: 64-72.

American Ornithologists' Union. 1983. *Check-list of North American Birds*. A.O.U., Lawrence, Kansas: Allen Press.

Bailey, Florence Merriam. 1939. *Among the Birds in the Grand Canyon Country*. U.S.D.I., Washington, D.C.: GPO.

Ballard, Larry R. 1983. Western tanager. In *The Audubon Society Master Guide to Birding*, ed. John Farrand, Jr. New York: Alfred A. Knopf.

Banko, Winston F. 1960. *The Trumpeter Swan*. U.S.D.I., North American Fauna No. 63. Washington, D.C.: GPO.

Barnes, F. A. 1990. *Canyon Country Hiking*. Salt Lake City: Wasatch Publishers.

Bates, Henry Walter. 1962. *The Naturalist on the River Amazons*. Berkeley: University of California Press.

Bellrose, Frank C. 1976. *Ducks, Geese and Swans of North America*. Harrisburg, Penn: Stackpole Books.

Bent, Arthur Clevelend. 1958. *Life Histories of North American Blackbirds, Orioles, Tanagers, and Allies*. Washington, D.C.: Smithsonian Inst.

_____. 1963. *Life Histories of North American Flycatchers, Larks, Swallows, and their Allies*. New York: Dover Publications, Inc.

_____. 1964. *Life Histories of North American Jays, Crows and Titmice*. New York: Dover Publications, Inc.

_____. 1964. *Life Histories of North American Thrushes, Kinglets, and their Allies*. New York: Dover Publications, Inc.

_____. 1964. *Life Histories of North American Nuthatches, Wrens, Thrashers, and their Allies*. New York: Dover Publications, Inc.

Boschen, Nelson. 1986. Report on the bird surveys performed at the Island Mesa and the Moab Sloughs in 1984 and 1985. Report to the National Park Service.

Bowers, Janice E., and Steven P. McLaughlin. 1987. Flora and vegetation of the Rincon Mountains, Pima County, Arizona. *Desert Plants*. vol. 8, no. 2: 51-94.

Brandt, Herbert. 1951. *Arizona and its Bird Life*. Cleveland: The Bird Research Foundation.

Brooks, Paul. 1980. *Speaking for Nature*. San Francisco: Sierra Club Books.

Brown, Bryan T., Steven W. Carothers, Stephen W. Hoffman, and Richard L. Glinski. 1990. Abundance of peregrine falcons in Grand Canyon National Park has implications for regionwide recovery. *Park Science*. Spring: 7.

_____, Steven W. Carothers, and R. Roy Johnson. 1987. *Grand Canyon Birds*. Tucson: University of Arizona Press.

Brown, Lauren. 1947. *The Audubon Society Nature Guides Grasslands*. New York: Alfred A. Knopf.

Burgess, Tony L., and David K. Northington. 1969. Plants of the Guadalupe Mountains and Carlsbad Caverns National Parks. Chihuahuan Desert Research Institute report no. 107. Report to the National Park Service.

Canadian Parks Service. 1984. *Alive in the Wet Belt*. Minister of the Environment. Gloucester, Ont.: T&H Printers.

_____. 1990. *State of the Parks 1990 Report*. Gloucester, Ont.: T&H Printers.

_____. 1990. *State of the Parks 1990 Profile*. Gloucester, Ont.: T&H Printers.

Carothers, S. W., and H. H. Goldberg. 1976. Life after the rain of fire. *Plateau.* vol. 49, no. 2: 14-21.

Carson, Rachel. 1962. *Silent Spring.* Boston: Houghton Mifflin Co.

Chadwick, Douglas H. 1990. The biodiversity challenge. *Defenders.* May/June: 19-31.

Chapman, Frank M. 1966. *Handbook of North American Birds.* New York: Dover Publications, Inc.

_____. 1968. *The Warblers of North America.* New York: Dover Publications, Inc.

Chase, Alston, and Debra Shore. 1992. Our national parks: An uncommon guide. *Outside.* June: 52-88.

Clark, Jim. 1991. Silent chorus. *Birder's World.* Oct.: 25-29.

Clark, William S., and Brian K. Wheeler. 1987. *A Field Guide to Hawks of North America.* Boston: Houghton Mifflin Co.

Clements, James F. 1991. *Birds of the World: A Check List,* 4th ed. Vista, Calif.: Ibis Publishing Co.

Collins, Henry H., Jr. 1951. *Birds of Montezuma and Tuzigoot.* Globe, Ariz.: Southwestern Monuments Association.

Collister, Allegra. 1970. *Birds of Rocky Mountain National Park.* Colorado: Denver Museum of Natural History.

Cook, Francis R., and Dalton Muir. 1984. The committee on the status of endangered wildlife in Canada (COSEWIC): History and progress. *The Canadian Field-Naturalist.* 98: 63-70.

Cook, Kevin J. 1991. Colorado dreaming. *Birder's World.* August: 15-19.

Correll, Donovan Stewart, and Marshall Conring Johnston. 1970. *Manual of the Vascular Plants of Texas.* Renner: Texas Research Foundation.

Council on Environmental Quality and Dept. of State. 1980. *The Global 2000 Report to the President.* Washington, D.C.: GPO.

Crandall, Hugh. 1978. *Grand Teton: The Story behind the Scenery.* Las Vegas, Nevada: KC Publications.

DeSante, David. 1983. Brewer's sparrow. In *The Audubon Society Master Guide to Birding,* ed. John C. Farrand, Jr. New York: Alfred A. Knopf.

Despain, Dod G. 1990. *Yellowstone Vegetation.* Boulder, Colo.: Roberts Rinehart Publishers.

Diamond, Antony W., Rudolf L. Scheiber, Walter Cronkite, and Roger Tory Peterson. 1989. *Save the Birds.* Boston: Houghton Mifflin Co.

Douglas, William O. 1961. *My Wilderness: East to Katahdin.* Garden City, NY: Doubleday & Co.

Duncan, Bob. 1990. Weather and birding. *Birding.* August: 173-175.

Dunne, Pete, David Sibley, and Clay Sutton. 1988. *Hawks in Flight.* Boston: Houghton Mifflin Co.

Ehrlich, Paul R., David S. Dobkin, and Darryl Wheye. 1988. *The Birder's Handbook.* New York: Simon & Schuster, Inc.

Ellis, David H., James C. Bednarz, Dwight G. Smith, and Stephen P. Flemming. 1993. Social foraging classes in raptorial birds. *BioScience.* 43: 14-20.

Elmore, Francis H. 1976. *Shrubs and Trees of the Southwest Uplands.* Tucson: Southwest Parks and Monuments Association.

Enderson, James H. 1992. Haven of safety. *Courier.* Sept.: 29.

Follett, Dick. 1986. *Birds of Yellowstone and Grand Teton National Parks.* Yellowstone Library and Museum Assoc. Boulder, Colo.: Roberts Rinehart Pub.

Freeman, Judith. 1986. The parks as genetic islands. *National Parks.* Jan./Feb.: 12-17.

Goodrich, Sherel, and Elizabeth Neese. 1986. *Uninta Basin Flora.* Ogden, Utah: U.S.D.A., Forest Service - Intermountain Region.

Graham, Frank, Jr. 1990. 2001: Birds that won't be with us. *American Birds.* Winter: 1074-1081, 1194-1199.

Griffin, Rebecca R. 1988. Fluctuating populations: A biologist looks for answers. *Bioloque.* Fall: 10-11.

Griscom, Ludlow, and Alexander Sprunt, Jr. 1957. *The Warblers of America.* New York: Devin-Adair Co.

Grossman, Mary Louise and John Hamlet. 1964. *Birds of Prey of the World.* New York: Clarkson N. Potter, Inc.

Gruson, Edward S. 1972. *Words for Birds: A Lexicon of North American Birds with Biographical Notes.* New York: Quadrangle Books.

Guggisberg, C. A. W. 1970. *Man and Wildlife.* New York: Arco Publishing Co., Inc.

Hagood, Allen. 1969. *This is Zion.* Springdale, Utah: Zion Natural History Assoc.

_____. 1971. *Dinosaur: The Story behind the Scenery.* Las Vegas, Nevada: KC Publications.

Halle, Louis J. 1947. *Spring in Washington.* New York: Harper and Brothers, Publishers.

Hansen, Wallace R. 1987. *The Black Canyon of the Gunnison: In Depth.* Tucson: Southwest Parks and Monuments Association.

Headstrom, Richard. 1951. *Birds' Nests of the West: A Field Guide.* New York: Ives Washburn, Inc.

Holt, Harold R., and James A. Lane. 1988. *A Birder's Guide to Colorado.* Colorado Springs: American Birding Association.

Houk, Rose. 1987. A guide to the Rimrock Drive, Colorado National Monument. Fruita, Colo.: Colorado National Monument Association.

Howe, Steve. 1992. Raptor redux. *National Parks.* July/Aug.: 28-33.

Hubbard, John P. and Claudia L. 1979. *Birds of New Mexico's National Park Lands.* Glenwood, NM: Tecolote Press, Inc.

Hutto, Richard L. 1988. Is tropical deforestation responsible for the reported declines in Neotropical migrant populations? *American Birds.* Fall: 375-379.

Jackson, Betty. 1941. Birds of Montezuma Castle. Southwestern national monuments, special report # 28.

Jackson, Earl. 1971. *Your National Park System in the Southwest in Words and Color.* Globe, Ariz.: Southwestern Parks and Monuments Association.

Jackson, Jerome A. 1992. Red-capped sap-tapper. *Birder's World.* Dec.: 24-27.

Johnsgard, Paul A. 1986. *Birds of the Rocky Mountains.* Lincoln: University of Nebraska Press.

Johnson, R. Roy, and Lois T. Haight. 1992. The importance of xeroriparian ecosystems to the wintering avifauna of Saguaro National Monument. In *Proc. of the Symposium on Research in Saguaro National Monument.* Tucson, Ariz., ed. Charles P. Stone and Elizabeth S. Bellantoni. National Park Service, Rincon Inst., and Southwestern Parks and Monuments Association.

Kaufman, Kenn. 1990. *Advanced Birding.* Boston: Houghton Mifflin Co.

Kirk, Ruth. 1973. Life on a tall cactus. *Audubon.* July: 12-23.

Knox, Margaret L. 1990. Beyond park boundaries. *Nature Conservancy.* July/Aug.: 16-23.

Kurtz, Don, and William D. Goran. 1992. *Trails of the Guadalupes.* Champaign, Ill.: Environmental Associates.

Lamb, Samuel H. 1971. *Woody Plants of New Mexico.* Santa Fe: New Mexico Dept. of Fish and Game.

Lanner, Ronald M. 1981. *The Piñon Pine: A Natural and Cultural History.* Reno: University of Nevada Press.

Lehman. Paul. 1983. Rufous-sided towhee. In *The Audubon Society Master Guide to Birding,* ed. John C. Farrand, Jr. New York: Alfred A. Knopf.

Leopold, Aldo. 1966. *A Sand County Almanac.* New York: Oxford University Press.

Ligon, J. Stokley. 1961. *New Mexico Birds and Where to Find Them.* Albuquerque: University of New Mexico Press.

Lowe, Charles H. 1964. Arizona landscapes and habitats. In *The Vertebrates of Arizona,* ed. Charles H. Lowe. Tucson: University of Arizona Press.

Marshall, Joe T., Jr. 1967. *Parallel Variation in North and Middle American Screech-Owls.* Monograph West. Found. Vert Zool. No. 1. Los Angeles: West. Found. Vert. Zool.

_____, Roger B. Clapp, and Joseph A. Grzybowski. 1985. Status report: *Vireo atricapillus* Woodhouse black-capped vireo. Report.

Martin, Dennis J. 1983. Fox sparrow. In *The Audubon Society Master Guide to Birding,* ed. John C. Farrand, Jr. New York: Alfred A. Knopf.

McClelland, B. Riley, Leonard S. Young, et. al. 1982. The bald eagle concentration in Glacier National Park, Montana: Origin, growth, and variation in numbers. *The Living Bird.* 19: 133-155.

McEneaney, Terry. 1988. *Birds of Yellowstone.* Boulder, Colo.: Roberts Rinehart Publishers.

National Audubon Society. 1966. *Audubon Field Notes.* vol. 20, no. 2. New York: National Audubon Society.

_____. 1980. The Eightieth Audubon Christmas Bird Count. *American Birds.* vol. 34, no. 4. New York: National Audubon Society.

_____. 1990. The Ninetieth Christmas Bird Count. *American Birds.* vol. 44, no. 4. New York: National Audubon Society.

_____. 1991. The Ninety-First Christmas Bird Count. *American Birds.* vol. 45, no. 4. New York: National Audubon Society.

National Fish and Wildlife Foundation. 1990. Proposal for a Neotropical migratory bird conservation program. Report.

National Geographic Society. 1987. *Field Guide to the Birds of North America,* 2nd ed. Washington, D.C.: National Geographic Society.

Nelson, Ruth Ashton. 1970. *Plants of Rocky Mountain National Park.* Estes Park, Colo.: Rocky Mountain Nature Association.

Nice, Margaret Morse. 1964. *Studies in the Life History of the Song Sparrow.* New York: Dover Publications, Inc.

Oberholser, Harry C. 1974. *The Bird Life of Texas.* Austin: University of Texas Press.

Palmer, Ralph S. 1988. *Handbook of North American Birds,* Vol. 4. New Haven: Yale University Press.

Paredes, Marcos, Raymond Skiles, and Douglas Neighbor. 1991. Peregrine falcon monitoring program Big Bend National Park & Rio Grande Wild and Scenic River 1991 season. Report.

Parrot, Lloyd P. 1970. *Birds of Glacier National Park.* Glacier Natural History Association. Kalispell, Mont.: Thomas Printing Co.

Patterson, Craig T. 1985. Bird and mammal inventory for the Bighorn Canyon National Recreation Area, Montana and Wyoming. Report.

Peterson, Roger Tory. 1961. *A Field Guide to Western Birds.* Boston: Houghton Mifflin Co.

Peterson, Wayne R. 1983. House wren; winter wren; Lincoln's sparrow. In *The Audubon Society Master Guide to Birding,* ed. John C. Farrand, Jr. New York: Alfred A. Knopf.

Pettingill, Olin Sewall, Jr. 1953. *A Guide to Bird Finding West of the Mississippi.* New York: Oxford University Press.

Petrides, George A. 1992. *A Field Guide to Western Trees.* Boston: Houghton Mifflin Co.

Phillips, Allan, Joe Marshall, and Gale Monson. 1964. *The Birds of Arizona.* Tucson: University of Arizona Press.

Phillips, Barbara G., Arthur M. Phillips, III, and Marilyn Ann Schmidt Bernzott. 1987. *Annotated Checklist of Vascular Plants of Grand Canyon National Park.* Ariz.: Grand Canyon Natural History Association.

Pough, Richard H. 1957. *Audubon Western Bird Guide: Land, Water, and Game Birds.* Garden City, NY: Doubleday & Co., Inc.

Ratcliffe, Bill. 1971. Canyonlands. *Audubon.* July: 32-51.

Raynes, Bert. 1984. *Birds of Grand Teton National Park and the Surrounding Area.* Wyoming: Grand Teton Natural History Association.

Reader's Digest. 1985. *Our National Parks.* New York: The Reader's Digest Association, Inc.

Rice, Larry. 1982. Journeying into the fold. *National Parks.* Sept./Oct.: 4-8.

Rich, Terry. 1989. Forests, fire and the future. *Birder's World.* June: 10-14.

Robbins, Chandler S., John R. Sauer, Russell S. Greenberg, and Sam Droege. 1989. Population declines in North American birds that migrate to the Neotropics. *Population Biology.* 86: 7658-7662.

Ruffner, George A., and Robert A. Johnson. 1991. *Plant Ecology and Vegetation Mapping at Coronado National Monument, Cochise County, Arizona.* NPS Coop. Park Study Unit, Tech. Report No. 41. Tucson: University of Arizona.

Seel, K. E. 1969. An annotated list of the avifauna of Waterton Lakes National Park, Alberta. Report.

Shafer, Craig L. 1990. *Nature Reserves Island Theory and Conservation Practice.* Washington, D.C.: Smithsonian Inst.

Shelton, Napier. 1985. *Saguaro Official National Park Handbook.* National Park Service, Washington, D.C.: GPO.

Simons, Ted, John Peine, and Richard Cunningham. 1989. Proposed migratory bird watch to encompass research, monitoring, and interpretation. *Park Science.* 9: 8.

Spangle, Paul and Elsie. (undated). *Birds of Walnut Canyon.* Globe, Ariz.: Southwestern Monuments Association.

Spence, John R. 1991. Spring birding in the Fruita historic area, Capitol Reef National Park. *Utah Birds.* vol. 7, no. 3: 41-51.

Spencer, Craig N., B. Riley McClelland, and Jack A. Stanford. 1991. Shrimp stocking, salmon collapse, and eagle displacement. *BioScience.* vol. 41, no. 1: 14-21.

Stoltenburg, William. 1991. The fragment connection. *Nature Conservancy.* July/Aug.: 19-25.

Sutton, Ann and Myron. 1974. *Wilderness Areas of North America.* New York: Funk & Wagnalls.

Taverner, Percy A. 1906. The yellow-breasted chat: A character sketch. *Bird Lore.* VIII: 131.

Terborgh, John. 1989. *Where Have all the Birds Gone?* Oxford: Princeton University Press.

_____. 1992. Why American songbirds are vanishing. *Scientific American.* May: 98-104.

Terres, John K. 1987. *The Audubon Society Encyclopedia of North American Birds.* New York: Alfred A. Knopf.

Terrill, Scott B. 1983. Western kingbird; pinyon jay. In *The Audubon Society Master Guide to Birding,* ed. John C. Farrand, Jr. New York: Alfred A. Knopf.

Udall, James R. 1991. Launching the natural ark. *Sierra.* Sept./Oct.: 80-89.

Van Tighem, Kevin. 1988. *Birding Jasper National Park.* Jasper, Alberta: Parks and people.

Vensel, Larry. 1986. Birding at Capitol Reef. *Utah Audubon Society News.* vol. 38, no. 1: 6-7.

Vickery, Peter D. 1983. Yellow warbler; vesper sparrow. In *The Audubon Society Master Guide to Birding,* ed. John C. Farrand, Jr. New York: Alfred A. Knopf.

Wauer, Roland H. 1971. Ecological distribution of birds of the Chisos Mountains, Texas. *The Southwestern Naturalist.* vol. 16, no. 1: 1-29.

_____. 1985. *A Field Guide to Birds of the Big Bend.* Austin: Texas Monthly Press.

_____. 1991. Avian population trends at Bandelier National Monument, New Mexico. Report to National Park Service.

_____. *Naturalist's Mexico.* College Station: Texas A&M University Press.

_____ and Dennis L. Carter. 1965. *Birds of Zion National Park and Vicinity.* Springdale, Utah: Zion Natural History Association.

_____ and John G. Dennis. 1979. Impacts of feral burros upon the breeding avifauna of a pinyon-juniper woodland in Bandelier National Monument, New Mexico. In *Second Conference on Scientific Research in National Parks, 26-30 November, 1979, San Francisco, California.* National Park Service, Washington, D.C.: GPO.

_____ and J. David Ligon. 1974. Distributional relations of breeding avifauna of four Southwestern mountain ranges. In *Transactions of the Symposium on the Biological Resources of the Chihuahuan Desert Region United States and Mexico,* ed. Roland H. Wauer and David H. Riskind. U.S.D.A., N.P.S., Trans. Proc. Ser. no. 3. Washington, DC: GPO.

_____, James Vukonich, and Steve Cinnamon. 1981. The breeding avifauna of Capulin Mountain National Monument, New Mexico. Report.

_____, and Terrell Johnson. 1981. La Mesa fire effects on avifauna: changes in avian populations and biomass. In *La Mesa Fire Symposium, Los Alamos, New Mexico, October 6 and 7, 1981.* Los Alamos, NM: Los Alamos National Laboratory.

Welty, Joel Carl. 1963. *The Life of Birds.* New York: Alfred A. Knopf.

Whitney, Stephen. 1985. *The Audubon Society Nature Guides: Western Forests.* New York: Alfred A. Knopf

Wilcove, David. 1990. Empty skies. *The Nature Conservancy.* Jan./Feb.: 4-13.

Wilkinson, Todd. 1991. Call of the trumpeter. *National Parks.* July/Aug.: 26-30.

Woods, John G. 1987. *Glacier Country, Mount Revelstoke and Glacier National Parks.* Vancouver, B.C.: Douglas & McIntyre.

Youth, Howard. Birds fast disappearing. In *Vital Signs 1992,* Worldwatch Institute. New York: W. W. Norton & Co.

Zimmer, Kevin J. 1985. *The Western Bird Watcher.* Englewood Cliffs, NJ: Prentice-Hall, Inc.

Zwinger, Ann H., and Beatrice E. Willard. 1972. *Land Above the Trees.* Tucson: University of Arizona Press.

INDEX

DeSante, David (in *The Audubon Society Master Guide to Birding*), Brewer's sparrow song, 36-37

Despain, Don, 92

dipper, American, 40-41, 44, 45, 57, 59, 64, 67, 70, 76, 102, 103, 117, 126-27, 165-66, 170, 192, 299

dove: mourning, 16, 86, 166, 176, 178, 192, 214, 228, 249, 260, 264, 277, 288, 300, 309, 321, 324, 338, 341, 356, 357, 369, 374; rock, 83, 87, 103, 154, 232; white-winged, 249, 254, 255, 260, 264, 385

duck: harlequin, 43, 64, 71, 75; ring-necked, 42, 72, 112, 151, 197; wood, 84; ruddy, 112, 222

Duffy, Katy, 113, 115

Dunne, Pete, David Sibley, and Clay Sutton (*Hawks in Flight*), golden eagle flight, 285

eagle: bald, 4, 37, 42, 74, 75, 81, 101, 109, 118, 169, 182, 293, 322; golden, 58, 73, 76, 81, **82**-83, 88, 96, 102, 124, 137, 161, 168, 169, 196, 215, 275, 284, 285, 289, 295, 307, 312

egret, snowy, 222

Ehrlich, John, David S. Dobkin, and Darryl Wheye (*The Birder's Handbook*): bushtit group behavior, 286; brown-headed cowbird parasitism, 384; American dipper feeding behavior, 40-41, 192; Canada goose display, 99; sage grouse courtship, 114-15, 137; sharp-tailed grouse display, 74; red-tailed hawk diet, 242; western kingbird courtship flight, 134; black-billed magpie diet, 314; Clark's nutcracker food storage, 303; Clark's nutcracker research, 27-28; pygmy nuthatch social order, 335; white-tailed ptarmigan foot feathers, 62; white-tailed ptarmigan nest protection, 143; Gambel's quail, 240; spotted sandpiper mating behavior, 151; varied thrush song, 57; verdin nest, 261; canyon wren nest, 226

Ellis, David, raptor behavior, 385-86

Endangered Species Act, 17

Enderson, James, 13

extinction/extirpation: general, 7-8; eastern peregrine falcon, 12

falcon: peregrine, 1, 12, 14, 18, 77-78, 81, 83, 88, 101, 103, 124, 139, 140, 168, 169, 181, 182, 188, 215-**216**-17, 222, 284, 285-86, 293-94, 300-01, 302, 338, 372, 385, 390; prairie, 64, 80, 81, 102, 146, 154, 168, 215, 284, 308, 386

field guides, 6-7

finch: Cassin's, 43, 116, 138, 154, 194, 195, 220, 242, 264, 338, 344; house, 136, 154, 163, 170, 176, 178-**179**, 180, 182, 183, 189, 192-93, 197, 198, 205, 215, 230, 233, 234, 247, 253, 254, 255, 260, 277, 287, 301, 309, 330, 349, 356, 357, 368, 373, 382, 389, 390

fire: general, 15-17; Bandelier, 16-17; Yellowstone, 16

fish: cutthroat trout, 97; kokanee, 74-75; snail darter, 18

flicker: "gilded," 257, 259, 264; northern, 17, 42, 148, 149, 152, 165, 176, 182, 194, 195, 197, 204, 214, 220, 228, 231, 257, 259, 266, 274, 275, 287, 306, 320, 330, 338, 342, 343, 350

flycatcher: Acadian, 14; alder, 42, 50; ash-throated, 16, 126, 135, 166, 176-77, 180, 182, 189, 191, 214, 228, 242, 249, 253, 259, 272, 275, 277, 309, 330, 338, 340, 349, 366, 369, 370, 383; brown-crested, 259, 275; cordilleran, 148, 149, 152, 191, 263, 307, 371, 374; dusky, 42, 51, 73, 116, 136, 194, 206, 300, 321; dusky-capped, 270; gray, 138, 176, 215, 230, 286-87, 289, 309, 340, 349; Hammond's, 42, 56, 70, 73, 116, 333; least, 42, 85; olive-sided, 39, 116, 195, 220, 373; sulphur-bellied, 270; vermilion, 3, 240, **388**, 389, 390; willow, 42, 51, 55, 73, 102, 110, 115, 152, 180, 215

Other Books from John Muir Publications

Asia Through the Back Door, 4th ed., 400 pp. $16.95 (available 7/93)

Belize: A Natural Destination, 336 pp. $16.95

Costa Rica: A Natural Destination, 2nd ed., 310 pp. $16.95

Elderhostels: The Students' Choice, 2nd ed., 304 pp. $15.95

Environmental Vacations: Volunteer Projects to Save the Planet, 2nd ed., 248 pp. $16.95

Europe 101: History & Art for the Traveler, 4th ed., 350 pp. $15.95

Europe Through the Back Door, 11th ed., 432 pp. $17.95

Europe Through the Back Door Phrase Book: French, 160 pp. $4.95

Europe Through the Back Door Phrase Book: German, 160 pp. $4.95

Europe Through the Back Door Phrase Book: Italian, 168 pp. $4.95

Europe Through the Back Door Phrase Book: Spanish & Portuguese, 288 pp. $4.95

A Foreign Visitor's Guide to America, 224 pp. $12.95

Great Cities of Eastern Europe, 256 pp. $16.95

Guatemala: A Natural Destination, 336 pp. $16.95

Indian America: A Traveler's Companion, 4th ed., 448 pp. $17.95 (available 7/93)

Interior Furnishings Southwest, 256 pp. $19.95

Mona Winks: Self-Guided Tours of Europe's Top Museums, 2nd ed., 448 pp. $16.95

Opera! The Guide to Western Europe's Great Houses, 296 pp. $18.95

Paintbrushes and Pistols: How the Taos Artists Sold the West, 288 pp. $17.95

The People's Guide to Mexico, 9th ed., 608 pp. $18.95

Ranch Vacations: The Complete Guide to Guest and Resort, Fly-Fishing, and Cross-Country Skiing Ranches, 2nd ed., 396 pp. $18.95

The Shopper's Guide to Art and Crafts in the Hawaiian Islands, 272 pp. $13.95

The Shopper's Guide to Mexico, 224 pp. $9.95

Understanding Europeans, 272 pp. $14.95

Undiscovered Islands of the Caribbean, 3rd ed., 288 pp. $14.95

Undiscovered Islands of the Mediterranean, 2nd ed., 224 pp. $13.95

Undiscovered Islands of the U.S. and Canadian West Coast, 288 pp. $12.95

Unique Colorado, 112 pp. $10.95 (available 6/93)

Unique Florida, 112 pp. $10.95 (available 7/93)

Unique New Mexico, 112 pp. $10.95 (available 6/93)

A Viewer's Guide to Art: A Glossary of Gods, People, and Creatures, 144 pp. $10.95

The Visitor's Guide to the Birds of the Eastern National Parks: United States and Canada, 410 pp. $15.95

2 to 22 Days Series

Each title offers 22 flexible daily itineraries useful for planning vacations of any length. Aside from valuable general information, included are "must see" attractions *and* hidden "jewels."

2 to 22 Days in the American Southwest, 1993 ed., 176 pp. $10.95

2 to 22 Days in Asia, 1993 ed., 176 pp. $9.95

2 to 22 Days in Australia, 1993 ed., 192 pp. $9.95

2 to 22 Days in California, 1993 ed., 192 pp. $9.95

2 to 22 Days in Europe, 1993 ed., 288 pp. $13.95

2 to 22 Days in Florida, 1993 ed., 192 pp. $10.95

2 to 22 Days in France, 1993 ed., 192 pp. $10.95

2 to 22 Days in Germany, Austria, & Switzerland, 1993 ed., 224 pp. $10.95

2 to 22 Days in Great Britain, 1993 ed., 192 pp. $10.95

2 to 22 Days Around the Great Lakes, 1993 ed., 192 pp. $10.95

2 to 22 Days in Hawaii, 1993 ed., 192 pp. $9.95

2 to 22 Days in Italy, 208 pp. $10.95

2 to 22 Days in New England, 1993 ed., 192 pp. $10.95

2 to 22 Days in New Zealand, 1993 ed., 192 pp. $9.95

2 to 22 Days in Norway, Sweden, & Denmark, 1993 ed., 192 pp. $10.95

2 to 22 Days in the Pacific Northwest, 1993 ed., 192 pp. $10.95

2 to 22 Days in the Rockies, 1993 ed., 192 pp. $10.95

2 to 22 Days in Spain & Portugal, 192 pp. $10.95

2 to 22 Days in Texas, 1993 ed., 192 pp. $9.95

2 to 22 Days in Thailand, 1993 ed., 180 pp. $9.95

22 Days (or More) Around the World, 1993 ed., 264 pp. $12.95

Automotive Titles
How to Keep Your VW Alive, 15th ed., 464 pp. $21.95
How to Keep Your Subaru Alive 480 pp. $21.95
How to Keep Your Toyota Pickup Alive 392 pp. $21.95
How to Keep Your Datsun/Nissan Alive 544 pp. $21.95
The Greaseless Guide to Car Care Confidence, 224 pp. $14.95
Off-Road Emergency Repair & Survival, 160 pp. $9.95

TITLES FOR YOUNG READERS AGES 8 AND UP

"Kidding Around" Travel Guides for Young Readers
All the "Kidding Around" Travel guides are 64 pages and $9.95 paper, except for **Kidding Around Spain** and **Kidding Around the National Parks of the Southwest,** which are 108 pages and $12.95 paper.
Kidding Around Atlanta
Kidding Around Boston,2nd ed.
Kidding Around Chicago, 2nd ed.
Kidding Around the Hawaiian Islands
Kidding Around London
Kidding Around Los Angeles
Kidding Around the National Parks of the Southwest
Kidding Around New York City, 2nd ed.
Kidding Around Paris
Kidding Around Philadelphia
Kidding Around San Diego
Kidding Around San Francisco
Kidding Around Santa Fe
Kidding Around Seattle
Kidding Around Spain
Kidding Around Washington, D.C., 2nd ed.

"Extremely Weird" Series for Young Readers. Written by Sarah Lovett, each is 48 pages and $9.95 paper.
Extremely Weird Bats
Extremely Weird Birds
Extremely Weird Endangered Species
Extremely Weird Fishes
Extremely Weird Frogs
Extremely Weird Insects
Extremely Weird Mammals (available 8/93)
Extremely Weird Micro Monsters (available 8/93)
Extremely Weird Primates
Extremely Weird Reptiles
Extremely Weird Sea Creatures
Extremely Weird Snakes (available 8/93)
Extremely Weird Spiders

"Masters of Motion" Series for Young Readers. Each title is 48 pages and $9.95 paper.
How to Drive an Indy Race Car
How to Fly a 747
How to Fly the Space Shuttle

"X-ray Vision" Series for Young Readers. Each title is 48 pages and $9.95 paper.
Looking Inside Cartoon Animation
Looking Inside Sports Aerodynamics
Looking Inside the Brain
Looking Inside Sunken Treasure
Looking Inside Telescopes and the Night Sky

Multicultural Titles for Young Readers
Native Artists of North America, 48 pp. $14.95 hardcover
The Indian Way: Learning to Communicate with Mother Earth, 114 pp. $9.95
The Kids' Environment Book: What's Awry and Why, 192 pp. $13.95
Kids Explore America's African-American Heritage, 112 pp. $8.95
Kids Explore America's Hispanic Heritage, 112 pp. $7.95

Environmental Titles for Young Readers
Rads, Ergs, and Cheeseburgers: The Kids' Guide to Energy and the Environment, 108 pp. $12.95
Habitats: Where the Wild Things Live, 48 pp. $9.95
The Kids' Environment Book: What's Awry and Why, 192 pp. $13.95

Ordering Information
Please check your local bookstore for our books, or call 1-800-888-7504 to order direct from us. All orders are shipped via UPS; see chart below to calculate your shipping charge to U.S. destinations. **No P.O. Boxes please; we must have a street address to ensure delivery.** If the book you request is not available, we will hold your check until we can ship it. Foreign orders will be shipped surface rate unless otherwise requested; please enclose $3.00 for the first item and $1.00 for each additional item.

For U.S. Orders Totaling	Add
Up to $15.00	$4.25
$15.01 to $45.00	$5.25
$45.01 to $75.00	$6.25
$75.01 or more	$7.25

Methods of Payment
Check, money order, American Express, MasterCard, or Visa. We cannot be responsible for cash sent through the mail. For credit card orders, include your card number, expiration date, and your signature, or call (800) 888-7504. American Express card orders can be shipped only to billing address of cardholder. Sorry, no C.O.D.'s. Residents of sunny New Mexico, add 6.125% tax to total.

Address all orders and inquiries to:
John Muir Publications
P.O. Box 613
Santa Fe, NM 87504
(505) 982-4078
(800) 888-7504